IVECO STORY

© Raffaele Sanguineti - Carlo Felice Zampini Salazar
Norden Publishing House Ltd.,
St. Gallen, Switzerland, 1994
ISBN 3-907150-21-X

Editorial coordination:
Roberto Thöni
Graphics and typesetting:
Marco Rostagno
Jacket:
FTG (Turin)
Photo composition:
Technical Graphics Ltd., Stockport, UK.
Photolitho, printing and binding:
G. Canale & C. S.p.A., Borgaro Torinese (To), Italy

The photographs published in this book were kindly supplied by:
IVECO archive (Turin),
Sanguineti archive (Turin),
Zampini Salazar archive (Pino Torinese, To),
Negri archive (Brescia),
Fiat Historical Centre (Turin),
Cinefiat (Turin),
Publifoto (Turin),
Mauro Raffini (Turin),
ESA-ESRIN (TIROS-AVHRR).

IVECO STORY

THE WORLD OF TRANSPORT

Text by Raffaele Sanguineti
and Carlo Felice Zampini Salazar

NORDEN PUBLISHING HOUSE LTD.

Contents

WHY A "HISTORY" OF IVECO

When the idea of going to press with the "history" of Iveco was mooted we thought long and hard. It did not really seem appropriate to describe the succession of events which only started in 1975, less than twenty years ago, as "history", however important those events might be for us.

Moreover, when we considered the succession of external events which have taken place in recent years, we realised that they had gathered pace over such a short time span that in the not too distant past they would have had their impact on the human race over the course of a century. The concept of "history", therefore, is difficult to distinguish from that of "news".

In about thirty years man has walked on the moon, faced and resolved the oil crisis which could potentially have upturned our whole way of life, eradicated some illnesses and seen the appearance of others hitherto unknown, seen the opposition between the superpowers dissolve, experienced the distruptive effects of information technology and telecommunications and much more besides.

So, we came to the conclusion that, if related to the industrial world, the birth, development and establishment of our company's reputation had passed through these stages much more quickly than would have been permitted by economic, technological and industrial advancement in the past.

In view of this, we also decided to write a chapter on the "history" of the industry.

The rapid succession of events is such that a decision taken today, to a greater degree than ever, implies, in fact, that it will impact on the future, for better or worse.

Viewed in this light, the original idea behind the creation of Iveco has de facto contributed to the creation of a part of Europe whose birth and strengthening we are witnessing daily.

This decision was based on faith in a product, the truck, which may have seemed to many as if it would be superseded. The truck could, in some futuristic logic, have been abandoned by the human race in favour of other methods of goods transport and more advanced technology: high speed trains, boats of all kinds, air carriers etc.

So, from 1975 until the present day the modern system of goods transport has continued to call on the truck which remains the most widespread form because it is flexible and economical. The truck has been able to respond to the infinite demands for specialisation necessitated by the enormous range of goods to be transported.

The truck has changed in terms of its structure and on board technology: it has been made more environmentally friendly and safer in traffic: it offers comfort comparable to a car and is destined to enter the next millennium as a key player in the transport world.

Iveco is one of only a handful of companies in the world who deal with this fascinating product: but, unlike its perhaps most famous competitors, the basis of its planning, implementation and production is built on the wide-ranging experience of people from different traditions and cultures throughout Europe.

If it is true that the companies which gave birth to Iveco have their roots in the last century: that the new companies which have come to join and enrich Iveco in recent years have many years of experience: it is nontheless certain that the same Iveco is fully justified in deeming itself a new reality which differs from the parts from which it was formed.

Today, as we stand on the threshold of the year 2000, the company has given birth to a new product which like itself has been projected into the future, and has been conceived precisely for this.

Iveco people, irrespective of their nationality, have put their past behind them and been able to produce together an integrated range of vehicles within which a very high degree of specialisation is available. This range, to give credence to the origins of Iveco, was born of Europe, for Europe and with the "Euro" prefix as part of its name, is intended to be introduced as the first, and for the moment only, truly European vehicle.

This product is the first born of the ideal and underlying Iveco: a company which from the start way back in 1975 tried to anticipate European development. It comes into being on "day one" of the new European history.

It is visible proof of a brief yet intense "history" in which we have all enjoyed being involved.

Iveco

PREFACE

*T*he purpose of this book is to retrace the history, now spanning almost 20 years, of the birth and development of a major industry. A complex organisation in a continuous state of change, a living organism which embodies the choices, doubts and expectations of those tending and guiding it. Through the language of numbers and, even better, the voices of the protagonists, let us relive the events which have helped nurture the growth of the company which we all know today.

The pieces have been gathered; the history of IVECO has been put together. Giving us a chance to analyse "from behind the scenes" an industrial adventure which, without rhetoric, is one of the most articulate and significant of our time. One which, as we shall see, is often troubled, with some cliff hanger passages, but with a happy ending for all that.

Because today, IVECO is a solid industrial reality, a leading company among manufacturers of industrial vehicles and diesel engines, with an enviable wealth of people and managerial, technical and technological know-how.

A reality which is all the more positive because, in spite of a "Europe without frontiers" and lofty talk of joint companies, IVECO remains one of the very few examples of true "transnationality", not a simple cooperation or acquisition between companies, but a true integration of the human and managerial cultures of different nationalities. And this at a time when, in spite of everything, a united Europe has still not succeeded in transforming the ideal of pan-European, transnational corporate management into a material reality which embodies laws and standards.

This also epitomises the modernism of the industrial concept on which IVECO is based and to which IVECO bears testimony today.

We shall try to relate this story, not just as a chronicle of facts, although these are important, but as a fabric woven from situations and choices, relations and strategies, conditioning and achievements.

Because the IVECO of today is a result of all this. Of a positive will - even if not always unambiguous and coherent - to build an industrial reality projected towards the future, one which is rich in people and resources, one which is modern and efficient. A competitive reality in terms of size, structure and strategy, capable of gaining a strong foothold in the future in an increasingly selective and competitive environment in Europe and throughout the world.

We shall try to tell the story with the accuracy of a historian and the objectivity of a reporter: the why, the how and when of the road travelled since that day on the 1st January 1975, now a long time ago.

The Authors

IVECO
A CONCEPT AND AN IDEAL
PROJECTED TOWARDS THE FUTURE

In the context in which it was announced - the middle of the '70s - the birth of a transnational group like Iveco was an industrial event of undoubted importance; an event made possible by an innovative managerial spirit and one intelligently projected towards the future.

To say this today, after the collapse of the physical and ideological barriers which, for decades, had divided the daily reality of our continent, and at the time of the move towards the Europe of 1993, may seem strange.

But in the reality of the Seventies the aim was ambitious. They were trying to remove deeply rooted cultural barriers, to remodel part of themselves to create something different, in search of wider horizons and a competitive future.

This was the major challenge taken up by Iveco: how to transform into a coordinated and coherent line of action the boiling magma of the nationalistic and managerial identities of five companies in three different countries which had been brought together in the holding company: Fiat, OM and Lancia in Italy, Unic in France, Magirus in Germany.

The road taken to achieve this goal has not been easy. From the negotiations between the partners - Fiat in Italy on the one hand, KHD (Klöckner-Humboldt-Deutz) in Germany on the other - to the initial cohabitation period with the millstone of party interests and problems created by misunderstanding between people, the differences between mentality and method were in some instances considerable.

It's a complex plot which has introduced a down-to-earth element into the "fairytale" which we wanted to write. True, we wanted realism, but idealism has its place, too.

All this in a socioeconomic and entrepreneurial climate which was unprepared in both attitude and structure for such a modern event as the birth of a transnational holding company. Also at a time when the ideal of a united Europe, a common market, in which the major manufacturers would face each other freely without nationalistic monopolies, no longer generated the enthusiasm of the previous decade.

However, some motivation was provided by the basic conviction that it was up to industry to play a leading role in the political happenings, and that only by setting up true pan-European companies would it be possible to promote economic integration.

If we also add that the Italian market on its own, or the French market on its own, was not considered adequate to support a manufacturer of sufficient size to meet future challenges, we have a reference point for the strategic motivation which led to the formation of Iveco.

Whilst these steps were being taken, the powers existing in the various countries - government, legislation, taxation, bureaucracy, etc. - showed no interest in a development of this type, because they were not able to imagine a company which might operate at transnational level.

Also, there were no instruments - neither legal, fiscal nor social - to be able to sustain such a far-reaching entrepreneurial initiative. Consequently, Iveco was born and nurtured with a pan-European idea, whilst the rest of society was still far from providing real, let alone ideological support.

The Fiat stand at the Turin Fair in 1971. On the opposite page a picture of the Fiat 682.

THE MARKET AND THE INDUSTRIAL VEHICLE INDUSTRY AT THE BEGINNING OF THE SEVENTIES

The scene is that of the early '70s, when Fiat in Italy and KHD in Germany - the future partners of the holding company - started to look around in search of a new dimension for their business in the industrial vehicle sector, i.e. that of Gruppo Veicoli Industriali and Magirus-Deutz.

At that time the main European markets were in the grip of an almost total monopoly of the national industries with shares even exceeding 80%.

The cake was divided between fifteen manufacturers, including five of the world's largest vehicle producers, both European and American (with their subsidiaries); then there were forty or so minor companies of mainly local importance.

Italy was dominated by Fiat which had integrated its own activities and those of OM, Brescia and Lancia, Bolzano into the Gruppo Veicoli Industriali. Alpha Romeo also had a small operation at its Pomigliano factory near Naples, following agreements with Renault-Saviem, for the production of commercial vehicles.

In France, there was the state-owned Renault-Saviem group and there was Fiat which owned Unic and had shares in Citroën and Berliet (which at that time, belonged to Citroën).

It is worth inserting a small paragraph here to tell of an event which was to have major repercussions on the future attitudes of the industry.

In 1970, Fiat and Michelin set up a joint holding company (49% and 51%, respectively) to control Citroën. And as Berliet had been absorbed by Citroën in 1967, there was a possibility that the latter would be integrated into the Gruppo Veicoli Industriali along with Unic.

But in 1973 the agreement collapsed and Fiat sold its shares to Michelin and withdrew from the partnership. So when, the following year, Citroën entered the sphere of influence of Peugeot at the request of the French Government, Berliet was sold to Saviem, controlled by Renault, and Renault Véhicules Industriels was born.

Returning now to the market situation, Daimler-Benz which had absorbed Hanomag-Henschel in 1969, was the market leader in Germany. There was also MAN, which had incorporated Büssing in the meantime, and Magirus-Deutz. Great Britain had four groups: BLMC, controlling AEC, Albion, Austin-Morris, Guy, Leyland, Scammel and Thornycroft; Ford; General Motors, including Bedford; Chrysler, which included Dodge and Karrier.

There were then companies like Seddon-Atkinson, Foden and ERF, small heavy vehicle conversion companies (with a production of between 4000 and 5000 vehicles a year) of mainly local interest.

Sweden had Volvo and Scania, two companies whose influence on the market far exceeded their actual industrial size.

In the case of Volvo, this was the result of its very active policy, comparable with that of the Americans, of setting up production units and efficient distribution networks in the main European and world markets.

As for of Scania, which concentrated on the production of heavy vehicles, particularly road vehicles, its strength was based on its excellent image and the strong position on the market acquired in this field.

In view of the size of the Swedish market we also have to remember that Scania and Volvo were (and still are) among the most export-oriented companies in the industry, with figures already approaching 80%. Another factor which was to have considerable significance in the years to come.

In Holland there was Daf, which had entered into a cooperative arrangement with the American company International Harvester, with the aim of opening up other markets.

The European picture was completed by some minor manufacturers of very limited influence: in Spain there was Barreiros (a member of the Chrysler group), Enasa, with Pegaso and Sava, and Mevosa. In Austria there was Steyr, Saurer in Switzerland and Sisu in Finland.

This was the scene in Europe. And now a word about the other two major markets and production centres of the industrialised world: USA and Japan.

As far as the United States was concerned, ten manufacturers were active on a market more or less the same size as Europe: General Motors, Ford, Chrysler, International Harvester and Paccar plus some large specialist companies, including White Motors and Mack, mainly concerned with maintaining a presence on the national market. However, 80% of the production was in fact concentrated on the three big names: Chrysler, Ford and General Motors.

This situation had allowed the American industry to develop an efficient process of rationalisation and reorganisation aimed at achieving an industrial dimension and technological capability suitable for large volume production.

One basic aspect of this re-organisation was the "devert-icalisation" of the components industry: engines, gearboxes, axles were standardised and produced by specialist companies which allowed considerable economies of scale.

Japan had followed the example of North America, achieving a considerable expansion capacity, (though not comparable with that of the American industry), particularly with regard to the various market volumes available. Production was concentrated at a small number of manufacturers headed by Nissan, Isuzu, Hino and Mitsubishi. These four companies were poised to launch themselves on the international scene and had already entered into the first agreements with the Americans.

A NEW EUROPEAN AWARENESS IS ALIVE AND KICKING

If this was the scenario at the beginning of the '70s, we need to understand the events which had engineered this. The European scenario had already started to change, starting in the previous decade.

The birth of the Economic Community had encouraged an increase in interchanges between countries, whereas the decline of the colonial powers with the loss of privileged markets, had made the old continent stand on its own feet and therefore make maximum use of its own production and market facilities.

European industry needed to acquire a suitable size, a necessary precondition although not sufficient in itself, to achieve through economies of scale and specialisation, greater competitive-ness on an increasingly penetrable and strongly com-petitive market.

Therefore, the start of the '60s - through the effect of the pressure by the leading American producers (as already mentioned, present in Europe through their subsidiaries) - heralded an era of commercial and manufacturing agreements and concentrations between companies concerned with finding a dimension which would allow them to face the future with greater certainty. It was to be a long process (and is still going on to some extent) and not without its traumas; one which was to create a close weave of new industrial relations both at national and international level and also on both sides of the Atlantic.

However, when reading through these events, it is easy to under-stand that nothing compares neither in spirit nor in industrial dimension, with the experience of Iveco as a transnational holding company in which different nationalities integrated their respective cultures for the common good.

It is also important to note how in this fabric of new relations, the desired dimensional leap has not always been made and how greater efficiency has not always been achieved with an improved dimension.

Looking at what has happened, it can be seen that if a cooperation agreement is to be both lasting and fruitful, it is necessary for the partners to offer mutual advantages, a complementary base (of products, ranges, technologies), reciprocal contributions (experience, know-how, plant, networks, image), and above all, the willingness of people to cooperate and integrate.

These were the conditions and stimuli which Fiat in Italy and KHD in Germany had to draw from within, when, becoming aware of the need to find a new approach to their respective activities in the industrial vehicle sector, they started to look round in search of a partner.

We will see later the motivating forces which induced both companies to make a strategic choice of this type. Remembering when reading through these events, that there existed a substantial basic difference.

So Fiat, having created the Gruppo Veicoli Industriali (the structure and role of which will be analysed in the following chapters) had already laid down and partly achieved an organisational plan and an important reorganisation measure between Fiat, OM, Lancia and Unic.

Whereas Magirus, apart from making the Club range within the "Club of 4" agreement (we will discuss this later), found itself in an economic and structural situation which was anything but flourishing and with few prospects of a solution at national level.

FIFTEEN YEARS
OF AGREEMENTS AND INCORPORATIONS
BETWEEN COMPANIES

First of all, a brief summary of the most important industrial relations which preceded the formation of Iveco between the beginning of the Sixties and the middle of the Seventies.

Let us start with 1963, a year in which the German company MAN and the French company Saviem agreed on an industrial cooperation programme and in the car industry, the American company Chrysler took control of the French company, Simca.

The following year Chrysler acquired control of the Spanish company, Barreiros. Two important historical events occurred in the car industry: the agreement between the German company NSU and Citroën of France to develop the Wankel rotary piston engine and, in Germany, the sale by Daimler-Benz of its majority holding in Auto Union to Volkswagen.

Two years later in 1967, Citroën absorbed Berliet, whilst in England, Leyland absorbed Rover. 1968 was a year full of initiatives: Alfa Romeo acquired control of the Brazilian company FNM; Fiat acquired a holding in Citroën; Daimler-Benz absorbed F. Krupp; in Sweden, Saab incorporated Scania-Vabis and in England, Leyland was formed with the British Motor Holding Company thereby creating (also with resources from the public purse) the British Leyland Motor Corporation. All the British owned companies (thus excluding the Ford companies, General Motors and Chrysler) were progressively incorporated into BLMC, except for a few small British producers, such as Atkinsons.

The following year Daimler-Benz incorporated Hanomag-Henschel and MAN incorporated Büssing; in the car sector, Fiat acquired Lancia and also a share in Ferrari, whilst Volkswagen took control of NSU and set up a joint company with Porsche; the Japanese also arrived on the scene with the Chrysler/Mitsubishi and Ford-Nissan-Tokyo Kogyo agreements.

We are now at the beginning of the Seventies. This decade opened with an agreement between Daimler-Benz and MAN to produce engines and axles; in the car industry Chrysler France absorbed Simca, whilst Nissan and NSU agreed to produce Wankel engines under licence in Japan. Fiat and Michelin acquired a share in the Citroën holding company.

1971 was the year of the "Club of 4", a cooperation agreement between DAF, Magirus-Deutz, Saviem and Volvo in the medium vehicle field. A new Saviem-MAN agreement was also signed for the production of vehicles. The car industry saw the Peugeot-Renault-Volvo agreement (which was to produce the three litre six cylinder V engine, known as the "PRV"), whilst General Motors acquired a shareholding in Isuzu Motors and Chrysler a holding in Mitsubishi.

1972 saw the arrival in Europe of the American company International Harvester, which signed an agreement with DAF. At the same time, in the car industry, DAF entered into a share partnership with Volvo.

In 1973, Fiat took over a large share in FNM from Alpha Romeo (which remained the majority shareholder).

1974 is the year when SO.F.I.M. was born (Società Franco-Italiana Motori), formed between Fiat, Alfa Romeo and Saviem for the production of diesel engines. International Harvester acquired the majority holding in the British company Seddon Diesel. In France, cooperation agreements were signed between Citroën and Peugeot, and Berliet (Citroën industrial vehicle sector) was transferred to Renault-Saviem (also with the aid of state funds).

1975 brings us to the year of Iveco. The European scene is much changed, the concentration phenomenon is radically transforming the competitive line up and the structure of the supply industry.

FIAT
veicoli industriali

VEICOLI SPECIALI

UNIC

OM

MAGIRUS
DEUTZ

FIVE INDUSTRIAL CULTURES
FORM A NEW
EUROPEAN COLOSSUS

The Iveco of today is an organisation with a strong and well-defined personality. The fundamental idea, that of transnationality (the integration of different industrial human resources and cultures), has been consolidated to create the reality of a modern, homogeneous company as we know it today. Iveco today is truly what they wanted it to be, what they hoped it would become. But for much of its almost twenty year history, it was not. Why? For numerous reasons, many of which - rhetoric and vision apart - were more of the natural order of things. It could not have been otherwise.

We hope that this will be clear from the following pages. For now, suffice it to say that the process of integration - a long and difficult one in the first few years - has today produced all the fruits hoped for.

But first and foremost, Iveco is what it is. In particular it exists today because previously, before that day in 1975, before the '70s, before ... from the beginning of the age of the motor car, other industrial and manufacturing companies existed. Very different from the Iveco of today and very different from each other. Each with its own unmistakable identity.

Our story actually starts here. It is the story of the five "makes" - Fiat, OM and Lancia in Italy, Unic in France and Magirus-Deutz in Germany - which, at different times and in different situations, saw their paths meet. And Iveco was born. Five companies which put down their roots before this century at the close of the 1800s, and which between them created much of the history of the industrial vehicle in Europe.

To respect the atmosphere and to recreate, at least partly, the style of those years, so different from our own and so rich in tradition, we will write about two different times and two different perspectives.

Let us start by retracing the history from the beginning to the post war period - to the Sixties and the beginning of the Seventies - in particular by remembering the vehicles produced over the years.

It is, in fact, the vehicles which mark the development of the producers and of our industrialised society. From the first awkward, bumbling ancestors to the still unsophisticated trucks of the post war period, to the first true industrial vehicles, which were more efficient, with better defined characteristics and ranges; those which were being produced when the idea of Iveco was about to become a reality. So let us embark on our road of discovery of Iveco, by going back a few years to rediscover the slightly naive ethos of an industrial era which was still young and which was proudly revealing the marvels of engineering to the world.

FABBRICA - ITA
LIANA DI AVTO
MOBILI TORINO
FIAT N

Il Conte Emanuele Cacherano di Bricherasio
IDEATORE E PROPUGNATORE PRIMO
DELLA PRIMA FABBRICA ITALIANA di AUTOMOBILI "LA FIAT"

More than 90 years have passed since the 11th July 1899, when "Società Anonima Fabbrica Italiana di Automobili", or Fiat as we know it, was founded in Turin.

All the Italian papers of the time carried the news in the next day's editions. And, as could be expected, the Turin daily newspapers paid particular attention to the event; the "Stampa-Gazzetta Piemontese" and "Gazzetta del Popolo" both published an article which was more or less the same and even had the same heading: "*Economic*

Movement in Turin".

We have transcribed the article which appeared on page 3 of the "Stampa-Gazzetta Piemontese" on Wednesday 12th July 1899, under the heading "*A New Car Factory for Turin*".

"*Yesterday, Tuesday, at the Banco di Sconto e di Sete, in a document drawn up by Sig. Torretta, a joint stock company was formed under the name Fabbrica Italiana di Automobili, with a capital of 800,000 Lire divided into 4,000 shares of 200 Lire each, and backed by the aristocratic, industrial and financial*

fraternity of our city.

The signatories of the deed of formation included Conte Biscaretti di Ruffia, Marchese Ferrero di Ventimiglia, Conte di Bricherasio, Conte Falicon, Avv. Scarfiotti, Avv. Racca, Avv. Goria-Gatti, Cav. Aymonino, Cav. Foa, Ing. Marchesi, Cav. Agnelli. Of the financiers involved in the formation, we would mention in particular the Banco di Sconto e di Sete, Messrs. Fratelli Ceriana, Cassinis, Sormani e Deslex, Kuster, Cav. Giaccone, Maffei, Comm. Vercellone, Luigi Damevino, Comm. Mioglia,

Fabbrica Italiana d'Automobili

SOCIETÀ ANONIMA CON SEDE IN TORINO

F. I. A. T.

PESO DEL CARRO · · ·	KG.	2000
LUNGHEZZA TOTALE · ·	M.	5,25
LUNGHEZZA DEL PIANO	„	4,00
LARGHEZZA DEL PIANO	„	2,00
CARICO UTILE · · · ·	KG.	4000
VELOCITÀ MASSIMA · ·	KM.	12
PREZZO · · · · · · ·	L.	

Carro da trasporto con motore di 24 cav. ind.

ABOVE: The first real Fiat truck designed and manufactured in 1903 as a "vehicle for transporting goods"; the construction was of the forward cab type, to make better use of the space available; 4 cylinder split block engine with a total cylinder capacity of 6,370cc, able to develop a power of approximately 24 HP.

OPPOSITE PAGE: The "Fiat Founders", painted by Lorenzo Delleani, the distinguished Piedmont painter (1840 - 1908); right to left, seated: Conte Biscaretti, Avv. Racca, Conte Bricherasio, Cav. Ceriani, Giovanni Agnelli, Avv. Scarfiotti, Marchese Ferrero; standing: Luigi Damevino and Avv. Goria Gatti.

Società Elettrotecnica Italiana, to name but a few.

The name itself states the aim of the company. The backers have assured themselves of an able management and are building a large factory in our city. The company has already received several orders and the industry seems destined for major development and a prosperous future. The first Board of Directors is made up as follows: Chairman: Cav. Avv. Ludovico Scarfiotti; Vice Chairman: Conte Emanuele Cacherano Di Bricherasio; Secretary: Cav. Giovanni Agnelli; Directors: Cav. Michele Ceriana-Mayneri, Marchese Alfonso Ferrero di Ventimiglia, Avv. Cesare Goria-Gatti, Conte Roberto Biscaretti di Ruffia, Avv. Carlo Racca, Luigi Damevino; Auditors: Cav. Alessandro Aymonino, Prof. Carlo Core, Cav. Tommaso Boarelli".

The statement that "they are building a large factory" immediately followed by "the company has already received several orders" may give rise to some confusion. However, the paradox is merely superficial. Just prior to its formation, the new Fiat company had acquired patents relating to the "Welleyes" vehicle designed by Ing. Faccioli and built by Ceirano & C. in its small factory in a stable courtyard in Corso Vittorio Emanuele II, near the Parco del Valentino. The "Welleyes" vehicle had made its debut with modest success at one of the first Italian car races, which was the endurance test held on the 30th April 1899 over 90 kilometres of the Turin-Pinerolo-Avigliana-Turin road. Driven by Avv. Cesare Goria-Gatti - a partner of Giovanni Battista Ceirano, and also founder and director of the journal "L'Automobile" - it took 3 hours, 10 minutes and 9 seconds to cover the course, which was not always easy, ending in second place in category III, reserved for 2 seater vehicles weighing between 200 kg and 400 kg.

On acquiring the "Welleyes" patents, Fiat had also assured itself of the cooperation of the major part of the staff of Ceirano. So, after fairly difficult negotiations with the Comune of Turin, and before even deciding on the site for the new factory (it was eventually to open on 19th March, 1900 in Corso Dante on the edge of the Parco del Valentino) - both the production and the design of new models were started.

The young Fiat make soon acquired fame, and not just in Italy, thanks to active participation and excellent results in the increasingly popular car races which were being organised all over Europe.

The successes gained with the vehicles, and the awareness of the opportunities offered by a developing market which, demanded more efficient and more versatile vehicles from the industry, convinced the directors and engineers of Fiat to extend their range of activity to transport vehicles both for goods and passengers.

A first - albeit timid - demonstration of this trend was seen in May 1901 at the "Esposizione Internazionale di Allevamento e Sport" in Milan, where Fiat exhibited two buses and a fire engine trailer, alongside other vehicles on its stand in the "Automobile and Cycle" hall. Soon afterwards, a "postal service vehicle" was to be made for the Italian Ministry of Postal Services and Telecommunications.

These were still vehicles directly "derived" from standard production vehicles. Until finally, in 1903, barely four years after it had been founded, Fiat was able to launch a transport vehicle specially designed for use - including heavy-duty use - in the haulage sector.

This vehicle, while obviously maintaining the style and overall image of the car, had features which were original and also technically advanced for the time. The chassis, consisting of two

TOP: After the truck came the buses; this is a 24/40 HP type with forward cab, double decker body made in 1906, depicted here with the special adornments for the official presentation.
ABOVE: Typical "charabancs" of 1908 made on a chassis with the cab set back and the characteristic Fiat bonnet of the time; note the absence of passenger doors and the slightly raised seats giving the passengers at the back a good view to the front.

longitudinal members with bent and shaped steel cross members, was suspended over the axles by means of strong leaf springs. The engine, a 6,370 cc, four cylinder split block model, projected beyond the front axle.

The gearbox arrangement was original; it had four forward gears plus reverse, and was installed in the middle of the chassis immediately under the loading platform. It was connected to the engine by means of a transmission shaft and to the rear wheels by chains.

The driving seat, in a very forward position, allowed a loading platform of a good 4 metres x 2 metres. The vehicle weighed 2,000

kilogrammes and could transport twice that at a speed of approx. 13 kilometres an hour.

In 1904, one of these vehicles with a load of 3,300 kilogrammes, completed a demonstration run on the Turin-Genoa-Turin road, maintaining an average speed of just over 10 kilometres an hour.

In 1905, a time of many military manoeuvres, the Italian Minister of War had started the gradual motorisation of the army and wanted to try out two of these vehicles, using them very successfully for the transportation of various goods on very demanding daily journeys.

Encouraged by the success of its goods vehicles, Fiat turned its

TOP: A substantial "fleet of military machines" made up of "Fiat type 15 bis Libia" and "15 Ter" trucks near Tripoli at the beginning of the Italo-Turkish war of 1911-12.
ABOVE: A "type 15 bis Libia" fitted with benches and used as a reconnaissance vehicle.

attention to passenger transport. And so the first buses were born. Between 1907 and 1910, the Turin company produced two basic bus versions: a light version with an 18 HP - 24 HP engine and a 12 - 24 passenger capacity, and a heavy version able to transport 28 - 30 people. The first managed a speed of 27 kilometres an hour, the second 39 kilometres an hour.

The body was fitted out according to the customer's requirements and depending on the climatic conditions of the area in which the vehicle was to operate. It could be open, with a hood to protect the passengers in bad weather or closed, with sliding windows in the sides.

There were also double decker vehicles, and it was not rare - particularly for completely or partly suburban services - to have two different classes: first class was towards the driver, and passengers boarded at the front, second was towards the rear and accessed from the back.

So within 10 years from the date it was founded, Fiat had managed to cover practically all the transport requirements, both in the civilian field and in the military field. And when, in 1911, Italian forces were in Libya engaged in the Italo-Turkish conflict, Fiat was able to provide the army with the means of transport it needed.

Within a short period it had fitted out the light "15 Bis" truck, also known as the "Tipo Libia", which differed from the basic "15" type through the use of twin rear wheels, allowing greater manoeuvrability on the roads through the desert.

From the "15 Bis", which had a 3,053 cc, 4 cylinder engine with a power of 16 HP, was derived the "15 Ter" which had a higher cubic capacity engine - 4,398 cc to be precise - with consequent increases in power (of approx. 40 HP) and in speed.

TOP: The "17 A" derived directly from the "17" model in 1913.
CENTRE: The military "15 Ter" which remained in production in this version
more or less to the end of the First World War.
ABOVE: Original "mobile searchlight" on a "Fiat 15 Ter" chassis.

Many of these vehicles were equipped with special bodies, in particular the ambulance version. And so, on the 8th June 1912, during the Battle of Zanzibar, the "15 Bis" and the "15 Ter" were the first vehicles in history to be used in a war zone.

In the period 1911 to 1912 more than 200 of these vehicles were supplied to the Italian army fighting in Libya.

In the meantime, Fiat continued to launch new passenger vehicles and in 1912, managed to set up its own transport company, S.I.T.A., ("Società Italiana Trasporti Automobilistici").

In just three decades, from the initial 54 kilometres of transport routes covering approx. 95,000 kilometres a year, S.I.T.A. progressed to operating 450 regular services and 85 tour services for 20 million kilometres a year. They had a pool of 2,000 vehicles by the beginning of the sixties.

But let us go back to Fiat and its truck production.

First of all, we wish to emphasise that for reasons of space, and not wishing to digress, no reference is made to the activities of the Turin company in the car sector, nor in other sectors associated with the motoring world.

The excellent service which the first vehicles had provided in the field motivated the Ministry of War to set up a vehicle park which was adequate for future requirements. And the most substantial orders were placed with Fiat.

On the eve of the First World War, apart from the "15 Ter" vehicles mentioned, which had been modernised in the meantime, the light "18 M" vehicle and the medium and heavy "18 P", "18 BC", "18 BL" and "18 BLR" vehicles went into production, up to and including the large "20 B" and "30" tractors capable of towing weights of up to 100 tonnes.

Practically all these models allowed for special conversions: trucks for the ground services and for the emerging air squadrons, tankers, ambulances and mobile hospitals, searchlights and buses with different seating capacities.

Of all these vehicles, the most popular, intended for a wide range of uses, were the medium size "18 P" and the heavy "18 BL" vehicles together with the versatile "15 Ter".

However the true champion of the history of the Italian vehicle industry was the "18 BL". In just 7 years, until 1921, nearly 20,000 of these vehicles were made, a very high number for the time. The "18 BL" had a payload of three and a half tonnes. The transmission used was still a chain transmission, but the vehicle as a whole already had a more modern appearance: driving cab protected by a windscreen, box body with drop sides and hoops for the canvas.

The engine used was a 5,650 cc, 4 cylinder engine with a power of 38 HP at 1,300 r.p.m. In the "BLR" version (where "R" stands for reinforced), the engine was still the 4 cylinder version, but this time it had 6,230 cc and a power of approximately 40 HP. With a payload of 4,500 kg, it was able to reach speeds exceeding 25 kilometres an hour.

When the First World War broke out, Fiat received a first large order from the Ministry of War for 1,677 vehicles, of which 106 were to be ambulances and 1,571 trucks (in particular the "15 Ter" light truck), the medium truck ("18 P") and the heavy truck ("17 A" first of all and then the "18 BL"). To give an idea of the size of the order placed with Fiat, it is sufficient to say that only 723 vehicles were ordered from all the other Italian vehicle producers put together - Isotta Fraschini, Itala, Spa and Züst. Other orders were to follow (it is not necessary to list them here), but it must be remembered that the Italian industry, and mainly Fiat, also supplied the allied forces. In France, for example, during the First World War, more than 25% of the trucks in active service were made in Italy. And these were almost exclusively vehicles supplied in several stages by Fiat. The percentage of Italian vehicles used by the English armed forces was not so high, but was none the less significant. All in all, Fiat supplied some tens of thousands of vehicles to the allied armies.

TOP: "Fiat 18 BL" chassis produced between 1914 and 1921 in numerous versions, both civilian and military.
CENTRE: Notable for the times, exports of the "BLR" versions (where "R" stood for "reinforced").
ABOVE: This impressive "20 B" artillery tractor dates from 1915; the engine was a split block 4 cylinder engine with a total cylinder capacity of 10,818 cc able to develop a power of 60 HP; rear wheel drive with differential lock was controlled by the driver; the rear wheels could also be equipped with tracks consisting of hinged plates.

On the other hand, on examining Fiat's annual truck production statistics, the numeric progression is very evident. It goes from 1,408 vehicles in 1914 to 6,657 in 1915, 12,225 in 1916, arriving at 17,217 in 1917, a remarkable achievement for the time. It was an all-time record and was only just beaten 38 years later in 1955. Fortunately, the war ended in 1918 and the production of military vehicles dropped to 14,304 vehicles.

But these figures show the impressive production levels reached by Fiat after less than two decades of activity in the transport vehicle sector.

As a result, the Turin company, and with it Italian industry as a whole, soon managed to gain ground in other countries, even though they too had had high production capacity at the time.

At the end of the First World War, a start was made on the long and difficult task of rebuilding the areas more directly affected by the events of the war, and the re-organisation of country's political, social and economic systems.

The climate was made difficult by political and social tensions and, naturally enough, by shortages and uncertainty in the economic and industrial fields. The vehicle industry was hit in particular, both as a whole and in the industrial vehicle sector. This was due to the gradual disposal of the military vehicles left in store after demobilisation, resulting in a saturation of the market. Fiat, which at the beginning of the twenties was still one of the leading European

TOP: Curious, yet advanced for the times, these armed vehicles made on the "15 Ter" chassis were supplied to India in 1918.
ABOVE: Original photographic montage, proclaiming Fiat's presence "on land, on sea and in the air" at the time of the First World War.

car makers, continued its gradual expansion, but was also beset by difficulties and unknown factors.

It completed the building of the new factory at Lingotto, a futuristic structure for the time, and one still admired today for its architectural and functional design (we would also mention the test track on the roof of the building and the two majestic spiral ramps). It was officially opened on the 22nd May 1923 when it had already been in operation for a few months.

At the same time, Fiat intensified its production of cars and started the design and manufacture of new vehicles suitable both for transporting goods and for special applications and services.

Naturally, they did not neglect the passenger transport sector either. Consequently, from 1923, new types of medium and light vehicles with payloads of between 500 kilogrammes and 1,500 kilogrammes were introduced onto the market.

They started with models equipped with engines used in cars, but they were almost always mounted on suitably designed chassis for the more rigorous use for which the vehicles were intended.

For example the "502 F" and "505 F", equipped with 1,460 cc and 2,296 cc 4 cylinder engines and with a payload of 750 kilogrammes and 1,200 kilogrammes, respectively.

In 1924 the company launched the "van" version of the "509" and the "603" truck, with a payload of 2,000 kilogrammes, and equipped with the same "505" engine already mentioned. A "coach" version of the same chassis was also made, the "603 S", but this had a 3,446 cc, 6 cylinder engine and was capable of accommodating 23 seats.

In 1926 the same 6 cylinder engine was used on the new "605" trucks and buses. A version with a 6 cylinder engine but with a cubic capacity of 3,739 was also produced. Other models followed which could still be defined as derivatives of these vehicles. Of these we would mention the "514", light transport vehicles which were very popular because they were very economical. And a "614" version launched in 1930, with twice the payload i.e. approx. 1,000 kilogrammes

But the true turn came in 1929 when Fiat decided to rationalise its production, make its selling organisation more efficient and promote the use of the truck in all its possible variations. This gave rise to the "621", a vehicle of very modern design with stamped steel chassis, which remained in production until 1939 in different versions and with different engines.

The basic model was a truck with enclosed cab and hinged sides and tailgate (also steel) which could be removed.

The engine, still fuelled by petrol engine, was a 6 cylinder unit with a total cylinder capacity of 2,516 cc and was capable of developing a

TOP LEFT: The "Giardiniera" in South Africa in 1921, made (probably at the request of the local representative) on a "502 F" chassis.
TOP RIGHT: Elegant van on "509 F" chassis in 1925, supplied to a fashion house in Turin.
CENTRE AND ABOVE: A refined coach made on the "603 S" chassis with deluxe decor, complete with "drawing room".

27

TOP: The "621", born in 1929. This was the first modern truck with stamped steel chassis; initially equipped with a 2,516 cc petrol engine, it was subsequently also equipped with a diesel engine, still a 4 cylinder model, with 4,580 cc.
ABOVE: Directly derived from the above , the "621 P" was the first standard Fiat truck with 3 axles," 6x2", which made it possible to increase the payload from the 2,000 kg of the basic model with 2 axles to 3,500 kg; launched in 1930, it gave rise to the "621 PN" version in 1934, still equipped with the above diesel engine. The payload of this new version was increased to 4,000 kg.

power of approx. 45 HP at 2,600 r.p.m. The maximum speed was 60 km/h and it had a gradeability of 19.5%. The consumption was 24.5 litres per 100 km and the payload, 1,700 kg, which could be increased to 2,500 kg on the version with twin rear wheels.

It had a single plate clutch; 4 speed box plus reverse, with central clutch lever; transmission shaft with 2 universal joints at the ends; rear axle with "Gleason" reduction gear; leaf spring suspension with shock absorbers; irreversible type steering; pedal controlled expansion brakes on all four wheels and a handbrake acting on the rear wheels.

As mentioned, there were several versions available, including the "621 P", the first Italian truck with 3 axles which was in production from 1930 and, in 1934, the diesel engine version and also the "621 RG" in 1938, complete with gas generator.

In the meantime, in 1929, an important event occurred: the founding of the "Consortium Fiat Veicoli Industriali", finalised in 1930, which concentrated

production and marketing control of commercial vehicles at the Fiat organisation. This included the "Spa" and "Ceirano" industrial vehicles.

Once this consortium was in place, Fiat was able to offer suitable vehicles, both military and civilian, for a variety of applications at competitive prices. Vehicles for haulage, passenger transport services, fire brigades, rescue and medical services, refrigerated transport, mobile shops, military field kitchens - even vehicles with tower superstructures for maintaining overhead power lines and many other uses.

It is worth pointing out that apart from the consortium, a very valuable technical consultation service was also created which was able to provide useful information on these vehicles: instructions and advice on the use of the vehicles, conversions and the various equipment available, practical advice, and much more besides.

But, during those years, the most important technical event which was to radically alter the transporting of goods and people by road was quietly simmering away. It was the advent of the diesel engine for commercial vehicles. Fiat already had considerable experience in this sector, having built diesel engines for ships since 1908. But the application of this engine to motor vehicles required very special studies and investigations.

In the period between 1925 and 1930, "Fiat Grandi Motori" started to manufacture a fast engine - a 4 stroke direct injection engine with small cylinders and a high engine speed which was able to develop impressive drive power.

They also made engines for railway locomotives, with 6 cylinders and a bore of 200 mm. Capable of developing 200 HP at approximately 800 rpm, these were followed by engines which were even smaller.

Finally, in 1930, they arrived at the first diesel engine for road vehicles which had been entirely designed and built in Italy.

For the first experiments, using a "Ceirano" chassis with a load

capacity of 8 tonnes, they used a 6 cylinder direct injection engine which was equivalent in terms of performance (80 HP), if not in size and weight, to the petrol engine which was used to power the original version of this vehicle.

The first tangible fruit of these experiments was the manufacture of two new trucks, equipped with diesel engines which were way ahead of their time: the "632 N", with a payload of 4 tonnes and the "634 N" with a payload of 6 tonnes. The letter N stood for the word "naphtha", used by Fiat to indicate models equipped with a diesel engine.

Both were then launched at the International Motor Show in 1931 which, at that time, was held as part of the Milan Fair.

The "632 N" was equipped with the "350" type diesel engine, a 4 cylinder, 5,540 cc engine able to develop a power of approximately 55 HP at 1,600 - 1,800 r.p.m. The "634 N", on the other hand, used the "355" diesel engine which was a 6 cylinder 8,310 cc engine producing 75 HP at 1,600 - 1,700 r.p.m.

The two engines - both direct injection, 4 strokes - had similar design and operating characteristics: vertical in-line cylinders, monobloc construction, with a bore and stroke of 105 mm x 160 mm; lubrication via two geared pumps (one feed and one recirculation); water cooling via a single centrifugal pump; starting via two 24 V electric motors.

It is worth mentioning that on these engines each cylinder, with pressed-in liner and removable head, had a decompression valve, and that the engine shaft was equipped with a flywheel to take up the torsional stresses. The distributor was the overhead valve type with adjustable tappets, and the timing shaft was controlled by the same chain which operated the fuel pump and the centrifugal governor.

Other technical characteristics common to both trucks were: dry multiple disc clutch; 4 speed box plus reverse with central control lever; 3 part transmission shaft, the first section of which (the horizontal section) was connected to the centre section via flexible

TOP: The "632N" was presented at the Milan Motor Show in April 1931, with the "634 N"; the first had a 5,540 cc four cylinder Diesel engine and the second had a 8,310 cc six cylinder Diesel engine.
CENTRE: About half-way through the 30s, at the time of economic self-sufficiency and sanctions, the "634" also had a version with a "gas generator" plant, produced by Fiat itself.
BOTTOM: The "635 RNL" bus (1933-39).

couplings, while the rear section (connected to the axle) was equipped with universal joints; rear axle with reduction worm gear; and differential unit and reduction gear mounted on adjustable taper ball bearings to form a single unit. Also, half-elliptic spring suspension with grease nipples at the joints, rubber shock absorbers, rear springs with two degrees of

flexibility; worm and sector steering gear; expansion brakes on all four wheels, controlled by a pedal via three vacuum servo-brakes (one for the front brakes, the other two for the rear brakes) and also an emergency hand brake acting on the intermediate transmission shaft.

In both vehicles, the chassis (slightly different dimensions in each case) was made from

The giant and the pygmy: nothing frightened the tiny "508 Balilla" truck which was faster than the gigantic "634 N" with trailer.

stamped sheet steel with reinforced cross members and flexible couplings for towing a trailer if required.

The body consisted of an internal front cab (the "634 N" equipped for the first time with a bunk) with two doors, wind-down windows, a two part windscreen which could be opened and fixed with suitable clips and also a large box body with drop sides.

From 1933, the "632 N" was also made as the "633 N" civilian and military versions, which remained in production until 1936. At the request of the ministry concerned, the "633" was also equipped as a military vehicle, using a four cylinder 6,647 cc petrol engine capable of 80 HP at 2,100 r.p.m.

In 1933 there was also a new version of the "634 N" with some of its characteristics modified and improved. Still with the 6 cylinder engine, but this time with 8,355 cc and the power increased to 80 HP at 1,700 r.p.m., this vehicle remained in production until 1939 and, during that period, Fiat also made a version with a 6 cylinder, 9,972 cc engine.

At the 1931 show, Fiat presented another interesting development - a coach with a petrol engine - 6 cylinders, 5,262 cc and also 6,220 cc (from 1932). This was the "635 R"

which offered 30 comfortable seats and was specially designed for travel companies. This could be increased to 35 seats, and in the case of the deluxe version, with a roof which opened completely. The "635 R", eventually also available with diesel engine and gas generator, remained in production until 1939.

In 1932, a particularly important year for Fiat, a vehicle was born which was destined to become the famous "508", the "Balilla", the first real "utility" vehicle in the history of Italian automotive engineering. This small, prestigious vehicle which remained in production until 1945, was to mark the history of the car for many years to come through the Fiat "1100" family and its many variations, including the bigger engines which were basically derived from it.

For example, from the "508" was derived a truck with a payload of 450 kg and a van with a payload of 400 kg.

During the first half of the thirties, the lengthy studies made of the manufacture of trucks (particularly, but not exclusively, for military use), which could operate on any type of terrain - hence the name "Dovunque" ("Anywhere") - resulted in the first satisfactory solution to this problem with the production of a

three axle truck with 4 rear wheel drive (in other words 6x4). This was the "Spa Dov. 33".

With intelligent originality the spare wheels, one on each side of the vehicle, "idled" between the driving seat and the body: this arrangement allowed the vehicle to negotiate even difficult obstacles with a certain amount of agility.

The engine was a petrol engine of approximately 40 HP. It had a 4 speed box plus reverse with reduction gear. The payload was 2,500 kg on the road and 2,000 kg off highway. The maximum speed (on road) was just over 50 km/h and the maximum gradeability in first reduced gear was around 60%.

This first model was followed in 1936 by the "Dov. 35", still with a petrol engine, but with a higher cubic capacity and a power of approximately 60 HP and in 1943 by the "Dov. 41" (6x4 and also 6x6) with a payload of 6,000 kg, equipped with a 6 cylinder, 9,365 cc diesel engine with a power of 115 HP.

From this, in 1945 the very famous "Spa 10000" was derived with identical drive line and a payload of 10,000 kg. It was available in both military and civilian versions, 6x4 and 6x2. In 1950 the "Dov. 50" derivative was launched with a 6 cylinder, 10,170 cc diesel engine.

TOP: At the request of the military authorities, Fiat made this interesting off-highway vehicle; christened the "Fiat/Spa Dovunque 33", it had 3 axles, with rear wheel drive (i.e. 6x4). A curious but efficient feature were the spare wheels (on each side between the cab and body). These "idled" to help the vehicle negotiate humps and various obstacles.

CENTRE: The "633 N.M.". This was the first diesel truck supplied to the Italian Armed Forces; the engine was the same as for the "632 N" civilian version. However, there were also versions with petrol engines and gas generators.

ABOVE: A small van with a payload of approximately 300 kg was derived from the tiny Topolino of 1936.

Also around the mid thirties, the medium "618" and "38 R" trucks went into production. These were equipped with petrol engines and had a payload of around 2,500 kg. The range consisted of the "Spa TL 37" military trucks, with 4 wheel and independent wheel drive, the "Spa CL 39" (also called the "Autocarretta Spa 39"), with a 1,628 cc, 4 cylinder petrol engine and the medium artillery tractor "Spa TM 40", using a 9,365 cc, 6 cylinder diesel engine. These vehicles, also available in civilian versions, remained in production until 1948.

We would also like to mention the arrival of the small "Topolino" in 1936. Another vehicle destined to become famous and mark an era, it was subsequently used as the basis for a small van with a payload of approximately 300 kg.

The following year, 1937, was a very important year for the future development of commercial vehicles in Italy.

At the end of that year, the Italian Government issued a ministerial decree containing the basic regulations for limiting the production of industrial vehicles to three categories only, conforming to clearly specified requirements.

In order to qualify for these regulations, the future "standardised vehicles" were granted a three year exemption from road tax and also a reduction of the transport tax in force at the time for a further six years.

In response to these regulations, just over a year later, Fiat presented the standard medium model, the "626 N" and the standard heavy model, the "666 N".

These two new vehicles were characterised by the use of a forward cab, something which Fiat had already used as long ago as 1903 on its very first vehicle, as we have already mentioned.

Both new models had a 4 stroke diesel engine with 6 vertical cylinders in line and injection in high turbulence combustion chambers, but with different cylinder capacities and power.

The "626 N" engine had a cylinder capacity of 5,750 cc and was able to develop a maximum of 70 HP at 2,200 r.p.m., whereas

FIAT 666 N

the one used for the "666 N" had 9,365 cc, developing 105 HP at 2,000 r.p.m.

The cabs were essentially the same except for the dimensions. This also applied to the chassis which were of the straight longitudinal member type.

The "626 N" had a five speed box plus reverse whereas its big brother, the "666 N", had an 8 speed box plus 2 reverse gears independent of the engine/clutch unit and a rear axle with double reduction gear.

The "626 N" offered a payload of 3,140 kg (and could tow approximately 6,500 kg). It was able to reach a maximum speed, when fully laden, of 62 km/h with a standard consumption of 18 to 20 litres of diesel per 100 km. Military versions of this model were made (with a petrol engine) and also buses and coaches.

The "666 N" on the other hand, had a payload of 6,240 kg and was able to tow 12,000 kg. It had a maximum speed of 55 km/h, and a consumption of 29 litres of diesel per 100 km. Various civilian and military versions and also some bus versions were made of this model up until 1948.

In the meantime, in the May of 1939 to be precise, the new and impressive "Mirafiori" factory had been officially opened on a site measuring around a million square metres, including 300,000 square metres of floor space.

But, on the first of September of the same year, the Second World War erupted. The sad sequence of those events is well known. In the first stage, Italy was not involved in the hostilities, but on the 10th June 1940, it allied itself with Germany.

As far as Fiat was concerned, in the years between 1940 and 1945, its production was more or less limited to the needs of war and was gradually geared down. This was also as a result of the damage inflicted on its factories during the war.

Finally, in 1945, with almost 30 million people dead and with destruction valued at approximately 1,500 thousand million dollars, the Second World War finally ended. Again Italy was faced with all the problems of rebuilding, but this time it was made worse by the fact that the whole country had been involved in the fighting.

In addition, the work of rebuilding and starting up the factories again, even if theoretically possible, was hampered by the almost complete lack of raw materials and by the need to rebuild or renew most of the plant and equipment. In addition, there were complex political and social tensions.

As far as the automotive industry was concerned, a further difficulty was caused by the fact that the vehicle park had not only been decimated, but was also extremely fragmented because it was mainly made up of military leftovers.

These leftovers were mainly of American origin and therefore were equipped with very thirsty petrol engines. In this situation, Fiat started up production again, amid extreme difficulties, using the pre-war models such as the "626 N", the "666 N", the "Spa 10000" and, for light transport needs, the various versions of small trucks and vans such as the "1100" and "500".

At the same time, production of

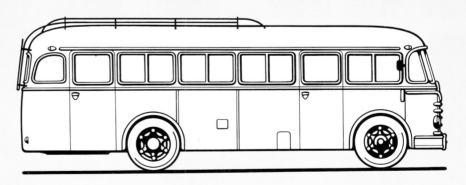

ADJACENT PAGE: On the basis of precise Government regulations, in 1939 the "Fiat 626 N and 666 N standardised" trucks appeared, these being characterised by the introduction of "forward" cabs; the "626" (top left) was in the medium-weight class, with a 5,750 cc six cylinder Diesel engine, a carrying capacity of 3,140 kg and towing weight of 12,000 kg; the "666" (bottom) had a 9,365 cc six cylinder Diesel engine, a carrying capacity of 6,240 kg and towing weight of 12,000 kg; the drawing at top right shows how easy it was to remove the engine for maintenance or repairs (on the "626" and "666").

TOP OF THIS PAGE: The splendid "Fiat/Spa mod. A 10,000" with 3 axles, available in the 6x2 and the 6x4 version, which went into production in 1945. The drive chain was the same as that of the "666 N" and the payload was 10,000 kg.

CENTRE: This van version, the "1.100 ALR", dates back to 1947 and was the last of the series equipped with the "508" 1,089 cc engine; there were innumerable new versions and new models in production until 1971.

ABOVE: Intercity bus, the "640 RN" from 1949 which, like the "640 N" truck, had a 6 cylinder, 6,032 cc diesel engine, the same as used for the "670 N".

commercial vehicles was concentrated at the Turin factory in Corso Ferrucci. It belonged to "Spa" which Fiat had controlled since 1926 and which was finally incorporated in November 1947.

Work then started on designing models to meet the new requirements of road transport: more powerful engines, bigger payloads, higher speeds, greater reliability and fuel economy.

So, between 1948 and 1951, the basic models of the medium and heavy trucks, which were the "640 N", "670 N", and the "680 N", plus the special "639 N" with all wheel drive and the light "615", were launched on the market in rapid succession.

The "640 N" had a 6 cylinder, 4 stroke engine with direct "combustion chamber injection" made in the piston heads, 6,032 cc, and a power of 72 HP at 2,200 rpm.

The payload was 4,300 kg, unladen weight 4,200 kg, and gross vehicle mass 8,500 kg. This truck was able to tow a trailer with a maximum total weight of 6,500 kg. The "train", i.e. the tractor plus trailer, had a total fully laden weight of 15,000 kg. The maximum speed in fifth gear was given as more than 60 km/h.

The cab, which was spacious and comfortable, complete with bunk, was more or less the same as the one designed for the "666 N". Some bus versions were also made of this particular model.

The "670 N" had the same engine as the "640 N". But these models differed in terms of dimensions, payload and axial ratio. The "670 N" had a payload of 7,000 kg, a gross vehicle mass of 12,700 kg and a maximum speed when fully laden of 57.2 km/h in fifth gear.

The most powerful model was the "680 N", equipped with a 10,170 cc, 6 cylinder diesel engine with a power of 123 HP at 1,800 r.p.m. Its cylinder head, with 4 overhead valves per cylinder, (two inlet valves and two exhaust valves), also featured a timing shaft in the base.

The payload was 7,700 kg and the weight which could be towed was 14,000 kg.

It had a four speed box plus reverse with reduction gear. Maximum speed when fully laden, in normal fourth gear, was just over 40 km/h

with an average consumption of 22.8 litres of diesel per 100 km (32.5 litres for the "train" version). Bus versions were also made of this model.

The original and technically advanced "639 N", the 4x4 truck derived from the military version, was equipped with a 6 cylinder, 4 stroke 6,032 cc diesel engine with a power of 72 HP at 2,200 r.p.m.

It had a dry single-plate clutch and four speed box plus reverse with reduction gear. The trans-mission unit for the front wheel drive, arranged between the gearbox and the rear axle, consisted of three permanently engaged helical gears and a free wheel controlled by a lever.

It was equipped with a load bearing

type front axle, bevel gear with spiral toothing, front wheel transmission via twin universal joints, load bearing rear axle and differential lock. Payload on the road was 3,640 kg and 3,000 kg off highway, with maximum speeds of 58.5 km/h and 43.3 km/h respectively.

Finally, the 615 was proudly launched by Fiat as the "one and a half tonne truck with many uses, fast and economical".

It was also emphasised that, although it could be classed as a light vehicle, it was not a derivative but a true industrial vehicle for fast transport. It was available both as a truck and as a chassis cab or chassis on its own.

The chassis offered vast conversion possibilities: fire engines, hotel buses, ambulances, parcel delivery vans, vehicles for maintaining overhead telephone and cable lines, for distributing milk, drinks, and for many other uses besides.

The first basic version of the "615" was equipped with a 4 stroke petrol engine with 1,395 cc and 39 HP at 3,800 rpm. It had a 4 speed gearbox plus reverse, with 2nd, 3rd and 4th gear synchronised and controlled by a gear lever underneath the steering wheel. The chassis had longitudinal members which were reinforced and connected by a central cross-member. It had an all steel cab with removable bonnet, bench seat for 2 or even 3 people, left-hand drive, ventilated hydraulic brakes on four wheels and a handbrake on the rear axle, plus disc wheels with rear double rubber shock mountings.

However, in 1952, less than a year after its launch, the "615" became the "615 N" through the use of a diesel engine or, to be more precise, the engine which a few months later, was to be used on the "Fiat 1400" diesel, the first Italian vehicle to use a diesel power train. This was a 1,901 cc, 4 cylinder engine capable of developing a power of 40 HP at 3,200 rpm, featuring overhead valve distributor and indirect injection with a Ricardo Comet type pre-combustion chamber. The consumption was just 7.8 litres of diesel per 100 km.

Again in 1952, the "642 N" and "682 N" trucks went into production, later also available as semi-trailer tractors and buses. The first was derived directly from the "640 N", using an engine with a slightly higher cylinder capacity and with the power increased to 92 HP at 2,000 rpm. The second version however, was derived from the "680 N" which used this engine initially. This was followed almost immediately by a derivative which had a higher cubic capacity and power, namely 10,676 cc and 140 HP at 1,800 rpm.

It is worth mentioning that between 1960 and 1963 the "642 N/65" version was derived from the "642 N". This still had a 6 cylinder engine, but this time with

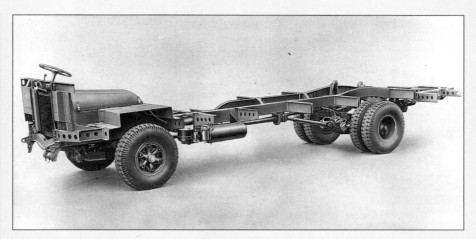

TOP OPPOSITE PAGE: The robust chassis of the "680 N" launched in 1949. The engine was a 6 cylinder, 10,170 cc diesel engine which had four valves per cylinder and a power of 123 HP at 1,800 rpm.
BOTTOM: The agile and versatile "615" light truck launched in 1951 as the "one and a half tonne truck with many uses, fast and economical".
TOP OF THIS PAGE: The indestructible and reliable chassis of the "682 N", the truck which made history for Fiat and which remained in production - with subsequent modifications and improvements - for a quarter of a century.
BOTTOM: The assembly line for the "682 N2" in 1955; the "642 N" models were also assembled on the same line.

7,298 cc and 120 HP at 2,200 rpm. But the truck which really makes Fiat's history at this time is the "682". When it was born it had a 10,676 cc 6 cylinder engine with a power of 140 HP. The truck versions had payloads of approximately 8,000 kg, with a fully laden towing capacity of 14,000 kg. The tractor version was able to pull semi-trailers with a total weight of around 30,000 kg.

These were followed by an increase in power and, from 1962, a 6 cylinder diesel engine was used with the cubic capacity increased to 11,548 cc and with a power of approximately 180 HP.

Naturally, there were also bus versions, with variable payloads and with 55 seats and more.

This vehicle, and also the subsequent versions, was to be passed on to Iveco and remained in production until the end of the eighties.

Between 1953 and 1955 various local and long distance bus variants were produced; the "404 UP", a 60 seater, with the same engine as the "642 N", the "401 UM" and the "306" which had the "682 N" engine.

In 1955, on the basis of the NATO standard, a special military version of the "639 N" 4x4 already mentioned went into production. This was the "639 N2", which was commonly referred to as the "6600", with a 6,650 cc engine and the power increased to 92 HP at 2,000 rpm. It had a payload of approximately 5,000 kg.

The next year it was the turn of a new heavy truck with 4 wheel drive specially designed for transporting goods in the NATO "10 tonne 6x6" category. This was the "CP/56", also commonly known as the "6601".

This truck used a different version of the engine used on the "682 N" civilian vehicles; the cylinder capacity was the same, but the power had been increased to 220 HP at 2,600 rpm.

It is curious that this model, entirely designed at Fiat, was then transferred for production to OM, a make which had already become part of the Fiat Group.

FROM THE TOP: Launched in 1958, the medium/light "C 40 N" and "C 50 N" which enjoyed immediate success; powered with a 6 cylinder 4,678 cc diesel engine with 90 HP, they were able to transport 4,000 kg and 5,000 kg respectively; the photograph shows a "C 50 N" in the classic box body truck version. The "309s" were buses equipped initially with a 6 cylinder 7,298 cc diesel engine and, two years later (1961) with a 6 cylinder diesel engine, but this time with 9,161 cc. The next photograph shows, a "309 Granluce", in the long distance truck version. Still in 1959, the new "645 N", equipped with the same engine as "C 40 N" and "C 50 N", had a payload of 4,500 kg. The bottom illustration shows the ultra-modern, robust and pure lines of the light "625 N".

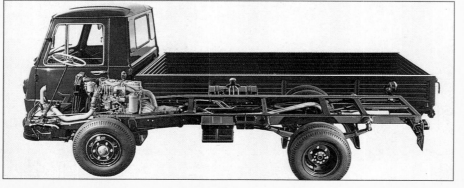

In the sixties there were other special vehicle versions still in the NATO categories, but we will discuss these later.

To go back to the civilian versions, in 1958 the medium/light "C 40 N" and "C 50 N" vehicles went onto the market, both featuring a 4,678 cc, 6 cylinder diesel engine with a power of 90 HP at 3,000 rpm. Basically these differed from each other in transport capacity; 4,000 kg and 5,000 kg respectively with fully laden weights of 7,465 kg and 8,700 kg. There were numerous versions with different wheelbases to meet the varied demands of customers.

1959 was an important year for the Italian vehicle industry. The much awaited new version of the Highway Code was finally published with the corresponding regulations which, although not perfect, laid down the standards for the manufacture of new vehicles.

Other significant events were the launching of vast road-building programmes and a slight relaxation of excise pressure on fuels. As is easy to imagine, these events formed the basis of an incentive policy in favour of vehicle and road transport in general.

In that year, Fiat also launched new bus models: the "314", equipped with the same engine as the "C 40 N" and "C 50 N" vehicles already mentioned; the "410", equipped with a variant of the engine used for the "682 N" trucks (10,676 cc and a power of 150 HP at 2,000 rpm) and, from 1962, also with an 11,548 cc, 6 cylinder diesel engine with a power of 176 HP at 1,900 rpm. Still in 1959, the company launched the "309" with a 7,298 cc, 6 cylinder diesel engine, 115 HP at 2,200 rpm (and, from 1961, 9,161 cc, 156 HP at 2,400 rpm), and also the medium transport trucks "645 N", with a payload of 4,500 kg, equipped with the same engine as the "C 40 N" and "C 50 N" already mentioned.

Various versions with different wheelbases and also restyled models were based on the "645 N", until (in 1960) the "650 N" with a payload of 5,000 kg upwards arrived.

At the beginning of the sixties there was clear evidence of

In the demanding heavy military vehicle sector, the "6607 CP 6x6" is worthy of mention. Fiat designed it for transporting land-air missile batteries. This vehicle belongs to the NATO 8 tonne 6x6 category and was mainly derived from the previous model, the "6602 CP 4x4", in the NATO 6 tonne 4x4 category.

considerable development internationally following specific road transport agreements, and therefore many skilful cards were played for offering suitable long distance and long haul vehicles in this difficult heavy vehicle sector.

As long ago as 1960, Fiat was offering the powerful 3 axle "690 N" with two front steering axles, which was able to transport more than 10,000 kg in the truck version and was capable of towing up to 2,500 kg in the semi-trailer tractor version (launched the following year). The engine in this case was a 10,676 cc, 6 cylinder engine with a power of 152 HP at 1,900 rpm.

This vehicle remained in production for nearly fifteen years with various versions, different wheelbases and new diesel engines. These were still the 6 cylinder, but of 3 different cylinder capacities: 11,548 cc and 177 HP, 12,883 cc and 180 HP and 19,819 cc and 200 HP, all at 2,500 rpm.

This model was highly successful and was widely used by specialist companies in the industry especially for conversion to 4 axle vehicles.

At the other end of the payload scale Fiat launched the "600 T" van in 1961 (when the T stood for transport), as the direct de-

scendant of the "600 D" utility vehicle introduced on the market the previous year (a bigger version of which had been produced from the original version of 1955).

This had a load capacity of approximately 600 kg and had a self-supporting body with ample loading space compared with the overall compact dimensions. The engine was a rear-mounted, 767 cc 4 cylinder petrol engine with a power of 32 HP at 4,800 rpm giving a maximum speed of approximately 95 km/h.

20 different versions of this interesting vehicle were offered, each suitable for solving specific problems concerned with the transport of goods or passengers both in town and out in the country.

In 1962, an interesting new military vehicle in the NATO 6 tonne 4x4 category was launched: this was the "CP/62" heavy vehicle known as the "6602". It had a payload of 5,000 kg and could tow up to 10,000 kg. Its speed exceeded 65 km/h and it had a range of approximately 500 km plus a gradeability of 60% and wadability of 85 cm.

Some time afterwards, following the adoption of land/air missiles by the Italian army, the Turin company was given the job of designing a vehicle suitable for

LEFT: The "683 N" 3 axle 6x4 of 1965 had a powerful 6 cylinder diesel engine with 12,883 cc, able to develop a power of 210 HP at 1,900 rpm; available in various versions, these were excellent vehicles not only for use on the roads, but also for heavy work in quarries and building sites; the photograph shows a three sided tip-up tractor for semi-trailer use.
BELOW: In the so-called "vehicle derivative" sector, 1966 saw the launch of the "238" (in the photograph) and the "241" with payloads of 1,000 kg and 1,400 kg respectively, with diesel and petrol engines.

this new type of service. Mainly derived from the "6602", the result was the Fiat "6607" 6x6 truck, belonging to the NATO 8 tonne 6x6 category.

Production of this vehicle went to the S.p.A. division of that time, which moved from its own factory in Corso Ferrucci, Turin, to a new complex exclusively intended for the production of industrial vehicles. These premises were near the river Stura, on the edge of the city of Turin.

In 1963 the "662 N" and "643 N" models were launched. They remained in production in various versions with different wheelbases for around 10 years.

The first had a payload of approximately 6,200 kg and was equipped with the same 4,678 cc diesel engine already used for the "645 N" models (the first version, with a payload of approximately 4,500 kg, was launched in 1960).

The second version used the 9,161 cc, 6 cylinder diesel engine with a power of 160 HP at 2,400 rpm, also used on one of the versions of the "309" bus brought out in 1962. The payload was 7,500 kg for the truck version and approximately 21,800 kg for the semi-trailer tractor version.

Numerous new versions were also launched in 1965, starting with the "693 N" 3 axle heavy vehicle with two rear drive axles (in other words a 6x4), which was also suitable for particularly heavy duty work in quarries and on building sites. Available in truck and tractor versions, it was powered by a 12,883 cc, 6 cylinder diesel engine with a power of approximately 210 HP at 1,900 rpm.

Two light vehicles also went into production: the "616 N", with a payload of 1,750 kg in the truck version and 1,650 kg in the van version; and also the "625" with a payload of 2,500 kg in the truck version and 2,000 kg in the van version. There was also a 24 seater bus version of this vehicle.

Both were equipped with a 4 cylinder diesel engine, 2,693 cc initially, with 66 HP at 3,500 rpm and later 3,119 cc with a power of 70 HP at 3,200 rpm, and later still 3,455 cc with a power of 81.5 HP, still at 3,200 rpm. In 1970 a 4 cylinder petrol engine version of this vehicle went into production. This had 2,125 cc and a power of 65 HP at 4,000 rpm.

Still in 1965, there was also the "416" 52 seater bus using the same engine as the "C 40 N", which, from 1968, was also used for the "414" series 60 seater buses.

In 1966 two interesting new light trucks went onto the market, these being the "238" and "241", of which many versions were made for numerous applications.

The "238" had a payload of approximately 1,000 kg and in the period of its production was equipped with different engines: a 1,221 cc, 4 cylinder diesel engine plus 1,197 cc and 1,428 cc, 4 cylinder petrol engines.

The "241" had a payload of 1,300/1,400 kg and was equipped either with a 4 cylinder 1,438 cc petrol engine or a 4 cylinder 1,895 cc diesel engine.

In 1967 the new models - truck and semi-trailer versions - were also equipped with the same 12,883 cc diesel engine used for the "693 N". This was the "683 N" with a fully laden weight of 14,000 kg and 32,000 kg.

1969 was a difficult year for Fiat. This was the year of the "hot autumn", the culmination of a long, difficult period of social and industrial unrest, certainly the most difficult period Italy had faced since the end of the war.

As was inevitable, these events had a detrimental effect on the productivity of all large and medium-sized industries, resulting in a worrying increase in production costs.

The repercussions on Fiat itself

were particularly serious, since the company had only just taken over the other large automotive company in Turin, Lancia, which was then faced with extremely serious internal difficulties, both financial and organisational. Also, this was a time when international competition was becoming more and more aggressive.

The situation was dealt with by imposing a vast reorganisation programme on the Group aimed at regrouping its various production divisions. As a result, the Fiat Veicoli Industriali section was reorganised as an independent division concentrating on the Fiat and OM products and also those of the French company Unic.

This new organisation was the stepping stone for the rationalisation of the production organisation and the range of vehicles to be manufactured in the medium and long term.

In an initial stage, the existing models were modified and improved, but soon models of a new generation were to be added to the Design and Production departments.

And so the "619 N" was born, a truck and semi-trailer tractor, and also the "691 N", a 3 axle vehicle with 2 front steering axles.

Both models used an excellent 13,798 cc, 6 cylinder diesel engine in 260 HP and 225 HP versions at 2,200 rpm.

Depending on the version, the "619 N" had a payload of 6,350 to 7,150 kg (and 11,250 to 12,150 kg) and the semi-trailer tractor version was able to tow a weight exceeding 25,000 kg.

The "691 N" also had a payload exceeding 10,000 kg and the semi-trailer version was able to tow weights of up to 25,000 kg.

As far as their design and technical characteristics were concerned, both vehicles were suitable for numerous special applications and could also accommodate additional axles.

The "697 N", a truck and semi-trailer tractor with 3 axles, including 2 rear drive axles, was equipped with the same engine as already mentioned. This vehicle was capable of payloads up to just under 10,000 kg and, in the case of the semi-trailer tractor, was able to tow weights up to 23,600 kg.

TOP: The generous 8210.02 engine used from 1970 on the "619", "691 N" and "697 N" and also on the "421 A" and "421 AL" buses; this was a 6 cylinder diesel with 13,798 cc, and power of up to 260 HP at 2,000/2,200 rpm.
ABOVE: Semi-trailer truck "697 N" with 3 axles, rear wheel drive, 6x4, with tip-up mechanism for quarry and site work.

Numerous special uses were also made of these models (with more or fewer axles), such as heavy duty quarry work.

In 1970 we saw the "672 N", equipped with a 5,183 cc, 6 cylinder diesel engine with a payload of up to 7,100 kg, the "673 N", with a 7,412 cc, 6 cylinder diesel engine and payloads of up to 7,650 kg, and the "684 N", equipped with 9,819 cc, 6 cylinder diesel engine with a power of 200 HP at 2,500 rpm. These could carry

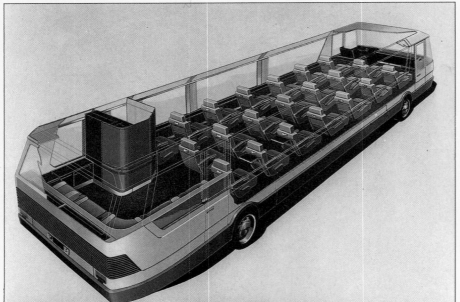

TOP: Restrained but extremely elegant, the "343" 51 seater long-distance bus;
with 6 cylinder 9,818 cc diesel engine.
ABOVE: Using a "343" chassis, Fiat also made this outstanding deluxe coach.
Note the internal decor and the elegance of the seats.

payloads of up to 7,800 kg, and the semi-trailer tractor versions could tow up to 26,000 kg.

In the same year, Fiat Auto launched its "850 T" van with rear engine, a 903 cc, 4 cylinder petrol engine able to develop 33 HP. The variants offered numbered 20 in all and some body-makers also fitted out truck versions.

Almost at the same time, Fiat Veicoli Industriali launched a range of new buses: "308" and "343" long distance and tourist buses and the "418" local buses, all using the same engine as the "684 N" truck. There was also the "421" local bus equipped with the same engine as the "697 N" truck.

In 1973 new models of medium and medium/high range trucks were launched on the market in the personalised Fiat and OM versions. Of these we would mention the "50 NC" and the derivatives "55 N" and "65 N", equipped with 3,455 cc, 4 cylinder diesel engines capable of 81.5 HP at 3,200 rpm and with payloads of up to 3,000 kg.

These were followed by the "80 NC", "90 NC", "100 NC", "110 PC" and "110 NT", all with a 5,183 cc 6 cylinder diesel engine and a power of 122 HP at 3,200 rpm. They had payloads of approximately 2,100 kg to more than 7,000 kg for vans and trucks, and

a maximum towing weight of 14,200 kg for the "110 NT" trailer version.

The "130 NC", equipped with a 7,412 cc, 6 cylinder diesel engine capable of 145 HP at 2,600 rpm, was also launched in various versions (truck, semi-trailer truck, cab chassis and with different wheelbases).

The gearbox used was a 5 speed box which became a 10 speed box in the "NR" versions (designed for towing a trailer) and the "NT" version (semi-trailer tractor).

Although belonging to the medium category, these models were equipped for the first time with many devices which, up to that time, had been reserved for vehicles intended for heavy duty transport applications. However, they maintained the advantages of a more manoeuvrable vehicle with lower operating costs and generous loading capacities.

In the October of 1973 at the Industrial and Commercial Vehicle Show in Turin, Fiat Auto presented, as an absolutely new line, the "242" front-wheel drive vans with a payload of 1,500 kg and 1,800 kg. These were the fruit of the technical cooperation agreement signed between Fiat and the French company Citroën. In Italy, the first was marketed with the Citroën diesel engine only. This was the 2,175 cc, 4 cylinder engine with a power of 61.5 HP at 4,500 rpm; the second could be equipped with either the Citroën diesel engine or a Fiat petrol engine - the 1,995 cc 4 cylinder in line version with a power of 68 HP at 4,300 rpm (derived - with modifications - from the Fiat "132" car engine).

Apart from the vans, a pick-up version with fixed sides was also produced. All the basic versions were available with numerous special items of equipment in order to increase the range of use and improve the economy of the vehicles under a very wide range of service conditions.

Also at the show, Fiat Veicoli Industriali presented its new 4x4 amphibious truck, the "6640 A", as a completely new line.

This remarkable vehicle, with sealed integral body, had been designed according to specific service requirements for transporting

THE TOP TWO PHOTOGRAPHS: In 1973, a new standardised range of trucks for medium-weight transport was presented; on the left, the "50 NC", "80 NC" and "90 NC" models and, on the right, the "100 NC"; the carrying capacities ranged from approximately 2,000 to 6,000 kg.
CENTRE LEFT: The new "130 NCs", being vehicles featuring advanced technology, were fitted with 7,412 cc six cylinder Diesel engines capable of delivering 145 HP (DIN) at 2,600 rpm.
CENTRE: The new "242" front wheel drive light commercial vehicles, which are the result of an agreement with Citroën, were made by means of joint production in two base models with carrying capacities of 1,500 kg and 1,800 kg and were either petrol or Diesel engined.
BOTTOM: Original "Amphibious 4x4" truck made for the Italian Ministry of the Interior's Civil Protection and Fire-fighting Services Department; a 5,184 cc six cylinder Diesel engine, road speed in excess of 90 km/h and, in water, by means of propeller, 11 km/h (in shallow water, with drive through the wheels: 5 km/h).

personnel and goods both on land and on water. It was also of interest to the civil defence authorities. Equipped with a 6 cylinder in-line direct injection diesel engine with a cubic capacity of 5,184 cc, and power of 177 HP at 3,200 rpm, it had a payload of 2,140 kg and a 6.26 m² loading platform.

On the road it could reach 90 km/h; in water, it was able to navigate with a screw propeller at a speed of 11 km/h and drive at 5 km/h through shallows.

Finally, in 1974, in the first fort-night of July, the agreement between Fiat and Klökner-Humboldt-Deutz of Cologne was announced for setting up the Iveco multinational holding company (Industrial Vehicles Corporation). The majority share of the equity was in the hands of the Fiat Group, its registered offices were in Holland and the company was operational from the 1st January 1975. And this is where another story begins.

Production of the famous OM "mark" cars started immediately after the First World War with the purchase of Fabbrica Automobili Ing. Roberto Züst in Brescia by Società Anonima Officine Meccaniche of Porta Vigentina, Milan.

The official date for the transfer of ownership was the 1st October 1917, but the first vehicle to bear the OM mark saw light of day at the end of 1918.

Therefore it is 1918 and not, as stated by some, a time vaguely beween 1902 and 1906, which is to be regarded as the year when OM the car maker was born.

If opinions in this respect differ, it is because - as we shall try to explain, although briefly - OM was the result of a complex interweave of mergers between companies in the metallurgical and metalworking sector, the oldest of which dated back to the second half of 1800.

Società Anonima Officine Meccaniche was founded in Milan in 1899 at the Credito Italiano in Via Manzoni before Vincenzo Strambio, a notary. The share capital (5,500,000 lire in 55,000 bearer shares with a face value of 100 lire each) was divided between 15 subscribers with slightly more than 40% in the hands of Credito Italiano, Genoa.

In practice, the new company (whose aims were stated as "*foundry engineering, metal constructions, railway and tram fixtures and rolling stock*") was the result of the merger of two famous old Milan companies, Grondona Comi & C. and Miani Silvestri & C.

Grondona Comi & C. descended (even if by way of subsequent company trans-formations and capital brought in by third parties) from a craftsman company founded in 1849 by a certain Benedetto Grondona who had started to build carriages and landaus at a laboratory-cum-factory outside Porta Nuova in Milan.

Through the refined and elegant design of its products, the small company soon acquired considerable fame until, in 1857, Felice Grondona, son of the founder, set up a company for "producing vehicles of all kinds and work relating to railways" with Giovanni Miani and Paolo Zambelli, both engineers. The share capital was 40,000 Austrian Schillings.

In 1880, Miani left Grondona and, together with Gerolamo Silvestri, also an engineer, and Prospero Venturi, set up Miani, Venturi & C., at Porta Tenaglia, still in Milan, for building railway locomotives, carriages and wagons. The new company started its activities by building - to the designs of a Viennese company - a locomotive with four coupled compartments and a 3 axle tender which was subsequently shown at the Milan exhibition in 1881 and later supplied to the Strade Ferrate Alta Italia.

On the death of Venturi in 1882, the company changed its name to Miani Silvestri & C.

In 1890, on their 100,000 m² site just outside Porta Vigentina, they started work on a new factory. It was here, in 1897, that the first steam locomotive entirely designed by Italian engineers was built and, in 1889, the first Italian electric tram, which went into operation on the Firenze-Fiesole run.

As far as the "Fabbrica Automobili Ing. Roberto Züst" is concerned, its origins can be traced back to 1854, when Fonderia Guller & Croff was founded in the vicinity of Intra, in the district of Selasca.

In 1858, the company became Guller & Greuter and was gradually expanded and modernised. This company produced forgings and castings which were large for the technology of those times, such as guns, the engine and hull of the ship Umberto I, sailing on Lake Orta and, in 1882, the engine and boiler for the Eridano, destined for Lake Maggiore.

In 1878, a Swiss engineer from Zürich, Roberto Züst, who had been living in Intra for a few years, joined Greuter. He extended the company's range of activities to spinning and weaving machines and also hydraulic turbines. In 1893 he became the sole owner of the company, changing its name to Ing. Roberto Züst.

In the next few years, the company's activities were expanded further to include in particular the design and manufacture of precision machines for machining metal.

In 1897, at just 54 years of age, Züst died. The company, which had become a private partnership, was then managed by his sons who soon decided to start making cars. So, in 1903 (some say 1902), the company to be known as "Züst Ing. Roberto - Fabbrica Italiana di Automobili - Società Anonima" was set up at Intra. But the factory at Intra was no longer adequate to meet the needs of increased production, so it was decided to open a second factory. This was set up at Via Borgognone 34, Milan, between 1904 and 1905.

The first Züst cars rolled out of this factory in 1905, accompanied almost immediately by industrial vehicles equipped with the same engine as used for the cars.

In March of 1906 Züst was involved in the founding of the new company Brixia Società Anonima with a registered capital of 1 million lire (300,000 lire paid up), which was in

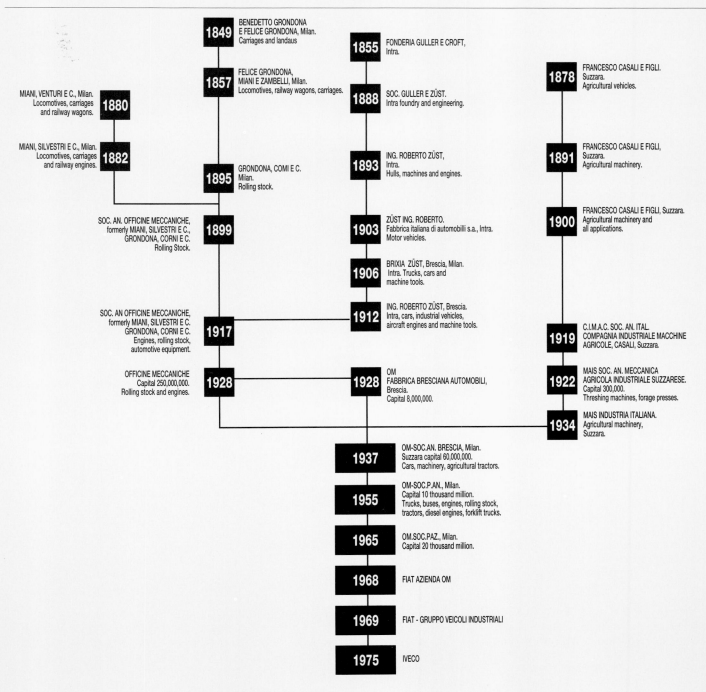

MIANI, VENTURI E C., Milan.
Locomotives, carriages
and railway wagons. **1880**

MIANI, SILVESTRI E C., Milan.
Locomotives, carriages
and railway engines. **1882**

1849 BENEDETTO GRONDONA
E FELICE GRONDONA, Milan.
Carriages and landaus

1857 FELICE GRONDONA,
MIANI E ZAMBELLI, Milan.
Locomotives, railway wagons, carriages.

1895 GRONDONA, COMI E C.
Milan.
Rolling stock.

SOC. AN. OFFICINE MECCANICHE,
formerly MIANI, SILVESTRI E C.,
GRONDONA, CORNI E C. **1899**
Rolling Stock.

SOC. AN OFFICINE MECCANICHE,
formerly MIANI, SILVESTRI E C.
GRONDONA, CORNI E C. **1917**
Engines, rolling stock,
automotive equipment.

OFFICINE MECCANICHE **1928**
Capital 250,000,000.
Rolling stock and engines.

1855 FONDERIA GULLER E CROFT,
Intra.

1888 SOC. GULLER E ZÜST.
Intra foundry and engineering.

1893 ING. ROBERTO ZÜST,
Intra.
Hulls, machines and engines.

1903 ZÜST ING. ROBERTO.
Fabbrica italiana di automobili s.a., Intra.
Motor vehicles.

1906 BRIXIA ZÜST, Brescia, Milan.
Intra. Trucks, cars and
machine tools.

1912 ING. ROBERTO ZÜST, Brescia.
Intra, cars, industrial vehicles,
aircraft engines and machine tools.

1928 OM
FABBRICA BRESCIANA AUTOMOBILI,
Brescia.
Capital 8,000,000.

1878 FRANCESCO CASALI E FIGLI.
Suzzara.
Agricultural vehicles.

1891 FRANCESCO CASALI E FIGLI,
Suzzara.
Agricultural machinery.

1900 FRANCESCO CASALI E FIGLI, Suzzara.
Agricultural machinery and
all applications.

1919 C.I.M.A.C. SOC. AN. ITAL.
COMPAGNIA INDUSTRIALE MACCHINE
AGRICOLE, CASALI, Suzzara.

1922 MAIS SOC. AN. MECCANICA
AGRICOLA INDUSTRIALE SUZZARESE.
Capital 300,000.
Threshing machines, forage presses.

1934 MAIS INDUSTRIA ITALIANA.
Agricultural machinery,
Suzzara.

1937 OM-SOC.AN. BRESCIA, Milan.
Suzzara capital 60,000,000.
Cars, machinery, agricultural tractors.

1955 OM-SOC.P.AN., Milan.
Capital 10 thousand million.
Trucks, buses, engines, rolling stock,
tractors, diesel engines, forklift trucks.

1965 OM.SOC.PAZ., Milan.
Capital 20 thousand million.

1968 FIAT AZIENDA OM

1969 FIAT - GRUPPO VEICOLI INDUSTRIALI

1975 IVECO

*The extremely complex "family tree" of OM, the leading automotive company in the early Thirties,
which dedicated itself exclusively to the production of commercial and industrial vehicles.*

Brescia. Brixia (the old name of Brescia) was one of the few car companies which also went in for the production and application of engines with three vertical cylinders.

But in spite of the success gained with its products, the young Brescia company was soon in financial difficulties and went into liquidation in 1911.

In 1912, Züst of Milan took it over and at the same time, changed the name of the company to Fabbrica Automobili Ing. Roberto Züst with a fully paid up capital of 2,500,000 lire and a registered office in Milan. Arturo Züst became chairman.

After extending the factory in Brescia and installing more modern equipment, Züst transferred the work which, up to then, had been done at the Milan factory in Via Borgognone, and this factory was closed not long afterwards.

The Brescia factory came under the management of Silvio Züst, who was joined by Ottavio Fuscaldo from 1913 (a general inventor known for making car prototypes with wheels which had a "rhombus" configuration). He was in charge of the technical department. With the imminent involvement of Italy in the First World War, Züst not only accelerated the manufacture of industrial vehicles, but also set up an aeronautical division.

And, it would seem, this was also the reason for transferring the now militarised company to Società Anonima Officine Meccaniche of Milan, in other words OM.

In fact, after the Brescia factory had accepted an order for supplying a large batch of aircraft, it was found that the existing plant was not adequate to start up production at the rate required. Therefore, it was decided to involve OM, which had more facilities and which had already been able to gain sufficient experience with working in wood (aircraft at the time were made using wood and canvas).

The change of ownership (which, if some sources are to be believed, was a good deal for OM, since the Brescia company was bought at a price of 3 million lire, i.e. little more than the share capital) took

place officially on the 1st October 1917. With this change of ownership, the make of Züst disappeared finally to give way to OM.

As already mentioned at the beginning, the first vehicle bearing the OM mark was launched at the end of the following year, 1918. Known as the "S 305" and powered with a four cylinder 4,712 cc engine, its design was essentially similar to the typical design of the Brixia vehicles.

This model was immediately followed by an original vehicle, the "465" (the first number "4" indicating the number of cylinders and the following two, the bore of the cylinders), which was equipped with a 4 cylinder engine of just 1,327 cc. The next of the OM 4 cylinder family duly followed with a 1,410 cc engine for the "467 S" and 1,496 cc version for the "469".

In 1923, OM launched the "665", its first 6 cylinder engine, with 1,991 cc and a power of approximately 40 HP. From the beginning, some of the chassis of

these vehicles were used (by outside manufacturers it appears) for equipping industrial vehicles, mainly buses.

What is certain is that the actual production of industrial vehicles and buses was officially started by OM in 1925 using the very good petrol engines used for the cars, as already mentioned. The one and a half litre engine was used on the "469 C" and "469 F" vehicles produced until 1930, and also on the "469 F1" produced between 1931 and 1935 and equipped with a 1,496 cc - 1,570 cc engine. However, the 2 litre engine was adopted by the "665 F" produced until 1930 and by the "665 F1" produced between 1930 and 1933, with 1,991 and 2,221 cc respectively.

All these vehicles, which differed from the originals in a few chassis details, gearbox and axle ratio and the size of the wheels. They were produced not only in the truck and van versions, with different payloads, but were also used for fire engines, ambulances, special trucks and buses, both for hotel services and public and tourist services.

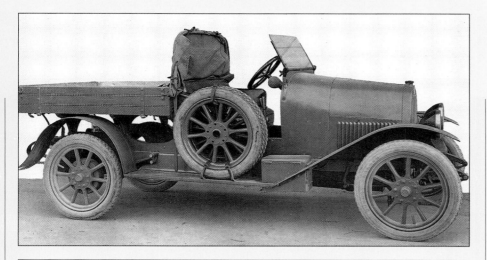

OPPOSITE PAGE: Züst truck of 1907 with chain transmission; note the original use of two radiators to guarantee efficient cooling of the engine, particularly at low running speeds.
TOP OF THIS PAGE: One of the first OM trucks derived directly - probably on the initiative of a customer - from a car.
CENTRE: Original refuse vehicle with tip-up body made on an "OM 469 F" chassis, with 4 cylinder, 1,496 cc engine.
ABOVE: Classic and elegant van on the "OM 665 F" chassis, with 6 cylinder, 1,991 cc engine.

The success achieved in this sector encouraged the directors of OM to put more into the research and development of new vehicles, as was logical, and also the use of diesel engines, which were beginning to reveal their potential more and more in this specific sector.

Meanwhile, and perhaps in anticipation of future developments, an important change occurred in 1928: the split between the factories in Milan and Brescia, which then continued their respective activities under different names.

In Milan, Società Anonima Officine Meccaniche continued with the production of railway engines and equipment, whereas OM Fabbrica Bresciana di Automobili was set up in Brescia with a capital of 8 million lire, and was to build vehicles only.

One of the first decisions of the new management at Brescia, led by Ing. Corrado Orazi, was to enter into a cooperation agreement with the Swiss company Adolph Saurer in Arbon, which was experienced in the production of industrial vehicles equipped with 4 stroke direct injection diesel engines with compression ignition.

These were now fully reliable after years of trials and improvements. The agreements with the Swiss company were for production under licence, but, whilst awaiting the installation of adequate production plant, OM started to import directly.

As a result, in April 1929 at the Industrial Vehicle Show held under the umbrella of the Milan Sample Fair - that year the car show, reserved for cars only, had been moved to Rome (30th January to 10th February) for reasons of space and political grandeur - OM presented a Saurer truck with a 6 tonne payload equipped with a 6 cylinder 8,550 cc diesel engine able to develop approximately 80 HP at 1,600 rpm.

This engine was the type with in-line cylinders, pressed-in steel liners, aluminium monobloc construction, cast in a single piece with the base. A cast iron cylinder head with vertical overhead valves (2 per cylinder) was controlled by a camshaft in

AUTOCARRO A MOTORE DIESEL "O. M.-SAURER 5 BLD,,

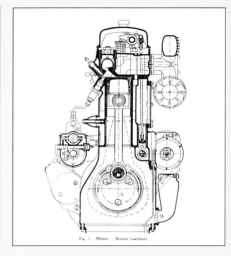

Fig. 1 - Motore - Sezione trasversale.

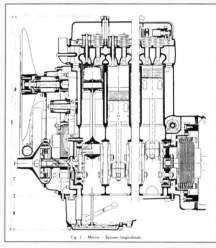

Fig. 2 - Motore - Sezione longitudinale.

TOP LEFT DOWNWARDS: OM-Saurer truck, the "5 BLD", equipped with diesel engine, made under Saurer licence; payload 5 tonnes.
OM-Saurer truck, "6 BLD", equipped with the same engine as the previous version (6 cylinders, 8,550 cc); however, the payload was increased to 6 tonnes.
OM-Saurer truck, type "3 BOD", equipped with 4 cylinder, 5,700 cc engine, power 65 HP; payload approximately 5,000 kg.
Bus "4 FA1" type, 1933, photographed in front of one of the entrances to the Brescia factory; the engine was a 4 cylinder petrol engine with 1,680 cc.
TOP: Cross section and longitudinal section of the "OM Diesel" engine, made under Saurer licence.

the base by means of rods and rockers; aluminium pistons, crankshaft on 7 roller bearings with front shock absorber. The combustion chamber was of the precombustion type (Acro system) with injection pump and injectors (placed on the side of the engine) of the Bosch type. Water cooling was by means of a centrifugal pump and radiator with

removable elements. The electric start was facilitated by suitable glow plugs.

A chassis with straight longitudinal members in two wheelbases, (4.50 and 5.00 metres), supported wheels with "Simplex" type spokes, twin-mounted on the rear axle with 40 x 8 tyres (or 36 x 8.25).

The transmission included a dry multi-plate clutch; gearbox in a block with the engine, four gears plus reverse; transmission shaft in two parts with 3 universal joints; rear axle stamped in sheet steel with cast steel differential box, bevel gear transmission.

The braking system was a dual circuit system: one system, equipped with vacuum servo brake, had pedal control acting on the four wheels, and the other system was a handbrake acting on all rear wheels.

When fully laden, the truck was able to reach speeds of around 45-50 km/h with a consumption of 28 litres of fuel per 100 km.

In addition to the truck, there was also a model intended in particular for buses which had a lowered chassis (top edge just 62 cm above the ground), a wheelbase of 5.00 metres and a slightly reduced track.

Records indicate that the first OM vehicles equipped with diesel engines produced under the Saurer licence were launched at the Motor Show in Milan in 1931. These were chassis for the "5 BLD" type 5 to 6 tonne truck and for the "3 BLD" 30-36 passenger buses, both equipped with the 6 cylinder, 8,550 cc diesel engine with a power of approximately 80 HP.

Publicity from the time shows that both chassis were sold at the same price of 115,000 lire, including 7 wheels with tyres. The "469 F3" petrol driven trucks and buses with the well-known 1,600 cc, 4 cylinder engine also appeared at the same show.

Here are the prices of some of the versions (complete with 6 wheels with tyres and 2 spare rims): chassis 25,000 lire, lorry with closed cab 30,000 lire, de luxe type hotel bus, 12 seater, 40,000 lire, 12/14 seater bus 41,000 lire, and 15/17 seater bus 42,000 lire.

At the show the following year, in 1932, OM attracted not just the

attention of visitors, but also that of its rivals, with an impressive 3 axle chassis with the 2 rear being driven and a payload of 14 tonnes. Known as the "12 BLD", this vehicle was powered by a 6 cylinder 8,550 cc diesel engine in the 85 HP version, still at 1,800 rpm. The chassis weighed 8,000 kg; the fully laden weight of the vehicle was 22,000 kg.

Next to this giant was an impressive 50 seater bus intended for the Rome authorities. This vehicle was also equipped with the 6 cylinder diesel engine and was known as the "5 BLD PL".

Another important achievement for OM that year was the interesting "autocarretta 32" with 4-wheel drive, equipped with the 4 cylinder 1,615 cc petrol engine with forced air cooling.

It should be mentioned that the prototype of this agile off-road vehicle had been built more than four years earlier by Ansaldo, a Genoa company with a factory in Turin. When this company ceased its activities in the automotive sector all the equipment went to OM which completed the development of the vehicle and put it into production.

OM also had novelties stored up for the 1933 show: trucks and buses of the "OD" family equipped with a 4 cylinder diesel engine (still under Saurer licence) with a cubic capacity of 5,700 cc and approximately 65 HP - the younger brother of the 6 cylinder engine already mentioned.

The payload of the truck versions reached 5,000 kg, with the possibility of towing a trailer with a payload of approximately 6,000 kg.

Depending on the wheelbase, the

Special military vehicle designed for operating in mountainous zones: the "OM 32" truck with 4 wheel drive and 4 steered wheels; 4 cylinder, 1,615 cc engine, power just over 20 HP, forced air cooling, 4 speed box plus reverse with reduction gear and differential lock; kerb weight 1,615 kg.

Il nuovo Autoveicolo

1 CRD

Diesel "OM" (licen. Saurer)

bus versions were able to transport 32 to 45 passengers with the 6 cylinder "LD" version and approximately 30 with the 4 cylinder "OD" version.

OM also made trailers for these vehicles. These were the traditional type for trucks and, with the correct turning circle, for buses.

In the light vehicle sector, and using a petrol engine, they then launched the "4 F1" and "6 F1"

TOP LEFT: The impressive "3 BOD-PL" coach of 1933; a 65 HP four cylinder Diesel engine (under licence from Saurer), a speed of 50/60 km/h; seating capacity: 30.
TOP: A page advertising the "1 CRD" presented at the 1934 Turin Motor Show; a 4,500 cc four cylinder Diesel engine developing 60 HP; the truck version had a carrying capacity of approximately 3,000 kg and the bus had a seating capacity of 25.
ABOVE AND RIGHT: With the same engine as in the "1 CRD", the "C 30" buses, (right) of almost the same carrying capacity, were produced from 1936.

vans with payloads of 1,800 kg and 2,300 kg and also the "4 FA1" and "6 FA1" buses with a seating capacity of 15 and 18.

These vehicles were equipped with 1,580 cc, 4 cylinder engines, developing 35 HP at 3,600 rpm, and 6 cylinder engines with 2,250 cc and 40 HP at 3,600 rpm.

But 1933 was an important year for OM, and not just for its products. It was also important - and to a much greater extent - because of the agreement which marked the transfer of the Brescia factory to the control of the Fiat Group.

For OM, this meant having the capital it needed for modernising its plant and strengthening its programmes in the industrial vehicle sector, a sector which showed sure signs of safe, favourable developments in the future.

However, this event also had its sadder side in the cessation of car production; a decision made worse in view of the sporting - and other - successes of OM cars. But then like now, the market made its own rules and the moment was right for concentrating efforts in one sector only. In spite of the extensive reorganisation of the company, in 1934 OM still managed to offer new products at the traditional show.

There they showed the 3 axle 60 seater bus with the "LD" 6 cylinder engine, this time with an upgraded 100/110 HP version and a maximum speed of approximately 60 km/h.

They also presented a new medium transport vehicle known as the "1 CRD" which was equipped with a diesel engine (still under Saurer licence) with 4,500 cc, a power of 60 HP and a consumption of just 170 grammes of diesel per HP/hour.

The vehicle was equipped with a gearbox with 5 forward gears plus reverse and hydraulic brakes. The truck version had a payload of 3,000 kg and a maximum speed of 70 km/h. The bus had 25 seats and could reach speeds of 75 km/h.

In 1936, the same engine was to be used for the "C 30" truck with a payload of 3,000 kg.

At the 1935 show, apart from the engines for locomotives, OM

TOP: This new OM "BUD" was launched at the 1936 Motor Show; equipped with a 6 cylinder, 11,538 cc, diesel engine, power approximately 130 HP, payload 7,500 kg, capable of towing 14,000 kg.
CENTRE: In 1937 a new version of the truck shown above, (same drive train) was christened the "Titano 137"; the photograph shows a 3 axle chassis fitted out by an outside contractor but nevertheless included in OM's official price list in 1938.
ABOVE: This interesting and manoeuvrable truck of 1938 (other versions were also made) was called "Taurus". It had a 4 cylinder, 5,320 cc engine of which there were also many military versions. The payload was just over 3,000 kg.

presented the new "BUD" chassis with a wheelbase of 4.500 metres and a payload of up to 7,500 kg. This vehicle was equipped with the "UD" 6 cylinder 11,536 cc diesel engine capable of developing approximately 130 HP.

The same engine was also used on the bus chassis with a "4 CPO" longer wheelbase and, from 1937,

also on the "Titano 137" truck of which a 3 axle version was also listed in the following year.

The "Titano 137" vehicles remained in production until the outbreak of the Second World War and the same name, but without the number "137", was used again for a new range of heavy vehicles in 1961. In 1939 the company presented

the latest "Taurus" in truck and bus versions, equipped with the 4 cylinder diesel engine, bore and stroke 110 mm x 140 mm, 5,320 cc, with 5-speed box plus reverse and a payload of 3,100 kg.

They also started to produce the "Ursus" truck with a 6 cylinder 7,980 cc diesel engine, a power of more than 100 HP at 1,800 rpm and a payload of 6,400 kg.

But the most important event of 1937 was, without doubt, the reunification - still within the Fiat Group - of OM in Brescia and OM in Milan. Together with the Società Industria Italiana Macchine Agricole in Suzzara (near Mantova), bought not long before, the three companies were grouped under the new name of OM Società Anonima with a share capital of 60 million lire, a registered office in Milan and administrative offices in Brescia. The deed of formation of the new company was signed on the 6th September 1937 (this is the date given in the Decree of the Ministry responsible for official approval) and if some sources indicate the following year, this is probably due to the fact that the notice did not appear in the Official Gazette until the 9th January 1938.

In particular, we wish to record that the founding of OM Società Anonima united three important factories:

i) the Milan works, housing the cast iron, aluminium and bronze foundries; the production of rolling stock (carriages and wagons, locomotives, electric and diesel); structural steel work, (including railway engineering) and the production of sheet metal parts intended for the industrial vehicles produced at the Brescia factory; the production of "slow" diesel engines for the navy; the production of agricultural tractors and a special division for vehicle bodywork.

ii) the Brescia factories, producing industrial vehicles, buses and diesel engines, both for road vehicles and for marine and railway applications.

and iii) the factory at Suzzara, specialising in the production of

agricultural equipment (threshing machines, forage presses, shellers), irrigation equipment and various structural steelwork. Benefitting from a strong, motivated management team and, something not usual for the day, a mentality already geared to marketing, i.e. sensitive to the needs of the customer, the new OM was born with ambitious development programmes.

These programmes were supported by an efficient industrial structure and an innovative concept - ahead of its time - of the design and development of new products. Already by that time, for example, they were thinking of future ranges in terms of standardisation and modular construction, particularly with regard to cabs,

but also, to some extent, engineering.

Unfortunately all these projects had to be drastically re-scaled and postponed with the outbreak of the Second World War.

The production activities were converted to the needs of war. For example, they started to produce military versions of the "Taurus" equipped with a petrol engine instead of a diesel engine. And all the factories suffered extensive bomb damage. When the war was finally over, and in spite of innumerable difficulties, they set about the work of reconstruction immediately, and design and production work was resumed within a very short period.

A new "Taurus" went into production in 1945. Its construction was radically modified compared with its pre-war version: in line with the new modular concept, it was equipped with a forward cab instead of the type with "nose".

The new "Taurus" generation was known as the "Taurus 340" (truck versions) and the "Taurus 380" (buses).

In 1951 the "Supertaurus" was derived from these vehicles. Still with the forward cab, it was equipped with a 5,816 cc, 4 cylinder diesel engine with a power of 80 HP at 1,900 rpm.

The gearbox was of the 4 speed mechanical type with reduction gear and pneumatic pre-selection control. The hydro-pneumatic brakes, integrated with the engine exhaust brake and the double leaf spring suspension, offered variable flexibility. The payload of the truck was 5,000 kg. Two bus versions were also made with structural modifications (dimensions and wheelbase) and also changes to some mechanical units such as gearbox and suspension. A long distance, rear engine bus for 36 + 6 + 1 seats and a local bus, still with rear engine, with 31 + 1 seats + standing room for 21, were also made.

There were new forward cab versions of the "Ursus" vehicles too. In the meantime, in 1946, production started on a high payload vehicle known as the "Orione", equipped with an 8 cylinder diesel engine, 90° V, 10,640 cc with a power exceeding 130 HP at 2,000 rpm.

TOP: A truck trailer with the "Orione 400/8" drive train equipped with a 90° V8 diesel engine, 10,840 cc.
ABOVE: The true star of the Turin Motor Show in 1950 was the new medium/light truck "Leoncino" with direct injection diesel engine, Saurer double turbulence system, 4 cylinder, 3,770 cc, 52 HP. Father of numerous offspring for a quarter of a century.

It was 7.46 m long, 2.47 m wide, with a wheelbase of 4.00 metres, offering a 5 metre x 2.35 m box body and a payload of approximately 9,000 kg.

It should be noted that the structural strength of this truck would have allowed higher payloads (using suitable tyres), but standards in force in Italy limited the total weight to 14 tonnes.

The motor and gearbox of the "Orione" were also used for a 45 seater bus.

The "Orione 580" was then made, specially designed for buses. Pullman trains were also made using this chassis with a total capacity of 126 seats, 66 on the trailer, which featured steering axles.

Later, in 1955, the "Super Orione" truck and bus versions

il Leoncino

appeared, equipped with 11,630 cc engines and with a power of more than 170 HP at 1,900 rpm. The payload was increased by 8,000 kg and the total weight to 18,000 kg giving a total kerb weight of the vehicle train of 34 tonnes.

Both the "Orione" and the "Super Orione" were used, including the 3 axle versions, for special applications and for numerous other uses, including heavy duty applications.

1950 was another important year for OM because it signalled the start of a new medium light vehicle with a very modern design which was to characterise the production of the Milan company for another 20 years, and achieve great fame, not just in Italy.

Christened the "Leoncino", it fell into the 20-25 kg payload category, a category which, at least in this country, had been neglected for more than a decade in favour of vehicles with a higher payload.

OM was aware that the changing needs of the marketplace opened up new opportunities, even in this particular sector. And so it launched its light vehicle, stressing its reliability and economy in operation.

LEFT: A publicity page for the "Leoncino".
BELOW: Illustration of one of the first versions of the "Leoncino" adapted for local buses.

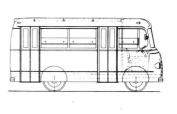

Two publicity pages of the new "Super Taurus" and "Super Orione",
published in the middle of the fifties.

The engine used was a diesel engine with direct injection, dual turbulent pre-mixing, Saurer system, 4 cylinder, 3,770 cc, able to develop a power of 52 HP at 2,100 rpm. It had forced circulation water cooling.

The transmission used a dry single plate clutch, a 5 speed gearbox plus reverse, and rear wheel drive with load bearing type axle. The suspension was a leaf spring suspension with constant flexibility for the front axle and variable flexibility for the rear axle, integrated with four double-acting shock absorbers.

Naturally the cab was of the forward type, with an all-steel structure and two comfortable seats. The standard series was right-hand drive. The maximum speed is given as around 75 km/h with a fuel consumption, fully laden over a variable surface, of approximately 10 litres of diesel per 100 km.

The Leoncino was also supplied with a 2,545 cc, 4 cylinder engine with a power of 59.5 HP at 2,900 rpm. Truck and bus versions with chassis and cabs options were also

designed.

This vehicle enjoyed an immediate success, as was demonstrated by the fact that as early as 1951, at the 33rd International Motor Show in Turin, the OM stand and various bodywork and equipment manufacturers, exhibited approximately 20 trucks, dumper trucks, vans, municipal vehicles, and no fewer than 10 buses all based on the "Leoncino" chassis.

In the following years, the range was extended with the introduction of four-wheel drive and front-wheel drive versions and also local and long distance buses with varying capacities. Lowered chassis were also intruduced.

In 1957, a more powerful diesel engine was adopted, still with 4 cylinders, but 4,156 cc and a power of 61 HP, still at 2,100 rpm. From 1963, both power and cylinder capacity were increased - 4,397 cc and 85 HP (and subsequently up to 92 HP) at 2,400 rpm. With the truck version, the payload increased to 3,500 kg for some versions.

At the end of the sixties, engines

with an even higher cubic capacity were installed: still diesel, with 4 cylinders, 4,561 cc and even 4,940 cc for some bus versions.

The "Leoncino" was the head of a family of models of similar style and structure, all named after animals.

1957 saw the "Tigrotto", initially powered with the 4,156 cc, 4 cylinder diesel engine, with a power gradually increased from 67 HP to 90 HP (for the bus versions, some of which had the engine at the back).

As with the "Leoncino", the "Tigrotto" was also equipped, at the times mentioned, with engines with increasing cubic capacity and power, 4,397 cc, 4,561 cc and 4,940 cc.

Apart from the basic truck and bus versions, there were also numerous variants such as the elongated cab with bunk, 4-wheel drive trucks and tractors for semi-trailers, the latter having a total weight of up to 18,000 kg.

The truck payloads varied between 3,500 kg (3,200kg for the van versions) to a maximum of 5,360 kg. The next year was the turn of the

55

more powerful "Tigre", equipped with a diesel engine, still a 4 cylinder unit with 6,870 cc, which was available both in the aspirated version developing 105 HP at 2,000 rpm and the super-charged version of 135 HP, still at 2,000 rpm.

The super-charger, which could be engaged or disengaged from the driving seat, was produced by means of a mechanical compressor of the helicoidal vane type, controlled via distributor gears. There was a hydraulic connector between the control gears and the compressor which was supplied with engine oil from the self-cleaning filter, which made it possible to engage or disengage the compressor very smoothly, without torsional vibrations. The engagement and disengagement were controlled by an electric valve which controlled a pressurised oil distribution box.

The "Tigre" trucks, equipped with aspirated engines, had a load capacity of approximately 6,300 kg and were able to tow trailers up to 12,000 kg. The super-charged versions had a load capacity of 7,300 kg and could tow trailers up to 11,000 kg.

In the following years there were increases in power and also 3 axle truck versions (with a payload of 11,150 kg and a total weight of up to 9,000 kg), tractors for semi-trailers (with a towable weight of 18,500 kg) and buses, some with rear engines arranged vertically or horizontally.

During the latter stage of their production, which ceased in 1967,

TOP: A light military truck of 1952; it was equipped with a "20-110" petrol engine with 4 cylinders in line, a cubic capacity of 2,545 cc and a power of 64 HP. The payload, including the driver, was 1,140 kg. This was known as the "Gippone" in military circles.
CENTRE: The "Tigrotto" launched in 1957 and originally equipped with a 4 cylinder 4,158 cc diesel engine. The payload was approximately 3,500 kg.
BOTTOM: 1958 saw the launch of the more powerful "Tigre" with a 6,870 cc diesel engine available both in the aspirated 105 HP version and the supercharged 135 HP version.

a 7,433 cc engine was also used on the "Tigre" vehicles.

In 1959, there was the "Lupetto", a light vehicle which initially had the 4,156 cc engine already mentioned, followed by the 4,397 cc and 4,561 cc versions.

The payload of the "Lupetto" varied between 2,000 kg and 3,000 kg in the case of the truck versions, and 1,750 kg and 2,600 kg for the van versions.

Many of these vehicles - including the bus conversions - had either front or rear engine.

It is also worth pointing out that some models - both truck and bus - were equipped on request with 4,156 cc and 4,397 cc engines with forced air cooling rather than water cooling.

In 1961, the vehicle series named after animals was temporarily suspended.

In that year, the name "Titano" was used again to christen a vehicle which, with its 230 HP - IGM (i.e. approximately 260 HP SAE) was, without doubt, the most powerful truck on the European market at the time.

The engine was a 6 cylinder in-line diesel engine with direct injection and 10,310 cc. From 1965 - 1966 this engine was complemented by a similar one with 11,150 cc and slightly higher power.

The "Titano" range offered directly by OM (many of the conversions made using these vehicles were in fact manufactured by outside bodywork and conversion companies), included all the possible configurations for trans-porting goods and passengers.

In fact, the company price list showed trucks and trailers for semi-trailers with 2 and 3 axles, with one or two engine shafts and a bus with a similar structure, with a vertical or horizontal rear engine.

In the truck sector there were also dumper trucks, since the "Titano" was widely used for heavy work at quarries and on building sites.

With regard to the payloads, quite briefly, these ranged from a minimum of just less than 7,500 kg to a maximum of 13,300 kg for a 4x4. The semi-trailer tractors allowed a maximum towing weight ranging from a minimum of 23,000 kg to a maximum of 25,800 kg.

TOP: The new "Lupetto" was launched in 1959; initially, it was equipped with the same engine as the "Tigrotto"; the photograph shows the van version with a payload of 1,750 kg.
CENTRE: A subsequent version of the "Lupetto" equipped with a 4,397 cc engine and then also with a 4,561 cc engine.
ABOVE: In 1981 the name of "Titano" was used again for the new OM heavy vehicles available in numerous configurations. In the photograph, a 3 axle, 6x4 semi-trailer tractor.

In the meantime, in 1964, production of the "animal" range of trucks was resumed.

There was the new "Cerbiatto", designed for truck, van and bus versions, and equipped with the 4,397 cc, 4 cylinder engine already mentioned, offering slightly more than 80 HP. Air-cooled engines were also subsequently used on the "Cerbiatto" instead of the water-cooled system and, from the end of the sixties, the 4,561 cc engine with a power of 87 HP (DIN) was installed.

The "Daino" with the same drive train was introduced at more or less the same time as the Cerbiatto. Over a period of time, the payload of the "Daino" varied from 3,900 kg to 4,500 kg in the truck version and 3,400 kg to 3,600 kg in the van version.

Many special versions were already being made by various bodymakers using the original chassis: mobile shops of every shape and size, drinks vehicles, refrigerated vehicles, vehicles for transporting "hanging" clothes, and vehicles for many other special applications.

However, there were no bus versions of this model.

In 1967, it was the turn of the "Orsetto" to launch itself on to the market; the last in the series of vehicles generally referred to as the "zoo". The "Orsetto" was also the lightest vehicle of the family: it had a diesel engine, still the 4 cylinder version, but with just 2,693 cc, and it was also available as a chassis and chassis cab intended for bodymakers and converters, and as a truck and combined vehicle (with normal wheelbase of 2.650 metres or a long wheelbase measuring 3.000 metres) in the original OM version.

The engine power was 64.5 HP at 3,500 rpm but, almost immediately, with the adoption of the 3,210 cc engine, the power rose to approximately 70 HP at 3,200 rpm.

At the 39th International Car Show held in Turin between the 1st and the 12th November 1967, the new "OM 150" truck made its debut, equipped initially with a 6 cylinder, 8,075 cc diesel engine with a power of 176 HP to 186 HP at 2,600 rpm and, from the sixth year of its production, with 8,905 cc

TOP: The "Cerbiatto" was capable of a payload of 2,000 kg and could tow a weight of 1,500 kg. Therefore, as can be seen from the photograph, it was possible to tow a small trailer.
CENTRE: Also the "Cerbiatto"; in spite of the small dimensions, many body makers used it to make mobile shops for various uses.
ABOVE: The "Daino" had the same 4 cylinder, 4,561 cc diesel engine as the "Cerbiatto" originally, but its increased transport capacity also allowed special conversions, as in the case of this refrigerated van intended for a Rumanian company.

TOP: The "Orsetto" ("Little bear") was the lightest of the family of OM trucks which were named after animals; it originally had only a 2,693 cc four cylinder diesel engine (subsequently increased to 3,210 cc), with a carrying capacity of 1,550 kg in the truck version.
CENTRE: The "150" of 1967, fitted with a 8,075 cc six cylinder diesel engine and delivering of over 175 HP, was offered with various different wheelbases and was suitable for conversion for special services and for town councils.
ABOVE: A "150" in a version suitable for operating in combination with a Piaggio "Ape" ("Bee") motor-tricycle with tipper body.

and 193 HP, still at 2,600 rpm.

The new "OM 150" vehicles were available in truck versions with a wheelbase of 3.485 metres, 4.095 metres and 4.715 metres and a payload of 8,270 kg (towable weight 17,000 kg), 9,230 kg and 7,980 kg (with more or less the same towable weights).

The tractor versions for semi-trailers were offered with one wheelbase of 3.485 metres and a towable weight of 14,000 kg, subsequently increased to 18,000 kg. Naturally, the range included the chassis and chassis cab versions, which were largely used by bodymakers, converters and equipment manufacturers for innumerable conversions, particularly those with a 3rd and a 4th axle added.

In 1968, OM was finally incorporated into the Fiat Group, for a short time as Fiat Azienda OM and then as Gruppo Veicoli Industriali Fiat, which combined Fiat and OM production and also that of the French company Unic. This, finally, was the culmination of the long process of integration and concentration of resources started by the Italian industrial vehicle industry some thirty years before, way back in 1933.

OM ceased to exist as an independent entity, but the Group inherited a make which enjoyed considerable prestige and an inestimable wealth of dynamism and commercial intelligence.

This wealth was safeguarded in full because, in view of the skill and know-how available in this sector, the major responsibilities of the new Group management were entrusted to the original OM directors.

As a result of this large scale reorganisation, there was a major shake-up of production and of the product range which soon resulted in standardised models. However, these were still distinct, identified as they were by the "badges" of the three original makes: Fiat, OM and Unic.

This reorganisation was to continue for the next six years until 1974, the year when Iveco was founded, when all the industrial identities merged in the new multi-national company and were standardised according to new regulations, new divisions

and classifications.

However, 1968 did not see the last exit of the original OM vehicles. In fact, the "OM 100" and "OM 120" trucks were still being marketed in 1970 and the heavy duty "OM 190" and "OM 260" in 1971.

Both the "OM 100" and "OM 120" were equipped with a 7,412 cc, 6 cylinder diesel engine offering 135 HP at 2,400 rpm and 145 HP at 2,600 rpm. The variants offered were truck, chassis and chassis cab.

The "OM 100" was available with variable wheelbase from 2.987 metres to 4.007 metres and with a payload of between 5,760 kg and 6,000 kg. However, the OM "120" had wheelbases of between 3.169 metres and 4.007 metres and a payload of between 7,850 kg and 8,000 kg.

In view of their dimensions, many of the chassis were used for making tankers and mobile cranes and also municipal vehicles (refuse vehicles, etc.).

The "OM 190" and "OM 260" (sold through Unic in France) were heavy vehicles equipped with a very interesting and sophisti-cated range of 8 cylinder V engines with 14,886 cc (bore and stroke 135 mm x 130 mm), direct injection and able to develop a horsepower of 292 HP (DIN) at 2,400 rpm and a maximum torque of 101 kgm at 1,600 rpm.

Since the dry engine only weighed 900 kg, its power to weight ratio was 3.3 kg/HP.

Both models were offered in truck and semi-trailer truck versions.

The cabs were 3 seaters and, for the first time on original OM vehicles, were of the fully tiltable type (60°), a design which made it possible to access the complete engine for any repair work.

The cab was tilted by a hydraulic mechanism with automatic lock which could only be released by operating a control on the dashboard.

The difference between the two models was the fact that the "OM 190s" were 2 axle 4x2 vehicles with a payload of up to 28 tonnes, whereas the "OM 260" was a 3 axle 6x4 vehicle for a combined payload of up to 44 tonnes.

Because of their strength, power and versatility these vehicles -

60

particularly the "OM 260" - were widely used in quarries and on building sites.

The history of OM as an independent manufacturer finally ended with the "OM 190" and "OM 260"; these were the last models designed and built exclusively by the companies of Brescia and Milan.

OPPOSITE PAGE: At the end of the eighties, the new "100" and "120" were launched. They had the same 6 cylinder, 7,412 cc diesel engine, with payloads of 6,000 kg and more than 8,000 kg, respectively.
TOP: The standard truck version of the "100" model.
CENTRE AND BELOW: Two versions of the "120", a 12,000 litre tanker and a bus destined for a Rumanian travel agency.
ON THIS PAGE: The last members of the OM family before it changed to IVECO were the "190" and "260" heavy vehicles equipped with the latest V8 diesel engine, 14,886 cc, approximately 300 HP; both had a forward cab which tilted 60°C.
TOP: The standard version of the semi-trailer tractor "190 N".
ABOVE: An extremely robust two-sided dumper truck with a 15 cubic metre capacity body on a "260 N" chassis.

The official date of birth of "Lancia & Co." Turin, is the 29th November 1906 when Ernesto Torretta, a solicitor, drew up the formation deed for the company in the names of Vincenzo Lancia and Claudio Fogolin with a capital of 100,000 lire paid up in equal shares by the two partners for the purpose of making motor cars.

Lancia assumed responsibility for the technical management, whilst Fogolin took on the administration of the company. The first factory was set up in part of a building (in via Ormea on the corner of via Donizzetti) which had already been the home of another Turin car maker with a great tradition, "Itala".

Going back a little, it is interesting to note that Vincenzo Lancia, who came from a wealthy family, was supposed to continue his studies to achieve at least a diploma in book-keeping which is what his father, Giuseppe, wanted. But the young Vincenzo preferred to spend his time in a workshop in the courtyard of his house rather than working on his school books. This was the factory where Giovanni Battista Ceirano made bicycles and also "Welleyes" cars from the end of 1898.

Such was Vincenzo's passion for anything mechanical that his father decided to allow his son - not yet seventeen years old - to work for "Ceirano", although officially it was said he was working as an "accountant".

In 1899, as we know, Fiat bought the small company or, to be more precise, the patents of the "Welleyes" cars.

So in March or April of 1900, Vincenzo Lancia was taken on by Fiat as a factory hand at a wage of 60 lire a month. The young man was quickly appreciated for his enthusiasm and intelligence and from the 1st January 1901,

his wage was increased to 100 lire a month, although he was obliged to work "special hours".

After proving himself in the inspection and testing of new vehicles, Vincenzo Lancia became Fiat's official driver, winning wide acclaim, even at international level.

Even after "his" company was founded when he was just 25 years old, Lancia continued to drive Fiat vehicles on the race circuits. That is until, at the Fiat Board Meeting on the 18th June 1909, the following statement was issued: "*Mr. Agnelli said that, as there were no car races, it had been decided not to retain the services of Messrs Wagner and Lancia*".

Fogolin too had worked at Fiat - from 1902 it seems - where his talents were quickly recognised, so that in 1903 he was sent to Milan to manage a planned subsidiary or sales agency.

But let us turn to "Lancia & Co.". The design of the first vehicle was ready in February 1907, just a few months after the company was founded. But a fire ravaged the factory and it was September in the same year before they were able to start tests on the "51", which then became the "18/24 HP" model and later the "Alfa". In view of the success of the tests, the chassis was entrusted to the Turin coach builder "Locati & Torretta" for its "investiture".

This first model was followed by others, all characterised by the search for innovative technical and design solutions.

The premises in Via Ormea soon became inadequate and in January 1911, the company moved to new premises in Via Monginevro with an area of just over 26,000 m² which had previously been occupied by "Fides Brasier", a small car factory which had had an

Vetture Leggere LANCIA & C.°
VIA ORMEA, 89-91
TORINO

The first Lancia factory in via Ormea, Turin.
It was situated near the Parco del Valentino which, without any doubt,
was the true cradle of the Italian automotive industry.

ephemeral life. It was in Via Monginevro that they started studying the manufacture of a small van using the strong chassis of the "Eta" model with suitable modifications, particularly strengthening of the suspension brackets.

Known as the "Z", this vehicle was equipped with a "Tipo (Type) 61" 4 cylinder in line engine of 4,940 cc able to develop a horse power of approximately 70 HP at 2,200 rpm.

The payload was given as 2100 kg, which was increased to 2200 kg for the "1 Z" military version, numerous models of which were used in the Italo-Turkish war in Libya from 1912.

At the outbreak of the First World War in 1914, the Lancia factory was declared part of the war effort. The production of cars for civilian use was more or less suspended and the study of new military vehicles was started.

In 1915, the "Jota" and "Diota" models were added to the "1 Z". These were equipped with the same engine already mentioned, the "Tipo 61".

Both models - which basically only differed in the length of the chassis - were mainly equipped as special military versions (artillery tractors, ambulances, mobile searchlights, guns, etc.) at the "Stabilimenti Farina" coach builders in Turin and also at "Ansaldo" for armour plating.

The "Jota", equipped with complete electrical equipment, can be regarded as the pioneer of a series of vehicles which was produced up to 1935. 2,131 of these extremely robust vehicles were produced during the First World War, up to and including 1918, with many also supplied to the allied armies.

The "Diota" model in particular was equipped as a bus and 170 of these vehicles were produced between 1915 and 1919.

In 1921, two new models were launched both using the "Tipo 64" engine (more or less the same as the "Tipo 61"). They were christened the "Triota" and the "Tetraiota", respectively.

Both vehicles had the same capacity, approximately 2400 kg, and were only produced in the chassis version. The bodywork

PEZZI CHASSIS TIPO 1 Z

TOP: A partial view of the factory in via Monginevro, Turin.
ABOVE: The first truck from Lancia, the "1 Z" in 1912.
TOP OF OPPOSITE PAGE: "Armoured machine gun version" of the first "1 Z Militare" made in 1915 in cooperation with Ansaldo of Genoa.
CENTRE: "Jota" in service during the First World War with the British Armed Forces.
BELOW: "Pentaiota", the first true heavy truck made by Lancia in the first half of the twenties.

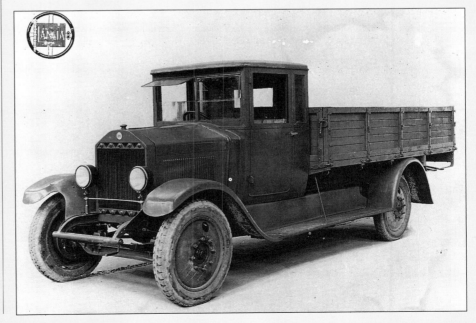

was produced outside, even by the customers themselves, both in Italy and abroad.

The "Triota" had a 3.350 metre wheelbase and just over 250 were produced between 1921 and 1922. The "Tetraiota" on the other hand, had a 3.850 metre wheelbase and approximately 420 were produced between 1921 and 1928, in particular for the manufacture of buses and coaches for the passenger transport sector.

Still using the "Tipo 64" 4,940 cc 4 cylinder engine, but after numerous improvements, Lancia presented its first heavy vehicle in 1924: the "Pentaiota" had the gearbox and central rear axle unit of the "Tetraiota", but the wheelbase had been increased to 4.310 metres. The loading area was 7.77 m² and the maximum payload 5300 kg.

In the ten years or so in which it

remained in production, 2,191 of these vehicles were produced, including numerous "bus" versions for local, long distance and tourist services.

At the request of the Comune di Milano, a new model, the "Esaiota" with a wheelbase increased to 5.180 metres, was derived directly from the "Pentaiota" bus chassis in 1924. This vehicle had the special feature of a chassis with low, shaped, longitudinal members to reduce the ground clearance and make boarding easier for passengers. It was also the first Lancia industrial vehicle to be equipped with brakes on the front wheels as well as the rear.

In spite of these qualities, because of the engine, which was now out of date and underpowered, the "Esaiota" was found unable to meet the increasing demands of a market which was asking for higher speeds. As a result, it was taken out of production after just 13 had been built.

However, in 1927, the old "Tipo 64" engine was judged suitable for equipping the new "Eptaiota", intended for economic use at low speed particularly for goods which were relatively light but bulky. With a wheel base of 4.724 metres and a box body 4.550 metres long, it had a useful loading area of almost 10 m². 1,827 vehicles of this model were made in 1935, including bus versions.

Still in 1927, Lancia launched a new, more powerful engine, a 6 cylinder 7,060 cc petrol engine able to develop a power of 91.5 HP at 1,600 rpm, for the new bus chassis known as the "Omicron". This engine, the first 6 cylinder engine for industrial vehicles designed and produced at Lancia, had a double overhead camshaft cylinder head and, as a further refinement, a centrifugal rev limiter which prevented the engine from exceeding the maximum speed.

The chassis version, or rather versions since there was a short chassis variant with a 5.125 metre wheelbase and a long chassis version with a 5.920 metre long wheelbase, were characterised by the use (for the first time at

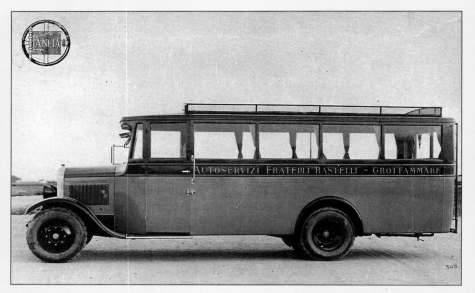

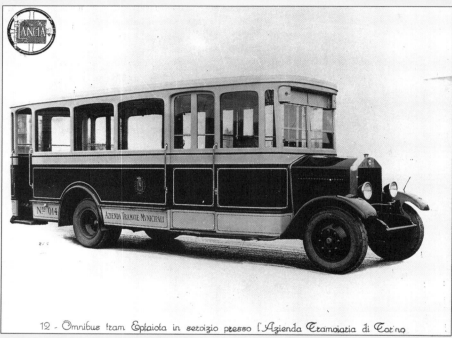

12 - Omnibus tram Eptaiota in servizio presso l'Azienda Tramviaria di Torino

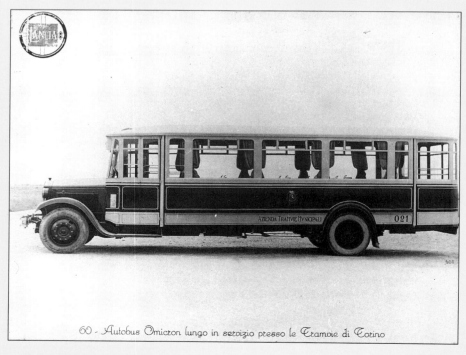

60 - Autobus Omicron lungo in servizio presso le Tramvie di Torino

Lancia) of a rear axle with supporting axle instead of a supporting shaft.

The brakes were mechanically assisted on 4 wheels (after making a hundred or so chassis with a "Dewandre" vacuum type servo brake). Between 1927 and 1935, 552 chassis of this type were produced which were mainly used for making buses for local, long distance and tourist services.

The public transport department in Rome bought a large number of these vehicles and was fully satisfied. The only disadvantage of this vehicle was the high fuel consumption - approximately 50-55 litres of petrol per 100 kilometres (urban cycle).

To solve the consumption problem, from the beginning of the thirties, Lancia too turned its attention to the diesel engine. After detailed studies of the best available on the market, it decided to acquire the manufacturing licence for the engine made by the German company, "Junkers".

And at the 25th International Motor Show in Milan, held in April 1932, Lancia officially launched its new powerful commercial vehicle, the head of the "RO" family, equipped with the "Junkers" diesel engine.

This engine was a 2 stroke 2 cylinder engine with 4 opposite pistons and 3,180 cc which - it was claimed - was distinguished by its limited size and weight and maximum simplicity. The maximum life of the engine shaft bearings, whose mountings were not stressed by combustion pressure, was further enhanced by the lack of cylinder valves. The "Junkers" engine also provided high performance thanks to a perfect combustion process, lack of exhaust fumes, ease of starting without the use of plugs or air heaters, fully automatic direct injection without a pre-combustion chamber and a power of approximately 65 HP at "only" 1,500 rpm.

A new type of transmission was used on the "RO" with a 4 speed, double reduction gearbox providing 8 forward gears and 1 reverse. A differential lock was also supplied on request. The foot brake, which had a system for

compensating the braking force plus a new type of servo brake, ("Westinghouse" compressed air system) and the handbrake, acted on all 4 wheels.

The chassis was characterised by lack of weight in relation to the payload: in fact it only weighed 3,500 kg with a payload of approximately 6,000 kg, or 12 tonnes when combined with the trailer.

Between 1932 and 1938 approximately 1,418 of the "RO" were produced in numerous wheelbase and payload versions and also in the bus version. It is not certain whether this figure also includes some or all of the military versions or any of the few special versions.

In fact, the "RO" military versions also included one with a

petrol engine - largely used in the war in Ethiopia - a 5,120 cc 4 cylinder version able to develop, a power of approximately 65 HP at 1,700 rpm.

In 1935, the "RO" was supplemented by the "RO-RO" version which was equipped with a new diesel engine - still a 2 stroke version produced under the "Junkers" licence - but with 3 cylinders in line, opposite pistons and a total cylinder capacity of 4,770 with a power of 95 HP at 1,500 rpm.

This engine was launched in 1934 and was immediately used on the "Omicron" bus, both as original equipment on the new vehicles and to replace the uneconomical petrol engine on those already in service in Rome. The "RO-RO" model was also

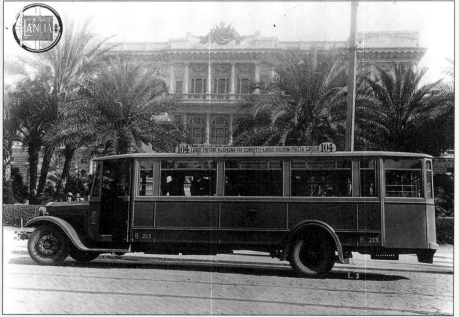

made in civilian and military versions, with some of the latter equipped with the petrol engine already mentioned in connection with the "RO".

Between 1935 and 1939, 301 "RO-ROs" were made, but again we do not know whether this figure includes some or all of the special military versions.

At this point, whilst recognising the excellent performance of the "Junkers" type engines as opposed to the complexity of their architecture which meant very high production costs, the first investigations were made for making an all Lancia diesel engine. Unfortunately, on the 15th February 1937, Vincenzo Lancia died suddenly at his home in Turin at just 56 years of age.

As might be expected, his death was a bitter blow for the company. The affairs of the company were entrusted to Vincenzo's widow, Signora Adele Lancia, and to his brother Arturo, who took over the general management.

At the end of the year the technical management was placed in the hands of Ing. Vittorio Jano, a design engineer who remained at Lancia until 1956 and then continued as a technical consultant for a few years.

Having overcome the initial shock of the untimely death of Vincenzo, Lancia set its sights on the future and in 1938 launched the "3 RO" truck equipped with the new "Tipo 102" diesel engine which was entirely its own design and manufacture. This diesel engine could be called a conventional engine made unconventional by the number of cylinders. They opted for 5 cylinders (four would have been insufficient in relation to the cylinder capacity), a 108 mm x 150 mm bore and stroke and a total cylinder capacity of 6,875 cc. The power output was 93 HP at approximately 1,800 rpm and the consumption was given as only 25 litres of diesel per 100 kilometres.

The "3 RO" was also made in numerous versions, both civilian and military, with different wheelbases and payloads, with or without trailer facility.

There were also many special versions with petrol, gas and

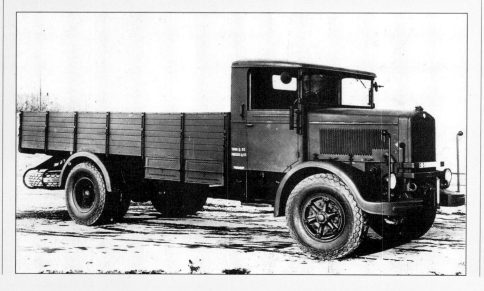

even methane engines. In 1941, because of the war, some models were equipped with 90 mm long range guns.

When peace was restored, the "3 RO" was equipped with a more comfortable cab and also a bunk for the second driver.

From what we know, and subject to the same reservations as expressed for the "RO" predecessors, approximately 15,200 "3 ROs" were built between 1938 and 1949, both in the truck and bus versions.

In spite of the war, 1941 saw the launch of the "800" light van which was derived directly from the "Ardea" vehicle of 1939. The engine, the same as the one on the original vehicle, was a compact 4 cylinder petrol "V" engine with 902.6 cc and a power of approximately 26 HP at 4,500 rpm.

Particularly interesting is the use of spherical segment heads with radial valves, radial plugs in a more or less central position, a double chain-controlled overhead camshaft with rollers, and the pinion on a spring cam.

In 1948, a small truck was added to the van, and from that date a new 5 speed box was installed in the commercial versions with fifth "multiplied" gear as used on the original vehicle.

The figures available indicate that between 1941 and 1953, 7,500 "Ardea" vans and trucks were produced, but this figure is not absolutely certain.

Also, in an attempt to overcome the fuel shortage, at least to some extent, two types of electric vehicle also went into production: the "E 290" twin axle version and the "E 291" triple axle version.

In view of the limited performance, both in terms of speed and range, it seems that not more than 200 of these vehicles were produced by 1948.

Even if not strictly belonging to the industrial vehicle category, the technical characteristics of the modern "Lince" armoured vehicle are worth mentioning. This vehicle was derived from a similar English armour-plated vehicle known as the "Dingo". Approximately 250 "Linces" were built.

It had a total weight of just over 3 tonnes, 4 wheel drive, inde-

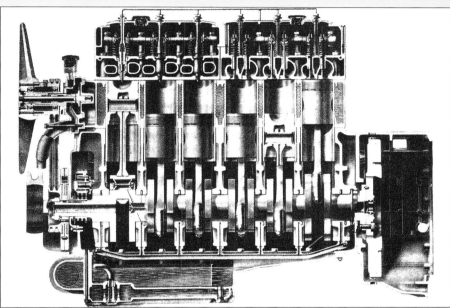

OPPOSITE PAGE TOP: New engine; the Junkers engine with 3 cylinders in direct line, derived from the original 2 cylinder engine of 1934.
CENTRE: This engine was first used in the "Omicron" buses to replace petrol engines and was then also installed in "RO-RO" trucks, both civilian and military.
BELOW: The new 5 cylinder diesel engine designed and built entirely at Lancia was used for the newest "3 RO" in 1938, here shown in the civilian version; the "3 RO" also used petrol, gas and methane.
TOP OF THIS PAGE: The "Lince" armoured vehicle with 4 wheel drive and 4 wheel steer, with 8 cylinder petrol engine, 2,817 cc, power 60 HP at 1,500 rpm. More than 250 of these vehicles were made during the Second World War.
CENTRE: Details of the direct injection 6 cylinder diesel engine with 4 valves per cylinder, 8,245 cc, intended for the new "Esatau" vehicles produced from 1947.
ABOVE: "Esatau" chassis in the 3 axle version.

pendent horizontal arm suspension and hydraulic shock absorbers. The engine was based directly on the 8 cylinder engine used on the "Astura". During the war, no fewer than 215 of these vehicles were made.

But, in the meantime, in the late Autumn of 1942, the massive bombing raids on Turin forced Lancia to transfer its main machining operations and assembly (mainly military vehicles, in view of the times) to premises at Bolzano which had been a factory since June 1937 and which was subsequently enlarged with an engineering shop.

In this respect it must be said that even if after the end of hostilities much of the machining and assembly work was moved back to Turin, in practice, the production of industrial vehicles remained at Bolzano.

Another typical wartime vehicle was the "Esaro" truck which was available in two versions and which was structurally identical to the "3 RO" model. Initially equipped with the same 5 cylinder engine re-converted to petrol, it was then, from 1946, produced with the original diesel engine but with the power reduced to 81 HP. Just over 2,000 of these vehicles were produced in all between 1942 and 1947.

In the post war period, Gianni, the young son of Vincenzo, joined the company to assist Arturo Lancia with the management and the hard job of reconstruction following the devastation inflicted during the war.

In 1947 the "Esatau" heavy truck went into production. This vehicle was also largely used as the basis for making buses, and was the first of a long series of different versions. 15,525 of these were made up to and including 1963.

Although it was a development of the "3 RO", more or less retaining the engine which was increased from 5 cylinders to 6 to give a total of 8,245 cc and a power of 124 HP at 2,200 rpm, this truck was perfectly adequate and even ahead of its time with regard to line - characterised by the long nose - and its reliability and economy of operation.

The consumption was amazingly low: just 20 litres of diesel for 100 kilometres even with a large payload exceeding 7,500 kg.

Although the technical specification more or less remained unchanged compared with the basic version, in 1949 a 3 axle

TOP: The military version of the "Esatau", commonly known as the "6 RO Militare", in 1948.
CENTRE: The very elegant forward cab which, from 1967, equipped the Esatau B"; a derivative of this was also used on the "Esatau A" from 1955.
ABOVE: The local "Esatau 703" buses with horizontal, 6 cylinder in-line engine, 8,867 cc.
TOP OF FOLLOWING PAGE: The light military truck, the "CL 51" with all-wheel drive.
BELOW: The last member of the "Beta" family was the "190" equipped with a 2 stroke, 1,963 cc 2 cylinder diesel engine boosted by a Rootes type compressor.

model was produced, the military version of which was called the "6 RO".

In 1953, the new "864 C" version went into production. This was equipped with a bigger and more powerful engine, but still with 6 cylinders. By increasing the bore from 108 mm to 112 mm, the cylinder capacity was increased to 8,867 cc and an increase in power of approximately 12 HP was achieved.

The innovations introduced in 1955, when the forward cab with engine compartment between the seats was introduced with the "864 A" model, were both substantial and immediately perceptible.

The new cab had rounded lines and the typical shield shaped grille on the front. As far as the engineering was concerned, modifications and improvements were principally made to the injection system.

The last version was made in 1957 when the model known as the "Type B" was introduced on to the market. This vehicle was complimented for the elegance of its design and the intrinsic mechanical and performance characteristics.

It had a modern design cab, made both attractive and elegant by the completely flat shape of the front with windscreen projecting beyond the radiator plane.

The cubic capacity of the engine remained unchanged but, thanks to some improvements, the power was increased to approximately 150 HP, still at 2,000 rpm.

The "Esatau" vehicles were mainly used for special conversions and various special types with additional axles as well as for passenger vehicles, as already mentioned.

Triple axle versions, tractors for semi-trailers and special chassis for buses were also produced in series at Lancia.

Returning to the chronicle of events, in 1950 Lancia returned to the light vehicle sector with a small rapid transport truck which was easy to manoeuvre and versatile and which had a payload of 2,500 kg.

Known as the "Beta Z 11" it was equipped with a petrol engine of superb construction: a 4 cylinder engine with a "U" rather than a

"V" arrangement (the cylinders being more or less parallel), single crankshaft, overhead valves and camshaft, and semi-spherical exhaust chamber.

With 1,908 cc, it developed 46 HP at 3,500 rpm and consumed 16 litres of ordinary grade petrol per 100 kilometres. The maximum speed was approximately 80 km/h.

In 1953, the "Z 50" went into production with a diesel engine instead of a petrol engine.

This small diesel was a 2 stroke engine with 2 parallel cylinders boosted by a low pressure "Rootes" type 3 vane compressor.

With 1,963 cc, it developed 42 HP at 2,000 rpm with a consumption of just 9.5 litres of diesel per 100 kilometres; maximum speed 72 km/h.

In 1957 a new range known as the "Beta 190" was introduced with a completely restyled cab, flywheel gearbox, improvements to the main mechanical assemblies, a more spacious body and a

payload increased to approximately 2,500 kg.

All these vehicles were produced both with simple chassis (mainly used for buses) and as complete vehicles or trucks with cab. There was also a 3 axle version, although very few of these were made. In all, in just less than 10 years, more than 2,600 of these vehicles were made (this figure is not absolutely certain).

If we go back a little, it is interesting to note that between 1951 and 1963, the "CL 51" and "TL 51" models were made, mainly with military applications in mind (the "TL 51" went out of production after 1956), equipped with 4 stroke, 4 cylinder petrol engines, 2,535 cc, 62.5 HP at 3,200 rpm.

This was a compact, forward cab vehicle with 4 wheel drive, a gearbox with 5 forward speeds plus reverse with reduction gear, self-locking front differential and rear differential lock. The maximum length was 4.480 metres, wheelbase 2.550 metres, kerb weight 2,680 kg, payload 1,800 kg; maximum speed 74 km/h; maximum grade ability 79%; standard consumption 25 litres of petrol for 100 kilometres. 4,162 of these vehicles were made (868 of the "TL" version which only differed from the "CL" by virtue of a different axle ratio), with a maximum speed of 60km/h. In 1954 production of the commercial "derivatives" of the well known "Appia" vehicle started. Equipped with a monocoque body, these vehicles were first available as a van version and then also as a truck from 1955.

The engine used was a 4 cylinder "V" engine, 1,089.5 cc, as used for the car but with the power reduced from 37.5 HP to 33 HP at 4,800 rpm.

1955 saw an important change in the company. The Lancia family decided to sell its majority holding to a finance group controlled by the cement industrialist Ing. Carlo Pesenti.

The management of the company changed at the same time as the shareholding: Massimo Spada became Chairman, Ing. Pesenti was Vice Chairman, while Ing. Antonio Fessia took responsibility for the general and technical management of the company.

After a very brief period of settling in, when new versions of the commercial derivatives of the "Appia 2nd series" vehicle were launched, (equipped with engine, a reduced power from 43.5 HP to 36.5 HP, still at 4,800 rpm), the research and development work on industrial vehicles was resumed with vigour. From then on, even if not of prime importance, this sector was generally significant for Lancia in terms of quality, quantity and finance.

The first industrial vehicles which were the fruit of the new management team were launched in 1959. These were the special vehicles known as the "506" and a medium/heavy vehicle which had been christened the "Esadelta". The "506s" were heavy vehicles with 4 wheel drive and were essentially destined for military and special civilian uses

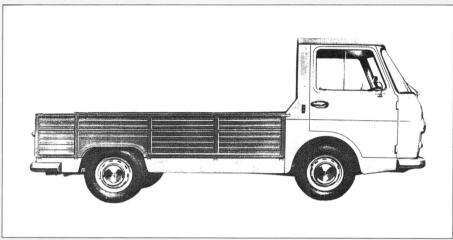

TOP: This agile "Jolly" van of 1959 was derived from the "Appia" car.
ABOVE: This commercial vehicle was the evolution of the "Jolly". The first made in Italy with front wheel drive, it was known as the "Superjolly", and was launched in 1963. It was available with two different wheelbases, both in the small truck version (in the photograph) and in the van version; it was also sold with the "Flavia 1,500" and "Flavia 1,800" car engines.

and also for very special vehicles such as fire engines. For the military version, the cab roof was removable and the windscreen folded down to meet the "stowage" requirements.

The engine, mounted at an angle of 30° in relation to the horizontal, was a 4 stroke, 6 cylinder in-line petrol engine with 6,786 cc and 170 HP at 3,000 rpm. There was also a version which used 115-145 octane "aircraft" type petrol with the power increased to 195 HP.

The vehicle normally operated with rear wheel drive but a clutch control in the cab could be used to engage the front wheel drive. Depending on the version, the maximum speed with rear wheel drive only was 70 km/h or 84 km/h. Even the payload varied, extending to 5,000 kg for

some vehicles, whilst the trucks suitable for towing had a capacity of 10,000 kg.

The "Esadelta" medium/heavy vehicle, designed to replace the now obsolete "3 RO" (not produced for some time), had a diesel engine derived directly from the one used on the "first series Esatau", a 6 cylinder, 8,245 cc engine, but with the power reduced from 122 HP to 115 HP at 1,850 rpm.

Available as chassis with cab, tractor for semi-trailer and truck, this was a vehicle of a very modern design which was soon acclaimed for its speed (maximum speed of more than 65 km/h) and low consumption: 14.8 litres of diesel per 100 kilometres (which was to be slightly higher for subsequent versions). Other qualities which were appreciated

74

TOP: *Two different applications of the special four wheel drive chassis versions of the "506" series.*
LEFT: *a "fire engine" designed for airport services.*
RIGHT: *A "Vento" type snowplough from the beginning of the sixties.*
ABOVE: *The medium/heavy "Esadelta" truck which was very successful because of its versatility, reliability and economy of operation right from its very first version in 1959.*

were the high payload, around 7,000 kg on average, and the possibility of towing a light trailer.

Still in 1959, the commercial derivatives of the "Appia" vehicle, now in its third series, were launched on the market. Known by the name of "Jolly" they were still equipped with the same 1,090 cc petrol engine, but with the power reduced from 48 HP to 36.5 HP.

With regard to the commercial vehicles, 1962 was a particularly important year for Lancia. It was then that a new version of the "Esadelta" was launched on the market with an engine upgraded to 126 HP. (In the following year, the power was increased again this time to 132 HP at 2,000 rpm). And in particular, because a new, powerful and modern industrial vehicle went into production: the highly successful "Esagamma" which was intended to replace the now obsolete "Esatau".

The "Esagamma" was a splendid vehicle with a forward cab, which was now the norm even at Lancia for this type of vehicle. It was equipped with a powerful 10,521 cc, 6 cylinder in-line diesel engine. Thanks to the innovative technical solutions adopted, including 4 valves per cylinder with a compression ratio of 16.5 to 1, this highly advanced engine was able to develop the considerable power of 187 HP at 2,200 rpm.

The truck version for the Italian market, with a 3.970 metre wheelbase, had a gross vehicle mass of 14,000 kg, a payload of 7,200 kg and was able to tow 18,000 kg. The semi-trailer tractor version with a wheelbase of 3.350 metres, had a payload of around 8,000 kg and could tow a weight of approximately 26,000 kg. In the following year versions with a third rear axle also appeared: in the case of the truck versions (wheelbase 3.970 metres + 1.350

metres), the payload was increased to 9,800 kg and the towing weight was 22,000 kg; in the case of the semi-trailer versions, the weight on the rear axle was 10,800 kg and the towing weight 24,800 kg for the Italian market.

The complete range also offered trucks and tractors for semi-trailers, 2 or 3 axles, with wheelbases other than those mentioned above.

In the commercial vehicle sector the "Jolly" was rechristened the "Superjolly" in 1963 and became the first Italian vehicle in this particular sector with front wheel drive which was directly derived from that on the "Flavia" car. The engine was the same petrol engine as for the saloon, with 4 opposed cylinders, 1,488 cc and a power reduced to 58 HP. A notable feature was the maximum speed, given as 115 km/h, and a low consumption: 14.2 litres of normal grade petrol per 100

kilometres.

A version of the "Superjolly" equipped with the "Flavia 1,800" engine was also made in 1966. The power was limited to 80.5 HP and it became the fastest van available on the market at that time, since it was able to develop speeds of around 135 km/h.

Because of this, the "Superjolly" was mainly used for fast delivery services and, in particular, for distributing newspapers within a small to medium radius. The "Superjolly" vehicles in general also found numerous applications as "mixed" vehicles, publicity vehicles and were also equipped for passenger transport in the form of taxis, school buses and minibuses.

In the years between 1964 and 1966, the "Esagamma" family was complemented by chassis and also complete buses for public transport services, both local and long distance. These became the "715" and the "718".

TOP: Many body makers made vehicles for special applications from the new "heavies" of the "Esagamma" family; in the photograph a dumper truck made by "S.A.I.M." on a converted chassis cab with 4 axles.
CENTRE: The "Esagamma" buses were very popular from the beginning of the sixties; in the photograph, a "718" long-distance bus with 4 automatic double doors.
ABOVE: The 3-axle "Esagamma E 520" of 1967.

Both used the same engine as the truck from which they were derived, but it was modified so that it could be mounted on the chassis in a central position. The "715" version kept the power of 187 HP, whereas on the "718", the power was increased to 237 HP. The choice of transmission also differed: a traditional mechanical 4 speed box plus reverse with integrated reduction gears for the "715" and an automatic box for the "718". 1967 saw new versions of both the "Esadelta" and the "Esagamma" vehicles.

The "Esadelta C" was launched on the market. These vehicles were equipped with a new series "402.000" engine: still a 6 cylinder diesel, but with a 122 mm x 135 mm bore and stroke, 9,469 cc and 176 HP at 2,300 rpm.

The truck versions, available with wheelbases of 3.580 metres and 4.090 metres, had a payload of up to 8,100 kilogrammes, whereas the semi-trailer tractor versions, with a wheelbase of 3.000 metres, had a towing weight of 18,000 kg.

The "Esadelta" vehicles were mainly used for special conversions carried out at companies specialising in this field, with longer chassis, additional axles, and numerous other applications.

They remained in standard production until the beginning of the seventies, although it is not possible to establish a precise date, because once Lancia joined Fiat (we will talk about this later), the production of industrial (and commercial) vehicles at Lancia was more or less only maintained until all orders in hand had been completed.

What is certain is that the last public appearance of the "Esadelta C" was at the second International Industrial Vehicle Show held in Turin between the 27th March and 4th April 1971.

As far as the "Esagamma" vehicles are concerned, the new series, known as "Esagamma E", had numerous improvements compared with previous versions, but it still kept the 10,521 cc engine, although the power had been increased to 209 HP at 2,200 rpm.

There were also 3 axle versions of

the "Esagamma E", both in the 6x2 and the 6x4 version, and these were put to numerous uses by specialist companies. A fourth axle was sometimes added and some versions had more than one steering axle.

Finally, new bus chassis appeared in 1969 which were known as the "Esagamma 718.441" (local) and "Esagamma 718.641" (long distance), still with the 10,521 cc engine installed centrally and with a power of 193 HP at 2,200 rpm. The transmission was automatic or semi-automatic.

But in the autumn of that year, the 29th October 1969 to be exact, the not totally unexpected takeover of Lancia by Fiat was officially announced.

We have said that this announcement was not unexpected because, for some time, Lancia had been in serious financial difficulties owing to a difficult national and international economic climate, with the added financial burdens imposed by development programmes already started.

After joining the Fiat Group, Lancia's production of industrial vehicles under its own name continued; particularly the buses at the Bolzano factory which came under the management of the "Fiat Veicoli Industriali" Group.

From July 1972, the Bolzano factory became "Lancia Veicoli Speciali" and was responsible for research and development connected with vehicles for special uses, in particular civil defence and military vehicles.

This brings us to July 1974 when the name Lancia appeared among those due to merge to form the new multi-national Iveco from the 1st January 1975.

"Esagamma" tractors equipped with "Easton" type semi-trailers for heavy quarry work.

For many of the car makers belonging to the period which can be described as the "pioneering age", it is not always a simple matter to establish their precise date of birth, or when a specific product began production. On the one hand there are no reliable records or documentation indicating the actual application of new inventions, and on the other, there is the difficulty of clearly distinguishing between the time of their "creation" and "actual embodiment".

Finally, to complicate things even further, there are the mistakes made - involuntarily or otherwise - by historians or reporters; mistakes which, when they appear in print, are perpetuated. And even if it is possible to achieve a high level of "certainty", doubtful interpretations still remain which give rise to - sometimes - endless debates.

Even the events at Unic do not escape this more or less inevitable rule of confusion. However, in this specific case, the doubt is more acute and directly concerns the date when the French company was founded. The date most commonly indicated is the 15th November 1906, the date on which the formation deed of the "Société des Automobiles Unic" was signed. But many reliable students of automotive history support the theory, which we also share, that the actual date of birth of Unic must go back to October 1904, when the private partnership "Georges Richard et Company" was set up to produce "Voitures Legères et Cycles Unic" (light vehicles and Unic cycles).

Therefore, in this case, the confusion is caused by two things: the founding of a company which includes Unic in its name and the creation of a product using Unic as its "mark".

As already stated, we think it correct to refer to the year as

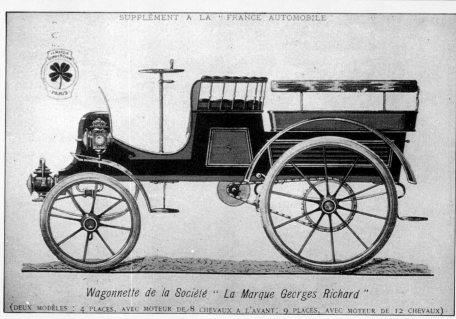

SUPPLÉMENT A LA "FRANCE AUTOMOBILE"

Wagonnette de la Société "La Marque Georges Richard"

(DEUX MODÈLES : 4 PLACES, AVEC MOTEUR DE 8 CHEVAUX A L'AVANT; 9 PLACES, AVEC MOTEUR DE 12 CHEVAUX)

TOP: One of the first achievements of Georges Richard, a "charabanc" dated 1897, with 6 HP engine.
ABOVE: Taken from a copy of "France Automobile", this illustration shows a wagonnette with an 8 HP engine; note the characteristic four-leaved clover symbol.
OPPOSITE PAGE: Brothers Max and Georges Richard taking part in a race in 1899. (Photograph by kind permission of the Automobile Club de France).

1904 even if, to be precise, it is necessary to point out that the first Unic prototype vehicle, made in "just four months", actually saw the light of day in February 1905, although it is not absolutely certain whether this first product from the new company carried the name of Unic.

The "1904 theory" is supported by the fact that, from the time when the company was founded, its founders stated that the choice of the name Unic was to signify that the aim of the new company was to produce vehicles which were as "unique" as possible and which were designed to be able to use the largest number of standard systems on several models. In short, a rationalisation of production. But the debates on the birth of Unic do not end there. Many in fact think that we should go back even further than October 1904, when Georges Richard started his adventures in the automotive field. In our opinion, this theory may be borne in mind, but only as a "relevant" source for a better understanding of the man and his vocation. Having completed this long preamble, we shall start our "chronicle" with a brief and certainly incomplete description of the merits of Georges Richard in those heroic times of the birth of the car. To avoid any confusion, we repeat that these events are merely referred to here as sources relevant to the actual history of Unic.

In 1893 Georges Richard, then thirty years old, and his brother Felix Maxime (called Max), seven years his senior, founded "Cycles Georges Richard" in Paris, a joint stock company with a capital of 500,000 francs and a registered office at 110 of Rue d'Angouleme. Even if not expressly indicated by the name of the company, the aims of the company as stated in

Article 2 of the Articles of Association were not just the "production and marketing of bicycles" but also the "manufacture and sale of motor vehicles". The four leaf clover was chosen as the good luck charm for all future vehicles.

The initiative was successful, and already by 1895 the company had been transferred to more spacious premises in the Auteuil quarter, to number 13 Rue Thé Gautier to be precise. In the following year, the first "Georges Richard" vehicle was launched, a two-seater powered by a 3.5 HP engine of "Benz" origin. It was a success. And so in 1897, the capital in the company was doubled and the corporate "aims" were extended to the "manufacture of mechanisms, engines and parts". Also, to be able to have more powerful engines quickly, an agreement was signed with the French engineer Vivinus who had set up his own company in Brussels, Belgium.

More or less in parallel with these events, the Richard brothers had started to take part in all the more important car races of the time. Consequently the name Richard soon acquired considerable fame. In 1899, with the help of some financiers, including F. Bentz Audéoud of Geneva, the capital was trebled from 1 million francs to 3 million francs. At the same time the company's name was changed to "Société de Anciens Etablissements Georges Richard" and a vast site was purchased at Ivry-Port (number 2 Rue De Galilée) on which the construction of a new factory covering approximately 5,000 m² was soon started. Production began with an initial labour force of 300 employees and a management which was the product of the growth in the manufacturing industry as opposed to the craftsmanship of the past.

Everything went well until, on the 25th May 1903, tragedy struck Georges Richard who, together with another 275 competitors, was taking part in the gruelling Paris to Madrid race. The race was so beset by serious accidents that the authorities decided to stop it at Bordeaux, at the end of the first stage.

Georges Richard, with his faithful mechanic Jeannot, was racing one

Between 1905 and the outbreak of the First World War, the majority of Unic commercial vehicles were equipped with this 4 cylinder petrol engine, the power of which changed over a period of time.

of their 12 HP machines. In the neighbourhood of Angouleme he was forced to take evasive action in order to avoid a careless spectator and left the road at high speed. His mechanic suffered slight injury to his right arm but poor Richard, who was thrown out of the car, suffered serious injuries particularly to his right leg. He was taken to hospital in Paris where he remained for several months, undergoing numerous operations.

During Richard's enforced absence, Henri Brasier, who had already assisted with the design of a 14 HP vehicle, took over the helm at Ivry-Port. First appointed Associate Director, in 1904 Brasier was appointed Chairman of the Board of Directors.

Georges Richard, still convalescing, was almost excluded from the company which he had created, so that in 1905, the Ivry-Port company took on a new name, "Société Automobiles Brasier", although it still kept the four leaf clover emblem. After other changes of name the

company finally put up the shutters in 1930 and, during the next year, the Ivry-Port factory was bought by "Delahaye", the well known French car company dating back to 1894.

In the meantime Georges Richard, still affected by the serious accident he had suffered, and deeply embittered by the misfortunes of his company, spent the days in his Paris home waiting for an opportunity for revenge.

And that opportunity arrived thanks to his friend, Baron Henri de Rothschild, who had already financed other initiatives in the car industry. And so it came about that in October 1904, the private partnership "Georges Richard et Cie" was set up with a capital of 400,000 francs (of which 300 shares were subscribed by de Rothschild and 100 shares by Richard himself) and with its head office at number 108 Rue Saint Maur, the home of the Richard family.

The first vehicle prototypes were made here: type "A", duly approved from February 1905 and

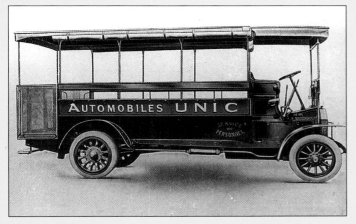

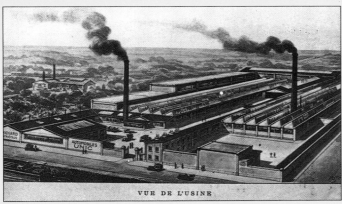

TOP LEFT: A bus made in 1909 by an outside bodywork company.
RIGHT: A "C 9 series F" 12/16 HP taxi of 1909.
ABOVE LEFT: A print showing a view of the Unic works in 1912.
RIGHT: A bus built on a 12 HP chassis (around 1913).

types "B1" and "B2", approved the following year.

All vehicles used 4 cylinder internal combustion engines with two cylinder capacities: 3,466 cc for the type "A" models and 2,607 cc for types "B1" and "B2" which also had the "Richard patent" constant atomisation carburettor (the only difference being the length of the chassis).

The favourable reception on the market of the new vehicles soon raised the problem of the need to increase production capacity. New premises were needed, and more funds.

Baron de Rothschild suggested moving the company to Puteaux, to 1 Quai National, the factories where the "Bardon" vehicles had been produced up until then, and also the "Pascal" between 1902 and 1903. (These had been designed by Baron de Rothschild under the pseudonym "Dr. Pascal").

Later, on the 15th November 1906, the capital of the company was increased to 2,500,000 francs and the name was changed to "Société

Anonyme des Automobiles Unic". Pierre de la Ville Le Roux was appointed Chairman of the Board, whilst the job of Managing Director went to Georges Richard. As was to be expected, the number of vehicle models increased, but it is difficult to establish with any certainty when the first vehicles for goods and passengers appeared. This is because, at the time, only chassis were made at Unic while the bodywork was entrusted to coach builders both by the company and by customers.

Of the more successful Unic models, we need to mention a special "taxi" which, through subsequent modifications and improvements, played a particularly important part in the history of the French company, and was also popular in other countries, particularly England. And it was in England in October 1907, that Unic, as the only French company, took part in the first Motor Show held in London. On that occasion they presented a chassis with a 3,791 cc

4 cylinder engine, developing 24 HP at 1,500 rpm, powered by petrol and alcohol. This was the first industrial vehicle designed and made at Unic for which we have a definite date.

From now on, we shall continue our story of Unic by concentrating exclusively on the production of industrial vehicles and buses, the subject of our present story, but would also point out that the production of cars continued almost to the outbreak of the Second World War.

To return to the "chronicle", we start with the production of a new truck chassis in 1909, the "H 24", with a payload of 2,500 kilogrammes, equipped with the same engine as the one exhibited at the London Show. This chassis, also approved in France in the same year, was used to make some "bus" versions, mainly for hotel services.

As we have not succeeded in obtaining definite information about the actual annual production at Unic (the only reliable information refers to the

CAMIONNETTE BACHÉE SUR CHASSIS TYPE C. 9. — SÉRIE L. 4.

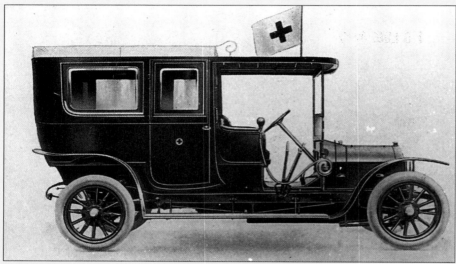

TOP: *Light truck with canvas on a "C 9 series L4" chassis with 35 HP engine, made in 1914.*
TOP CENTRE: *Vehicle for emergency services supplied to the Red Cross during the First World War.*
ABOVE: *Ambulance in service on the Eastern Front in 1917.*
TOP RIGHT: *Georges Dubois who, in 1922, replaced Georges Richard as Head of Unic. Richard had died on the 8th June the same year.*

production of the "taxis", of which 7,292 were produced in the three basic versions between 1906 and 1913), but wish to give an idea of its capacity, we would point out that at the Paris Motor Show in 1910, Unic exhibited 7 different types of cars and 9 industrial vehicles (trucks, vans and buses) on its enormous stand.

The engines used for the industrial vehicles were always the 4 cylinder type, but there were new versions of 3,061, 3,325 and 2,131 cc intended for trucks with payloads of 2,000 kg and 1,200 kg. The imminence of the First World War brought about the need for making large scale deliveries to the armed forces. This was how the production of ambulances started (type "B 8" with 2,131 cc, 4 cylinder engine) and military trucks (types "B 9 0" and "C 9 0"), the first with a 3,325 cc, 4 cylinder engine and the second with the 2,131 cc engine already mentioned. But with the start of hostilities, Unic was also obliged to adapt its activities to the war effort, in particular by producing shells for the artillery and the Air Force.

At the end of 1919, in spite of the many problems of a difficult post-war period, it was possible to restore a reasonably regular schedule of vehicle production.

The capital of the company was increased to 7,500,000 francs and production was resumed on the basis of the pre-war models.

It was only in 1922 that vehicles in the new "M 1" series with payloads of up to 2,000 kg went into production. These vehicles were equipped with 2,626 cc, 4 cylinder internal combustion engines. The models in the "L" series then followed, initially equipped with a 1,852 cc engine and with a payload of around 1,000 kg.

Unfortunately, on the 8th June of the same year, Georges Richard died in a tragic accident whilst he was working on the development of a new front wheel braking system. In the vicinity of Rouen, having stopped to check something, he was knocked down by his own vehicle which toppled over when the edge of the road gave way. Whereas his companion, Mathieu, escaped with a fractured collar bone, Richard broke his pelvis. He was taken to a hospital in Rouen, where he died three days later, when, at his request, he was about to be taken back to Paris.

Ing. Georges Dubois, who was already acting as Technical Director, was appointed to replace Richard on the board. He continued the programmes already started and, by following a direction which had been taken for some time, he furthered the production of industrial vehicles.

From a leaflet dated 1923-1924, it is seen that Unic offered the following basic types of chassis for commercial vehicles:

- Two "M 1" chassis equipped with 2,626 cc monobloc 4 cylinder engines, 4 speed gearbox plus reverse, universal transmission, right hand steering, potential body size 3.370 and 3.635 metres, total payload (including the body) 1,400 kg and 2,200 kg;

- Two "L 2" chassis with a 1,852 cc monobloc 4 cylinder engine, 4 speed gearbox plus reverse, universal transmission, left hand steering, brakes on 4 wheels, potential body size 2.750 and 3.200 metres, total payload (including body) 900 kg and 1,200 kg.

It should also be noted that all these chassis had a speed governor as standard and, if required, though at a surcharge, could be supplied with starter unit and electric lighting.

Between 1925 and 1926, production increased considerably at Unic, made possible by a consistent increase in personnel. In fact, at the beginning of 1925, the employees numbered approx-

imately 1,500, whereas at the end of 1926, they totalled 1,884 (made up of 1,422 workers, 308 apprentices and 114 women).

The employment of women (at least for the time) was something unique to Unic, and was all the more remarkable because many of them were responsible for road testing the vehicles produced. The factories were also expanded and modernised and maximum effort was made to increase sales abroad, at first in the colonies and French speaking countries. During those years the production of industrial vehicles, although increased in relation to car production, still did not exceed 20% of the total production of Unic vehicles.

In 1930, in the light of further possible developments, Unic acquired more factories, increased its capital to 14,550,000 francs and adopted the new name of "Société Nouvelle des Automobiles Unic".

It was precisely at that time, and in spite of the fact that the American depression of 1929 had finally hit the Old World, that the dogged advance of the diesel engine also reached France. Whereas some French manufacturers opted for producing "Junkers" or "Saurer" engines under licence, Unic preferred the

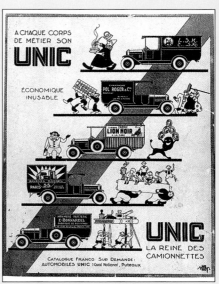

TOP: Female test drivers from the twenties.
CENTRE AND ABOVE: Advertisements showing "vans" of 1925 and 1929 respectively.

diesel engines of Mercedes Benz. However, the licence was not acquired directly from Mercedes itself, but through "C.O.D.R.A." (Compagnie des Diesel Rapides) which held the patents for it for France.

It was for that reason that the first Unic chassis equipped with the new diesel engines in 1931 bore the mark "C.D." which stood for "Codra Diesel".

The first models made were the "C.D.2" and the "C.D.3", both equipped with a diesel engine of the type with pre-combustion chamber, 6 split block cylinders, bore and stroke 105 x 165 mm, a total cubic capacity of 8,572 and a maximum power of 85 HP (increased to 90-95 HP for the "C.D.3") at 1,600 rpm.

The "C.D.2" type chassis had 2 axles with a wheelbase of 5.100 metres or 4.500 metres. The payload (including the body) was approximately 7,500 kg, to give a total weight of 12,600 kg; the towable weight was approximately 8,000 kg. Maximum speed 36-55 km/h, depending on the ratios and whether or not a trailer was used. In the years immediately following there was also a semi-trailer tractor version with a total payload of 17,000 kg.

The "C.D.3" chassis had 3 axles, wheelbase 5.650 + 1.350 metres or 4.850 + 1.350 metres, maximum payload 11,000 kg and total weights of 17,200 kg and 17,100 kg respectively. The maximum speeds were between 37 km/h and 46 km/h.

The advent of the diesel engine, which was also used to equip the special "M" series chassis, did not affect the production of the light and medium light vehicles in the "L" and "M" series with total payloads of between 900 kg and 4,200 kg, which continued to use 4 cylinder petrol engines with different cylinder capacities.

In 1936 a 4,942 cc, 4 cylinder diesel engine went into production which was intended to equip the first chassis for trucks and buses in the famous "Z" series. In the same year Unic also saw the first applications of charcoal, anthracite or coalite "gas generators".

In 1937 Unic launched its own diesel engine, the first diesel

TOP: Unic's first diesel engine made under C.O.D.R.A. licence, on the test bench in 1931.
CENTRE: The above engine installed on the new "C.D.2" and" C.D.3" (2 and 3 axles); photograph: C.D.2 truck, total kerb weight 12,600 kg.
ABOVE: Rear tip-up truck on a "C.D.2" chassis.
FROM THE TOP OF OPPOSITE PAGE: Van on "C.D.3" chassis.
1936 bus made by Carrozzeria Currus on an "M 24" chassis.
"G 40" van equipped with Gohin-Poulenc gas generator.
Unic Regresse "P 107", a semi-tracked military vehicle approved in 1938 and intended for the Engineering Corps.

entirely designed and made in France.

Curiously, this engine was also identified by the "C.D.26" mark, although "C.O.D.R.A." had nothing to do with it. This was a powerful 6 cylinder engine with pre-combustion chamber, bore and stroke 115 x 165, 10,283 cc, intended for equipping three different types of chassis with a total weight of between 15,600 kg and 19,000 kg, all equipped with an 8 speed box plus reverse.

In the meantime, the production of cars continued to decrease in favour of industrial vehicles. Evidence of this is the fact that on the eve of the Second World War, the Unic price list only included three types of chassis for cars (with 4 and 6 cylinder petrol engines) and 32 types of chassis for industrial vehicles. These were divided between 11 models with petrol engines (all with 4 cylinder) 13 with diesel engines (4 and 6 cylinder) and 8 with gas generators (4 and 6 cylinder).

In view of the times, the production of ambulances and military vehicles was also started. Of these, those worthy of particular mention include the well known "P 107 semi-tracked vehicle", made from the end of 1937 following an agreement with the "Société d'exploitation Ké gresse" which held the "track" patents.

The army purchased various versions of the "P 107", including the later "TU 1" version, still equipped with petrol engine.

Between 1938 and 1940, 3,276 of these very efficient semi-tracked vehicles were produced, practically all of which were intended for the army, except for a few supplied to the fire services.

With the outbreak of the war, again the production of vehicles for civilian use was interrupted and the production of artillery shells was started. However, on 3rd June, 1940, the factory was heavily bombarded and this was followed by the German occupation a few days later.

Production at Puteaux was resumed under very difficult conditions after a few months, under the supervision of the occupying forces.

As far as transport vehicles for civilian use were concerned, there

CHARGE TOTALE : 6.500 KG.

CHARGE UTILE 5.500 Kg.
POSSIBILITÉ TOTALE de
remorquage: 4.000 Kg. environ.
VITESSES MAXIMA :
63 Km/H avec démultiplicat. 10x59
57 " " " 10x62
POIDS DU CHASSIS NU
(en ordre de marche) 3.500 Kg.
*
TRACTEUR
POIDS TOTAL EN CHARGE
de la semi-remorque : 12.000 Kg.
environ.

QUELQUES UTILISATIONS
DES CHASSIS ZU-51
CITERNE 5 à 6.000 L. environ.
PLATEAU 12 m² environ.
LAITIER
BENNE BASCULANTE 3,5 m³.
TRACTEUR etc...
*
VENTE A CRÉDIT
Paiements échelonnés
jusqu'à 18 mois.

was only a limited production of trucks with gas generators. Installing gas generator equipment on chassis was taken on as contract work for other companies.

In December 1940 the government of occupied France, which wanted to harmonise the distribution of the scarce supplies of raw materials and to regularise the vehicle industry, set up a type of consortium between the car companies which had survived. In an initial period this consortium was known as the "Groupement Francais de l'Automobile" (known as "G.F.A.") and later, following the changes made in the immediate post-war period, it adopted the name "Société Générale Française de Construction Automobile".

This organisation gradually grew weaker until its final demise in 1951.

When the Second World War was finally over, regular production at Unic was gradually resumed but beset by many problems. It was finally decided to abandon cars and concentrate exclusively on the production of industrial vehicles.

In October 1944 a new series of chassis was produced known as the "ZU", which had a new 4 cylinder diesel engine with bore and stroke 115 mm x 150 mm. However, this engine was modified immediately, increasing the bore to 118 mm and then increasing the cubic capacity to 6,560 cc.

In 1946 a 6 cylinder diesel engine with a cubic capacity of 9,840 cc and the same bore and stroke also went into production. The trucks, equipped with the 4 cylinder engines, had total weights of between 9,000 kg and 12,000 kg; those with the 6 cylinder engine had weights of between 13,000 kg and 16,000 kg (including the semi-trailer tractor versions).

Gradually the 4 cylinder engines had powers of between 85 HP and 110 HP and those with 6 cylinders between 120 HP and 150 HP and even up to 180 HP when, in 1955, there was a version with a compressor.

However, in the meantime, in 1949 to be precise, the need to modernise all the production facilities at Unic factories required investments which exceeded the financial resources of the company.

"SIMCA" (Société Industrielle et Mécanique de Carrosserie Automobile), came to its aid. This company was founded in Nanterre (Paris) on the 2nd November 1934 on the initiative of Commendatore Pigozzi, for the assembly and distribution of some "Fiat" cars in France and, whilst maintaining a close link with the Turin company, it also designed and manufactured its own cars.

Simca not only provided Unic with its capital, but also various types of machinery and fixtures. From this first link - exclusively financial - closer relations soon developed, until an agreement was reached whereby Unic became the "Industrial Vehicle Division" of Simca.

All this happened in 1952 and, two years later, with effect from 1st January 1955, Simca also bought the business of "Ford France".

Following this last transaction, the production of what we would call "mixed" vehicles started, first at Poissey and then at Suresnes. These vehicles had mechanical systems and parts either belonging to the Unic models or the "Ford Cargo" models.

Between 1956 and 1966, approximately 35,000 truck models in the "Cargo" class were made at Suresnes, the majority of which were in the 4x4 military version.

Still in 1956, there was another important event: the Spring marriage of Unic and "Saurer France". In view of the proximity of the Puteaux and Suresnes factories, this union led to the formation of an industrial complex measuring 105,000 m². In addition, the combining of the respective sales networks of the two companies produced quite a significant capillary effect for the marketing and after sales services for that time.

Turning now to the product, a whole series of new, all steel cabs were made both for the 4 cylinder diesel engine trucks and also for the trucks with 6 cylinder engines. The latter were bigger and also included bunks.

Still on the subject of cabs, it was

at this time that, following reductions in the maximum weights per axle agreed at international level in order to lighten the vehicle tares as much as possible, chassis with semi-forward and forward cabs were made. But the "long nose" which had made the Unic trucks popular did not disappear altogether, particularly in the heavy vehicle sector.

In 1960, Simca, the owner of Unic, was divided into two separate companies, i.e. "Simca Automobiles" for the production of cars and "derivatives" (which were then gradually assigned to "Chrysler France") and "Simca Industries" which included the "Unic Industrial Vehicle Division", among others.

Therefore, Unic no longer produced light vehicles for Simca.

Consequently, at the end of 1960, in order to offer a complete range on the market, they started to import into France the light "Fiat 615" trucks (4 cylinder diesel engine, 1,901 cc, payload 1,800 kg) and also some trucks from the Brescia company "OM" (already owned by "Fiat") : the "Lupetto", "Leoncino" and "Tigrotto", all equipped with 4,156 cc, 4 cylinder diesel engines and with a total kerb weight of 4,250 kg, 5,600 kg and 6,900 kg respectively.

At the Paris show in 1964, Unic presented - mounted on a strong "Izoard" chassis designed for a total kerb weight of 35,000 kg - its newest 10,760 cc, 8V diesel engine which was capable of generating 225 HP at 2,600 rpm. Known as the "M 62", it was the result of 15,000 hours of design

work, 10,000 hours of tests on the bench and 500,000 km of road tests.

It should be noted that this engine kept the same bore and stroke (119 mm x 121 mm) as the previous Unic diesel engines: the 5,380 cc, 4 cylinder engine which developed 115 HP at 2,600 rpm, was launched in 1961, and the 6,730 cc, 5 cylinder engine generating 140 HP at the same engine speed was launched in 1963.

On 16th June 1960 "Simca Industries" was absorbed by "Fiat France", which at the same time assumed the name of "Fiat France Société Anonyme" (abbreviated to "F.F.S.A."), which also retained the "Divisione Veicoli Industriali Unic". Following this event, the exchange of products with Italy increased.

A few months later at the Paris Show, Unic presented, on an "Izoard" 6x4 3 axle chassis equipped with a newly designed forward cab, a development of the 8V engine. Identified as "M 62 S", it was equipped with the "Saurer" high-performance injection system and developed a power of 270 HP whilst maintaining an engine speed of 2,600 rpm.

In 1969, still at the Paris Show, and also to celebrate the 4,000th V8 engine produced, Unic launched a new generation of this engine known as the "V 85 S" (which was not marketed until September 1970): the bore and stroke was 135 mm x 130 mm for a total cubic capacity of 14,880 cc and it was able to develop 340 HP at 2,400 rpm.

In 1970 it was the turn of the new 6

TOP OF OPPOSITE PAGE: A powerful semi-trailer or tractor, the "Izoard", at the 43rd Tour de France in 1956.
BOTTOM: The splendid V8 diesel engine with 10,760 cc, 270 HP known as the "M62S", which made its debut at the Paris Motor Show in 1964.
TOP LEFT OF THIS PAGE: Van on Bonhomme chassis, semi-forward cab, "Saint Could" model.
RIGHT: Simca military truck from Ford France with four-wheel drive, in regular production at Unic in Suresnes.
CENTRE LEFT: Concrete mixer on a Saverne "MZ 36" chassis with semi-forward cab.
RIGHT: Semi-trailer tractor, the Izoard "T 270", with forward tilting cab.
ABOVE LEFT: "Izoard" V8 forward cab with refrigerated semi-trailer, leaving for the USSR.
RIGHT: The 4000th Izoard "270 A" with V8 engine, produced in 1969.

In 1986 Unic started to produce new diesel engines.
TOP LEFT: The 4 cylinder "32" type with a power of 135 HP.
RIGHT: The "42"; 6 cylinders, 200 HP.
CENTRE: "Izoard" semi-trailer tractor equipped with "M 62 S" engine.
ABOVE: A special truck made in 1966 on the "Vercors" chassis, fitted out for transporting iron bars.

cylinder diesel engine, the "V 63 S": bore and stroke 125 mm x 121 mm, 8,900 cc, power 240 HP at 2,600 rpm. In the meantime at Fiat in Turin, following a complete reorganisation, it was decided to create an industrial vehicle division which naturally included Unic. The exchange of vehicles and parts between France and Italy continued to increase.

Some production was also shared and a decision was made on the partial transfer of production from the Unic factories at Puteaux-Suresnes to Trappes, an important railway junction approximately 30 km from Paris on the Paris to Chartres road. The work on the new premises progressed quickly and between 1971 and 1973 the production of industrial vehicles was gradually transferred from Puteaux-Suresnes where just the engine production remained.

We think that we must mention the last "original Unic" product, the "8220", a beautiful engine with 6 cylinders in line, a bore and stroke of 125 mm x 130 mm, 9,572 cc and power of 201 HP at 2,600 rpm. The design work started in 1971, although the official launch of this engine did not take place until September 1975 at the Frankfurt Fair, already under the auspices of Iveco.

Just before changing to Iveco,

which was on the 18th December 1974, the Unic division of "F.F.S.A." was set up as a joint stock company under the name "Unic FIAT S.A.". And it was this company which, on changing to Iveco, handed over the following factories in France to this new multi-national:

- Trappes: total area 520,000 m², 110,000 m² of which are floor space; 1700 employees; production of medium and heavy trucks;
- Suresnes: total area 63,200 m², 58,000 m² of which are floor space; 2,500 employees; production of gearboxes and mechanical components;
- Bourbon-Lancy: total area 27,000 m², 88,000 m² of which are floor space; 1,600 employees; production of engines and truck components;
- Fourchambault: total area 80,000 m², 47,000 m² of which are floor space; 500 employees; production of stampings and spares for trucks.

Three different versions on the "Izoard" V8 chassis.
TOP: Semi-trailer tractor "T 270", 6x4, with rear tip-up mechanism for quarry and building site work.
CENTRE: Truck designed for heavy work in quarries and on building sites, the "P270", 6x6.
ABOVE: The special "270", 6x6 truck, photographed in Red Square, Moscow.

onrad Dietrich Magirus was
born on the 26th September,
1824, in Ulm, a German city
which, a few years previously,
had passed to Württemberg
under the Vienna Peace Treaty of
1809, and was famous for its
imposing Gothic style cathedral.
On completing his studies, the
young Conrad was sent by his
father, a well-known and influ-
ential merchant, to undergo a
harsh apprenticeship in the
world of business which led him
to make numerous journeys,
including several abroad. During
that period he spent some time in
Naples, where he had a brother-
in-law.
On returning to Ulm, Magirus
started to take an interest in
problems connected with fire-
fighting which, at the time, was
approached in a somewhat haph-
azard and not uncommonly
superstitious manner.
In 1847, aged just 23 years,
Conrad joined the newly
constituted Turngemeinde, a
sporting, cultural and, to some
extent, political institution,
which was destined to play an
important part in the development of the city of Ulm and
surrounding cities.
Very soon, in recognition of his
studies and the ideas he had
expounded on methods for
fighting fires, he was officially
given the job of reorganising the
citizens' fire services.
At the beginning of 1864,
Magirus joined the company
Fratelli Eberhardt as a partner
and authorised signatory with a
share of 10,000 Florins. For 10
years or so, this company had
been involved in the agricultural
machinery and equipment sector.
About the same period, Conrad
Dietrich Magirus also began his
activities in the fire-fighting
sector, initially limited to
equipment specifically designed

*TOP: Conrad Dietrich Magirus, doyen
of the German fire brigade and
founder of the company.
RIGHT: One of the impressive "Flying
Ladders" from Magirus.
BELOW: One of the last horse-drawn
"Flying Ladders".*

*A birdseye view of the Magirus factory in Via Schiller, Ulm,
where they produced special equipment for
fire engines and firemen.*

for fire brigades and then extended to new types of hoses and engines which were more efficient and easier to handle compared to those currently available.

On the 10th March 1860, Magirus registered himself in the commercial register and in the following year he placed an advertisement in a journal published by the German fire brigades announcing himself as a supplier of fire brigade accessories and equipment.

He was highly successful in his business, but it was a practical, lightweight free-standing ladder that brought him considerable fame in 1872.

Known thereafter as the Ulm ladder, it received the gold medal at the Vienna World Exhibition in 1873 and the name of Magirus became widely known, even in international circles.

In 1875, Magirus built himself a grand villa in the "Ulmer Promenade" which also housed a small factory.

Here innovations multiplied and were perfected so that in 1881, faced with an increasing demand, an "office" was set up in the vicinity of the villa and in 1885, a new factory was opened in Via Schiller, also in Ulm.

To give some idea of the fortunes of the "Fabbrica Equipaggiamenti Anticendio de C.D. Magirus", it is sufficient to record that in the "ladder" sector alone (perfected to a greater degree) no fewer than 175 variants were produced in all shapes and sizes for a variety of uses in the period from 1873 to 1885.

In 1887, in spite of still being at the peak of his powers (he was to die 8 years later on the 26th June 1895), Conrad Dietrich Magirus decided to hand over the reins to his sons Heinrich, Otto and Hermann, who had already been helping him in his work. The

technical management of the company went to Otto.

In 1890, the premises at Via Schiller were expanded, it having been decided to add new fire engines, first manual and then motorised, to the products already listed.

The first "Magirus motorised engine", mounted on a horse-drawn carriage, was officially launched at the fire-fighting equipment exhibition held at Monaco di Baviera in 1893.

It appears that a Daimler 12 HP twin engine was used ignited by means of two platinum glow plugs heated by a flame.

Other models followed, powered by steam engines and electric motors, until the gradual advance of the internal combustion engine resolved all the problems concerning the operation of the engines and their mobility, without having to rely any longer on animal traction.

Regarding this last point, many sources confirm that the first Magirus fire-fighting vehicle with an internal combustion engine was a "revolving ladder" mounted on a Morris chassis, which was supplied to Cape Town in 1906. And, still on this point, many make the mistake of saying that this motorised ladder, a photograph of which has been handed down, had an internal

In addition to ladders, Magirus also produced fire engines.
TOP LEFT: A manually operated engine; RIGHT: The first fire engine driven by a petroleum engine, launched in 1895.
CENTRE: Ladders and fire engines in production at the end of the nineteenth century; they were all designed to be horse-drawn.
ABOVE: The mysterious "Magirus ladder mounted on a chassis with petrol engine" in service in Cape Town in 1906; the ladder was certainly made by Magirus, but it was sold to an English company who produced firefighting equipment, (John Morris and Sons Ltd.), who installed it on a chassis which the company did not produce itself, and whose origin cannot be traced.

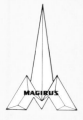

The first truck - chain transmission version - produced by Magirus in 1918 and below: photographs of both the inlet and exhaust sides of the "V110" petrol engine.

In 1911, on the 8th July to be precise, Magirus changed from a private company to a joint stock company with a capital of 1.5 million Marks.

And since the Magirus family did not have sufficient financial resources to cover the entire capital, approximately half was subscribed by a Berlin company, the "Berliner Handelsgesellschaft". The Magirus brothers were appointed to the company's Supervisory Board with Heinrich Magirus as Chairman.

Not long afterwards, the premises in Via Schiller having become inadequate, a plot of land was bought on the outskirts of Ulm which was to become the home of factory No. 2 (factory No. 1 being the one in Via Schiller).

When the First World War broke out, the Magirus company soon realised that it could no longer depend on outsiders for the supply of motorised chassis on which to install its fire-fighting equipment.

This gave rise to the idea of starting the independent production of vehicles which could also be used as transport vehicles, both military and civilian.

On the 1st May, 1916, Magirus took on the engineer Heinrich Buschmann, who had already earned himself a wide reputation at that time. Within a short period, he made a first vehicle prototype which underwent rigorous testing.

The first Magirus truck was officially launched in September, 1917. This was a truck with a 3 tonne carrying capacity and "cardan" joint (hence the name "3C"). A version with a chain transmission (known as the "3K", from "Ketten", chain in German), was made more or less at the same time.

In both cases, the engine was a robust 4 cylinder 6,082 cc petrol engine, bore and stroke 110 mm x 160 mm, able to develop 40 HP at just 1,100 rpm. The engine was christened the "V 110", the letter V indicating the number of cylinders (vier = 4) and the number, 110, being the cylinder bore in mm.

At the beginning of 1918, Magirus was invited to send vehicles to Berlin, to the army

combustion engine produced by the English car manufacturer Morris, but fail to mention that Morris the car maker did not arrive on the scene until 1912.

The truth is that at the beginning of the century, Magirus supplied fire-fighting equipment, particularly ladders, to the English company John Morris & Sons Limited, Fire Engine Works, Salford.

This company then proceeded to mount the revolving ladders first on horse-drawn carriages and then on chassis with internal combustion engines and to supply them to the countries of the Commonwealth.

Following research at John Morris, it was impossible to find out certain information concerning the identity of the company which manufactured the chassis and the engine actually used. Nevertheless, Magirus still proceeded to install its own

equipment on chassis, with engine or otherwise, supplied by outside manufacturers.

In 1907, following agreements made with another company, Magirus also started to produce camp kitchens for the army. This was the start of a relationship with the German armed forces which was destined to become much closer. In fact, Magirus was soon commissioned directly to supply observation towers for the artillery and also latticework and limbers for the telegram service.

This relationship also gave rise to a close cooperation with Telefunken and Siemens & Halske. And since these companies were in Berlin, Magirus was also obliged to set up an office in that city.

In 1909, the first company of all opened up a small office, followed in 1910 by a more elaborate office in the Tempelhof area on the outskirts of the city.

proving ground, and soon afterwards, they also started deliveries to "civilians".

In this period, the company also produced an interesting articulated tractor vehicle for motorised infantry, equipped with the "V 135" engine, a 4 cylinder petrol engine with a cylinder capacity of 10,306, bore and stroke 135 mm x 180 mm, developing 70 HP at 1,100 rpm. However, only two of these vehicles were made because the end of the war interrupted this initiative.

The post-war period was extremely difficult. Magirus tried to diversify into other sectors, but although there were some difficulties, they soon went back to the production of motor vehicles and enlarged the range to include buses, the demand for which was increasing.

The first Magirus bus was delivered on the 25th October 1919, to a transport company in Auendorf.

The superstructure was mounted on a "2 C" chassis (2 tonne payload, "cardan" transmission), equipped with the "V 110" engine already described, and provided seats for 18 passengers and standing room for 6. It was able to reach a speed of 26 km/h.

In the years which followed, by varying the bore and stroke dimensions, a whole family of engines with different cylinder capacities and powers was derived from the basic 4 cylinder version.

In fact, in that period, there were engines with cylinder capacities of 8,435 - 2,950 - 4,250 and 4,712 and power of 55 - 26 - 34 HP and, a new one providing 55 HP.

The chassis were also modified to some extent, motivated by the need to achieve a wider payload range.

In the ten year period between 1917 and 1926, approximately 4,000 Magirus 4 cylinder engines were built, about 3,000 of which were used to power lorries and buses, and the remainder for fire-fighting and military vehicles.

In the meantime, in 1922, Buschmann had left the company to take up the Chair of Mechanical Engineering at the State University in Esslingen. But in 1925, he was brought back to Magirus to start on the design of new engines and new vehicles. That which was inevitable had in

TOP: The 3 tonne truck with "cardan" transmission which completed the test drive from Ulm to Berlin.
CENTRE: The "Kraftprotze", the military off-highway vehicle tried out during the First World War.
ABOVE: In the immediate post-war period, Magirus also started to produce buses, still equipped with the "V110" engine.

fact occurred: the market demanded more modern vehicles, capable of improved performance, and not just in terms of power and speed, but also in terms of capacity and economy of operation.

Therefore, even though they were

still valid within certain limits, the old 4 cylinder engines had to give way to the 6 cylinder engines which were spreading rapidly among practically all competitors. Although he did not surrender his chair at the university,

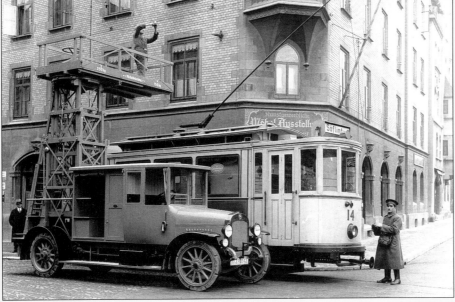

TOP: Dating from the early twenties, this slender bus with its long wheel base and four doors, was suitable for out-of-town services.
CENTRE: A truck from the same period equipped for maintaining overhead tram lines.
ABOVE: A refuse cart.

Buschmann started work and recommended that whilst awaiting the development of the new 6 cylinder generation of Magirus engines, the company should use the engines available on the market which had already been tried and tested.

The immediate choice was made in favour of the "OS 5" and "OS 6" 6 cylinder petrol engines made by Maybach Motorenbau in Friedrichshafen, which were then also made under licence, with slight modifications, at Magirus. The 2 engines were practically identical: 6 cylinder petrol engines bore and stroke 94 mm x 168 mm, 6,995 cc and a power of approximately 100 HP, weight (with oil and cooling water) 432 kg. The only difference between the two types was that the "OS 5" had a Maybach original carburettor, whilst the "OS 6" had 2 Solex carburettors.

From 1927 to 1928, these engines were used to equip the new chassis for the Magirus "M" series trucks and buses. In particular, there were the "MM 3" and "MM 4" chassis which were bigger and were used for making buses, an area in which Magirus had earned a considerable reputation, and the "MML" (ladder) and "MMS" (fire) engines. From 1931, they were also mounted on the "M 50" type chassis.

Between 1929 and 1932, Magirus also used the "W 2" type Maybach engine, a 6 cylinder petrol engine, but with 5,740 cc, 95 mm x 135 mm stroke and bore, 70 HP at approximately 2,200 rpm.

More or less at the same time, 150 type "16 C" engines were bought from Continental. These were 6 cylinder petrol engines, 4,068 cc, 85.72 mm x 117.47 mm bore and stroke, power 55 HP at 2,000 rpm. They were used to equip the "MI" chassis series (which were lighter than the "MM").

At the same time however, Magirus persevered with the development of its own 6 cylinder engines.

The first to see the light of day was the "S 85" petrol engine in 1929 (when, using the usual coding method, the letter "S" meant that it was a 6 cylinder engine "sechs" in German and the number represented the bore in mm). It had 4,255 cc, a bore and stroke of

The excellent reputation which the Magirus buses soon acquired led to an intensification of the programmes in this specific sector and to the manufacture of increasingly powerful and roomy vehicles.
TOP: An imposing coach of the "MM4" type belonging to the police force.
CENTRE: One of the first Magirus buses with an all-steel enclosed body (approx. 1930).
BELOW: The first "M" series truck with diesel engine produced in-house, launched in 1933.

85 mm x 125 mm and a power of 55 HP at 2,000 rpm.

The "S 88" types, increased to 4,562 cc and a power of 65 HP or 70 HP, and the "S 105", with 7,793 cc and a power of 110 HP were derived from this engine.

In the meantime, in 1930, a splendid 12 cylinder petrol engine was bought from Maybach, a reduced power version of which (100 HP) was used on the "MM 4" bus chassis with an all steel structure. The 100 HP limit was imposed by the need to use the original chassis engineering, particularly the gearbox and axle, without modification.

But the era of the diesel engine was now beginning and naturally Magirus started to work on engines of this type too.

The first to arrive on the test bench for final adjustment was a 6 cylinder engine based on the "S 88" petrol engine already mentioned. This was in December 1932. Since the fuel used was naphtha (crude oil, "Rohöl" in German), it was known as the "S 88 R". The cubic capacity and power were the same as for the petrol version: 4,562 cc and 65 HP at 2,000 rpm. The "S 110" 6 cylinder petrol engine was also transformed into a diesel engine with a pre-combustion chamber, and this was known as the "S 110 R". In this case too, the cylinder capacity and power remained the same as for the original model.

From 1933, the letter "R", used to distinguish engines running on naphtha, was changed to "D", meaning diesel. These engines were also used on the "M" series chassis and were available in a wide range of different versions in terms of dimensions, weights and payload capacities.

At the beginning of that year, in order to obtain wider sources of income to offset the consistent trading losses and the consequent indebtedness to banks which had accumulated during the depression, Magirus started to produce an original light vehicle which had a forward cab and compact overall dimensions. It was designed to increase the range of possible uses. This vehicle was known as the "M 10" and had a payload of approximately 1,000 kg. It was equipped with a small 2 stroke, 2

cylinder air-cooled engine supplied by Ilo-Werke GmbH in Pinneberg (in Schleswig-Holstein). Known as the "P 2334", its cylinder capacity was a mere 670 cc and it was able to develop a power of 18 HP at 3,000 rpm.

In the five years of production of this particular vehicle, the company managed to produce 1,022, many of which were equipped for special applications. In 1934, it was the turn of a powerful 3 axle 6x4 military vehicle known as the "M 206" which was equipped with the "S 88" tried and tested 6 cylinder engine in a slightly boosted version.

Lorry versions for civilian use and special military versions, known as the "M 206/a", were derived from the basic model. These were equipped with a second driving seat at the back (complete with steering wheel, gearbox, pedals, etc.).

After being "clad" in steel armour-plating by an outside contractor, these special military vehicles were supplied to the German army which used them as reconnaissance vehicles.

Still in 1934, the banks, which had almost become the major shareholder of Magirus, dismissed Adolf von Magirus from the office of Chairman of the Supervisory Board (he had succeeded to the office on the death of his brother Hermann in March 1928) and replaced him with Fritz Kiehn, the industrialist. From that time, the Magirus family no longer had any dealings with the company.

TOP: A curious vehicle "with forward cab" of the "M10" type launched in 1932: it had a "110" engine with a cubic capacity of 670 cc and was produced with different equipment; the fire engine is seen in the photograph.
CENTRE: This powerful military truck with 3 axles, the "M 206" made in 1934, was equipped with the "S 88" petrol engine.
BELOW: The diesel version of the M 206 engine with 6 cylinders in line.

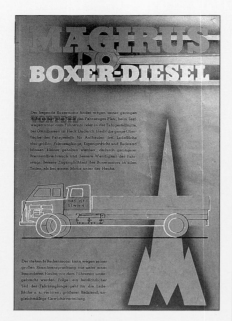

ABOVE: Two publicity pages on the splendid, compact 12 cylinder Boxer engine with a cubic capacity of 10,632 cc. Known as the "Z 95 D", it had a power of 150 HP and was used to equip trucks and buses of the "M65" heavy duty type.

TOP RIGHT: Bus equipped with the 12 cylinder Boxer engine in service in the city of Zittau around the middle of the thirties.

CENTRE: The lines of this tourist version, the "Strabus M 45" made in 1937, are streamlined and rounded.

BELOW: "S3000" type truck made under the Schell Plan. Note the circular "Klöckner-Deutz" symbol on the radiator.

In an attempt to remedy the difficult financial situation of the company, the new directors of Magirus decided to increase the production of diesel engines by also increasing the range available.

As a result, the "V 88 R" 4 cylinder diesel engines were created, followed by the "V 88 D", 3,040 cc, 45 HP at 2,200 rpm; the 6 cylinder "S 110 R" and the "S 110 D", 7,412 cc and 110 HP at 2,000 rpm and finally the "S 95 D" 6 cylinder version with 5,316 cc and 88 HP, still at 2,000 rpm.

The marriage of these last two engines produced a beautiful 12 cylinder Boxer engine with 10,632 cc which was able to develop approximately 150 HP at 2,000 rpm. Called the "Z 95 D", where, as usual, the letter Z stood for "Zwölfzylinder", i.e. twelve cylinders, this engine was used to equip lorry and bus chassis of the "M 65" heavy duty type with forward cabs.

In September 1935, there was an event which greatly affected the future of Magirus.

It was the signing of an agreement between Magirus AG and "Humboldt-Deutz-Motoren AG" of Cologne, an agreement which, in March of the following year, resulted in the complete merger of the two companies. Whilst maintaining a certain degree of independence, Magirus then became a division of Humboldt-Deutz-Motoren AG.

It may be interesting to give some details of the origins of the Cologne company. It was set up in the autumn of 1930 following the merger of two former companies: Deutz-Motoren AG, which dated back to 1864, and Humboldt AG, which arose in 1871 from a machinery factory which had been set up in 1865.

Still on the subject of the company history, in 1938, Humboldt Deutz-Motoren, linked by a financial agreement with Klockner-Werke AG of Duisburg, then became Klockner-Humboldt-Deutz AG (usually abbreviated to KHD).

This union favoured an increasingly generalised use of the excellent Deutz diesel engine, progressively abandoning those made by Magirus. To accommodate the new Deutz engines and the improved Magirus engine, a new series of chassis was produced, known as the "L" series, which did not replace the "M" series immediately. They remained in production for a few more years.

In the meantime, the German government had introduced a rationalisation plan for the production of transport vehicles, lorries and buses, essentially with an eye to future military requirements. Known as the "Schell Plan", from the name of the person who devised it, it laid down the standardised production of parts and rules for joint production between different companies. It also laid down a basic standard for various types of vehicle in terms of payload and application.

A typical example of a vehicle built jointly by several companies, including Magirus, was the "33 Gl" model, a 3 axle 6x4 vehicle made under the Henschel licence.

It was powered with the "F6M516H" 6 cylinder diesel engine produced by Deutz with 9,122 cc and approximately 100 HP at 1,500 rpm.

To paint a clearer picture, it is probably a good idea to explain the significance of the designations used to identify the Deutz engines. The first letter indicated the intended use of the engine (for auto-traction in the case of "F"). The first number indicated the number of cylinders, the second letter stood for the type of cooling ("M" for water, "L" for air), the last number related to the design number and the final letter indicated the position of the engine ("H" for rear engine) or the type of engine (if it was a petrol engine rather than a diesel engine, a "B" was used).

In the years between 1937 and 1941, Magirus produced 3,860 "33 Gl" vehicles with various equipment and bodies.

In the same period, the 3 axle 6x6 was also made, which was equipped with the Deutz "HWA526D" engine, still with direct injection, a 6 cylinder diesel engine with 6,234 cc and 80 HP at 2,400 rpm.

All in all, on the basis of the Schell Plan, Magirus produced 18,568 of the "3000" model (3 tonne class) between September 1940 and September 1944

Typical and sophisticated, these advertisements which go back to the eve of the Second World War are much sought after by collectors. On the sketch relating to the "M 27 - 2³/₄ tonne" truck, note a pair of horses faded into the background which symbolise transport methods old and new.

TOP: The "A330" four-wheel drive military truck from 1941.
CENTRE: Tractor with tracks specially designed for military use on the
Eastern Front.
ABOVE: The first two Deutz diesel engines with air cooling for industrial
vehicles; the 4 cylinder "F4L514", and right: The 6 cylinder "F6L514".
ON THE OPPOSITE PAGE: Publicity material from the beginning of the fifties.

(including the 25 pre-series models made in 1939). These vehicles were made up of the following versions:
- 7,990 series "S 3000" road vehicles in the following configurations: truck, semi-trailer tractor (the letter "Z" stands for "Zugmaschinen" or tractor vehicles), tip-up type (the letter "K" standing for "Kipper", dumper truck), the bus version ("O" for omnibus) and also military vehicles for various uses;
- 5,968 all-wheel drive vehicles, practically all in the truck version, military type. Only 5 were equipped as buses;
- 1,113 special vehicles for military use, all in the truck version;
- 1,750 chassis for fire engines;
- 1,747 "M 3000" semi-tracked military vehicles, known as the "Maultier", the "mule".

All these vehicles were equipped with the "F4M513" 4,942 cc Deutz engine which had a power of approximately 70 HP at 2,100 rpm. A petrol version of the same engine was only used for a few fire engines.

Where higher payloads were needed, up to 4.5 tonnes, the "GS 145" and "GA 145" vehicles were made, still in partnership with other companies. These were equipped with 7,274 cc, 6 cylinder diesel engines with 125 HP at 2,400 rpm.

From February 1943, and still working with other manufacturers, they started to produce a track-laying vehicle which had been specially designed for use on the Russian front.

There were two versions: the "RSO/01" and the "RSO/03". The first had a Steyr 8 cylinder air-cooled petrol engine with 3,517 cc and a power of 70 HP at 2,500 rpm. The second had a Deutz diesel "F4L514", which was also air-cooled (the first diesel engine for lorries produced by Deutz to use this cooling system), with 5,320 cc and a power of 65 HP at 2,100 rpm.

Both vehicles had a payload of 1,500 kg. When fully laden, the petrol model reached a speed of 17.2 km/h and was able to negotiate gradients of up to 70%. The version diesel engine reached a speed of 14.5 km/h and could negotiate gradients up to 50%.

By March 1945, the date when, with the advance of Allied troops, Magirus was forced to stop production, approximately 12,000 of these vehicles had been built.

At the end of the war, the city of Ulm, with 85% of its historical centre and at least two thirds of its outlying districts destroyed, including the Magirus factories, went through a period of almost total paralysis, even though the survivors, with typical German determination, set about the work of reconstruction immediately.

When it started up again, Magirus did a little of everything. They started to make ladders again. Tractors were made on behalf of the agricultural division of the parent company, KHD. They also made bus bodies on the basis of the General Motors Vehicles supplied by the American Occupying Forces.

In 1946, they also started to produce a curious semi-tracked vehicle with forward cab, which was directly derived from the "RSO" tractor already mentioned. Known as the "RS 1500", it was also known as the "Phöenix aus der Asche", or the phoenix rising from the ashes.

On this extremely versatile vehicle, the ordinary track had been shortened to provide space for a standard front axle with steered wheels. The payload was specified as 1,500 kg, but in practice, it was able to transport up to 2,000 kg.

In just two years, they made 1,460 of these vehicles which provided very valuable service on the semi-destroyed roads during that extremely difficult post-war period.

Under the guidance of Chief Engineer Adolf Wunsche, they then started to make trucks and buses again. These were based on the 3 tonne vehicles which had been developed during the pre-war Schell Plan period, but this time they were equipped with the new "F4L514" air-cooled engine already mentioned.

The chassis too, were the subject of important improvements which, among other things, made it possible to increase the payload to 3,500 kg. For this reason, these were christened the "S 3500" series. There were also the "O

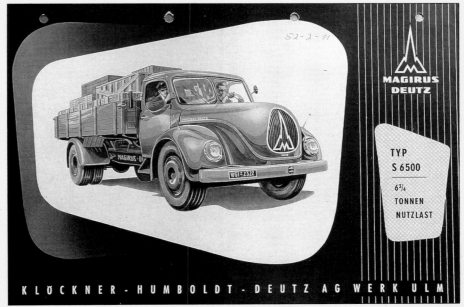

3500" bus versions and the truck versions which included a 4x4 and the semi-trailer tractor vehicle.

It was only in the April of 1951, at the Frankfurt Fair, that Magirus was able to launch its first authentic post-war models.

These vehicles had an imposing curved bonnet and were all equipped with Deutz air-cooled diesel engines. They were named after the planets and were very successful in other European countries and also outside Europe. The range included the "Mercury" and "Jupiter" models. The "Mercury" vehicles were produced in two versions with payloads of approximately 5,000 kg. They were equipped with a 5,322 cc, 85 HP 4 cylinder engine and a 125 HP, 7,983 cc, 6 cylinder engine. They also made bus versions with seating for up to 40 passengers.

Using the 7,983 cc, 6 cylinder engine mentioned above, they also produced "A 3500" versions of the truck with 4 wheel drive and a payload of approximately 4,500 kg.

The "Jupiters" were powered by a 10,644 cc, 8 cylinder engine with a power of up to 175 HP at 2,300 rpm. There were also truck versions, again with 4 wheel drive, with a payload of approximately 8,000 kg and a bus version able to carry up to 48 passengers.

But the Magirus achievement which was the highlight of the show was, without doubt, the highest revolving ladder in the world with an elevation of 52 + 2 metres.

It consisted of 6 mechanically operated telescopic sections all made of steel, plus a seventh section which was 2 metres long and could be extended manually to reach the height required.

The ladder was equipped with a special rotation mechanism and had a highly practical and reliable "lift" system.

The chassis used to transport the ladder was the "S 6500" equipped with the 175 HP, 8 cylinder engine used on the "Jupiter" models.

In 1953, KHD, the parent company of Magirus, bought a factory from Westwaggon AG in Cologne. This factory, which was in the city of Mainz, had a very long history.

It could trace its origin back to

TOP: A shot of the "grandtouring" coach from the early fifties characterised by the "round nosed" bonnet in fashion at the time at Magirus.
CENTRE: The "tallest rotating motor turntable ladder in the world" presented at the Frankfurt International Motor Show in 1951.
ABOVE: The compact Diesel-Deutz air-cooled 8 cylinder engine "F 8 L 614" also fitted to the turntable ladder above.

1777, when a certain Anton Gasti started up a saddlery in Mainz. One of his sons, who had changed his surname to Gastell, started to make coaches and carriages. He subsequently started to produce railway wagons and, from 1872, the company moved to the place where the factory bought by KHD is still located.

In 1928, Gastell merged with Westwaggon and from the middle of the thirties, the manufacture of buses was added to the manufacture of railway vehicles.

Several years later, in 1955 to be precise, KHD decided to transfer the entire production of Magirus buses to Mainz. The move was made very gradually, in order to make the effect on jobs in the bus division at the Ulm factory less traumatic.

The first stage was completed in the following year, 1956, when Mainz only made the bodies (the chassis continued to be made at Ulm). At that time, they started to produce modern bodies with "self-supporting structures", a novelty for Magirus. But it was not before the end of 1960 that the entire Magirus bus production was concentrated at the Mainz factory, although it was still being modernised at the time.

By the end of the fifties, the range of Magirus buses essentially boiled down to three basic models:

i) - the "O 3500 V 6": 7,893 cc, 6 cylinder, front mounted Deutz diesel engine with a power of 130 HP at 2,250 rpm and a capacity of 36 seats, which then became 32 seats + standing room for 11 in the "line" version;

ii) - the "O 3500 H": the same engine as the previous version, but this time installed at the rear. This model, with no forward engine compartment, had 44 seats + 9 spare fold-down seats;

iii) - the "O 6500 H": 8 cylinder, 10,644 cc rear engine in the long distance or tourist version, was able to accommodate up to 48 seats + 10 fold-down seats, whilst the local version offered a maximum capacity of 103 passengers, including those standing.

Taking a step back in time now, it is essential to record that in 1953, there was a further avant-

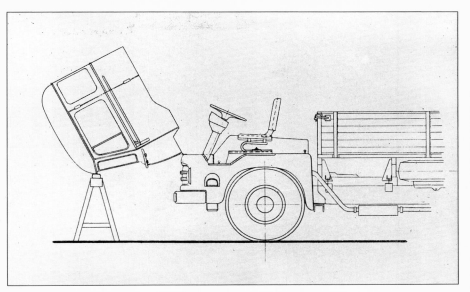

TOP: The tilting cab launched by Magirus in 1955; it did not have much success with hauliers; only much later, after the system had been improved, did tiltable forward cabs have a favourable reception in Germany.
ABOVE: One of the first large buses with self-supporting structure made at the Mainz factory; this was the "Saturn II" model.

garde achievement by Magirus in the field of fire-fighting equipment. This time, it was a 30 metre ladder which, for the first time, was equipped with a hydraulic rather than mechanical extension system.

The manufacture of original, highly advanced emergency vehicles for airports during those years is worthy of a mention.

Still in the area of special vehicles, in 1955, the Uranus heavy duty tractor, a 3 axle 6x4 vehicle (but, from what we can see, there were also 6x6 versions), mainly intended for military use (e.g. transporting armed trucks) is also worthy of a mention. Different drive trains

were used which were specific to each individual application, and this chassis was used as a mobile base for heavy duty cranes and equipment used in oil fields. In the meantime, the range of vehicles named after heavenly bodies has been extended at Magirus.

The new models included the "Sirius" with a 5,322 cc, 4 cylinder engine and a payload of 3,400 kg or 3,800 kg, and the "Saturn" with a 7,983 cc, 6 cylinder engine and a payload of approximately 6,700 kg. On some of the road truck versions in this range (trucks and tractors for semi-trailers), instead of the classic "nose", they changed to forward cabs.

The first model with a fixed cab, which was not really very successful, was followed in 1957/1958 by other models with a tilt cab and different front. However, particularly in the early stages, this type of cab was not used on many vehicles and the vehicles with the characteristic "nose" continued to be seen on the roads, particularly at quarries and building sites.

At the beginning of the sixties, Magirus was seen to undertake a vast renewal programme. As far as the product was concerned, the focal point was modular design, aimed at simplifying the production processes and achieving economies of scale. Also the range of vehicles was rationalised to encourage the standardisation of components.

At the same time, they intensified the campaign to promote the image and products of Magirus beyond national bound-

aries.

At the end of the fifties for example, an agreement was signed with the Yugoslavian company "Tovarna Automogilov in Motorjev" (TAM), Maribor, to produce some Magirus models under licence and others were then subsequently signed with

Argentina, Egypt, Turkey, Brazil and other countries, mainly for setting up bus assembly lines.

Within the scope of international development, we should also mention the company's first appearance - via an Italian importer - at the International Motor Show in Turin in November 1960.

Towards the end of 1964, the new modular range made its debut. Names were no longer used to identify the different models and types, but instead there was a series of symbols, where the first number indicated the maximum power developed by the engine, a capital letter indicated the type of vehicle (N for road vehicle, D for quarry/site) and a final number indicated the total kerb weight.

Other similar symbols were used for special vehicles and buses. However, with the room we have here, we will not give details of these.

The first obvious innovation was the total abolition of the "alligator" nose, which was replaced with a new square type bonnet design. There were also forward cab models which were more numerous than in the previous range.

It is also interesting to note that a modular structure had been studied for the cabs. From a single basic cab, with the addition of extra structural components at the back or on top, it had been possible to derive several versions, e.g. the bunk arrangement for long-haul vehicles. The chassis had also been completely redesigned on the basis of modular criteria.

Of the development initiatives at international level, it is now

TOP LEFT: *Original special bus with couchette for long journeys. It was made at the beginning of the seventies by an outside bodymaker.*
RIGHT: *Truck suitable for quarries and building sites; the "170 D 15 AK" of 1970 with the characteristic "square nose".*
ABOVE: *Four axle chassis, two of which are steering axles, were used for this "concrete mixer" version of the "315 D 28 FAB" with forward cab.*

interesting to point out what happened in Great Britain when, in 1964, an English company was granted an agency for this market. Since the company concerned proved inadequate for the task, in 1967, through the intermediary Frank Tinsdale, an agreement was signed with Seddon Diesel Vehicles Limited for the supply of Deutz engines to be used on vehicles intended to operate in Central America. But, for various reasons, this agreement did not last very long either.

Consequently, it was decided to give Tinsdale the job of setting up an assembly operation in England. The result was Magirus - Deutz GB Limited, which had a factory at Middleton, near Manchester.

Production was concentrated on 3 axle quarry and site vehicles, but an interesting 4 axle all-wheel drive prototype was also produced. This was an 8x8, a vehicle widely used in Great Britain.

This vehicle immediately revealed its excellent qualities and soon it was decided to produce it in Ulm as well, where higher production numbers could be reached. This would enable the company to meet demand from other countries.

Unfortunately, after only two years, fewer than 200 chassis had been built and logistic and financial reasons forced the company to stop production in England, leaving the English subsidiary in charge of marketing and after-sales operations only.

In the meantime, from 1969, new direct injection Deutz diesel engines - still air-cooled - went into production. A modern factory was set up at Ulm/Donau to build these engines where, a few years later, Magirus was to build a new factory for producing trucks.

In the meantime, the international economic situation was passing through an increasingly critical stage. In 1970, Dr. Heinz W. Hahn was appointed Managing Director in order to secure the future of the company.

Times were so difficult that they had to cancel the 1971 Frankfurt Show. In addition, in West Germany, the end of that year saw a damaging strike by metal-workers, and only after tough negotiations in a tense atmosphere was it possible to reach an agreement acceptable to both sides. But, as the proverb says:

"Necessity is the mother of invention" and so Magirus started to look at ways to get through these difficult times

In 1971, in spite of the situation, a new generation of trucks was launched, mainly intended for heavy work in quarries and on construction sites. The cab on these vehicles was set back and there was a more imposing front bonnet. At the same time, an important step was made in the light and medium truck range towards greater rationalisation and standardisation of some parts and components.

An agreement was signed between Magirus, the French company Saviem, the Dutch

**MAGIRUS
DEUTZ**

company DAF and the Swedish company Volvo to develop, produce and use fully interchangeable components.

The project was officially christened the Euro Truck Development Group, but in practice, it was also referred to as the "Club of 4". Through a series of setbacks which prevented the agreement from being implemented in full, it only became operative in 1974. Magirus used axles, springs and cabs (it only started to build cabs in 1975, which were also suplied to DAF).

In Moscow in 1972, Magirus started negotiations for supplying trucks and engines to the Soviet Union. The negotiations were successful, followed by the signature of a contract on the 7th of October 1974 for the supply of 10,000 trucks to be used in the construction of a railway in Siberia.

In the meantime, in 1973, in the light of new production developments, a new assembly line 600 metres long, was installed at the Magirus factory in Ulm.

More or less at the same time, Magirus, and through it KHD, started exploratory discussions with Fiat for the development of joint production programmes. Reeling from the effects of the first devastating oil shock at the end of the year, the discussions with Fiat took a number of turns until, towards the middle of 1974, these discussions suddenly built up. And in July of the same year came the official announcement of an agreement between Fiat and KHD for setting up a new supranational company involving Fiat, Lancia, OM and Unic on the one hand and Magirus on the other.

On the 18th of November 1974, KHD proceeded to transform its Magirus division into a totally independent company which was to be known as Magirus-Deutz-Motoren AG with a capital of 250 million Marks.

Magirus-Deutz-Motoren AG then transferred its Ulm and Mainz factories to the new multi-national, Iveco, operative from the 1st January 1975.

The industrial complex at Ulm was made up of three factories specialising in the production of light, medium and heavy trucks, with kerb weights of between 6

Rear dumper type "290 D 22 K", 6x4, part of the batch to be supplied to the USSR for building the Siberian railway.

tonnes and 12 tonnes. The site covered a total area of 835,600 m² which provided the necessary floor space, and employed 9,950 employees.

The Mainz factory, which specialised in the production of buses and special vehicles, had a site of 197,000 m², providing 76,000 m² of floor space, and employing 2,050 people.

So, on the 1st January 1975, a new era started for Magirus: this was to be the Iveco Era.

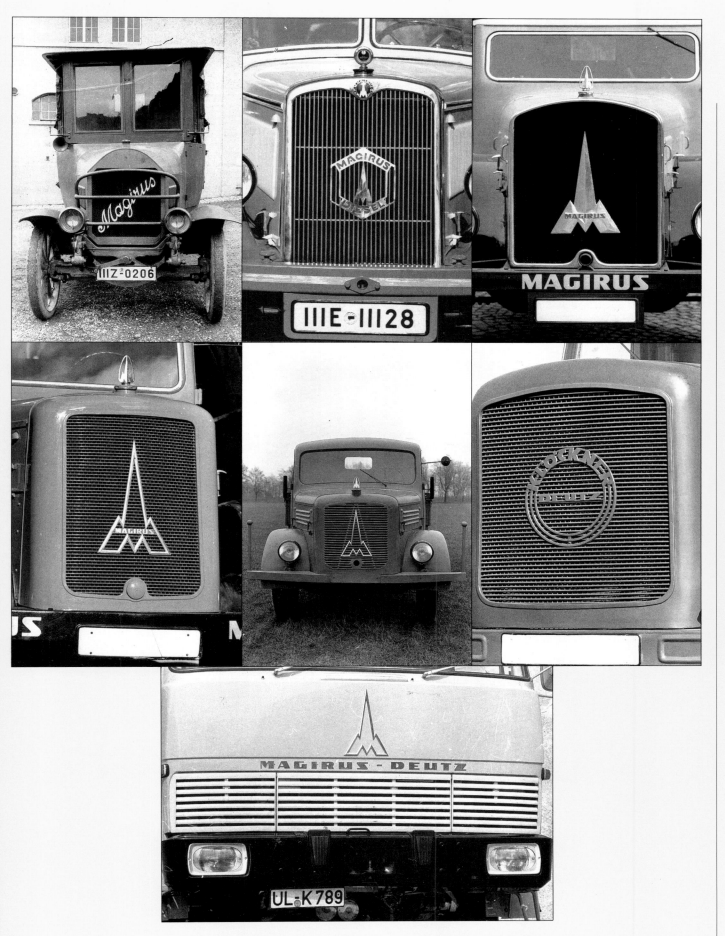

Some trademarks used to identify Magirus industrial vehicles. The use of a logo reminiscent - in stylised form - of the spire of Ulm cathedral was prevalent.

FROM THE CRISIS OF THE SEVENTIES, THE STIMULUS TO APPROACH THE FUTURE

The key to our story lies between the end of the Sixties and the beginning of the Seventies.

A time when Europe was in a state of paradox, with a sudden swing from the euphoria of the consumer boom to the backlash of 1968, and then the shocking reality of the first oil crisis triggered in 1973 by the Arab-Israeli war of Yom Kippur.

The repercussions were particularly severe for Italy where the problems were exacerbated by a socio-political and financial situation which was already weak. The struggle between the social parties took a dramatic turn - reaching its peak in the "hot Autumn" of 1969 and fuelling the dreadful phenomenon of terrorism - and the oil crisis had a devastating effect on an economy already debilitated.

In a few months the price of oil increased four times, prices rose 25% and inflation reached double figures (up to 20% in 1976, whereas the major industrialised countries did not go beyond 6%-7%).

And the worst was still to come - the second oil crisis in 1978, and in particular the deep recession which was to upset the industrialised world at the beginning of the Eighties. It also upset the economic equilibrium of the oil producing countries with the collapse of sales and the price of crude.

As far as the industrial vehicle is concerned, for the first time there was to be a crisis both for the domestic markets and for exports outside Europe. We were to wait until the middle of the decade to turn the corner.

This, briefly, was the context, the socio-economic climate in which Fiat in Italy and KHD in Germany became aware, more or less at the same time, of the need to strengthen their respective activities in the industrial vehicle sector and to start to look around for a partner. Their search went beyond their national confines, and so the concept of trans-nationality - and the birth of Iveco - came to be.

ON THE LEFT AND THE FOLLOWING PAGES, two emotional scenes which take us back to two historic landmarks in our still recent past: from the boom of mass car ownership in the sixties to the disruption of "Sundays on foot" experienced between fear and a bitter "leisure pursuit" in the mid seventies.

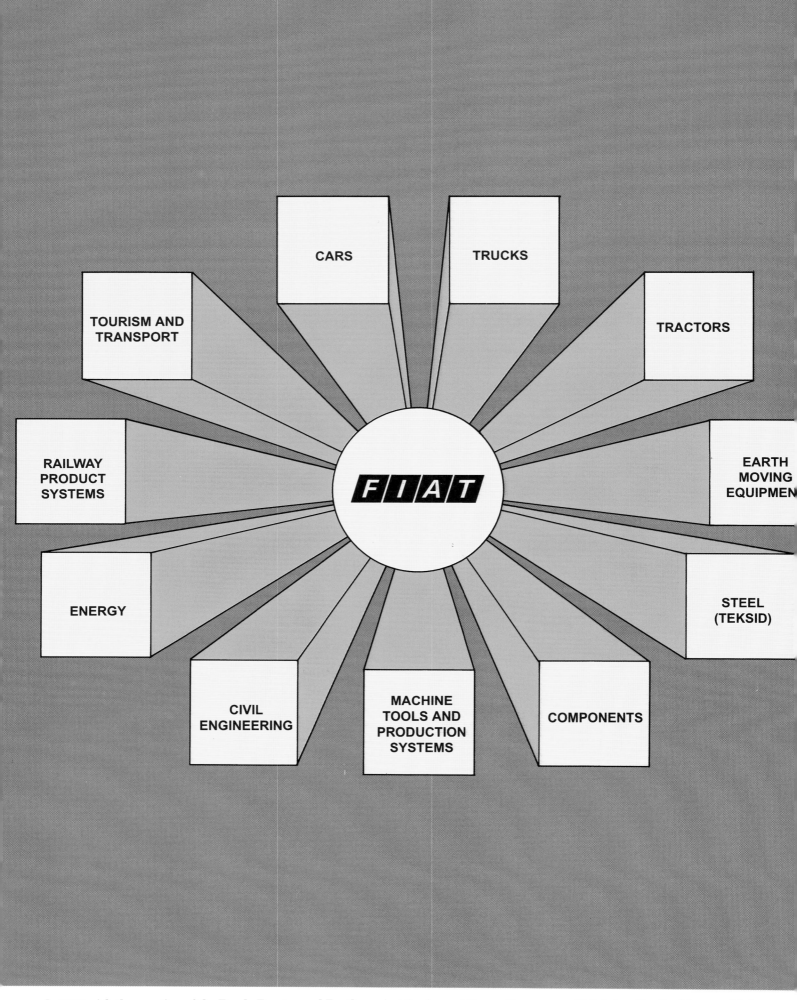

CARS

TRUCKS

TRACTORS

TOURISM AND TRANSPORT

FIAT

EARTH MOVING EQUIPMEN

RAILWAY PRODUCT SYSTEMS

STEEL (TEKSID)

ENERGY

CIVIL ENGINEERING

MACHINE TOOLS AND PRODUCTION SYSTEMS

COMPONENTS

In 1969 with the creation of the Truck, Tractor and Earth-moving Equipment Group the process of "divisionalisation" began which was to transform the "great Fiat" of the Valletta era into the industrial Group divided by product group that we all know today

THE "GREAT FIAT" IS TRANSFORMED INTO A MODERN INDUSTRIAL GROUP

I n Italy, the events which we have mentioned also had considerable consequences for Fiat. When we talk of Fiat, we mean Fiat as a whole, with the car division in pride of place. Fiat's financial situation after nearly twenty years of an exceptional boom, showed signs of a worrying downturn at the end of the Sixties. This reversal was confirmed by the market trend. Let us look at the figures: vehicle registrations in 1949 were just over 64,000 (cars, trucks and buses). In 1950 they had already exceeded 99,000. This was then followed by an impressive increase: 230,000 in 1956, 427,000 in 1960, passing the million mark for the first time in 1963.

1973 saw a record 1,553,011 vehicles. Then came the start of the decline: 151,000 vehicles down in 1974, a further drop of 257,000 in 1975. Recovery was to be slow, and the 1978 crisis was to kick the market while it was still down with nearly 30,000 fewer compared with the peak in 1973.

Consequently, Fiat was faced with the problem of obtaining new capital, which could not come just from the shareholders. It was necessary to draw financial resources from within. To achieve this the group had to be reorganised along the lines of decentralisation which would bring the management closer to the problems it had to deal with.

A complex task which was completed in two stages. The company started by breaking down the great Fiat into divisions, creating the car division, the tractor and earthmoving equipment division, etc.

The next step was to set up the individual companies by disincorporating them, endowing each of them with its own management and financial independence within a holding company guided by a parent company.

This second stage organised Fiat into the company we know today. At the beginning of the '70s, Fiat Allis was set up, a joint venture between Fiat and Allis Chalmers; 1975 saw the birth of Iveco followed by the last addition to the family, Fiat Auto, on the 2nd October 1978.

THREE INDEPENDENT ACTIVITIES IN THE INDUSTRIAL VEHICLE SECTOR

Fiat was faced with the problem of controlling its own future and the conclusion was that it needed to start a divisionalisation process based on a market-oriented product concept.

In the industrial vehicle and tractor sector at that time, the company was divided into three separate areas: those which, to all intents and purposes, and also from a corporate point of view, belonged to Fiat itself: engines (diesel engines), industrial vehicles & buses and agricultural tractors & earthmoving machinery.

And, as the result of acquiring Lancia's car business in 1969, Fiat was also in charge of the industrial vehicle, bus and military vehicle business of Lancia, with production facilities at the Bolzano factory.

Fiat also wholly owned OM in Brescia, a company with its registered office in Milan, three factories in three locations and with clearly defined production skills.

Brescia produced vehicles and their components, Milan produced anything not connected with industrial vehicles, i.e. tractors, forklift trucks, rolling stock (in particular diesel engines), and Suzzara, in the province of Mantova, specialised in bus and -

at a later date - van bodies.

OM was a company with a very long tradition whose activities also included diesel engines, industrial vehicles & buses, agricultural tractors and forklift trucks plus other activities which included equipment for the railway industry. Through Fiat France, Fiat controlled Unic (which once belonged to Simca), Someca and the Public Works division.

Unic was active in the field of diesel engines and industrial vehicles. Someca made tractors. Public Works specialised in earth moving machinery.

Finally, Fiat was also active in the railway sector, although this was not to be included in the diesel/industrial vehicle divisionalisation and so we will not discuss it here.

Three separate companies: Fiat (with Lancia), OM and Fiat France, without links with each other and each self-sufficient at every stage of the cycle (planning, production and sales network); only Public Works had an exclusively commercial connotation.

THE INDUSTRIAL VEHICLE GROUP IS BORN

In 1969, it was decided to set up a division for all the Fiat activities - in Italy and in France - which were connected with diesel power trains: this meant the engines, industrial vehicles & buses, tractors, earthmoving machinery and forklift trucks.

This division was given various names, but finally it became the Gruppo Veicoli Industriali, Trattori e Macchine Movimento Terra.

This was purely an organisational arrangement, not a corporate body controlling the activities of Fiat, OM and Unic in the industrial vehicle and diesel engine sector. In the process, OM lost its railway business, which was merged with that of Fiat, giving rise to an independent division, and eventually, the Gruppo Veicoli Industriali was to lose two of its market products as the result of two joint ventures/acquisitions: the earthmoving sector, following successful negotiations with Allis Chalmers, and the agricultural tractor sector, following negotiations with John Deere which, however, did not turn out well.

Following these two events, the Gruppo Veicoli Industriali - the product of the diesel engine concept and anything which uses a diesel engine - made a further move towards the market product idea, ending up with just the engines, industrial vehicles and buses & forklift trucks.

THE CHOICE OF THE MANAGEMENT

The running of the Group's affairs was essentially entrusted to the management of OM which, within Fiat and its controlled companies, had the best established history and culture in the industry because it had always been concerned solely and exclusively with industrial vehicles.

It was a highly dynamic management team, very aware of what the future might hold for the industry and with a clear vision of the demands of modern management; a management which was more market-oriented than Fiat at the time, and one which was particularly aware of organisational needs, both from the production and administrative points of view.

And it was a management with advanced ideas for the time in terms of product and production control, based on modularity and specialisation and also the use of the latest technologies available for industrial vehicles.

An attitude which was rooted in OM's history and expressed in terms of highly rationalised product ranges.

This was true European leadership in the range from 3.5 tonnes (the "Lupetto" vehicle) to the medium to heavy range with vehicles like the "Tigre" and the

"Titano". And in fact, once the "Group" was constituted, it suddenly registered a big profit, mainly due to the profitability of OM.

This was because, at the time, Fiat's activities in the industry were in decline in spite of the success of its range of heavy vehicles which clung tenaciously to its leadership on the home market (with a share of around 90%) and which was very highly regarded in markets outside Europe (particularly North Africa). However, a shrewd commercial strategy was to allow the "Group" to exploit the potential of the original Fiat product, thereby improving its profitability.

This was, in fact, the task assigned to the marketing division set up at the beginning of the '70s with the aim of responding to the mood of the market. It became the lynch pin between Production and the Commercial Division.

As far as our story is concerned, it is important to emphasise how this development of the Gruppo Veicoli Industriali spread way beyond its more immediate effects.

It became the tangible expression of a radical change in the relationship between producer and consumer, a stimulus which in the years to come, was to make everyone roll up their sleeves and get to work on laying the foundations for what was to become the reality, the new role of industry in the post industrial era. Before, concepts such as marketing and market strategies, sales incentives and service had been almost unknown quantities for both parties.

On the one hand, industry designed and produced its products on an "autarchical" basis, taking advantage of a technology in a continuous state of evolution. And on the other, there was the vehicle user, still loath to demand comfort or specialisation of the product.

From now on, however, these concepts were to make the difference, transforming both industry and the industrial ethos from a situation where a product is produced and, because it exists, will then be sold to one -

more inconvenient for industry - where the roles are reversed and the consumer takes control.

From now on no producer will be in a position to impose his products, but will have to organise himself to give the market what the market wants at the time and in the numbers which the market demands.

FIRST STEPS TOWARDS RATIONALISATION

The strategy of integration involved all the components and activities of the Group as a whole, but the rationalisation process was approached in successive stages.

The first measures concerned production allocations; the next step was to restructure planning and marketing, an innovative idea as we have already seen, and finally, rationalisation of the commercial management.

This approach was influenced by the way in which Fiat had been structured until then. Only one person was in charge of production, but as far as the car and industrial vehicle factories were concerned, never the twain should meet.

Consequently it was logical to start here because it was the easiest step to make, even though certainly not without its difficulties.

However, the work of rationalisation was found to be much more problematical with regard to planning. Whereas the OM and Unic structures were clearly definable, at Fiat, automotive planning was grouped together, except for tractors and to some extent, earthmoving machinery, which had its own history. However, car and industrial vehicles were as one: there was one planning centre and one manager.

Finally, rationalisation of the sales network was no less delicate, since it involved problems of image and mark.

So this part was left till last and was initially restricted to creating a level of coordination above the various distribution channels without attempting further unification.

This process of unification within

the Gruppo Veicoli Industriali took a long time, beset by not insignificant problems of integration not only between the Italians and the French, but also between the original management teams of Fiat and OM.

All this was inevitable because each of the companies merged into the group had its own history and culture to profess and defend.

However, the basic concept of this decision was overriding: to rationalise and create a single competitive entity from three activities competing with each other, each with its own planning, production and commercial structures and - the main point - each without a secure future individually.

THE GRUPPO VEICOLI INDUSTRIALI LOOKS TO EUROPE

The commitment to rationalisation and also to the renewal of internal resources and to the product did not make the management of the Gruppo Veicoli Industriali any less aware that it would have to come to terms with a basic strategic weakness: a limited presence outside the national confines, with excessive dependence within Europe on just two markets, namely Italy and France, and outside Europe, on the North African countries with the exclusion of the wealthy Middle East.

As far as Europe was concerned at that time, as we have seen, all the major markets were dominated almost exclusively by national manufacturers.

If we add up the shares of Daimler-Benz and MAN, we are talking about 80% of the German market. The situation in France was more or less the same for Saviem and Berliet and for British Leyland in England.

In Italy, Fiat and OM more or less had a monopoly (more than 90% of the market share) roughly at the rate of two thirds to one third respectively.

However, as far as the Gruppo Veicoli Industriali was concerned, a particular weak point was the almost total absence from the two major European markets,

Germany and England.

The problem was serious not just from a commercial point of view. Because the absence of confrontation, of direct competition, failed to stimulate the necessary development of products from the Italian group, which was in danger of lagging behind the level of sophistication and quality offered by leading European industries with the Germans in the lead.

Particularly in the heavy vehicle sector, the Italian products certainly could not boast qualities of excellence on the Continent. It came somewhere in the middle between Europe and outside Europe.

The situation in the light and medium/light sector from 3.5 tons to 10 tons GVW was different, but the validity and vitality of the OM product range was not backed by a suitable distribution organisation (and as we know, it is certainly not easy to create this from scratch).

The situation of the Gruppo Veicoli Industriali was better outside Europe, but even here it was not as strong as its major European competitors.

As we have mentioned, Fiat had a strong commercial presence in numerous African countries: Algeria, Libya, Ethiopia, and also Somalia, Kenya, Tanzania and Uganda, but not on the Middle Eastern markets, a territory conquered and held by German industry.

In this respect, it should be remembered that both before and during the creation of Iveco, and even before the first oil crisis, the German truck industry was exporting more than 50% of its output, even two thirds, and this, amongst other things, was the stimulus for developing both the products and the sales organisation.

IN SEARCH OF A PARTNER

So, at the beginning of the Seventies, the management of the Gruppo Veicoli Industriali was fully aware that the size of the group would remain vulnerable in the long term and that to be competitive in the future it would have to reinforce the company's commercial presence and also its image on the Continent.

Consequently, whilst the process of rationalising the internal structures and the product range progressed quickly and with profitable results, the Group initiated various contacts in Europe and beyond, to investigate the possibilities of cooperation.

The most important initiatives to be mentioned are the negotiations with the American company Mack, FNM of Brazil and, in Europe; British Leyland in England and KHD in Germany. Of these four initiatives, two were successful: the one with FNM and the one with KHD.

As far as North and South America were concerned, the Gruppo Veicoli Industriali wanted to extend its operating bases, knowing that in the key countries - United States and Brazil - it was necessary to have production/design presence and not just a commercial one.

And there was only one way to do this, find a local partner.

In the United States, negotiations with Mack did not bear fruit. The Gruppo Veicoli Industriali was not ready to enter a market which was to prove extremely difficult.

We should mention the creation of ITONA (Iveco truck of North America) in 1977, destined to cease trading at the end of the '80s. The failed commercial agreement with International Harvester never got off the ground because of a serious market and financial crisis which would force the American company (rechristened Navistar) to rescale its projects. This included abandoning its initiatives and also the attempt at an agreement with Ford in 1989, which did not succeed either, except in the agricultural sector.

But the Brazilian joint venture

was successful with the acquisition of FNM of Rio from Alfa Romeo in 1973.

The negotiations with the British were not destined to succeed either and it was nearly fifteen years - with the Iveco Ford agreement in 1986 - before the company was able to disembark on the other side of the channel.

That left KHD and the German market. Negotiations were to be long and difficult, but in the end an agreement was reached and the European industrial vehicle scene was to see a new and ambitious competitor, Iveco.

THE REORGANISATION OF THE FACTORIES STARTS

In the meantime, the process of reorganisation within the group proceeded at a brisk pace. In the case of the factories, it was a question of redefining the allocations and production technologies for improving the resources available. All this triggered a true revolution creating some - not insignificant - employment problems.

In Italy in particular, the situation was made more difficult by the need to support the Mezzogiorno development policy by transferring some of its production to the South.

Briefly, the first measures included the disincorporation of the foundry activities of OM in Milan and Lancia in Bolzano. This latter factory was a crucial issue which had to be resolved.

Bought at a peppercorn price of 1 Lire when Fiat took over Lancia's car activities, Bolzano was producing a few hundred vehicles a year and a family of engines which was interesting from a purely technical point of view, but largely obsolete, because they were too complex in design and too expensive to produce. The only value - if you can call it that - of Lancia was an informal agreement with the Italian army for the supply of a new generation of medium class four wheel drive vehicles. These were the highly mobile vehicles (ground clearance approximately 400 mm) which were to replace the now obsolete Fiat 639.

The basic specification of these vehicles was ready, the design was in the embryonic stage, but not a single prototype had been made. So it was a case of starting again from square one.

It was decided to terminate the production of industrial vehicles (the last "Esadelta" and "Esagamma" models rolled off the line in 1970) and buses (production of the "715" and "718" models ceased in 1971 to 1972), complete the design and start the production of military vehicles.

Bolzano was also to make the prototypes of new products for the entire Group.

The rationalisation process within the Group also involved tractors, which were produced at three factories at the time: by Fiat at Modena, OM at Milan and Someca at Bourbon-Lancy.

Production was concentrated at the Modena factory under the control of the agricultural tractor division (Società Trattori Agricoli, Fiat Agri and finally Geotec as the combination of Fiat Agri and Fiat Allis).

With this operation, the Milan factory of OM kept the production for the railway industry and forklift trucks, but the Someca factory at Bourbon-Lancy, which employed 15,000 people and had no other type of work, found itself embroiled in a job crisis.

But the French government had given its approval to transfer production to safeguard jobs ... we shall see later how it was possible to remedy this situation.

Regarding the earthmoving machinery, production was moved from Torino SPA to Lecce in support of the policy to develop the Mezzogiorno region of Italy. SPA too, found itself in the process of being reorganised.

In the meantime, with Fiat's acquisition of the factories of the same name, the entire activities of the railway sector were concentrated in Savigliano, leaving the OM factory in Milan with just the production of forklift trucks.

But, still in connection with the development policy for Mezzogiorno, it was decided to transfer the production of forklift trucks too; the production was moved to Bari and an attempt was made to

find a new role for the Milan factory.

Anticipating events which were to occur at the end of the decade, a further consequence of the Mezzogiorno policy was the transfer of the production of buses from the Cameri factory, in the province of Novara, to a new site at Valle Ufita in Campania. Cameri too, was to need a new production facility. The problem with this situation was that both in Italy and in France during this first reorganisation stage, it was not possible to close anything: in fact, only the foundries ceased to operate, whereas all the other factories had to be kept running some way or another. This caused numerous problems.

Practical solutions had to be found by transferring machining operations from one factory to another just to keep everybody occupied.

As we have seen, Bolzano made the prototypes and the production of military vehicles was concentrated there; that market was also to be hit by a crisis and again no one knew what to do. Milan was transformed into an engineering factory producing shafts and axles for the vehicles produced in Brescia.

In the case of Cameri, the solution will be seen later in connection with the Iveco and Rockwell joint venture for the production of axles. But that is another story ...

In France, at Bourbon-Lancy, they started to make engines. Machining operations were also transferred there which, until then, had been done at another French factory in Fourchambault. This factory was also converted, first for reconditioning engines and then for making bus bodies, initially for the army but subsequently for civilian, urban and interurban use.

To complete the picture of those years - still in France - we would also mention the transfer of Unic's production from Suresnes, on the outskirts of Paris, to Trappes. This followed the decision of the Paris Municipal Authorities to transfer all industrial activities to an area further away from the city.

A modern factory was built at Trappes for the purpose of accommodating the production of medium range vehicles for the entire Gruppo Veicoli Industriali. But, through the irony of fate, some ten years later, this was one of the three factories which Iveco was forced to close (together with SPA in Turin and Mainz in Germany). The commercial management of Unic and also a small design team was to remain at Trappes.

RATIONALISATION INVOLVES THE PRODUCT

The first reorganisation of production and of the factories having been started, the Gruppo Veicoli Industriali was able to dedicate its efforts to redefining the product ranges.

This process was carried out in three successive stages: first of all, the chassis (cab, chassis, power train) were standardised, maintaining the individual power trains and identities (name and vehicle logo) for the three makes of Fiat, OM and Unic. Then the engines were standardised, although maintaining the distinction between the name and identity. Finally, as the third and final step, the product was fully integrated except for the distinction between the name and the make.

The development of the new range, which we shall refer to as "standardised" (basically between Fiat-OM-Unic because, as far as Lancia was concerned, it was decided to cease the production of both its heavy industrial vehicles and buses) started and ended in the first half of the Seventies.

The process first of all concerned the light vehicles, the most important in numeric terms, and the heavy vehicles, which were strategically important, immediately followed by the medium vehicles. With regard to the engines, it was decided to cease production at Unic, because the numbers were too limited. This was a V8, used on Unic and OM heavy vehicles, an engine of recent design which was having teething problems and was therefore set aside.

And there was also a 10,000 cc, 6 cylinder in-line prototype called the "X200" which was transferred to Torino SPA and put into pro-

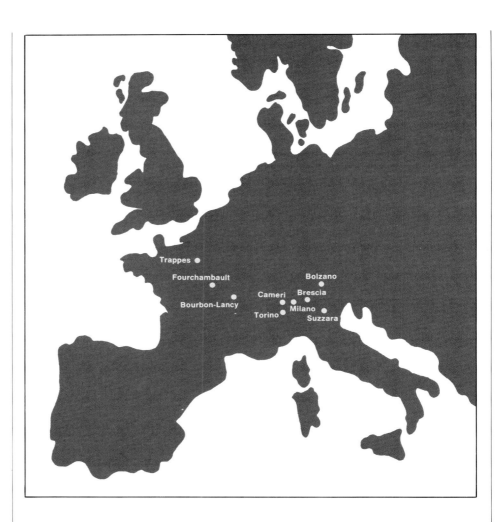

duction as the 8220.

From a production point of view this meant concentrating engine production in Italy at Brescia and Turin (of OM and Fiat-Unic origin, respectively) and also at Foggia where production started on the new light diesel engine, the 8100 of SO.F.I.M .

The Fiat, OM and Unic truck production centres immediately prior to the formation of Iveco.

THE STANDARDISED RANGE OF LIGHT VEHICLES

With regard to the vehicles, as mentioned, the rationalisation process first concerned the light vehicles. The development of the new standardised range started in 1970 and the vehicles were launched in 1972. The OM vehicle family was used as a basis, this range being known as the "zoo', because all the vehicles had been named after animals.

These were, in ascending order of capacity, the Orsetto 15, the Cerbiatto 20, the Lupetto 25, the Leoncino 30-35, the Daino 40-45 and the Tigrotto 50-55-65. It should also be noted that the OM name also indicated the payload, which was used in Italy at that time (and still is, for that matter) as a basis for calculating road tax.

Returning to the vehicles, it was a range which had achieved very considerable commercial success, at least on the Italian market; the modular design on which its development was based, placed it in the lead.

The cabs were modular, having a standard type architecture and using as many common components as possible. The sizes varied, obviously, from one range to the next (because of the different engine size and, in particular, the different wheel sizes), but many parts remained the same. For example the side panels and the doors and in fact much of the production, used the same cab.

Even the engines were of modular design: 3, 4 and 6 cylinder and all with the same cubic capacity. There was a certain flexibility with regard to the gearboxes, using units produced in-house or bought in (from ZF). Finally, the chassis were also of standard design (obviously the shapes, not the thicknesses). And today, we know how much the chassis is one of the main elements from the standardisation point of view: common cross members, common connectors, cab/chassis connection and all the accessories (tanks, etc.). Consequently, the seventies paved the way towards standardisation. How? Very

simply. The OM chassis (i.e. the complete OM base, the running gear without the body) was fitted with a new cab (a forerunner of the "Z" range cab), with an individual identity (apart from the logo, the name of the vehicle and the front grille) for Fiat and OM. So it was the cab which was new and different.

With regard to the engines, the OM and Unic vehicles used OM engines (with the exception of the "Orsetto and Cerbiatto", which already used the Fiat engine) and the Fiat vehicles used a Fiat engine.

These were the OM CO3, a 4.6 - 4.9 litre 90 HP short stroke version and a 100 HP long stroke produced in Brescia, the Fiat 8040, an 80 HP 3.4 litre 4 cylinder version and the "8060", a 122 HP, 5.2 litre 6 cylinder in-line version (the first engines of the series 8000) built at Torino SPA.

The lower end of the range (3.5-4.0 tonne) included the two newest members of the OM family, the Orsetto 15 and the Cerbiatto 20 (actually, the vehicles were the same, only the wheels were different: single or twin) equipped with the Fiat 804 and the Fiat 616 engines, a semi-forward cab version, initially powered by a 3 cylinder engine and then the 4 cylinder 804 engine. As a result of the rationalisation measure, the 616 was taken out of production, whereas the Orsetto and the Cerbiatto changed their name, becoming the OM 35/OM 40 and the Fiat 40 NC respectively, with an 80 HP, 3.5 litre 4 cylinder engine known as the "8040".

To simplify matters, we will not list the names of the Unic "personalised" vehicles here.

Going up to the 5 tonne vehicles, we have the OM Lupetto 25 (90 HP, CO3 engine) and the Fiat 625 (80 HP 8040 engine). Again through the effects of ration-alisation, this time the Fiat 625 was taken out of production, whilst the Lupetto chassis was fitted with a new cab to make the OM 50 and Fiat 50 NC which kept their original engines.

The 6-7.5 tonne range only consisted of OM vehicles: the OM 60-65 and OM 70-75 were derived from the Leoncino 30-35 and the

Daino 40-45 (90 HP, CO3 engine), again with a different cab.

In the 8-9 tonne range, we find the OM Tigrotto 50-55 (100 HP, CO3 engine) and the Fiat 645 and 650 (122 HP, 8060 engine). The Fiat vehicles were taken out of production, whilst the new OM 80-90 NC were derived from the Tigrotto.

Finally, from 1972, after Fiat had brought FNM from Alfa Romeo, the "645" and "650" cabs were to be used for the Brazilian range of vehicles.

In the 10 tonner range, the OM 100 and the Fiat 100 NC (122 HP 5.2 litre, 6 cylinder in-line engine 8060) were derived from the bigger version of the Tigrotto 65.

This was the standard range of light vehicles known as the "X" range which was born in September 1972. Production was concentrated at Brescia (whereas previously, the Fiat light vehicles were produced at Torino SPA) and naturally these vehicles were also sold by Unic, currently under the combined trade name of Unic /OM.

OPPOSITE: Some examples of light vehicles from the "unified" range in production since 1972.

THE STANDARDISED RANGE OF HEAVY VEHICLES

The range of heavy vehicles was rationalised at the same time as the light vehicles.

In the initial stage this was restricted to very limited measures, reducing the number of models and using the new "H" cab ("H" for standard version, "HC" for short version) on all the vehicles in the Fiat range, except for the 682.

Consequently, the range was broken down into two OM-Unic models and four Fiat models. With regard to OM and Unic, the ranges were already standardised. They had an OM cab, OM chassis and Unic engines. This was due to the fact that at the time Unic was selling the light OM vehicles, whereas before it became part of Fiat, OM used Unic engines on its heavy vehicles. These were the 19 tonne OM 190 4x2 and the 26 tonne 260 6x4 equipped with Unic chassis and engine (M62S, 240 HP, 14.9 litre V8) and the Fiat "H" type cab. Fiat had the 682 and the 690.

The 682 was a 17.5 tonne 4x2 truck equipped with a Fiat engine (the 160 HP, 11.5 litre 203) a special cab and chassis. There was also a corresponding bus version known as the 306.

At that time there was a vehicle (already no longer young) destined to have a very long career (it was not taken out of production until the end of the eighties) which will go down in history as the "King of Africa".

The "690" was an 18 tonne 6x2 truck with the "203", 177 HP engine. This was the basic vehicle according to the Italian licensing system. Produced as a 3 axle vehicle with a twin front axle (steering), it was almost always converted to a 4 axle vehicle. When coupled with 4 axle trailers, it became the famous "millipede", an 8 axle combination at the 44 tonne limit (because the Italian regulation allowed 22+22 tonne).

In 1971, the 690 was equipped with a new "H" cab and a new engine, the 260 HP, 13.8 litre 6 cylinder 8210 engine, which changed its name to the 180,

referring to the 18 tonnes allowed by the Italian regulation for 3 axle vehicles.

As we have seen, the vehicles were then converted to 4 axle vehicles (with an additional rear axle) to allow a GVW of 22 tons.

Also in the case of the 180, there was the 180 NC truck and the 180 NT tractor. This vehicle, plus a few 682's, constituted 100% of the heavy vehicle traffic on Italy's roads.

Finally, there was a standard range of two vehicles: the 619 (19 tonne 4x2 260 HP engine 8210) and the 697 (26 tonne 6x4 engine 8210; a vehicle derived from the previous 693), already equipped with the new "H" cab. These vehicles were created assuming a future European licensing code setting a limit of 19 tonnes for 2 axle vehicles and 26 tonnes for 3 axle vehicles. This code never got off the ground and the vehicles went for export.

They were European vehicles which, in the event, were only exported, with the exception of

the 6x4 which was converted to concrete mixers, etc. for use in the construction industry. This was not only because of the weight, but also because of the dual traction (otherwise the 3 axle version of the 682 was used as a 6x2).

Three years later in 1974, the Fiat 697, OM 260 and Unic Izoard were replaced by a standard vehicle known as the 300 PC/PT : PC if it was a vehicle with cab, PT in the case of a tractor (because the code allowed concrete mixers a "potential" of up to 30 tonnes).

Also, in the case of the heavy vehicles, the standardisation of the range coincided with concentration of the entire production at Torino SPA.

Some examples of heavy vehicles from the "unified" range in production since 1972.

126

THE STANDARDISED RANGE OF MEDIUM VEHICLES

In 1973, following the light vehicles and heavy vehicles, the third operation consisted of standardising the medium vehicles followed by the concentration of production at the new Unic factory in Trappes.

This range was based on Fiat chassis and a new cab, derived from the "H" cab of the standardised heavy vehicle range and christened the "HCS", representing a short, narrow version of the "H" cab. This was not an identical cab, but it was highly standardised (for example the doors were the same). The engines used were the OM "CP3" and the Fiat 8060.

At the bottom of the range (GVW 10 tonnes, the limit prescribed by Italian law for vehicles without power assisted steering), there were the Fiat 662 (122 HP 8060 engine) and the OM 100 (CP3 engine) from which were derived the Fiat 110 NR-NT-PC and the OM 110 R-T-P, all with a Fiat 8060 engine.

The Fiat range also included the 672 which in practice was the approved version of the 662 for 11 tonnes (10.99 to be precise, to satisfy French legislation). To explain the meaning of the name, the N stood for vehicles of the standard version (according to the Fiat tradition, N stood for naphtha, i.e. a vehicle with diesel engine), whereas a trailer was called NR, a tractor NT, construction vehicles NP and chassis cabs NC.

The 12 tonne category included the Fiat 673 (122 HP 8060 engine) and the OM 120 (CP3 engine), from which were derived the Fiat 130 NC-NR-NT and the OM 130 R-T with a 145 HP OM CP3 engine.

These were followed by two models launched in the September of 1973, also sold by Unic under a "Fiatised" name, i.e. using the familiar diamond, whereas OM kept the characteristic oval. To complete the range in ascending order, i.e. in the medium to heavy class (15 to 16 tonnes) we had the OM 150 (OM cab and chassis, Unic Izoard engine, 6 cylinder in-

line) and the Fiat 684 in the N and NP versions (already with the "H" cab, as the successor of the 643, with Fiat chassis and a 6 cylinder in-line engine 8220).

Following rationalisation, the OM 150 was taken out of production and replaced by the OM 160 which was derived directly from the 684 NP (cab, chassis and engine). This vehicle was to remain in production until the middle of the eighties, when it was replaced by the 175.24.

However, the N version of the 684, i.e. the road version, remained in production.

In this period, Lancia became part of the Gruppo Veicoli Industriali. As we have seen, its range of industrial vehicles and trucks, no longer considered competitive, was taken out of production.

These were the Esatau, a medium or medium to heavy vehicle like the OM 150 and the OM 160; the Esagamma heavy vehicle and the buses 703 and "718", the latter being vehicles with very interesting technical characteristics.

Some examples of medium vehicles from the "unified" range in production since 1973. At the same time Lancia in Bolzano ceased production in the truck and bus sector (top, an :Esatau B: from 1960).

KHD AND MAGIRUS:
250 YEARS COMBINED

In the previous chapter, we retraced the trials and tribulations of Fiat and its Gruppo Veicoli Industriali which was to become the future Italian partner of Iveco. We shall now look at the German side of the agreement, KHD, with its associate Magirus-Deutz.

Let us start on a cheerful note. In 1989, KHD and Magirus both celebrated 125 years in the industry.

Originally there was no link between the two companies: in fact, their respective histories only started to merge at the beginning of the Thirties.

Magirus-Deutz was founded in 1864 by a man with the same name in charge of the fire service in the German city of Ulm who had decided to build fire fighting ladders himself rather than buy them.

Other equipment was soon added to the ladders giving rise to an activity which continued until the First World War.

For around seventy years Magirus-Deutz specialised in the production of fire fighting equipment, first mounted on horse drawn carriages and then on steam engines and, following the advent of the internal combustion engine, on the first trucks.

Then, with the outbreak of the First World War, the engine driven vehicle suddenly appeared on the military stage: it was realised that the truck could play an important strategic role alongside the cavalry.

So, around 1916, Magirus-Deutz decided to produce a truck.

The design was entrusted to a young engineer at Benz (at that time the companies of Daimler and Benz were separate entities). The engines were purchased because Magirus-Deutz did not produce them.

After the war, in the Twenties, Magirus-Deutz passed through a period of serious economic difficulty (and was certainly not the only German company in such a situation) until, in 1934, it was bought by KHD, an Austrian company in Graz which specialised in the production of air-cooled engines for tractors.

KHD had also foreseen the possibility of fitting its engines on trucks. This it did in the years 1930 to 1940 and then during the Second World War, using them to power Magirus-Deutz trucks.

THE TRUCK INDUSTRY IN GERMANY AT THE BEGINNING OF THE SEVENTIES

This is the corporate story of KHD and Magirus-Deutz.

We shall now see why, in such different national and market contexts, the motivation to form a partnership in the industrial vehicle sector developed more or less at the same time in two companies completely different in terms of culture, industrial vocation and size; Fiat on the one hand and KHD on the other.

First of all, let us try to reconstruct the scenario of the industrial vehicle sector in Germany in those difficult first years of the Seventies.

As we have seen, at that time, German industry in this field was concentrated in just three companies: Daimler-Benz, MAN and Magirus-Deutz.

From the middle of the Sixties, Daimler-Benz had become the company we know today. After buying Krupp in 1967 and Hanomag-Henschel in 1969, it became the world's number one truck company and the country's fourth largest manufacturer.

It was the control of the latter which, towards the end of the decade, became the reason for fierce competition between Daimler-Benz and KHD, but Daimler-Benz won in the end.

In fact, at the beginning of the Seventies, this process of integration was to make a further step forward with the agreements between MAN and Büssing and later, with Daimler-Benz too.

Therefore, those years in Germany saw a lively process of industrial integration take place.

TWO OBJECTIVES FOR KHD

As far as KHD was concerned, it had to pursue two objectives: to guarantee an adequate commercial outlet for its production of air-cooled engines and to find a suitable place for Magirus-Deutz in the new industrial scenario which was beginning to develop in Europe. It was clear that the dimensions of the Group as configured at that time would not be able to secure a satisfactory future for Magirus-Deutz. Nor was there any precedent to believe that things could change without a partner being found.

It should be said that KHD was oriented more towards engines and agriculture than to industrial vehicles, so that Magirus-Deutz represented a collateral activity for it to some extent. Magirus-Deutz on the other hand, had two basic weaknesses.

First of all, it only produced vehicles with air-cooled engines, a type of engine which had earned its distinction throughout the world, achieving considerable success for site and off-highway use in general. Magirus-Deutz had acquired quite a high market share both in the construction industry - with more than 20% in Germany and with exports to two countries in particular where air cooling was an advantage - and in the military sector. But it was also an engine which, with the development of long distance transport, TIR transport, had started to reach its limits. With any type of service requiring greater horse power and a prolonged power output, rather than for brief periods as on construction sites, limitations emerged which had not previously been important or at least had gone unnoticed: noise, oil consumption, problems of non-uniform cooling between cylinders.

So, at the time when the large vehicle "fleets" started to appear and purchase decisions were made to set up new vehicle "parks", Magirus-Deutz found itself with an unsuitable product.

The other handicap affecting Magirus-Deutz was the fact that it had no medium and medium-light range, the one occupied by the Iveco "Z" vehicles. This was an "historic" weakness which the German company had tried to resolve by bringing in outside partners.

In the Sixties, Magirus-Deutz had sold a range of medium vehicles manufactured in cooperation with Eicher, a manufacturer of agricultural tractors which was also trying to extend its range. The chassis, engine and the main mechanical units were Magirus-Deutz whilst Eicher made the cab and a few minor components.

This had been Magirus-Deutz's first step into the medium and medium-light vehicle sector.

Later on, when it was time to renew its product range, Magirus-Deutz again tried to find a solution through cooperation by availing itself of many possibilities. Contact was made with Fiat to sell the vehicles in the Brescia range on the German market. And there were also contacts with the Japanese company Hino, whose vehicles also underwent trials in Germany. In the end, in 1971-1972, there was an opportunity for a four-way cooperation in Europe with Volvo, Daf and Saviem. And so the "Club of 4" was born, destined to become operative in 1975.

Two typical Magirus-Deutz vehicles, shown here already with the Iveco marking from the top, a medium truck from the "Club" range and a heavy conventional cab tipper lorry.

THEY THOUGHT ABOUT FINDING A PARTNER FOR MAGIRUS-DEUTZ

So KHD was faced with the problem of guaranteeing a future for Magirus-Deutz. There were two possibilities: to find a partner of more or less the same size as Magirus-Deutz or to integrate with a larger company.

They thought about a national joint venture. No longer with Hanomag-Henschel, since this company had been taken over by Daimler-Benz. So they started negotiations with MAN to set up a 50-50 company. But who would actually control the company? The answer was never found and the negotiations failed (about a year later, MAN signed a joint venture agreement with Büssing in which Daimler-Benz was also to be involved at a later date).

The alternative of integrating with Daimler-Benz remained. However, this would probably have meant that Magirus-Deutz would lose any chance to decide its future and therefore also its corporate identity and brand image. There was the very recent example of the fate suffered by Hanomag-Henschel whose engineering and commercial structures and even its sales network had been absorbed into Daimler-Benz.

This had created considerable anxiety at KHD both regarding the future of the works (it was said that Ulm would be converted to vehicle production), jobs and the Magirus-Deutz network. A power ratio to the obvious disadvantage of Magirus-Deutz, with all its consequences, was clearly a reason for concern.

Also, by choosing the integration of Magirus-Deutz with Daimler-Benz, another problem would have emerged, that of German anti-trust law: Daimler-Benz had 50% to 60% of the market and, with the 15% to 20% brought in by Magirus-Deutz, would have had a share of 75% and more.

THEY LOOK TO EUROPE FOR MAGIRUS-DEUTZ

Another possibility was to look beyond the national frontiers, to Europe and perhaps even beyond. Magirus-Deutz had already established the precedent of the "Club of 4" agreement signed, as already mentioned, at the beginning of the Seventies.

For the German company, the alliance with Volvo, Daf and Saviem had meant, in particular, a means to renew at least part of its range. It was now a question of assessing whether this cooperation could also be developed upwards, in the direction of the heavy vehicle range.

It soon became clear (from 1973) that this particular road was not a practicable one. The industrial scale and interests of the 4 partners were too different, and if the "Club of 4" had represented a step forward for Magirus-Deutz, it certainly could not become an adequate base for a long-term cooperation.

So another door closed. However, there were still several possibilities - it was merely a case of choosing the size of partner. A joint venture with one of the four large groups present in Europe - the British BLMC, the Italian Fiat, the American Ford and German Chrysler - would probably have meant a more or less considerable integration of Magirus-Deutz in these groups, with a subsequent loss of identity and decision-making power. However, there was a substantial difference compared with the national solution with Daimler-Benz: none of these possible partners had a network for distributing industrial trucks in Germany.

Fiat, Ford and GM had their own network in Germany, but only in the car sector. With regard to industrial vehicles, BLMC, Ford, GM, Chrysler and Fiat, to some extent, had networks - but not very wide-spread - in some countries of the EC.

There remained the alternative of a more or less joint agreement with some medium sized industry which would be able to offer the best guarantees for an independent future of Magirus-Deutz, in terms of management and mark, safeguarding jobs and the network.

However, for one reason or another, there were difficulties here too. There was Renault-Saviem in France which was a state controlled group; Seddon Atkinson, Foden and ERF in England, all independent manufacturers of modest size; Daf in Holland, at the time engaged in negotiations with the American company International Harvester, and Volvo and Scania in Sweden, both with the intention - although in different roles - of maintaining their independence and identity.

Finally, it could have considered some smaller companies in Europe, Steyr in Austria, Saurer in Switzerland or Sisu in Finland. But these were very small companies, and the Magirus-Deutz situation would not have changed significantly as a result of an agreement.

This was the choice, as far as Europe was concerned. What about the United States and Japan? For one reason or another there were very great problems to overcome.

As far as the United States was concerned, apart from the groups already in Europe (GM, Ford and Chrysler), and with the exception of International Harvester, already in negotiations with Daf, there were at least three companies which, in terms of size, might have been an interesting choice for Magirus: White Motors, Diamond Reo and Mack. But at the time, they were all biased towards the national market and in some cases, were forging the first links with the Japanese.

Finally, the four major Japanese groups: Nissan, Isuzu, Hino and Mitsubishi. They might have been interested in a cooperation, but of a more commercial nature, as was the case with the Americans: an outlet for Japanese products in Europe; support on the markets of East Asia and access to the Chinese market for Magirus-Deutz. The time was not right for a closer cooperation which would involve the development and production resources of the partners: the distances in terms of space and time were too great.

133

FIVE YEARS OF "TALK" BETWEEN KHD AND FIAT

These were the doubts and prospects for KHD concerning the destination of its subsidiary, Magirus-Deutz. But Magirus-Deutz had been negotiating with the Gruppo Veicoli Industriali of Fiat for a few years, in fact since 1969. The discussions revolved around two separate issues.

An interchange of components (shafts, axles, engines) for heavy vehicles. And the possibility of selling light and medium weight vehicles (absent from the German company's range) through the Magirus-Deutz network. Taken from the Fiat/OM range, they were to be equipped with Magirus-Deutz engines and logos. Hence a negotiation similar in substance, if different in spirit, to the one already concluded by Magirus-Deutz in connection with the "Club of 4".

The talks had reached deadlock at the beginning of 1973.

Fiat was interested in an agreement but Magirus-Deutz was indecisive, because it was afraid that the Italian product was not suitable for a sophisticated market like the German one. So at that time, it looked almost certain that nothing would be done about it. But one day, at the end of August, Fiat made a new proposal to Magirus-Deutz: forget the exchange of components and go for an agreement of cooperation, participation, even merger.

FIAT AND KHD AT THE NEGOTIATING TABLE

Fiat's proposal to set up a joint company bringing together the Gruppo Veicoli Industriali and Magirus-Deutz was quite unexpected.

Because as we have seen, after long, fruitless discussions, the "direct line" seemed to be interrupted in those months. But the Italians relaunched the initiative.

The idea was to set up a joint holding company - known as the "Truck Union" - with its registered office in a neutral country, in other words neither Italy, nor Germany, to which both companies would contribute business in the industrial vehicle sector.

Fiat would have the role of majority partner in a share ratio to be agreed with KHD. The holding company was to be the parent company of national affiliated companies - Fiat Veicoli Industriali S.p.A., Unic S.A., Magirus-Deutz A.G. and possibly other companies which were active in the component field and which could produce for both the holding company and for customers.

The general managers of the affiliated companies would have to be represented directly on the board of the holding company. The 1st of January 1975, was suggested as the date when the holding company would start to operate. These were the basic ideas. It was decided to set up committees to assess the possibilities and terms of an agreement. But the important thing was that contact between the Gruppo Veicoli Industriali and Magirus-Deutz had been resumed at a higher level, involving the parent companies, Fiat and KHD, directly.

When the first misgivings about the negotiations transpired, there were those within Fiat who tried to convince the top management and the owners of the company in favour of a national agreement.

Many of those at KHD were of the same opinion, but neither the owners of KHD nor the German financial "lobbies" indicated their opposition to an agreement in principle with Fiat. So it was possible to conclude the negotiations with Fiat successfully.

NOT AN EASY AGREEMENT

If they thought it was all plain sailing from then on, the negotiations soon proved otherwise.

Probably, neither party had the necessary experience to deal with such a complex matter. And the objectives which the future partners wanted to achieve were very different.

Fiat wanted to guarantee a size commensurate with the newly emerging European reality for one of the historically important activities of its industrial tradition. KHD was looking for a future for Magirus-Deutz, but it also wanted a commercial outlet for its main business, the production of air-cooled engines.

So the negotiations were to be dragged down by tactical moves aimed at obtaining partial benefits, with the result that - with hindsight - the contract which eventually sanctioned the agreement tied the management of the holding company to decisions not always in sympathy with the objectives to be pursued.

For example, the obligation to maintain separate distribution networks for the different makes, and a Magirus-Deutz range based on vehicles equipped with air-cooled engines.

THEY DECIDE ON THE TIME AND METHOD OF INTEGRATION

In singular contrast with the many differences between the parties in the course of negotiations, the operating structure of the future holding company and the time and method of integration seem to have been very clearly defined from the outset.

These are the main points as recorded in an internal report drawn up after the highly secret preliminary meeting held in Frankfurt at the beginning of September 1973.

At the time when Iveco was set up, Fiat S.p.A. was to divide its Gruppo Veicoli Industriali into two independent companies, Fiat Veicoli Industriali S.p.A. in Italy and Unic S.A. in France; KHD was to transform Magirus-Deutz into a legally independent company with its registered office in Ulm.

The corporate aim of Magirus-Deutz A.G. was still the production of trucks, buses, fire fighting equipment, military vehicles and other products such as components, possibly defined on the basis of agreements with the main holding company.

Magirus-Deutz was to continue to distribute vehicles with its own badge through its own commercial organisation both at home and abroad. This was one of the "sine qua non" required by KHD.

The Magirus-Deutz product was to retain certain qualities, mainly the air-cooled engine - another contractual condition required by KHD - irrespective of whether the vehicles were to be assembled in Ulm, Magonza or any other factory belonging to the holding company.

As far as the range was concerned, this was to be redefined on the basis of the pre-agreement range and integrated with Fiat vehicles.

Fiat declared itself prepared to install the air-cooled engines in vehicles intended for the Magirus-Deutz network at one of its factories or to supply the parts for assembling the vehicles to Ulm. Magirus-Deutz was to decide which engines to use.

As far as the Club range was concerned, since it would not have been possible for Magirus-Deutz to extricate itself from the contractual ties with the "Club" in such a short time, Fiat agreed to leave these vehicles in the Magirus-Deutz range alongside the Fiat and OM vehicles in the same categories.

Still in connection with the reorganisation of the ranges, it had to be assessed whether Magirus-Deutz vehicles could be replaced by Fiat vehicles, either because they were better or more economical to produce.

In this way, from the beginning of the cooperation, Magirus-Deutz was to have a wider range, even if it included units not yet standardised. On the other hand, Fiat was to have a chance to include Magirus-Deutz models in its own range, in which case Fiat engines were to be supplied to Ulm.

Dates were proposed to complete the harmonisation of the ranges: the last month of 1973 for the rationalisation studies; the first half of 1974 for completing the design work and production facilities; the sale of the ranges of both partners from January 1975.

At a future date, in connection with a further development of the cooperation agreement, they would start on standardisation and integration at component level within the limits considered to be convenient.

Regarding the Magirus-Deutz fire fighting range, it was proposed that this should remain an essentially Magirus-Deutz activity, possibly extended to include Fiat chassis to be supplied to Ulm and equipped by Magirus-Deutz.

At this stage the negotiations already took into account the organisational and management aspects. For example, it was suggested dividing production into two stages.

At the start of the agreement, the Magirus-Deutz factory in Ulm was to continue to produce its range of vehicles, including the "Club" vehicles. Apart from these, in order to make better use of the production capacity, Ulm was also to produce selected Fiat vehicles to integrate with the Magirus-Deutz range: Magirus-Deutz vehicles to be included in the Fiat range, Fiat vehicles from the Italian range, or even combinations of these ranges.

In this way it would be possible to guarantee job levels at Ulm in the initial stages of the co-operative venture without causing major disruption.

Looking at the final reorganisation of production within Iveco, four factories were named for the assembly operations: Brescia for lower medium category vehicles,

Trappes for the higher medium category, Turin for the heavy road vehicles and Ulm for medium and heavy construction vehicles, including all the models with a semi-forward cab.

It was decided to concentrate the production of the main mechanical units at a single factory still to be agreed.

Ulm was also to produce the cabs for the construction vehicles (possibly using components supplied by other factories), and also the chassis and the main components of units with a high technical content (basically axles). Should axle production be transferred to a different factory, it was suggested that the production of another component intended for the entire Group be concentrated at Ulm to fully utilise its engineering capacity.

HOLLAND IS CHOSEN FOR THE HEAD OFFICE OF THE HOLDING COMPANY

The decisions to be taken also included choosing the head office site for the holding company. As we have seen, the agreement stated that this was not to be in Germany or in Italy.

So they decided on Holland, because, apart from being convenient for Fiat, it also represented the most advantageous solution for KHD, for various reasons, not least the fact that Dutch legislation allowed the rights of the minority partner to be established in a contract, irrespective of the size of his share.

IVECO HAS ARRIVED,
BUT FINDS IT DIFFICULT TO "GROW"

The official date of birth of Iveco is the 1st January, 1975. The negotiations were nearing their close in the summer of 1974 and formal signing of the deed of constitution took place at Fiat's office in Geneva. Following the preliminary meeting in Frankfurt, the contract had been rediscussed and redefined in the preceding months in a series of meetings which were held in different European cities: Cologne, Stockholm, Rome, Turin, Paris and back to Rome.

And now, finally, Iveco was born, a "corporate" body. It was now a case of transforming it into an up and running reality. They needed a magic wand: from the 31st December, 1974 to the 1st January, 1975 everything, or nearly everything, was to be different from before. But, putting the "puzzle" together again was to take several years and was hard work. They had to solve both long term and everyday problems.

They had to fight a certain degree of "provincialism", a basic unwillingness to integrate. There was a willingness to impose their own way of doing things, but not the ability to merge their own culture with that of others to their mutual advantage; each thought it was the other that had to adapt.

But, of the three national companies forming Iveco, none was sufficiently strong to impose its own will.

The problem was less sensitive between the French and Italians, who had become accustomed to the state of coexistence which had developed throughout the first half of the Seventies within the Gruppo Veicoli Industriali.

However, the process of integration with Magirus-Deutz - determined to defend its identity - was a much more abrasive affair.

And production had to go on, the company had to "live"...

There was only one way: they had to find a way of "thinking" and "being" Iveco. It was necessary to integrate the structures and methods already consolidated with the Gruppo Veicoli Industriali with those of the new arrival, Magirus-Deutz. It was necessary to define and develop the strategies which were to guide Iveco towards its future.

The differences were many, too many. In all the documents recording those years, the same problem was always at the root of the discussion: how to standardise something which was historically different. The company was involved with this problem in all its aspects.

A great deal of time was spent on trying to understand both the extent of the problems and their nature: the different methods of interpreting a transnational company, the different approaches to the dilemma of integration or independence. The whole situation was burdened by the stereotypes of the different mentalities existing in the countries in which Iveco operated, sometimes also magnified by the inevitable misunderstandings due to the barriers thrown up by language and the different original cultures.

This was then the start of a difficult learning process concerning the spirit and interpretation of the words "transnational company". What did they mean?

A difficult subject to qualify - and quantify - in practical terms which could be usefully employed in the day to day management. Finally, the great distances which separated the various factories also play a negative role, making contact difficult.

This was a truly laboured and wearying process which, however, allowed the development of knowledge, experience and guidelines which were to be very valuable for the future development of Iveco.

TRANSNATIONALITY: A BATTLE FOUGHT ON TOO MANY FRONTS

As we have seen, Iveco was born in a difficult period in the socio-economic context of Europe. The markets were showing sluggish signs of recovery from the effects of the first oil crisis and the idea of a united Europe had been relegated to the limbo of good intentions by the serious problems which had to be faced.

The people at Iveco (and with them certain others in the world of industry) were in fact, "too European"; because in actual fact, nothing of the mentality and political will of the European nations had changed for a very long time.

But, in spite of it all, Iveco had succeeded in becoming a reality.

The problem now was to find an identity for it, to impose the values and ideals which had given substance to the idea. It was a question of imposing them on Iveco itself first of all, and then on the social, economic and political scenario in which the group would have to develop and operate.

An arduous task indeed, which had tested the endurance of the human and financial resources of the holding company in a battle which never seemed to end.

Such problems, which always arise when trying to combine different independent realities, were increased in Iveco's case by an additional variable which only now fully emerged: the problem of being a transnational entity belonging to three different nations and, paradoxically, over and beyond them.

Iveco was born to be European. This was to be its vocation, its true aim. It could not depend on rhetoric because its functional structure as an industry integrated between poles so far apart spiritually, would be transformed into a lethal "boomerang" comprising any possibility of efficiency and profitability.

As a transnational company, Iveco would have to confront the traditional physical, customs, legal and regulatory barriers in a much more complex manner and along different lines with regard to any import or export activity.

But it was to find an additional obstacle in the problem of communication; in preconceived ideas and misunderstandings which were rooted in the cultural differences which were as deep as they were historically entrenched.

A PROBLEM OF IMAGE FACES ITALIAN INDUSTRY

All in all, it was a case of convincing the people at Magirus-Deutz that if their company was to survive - (more than a century old, it was the biggest industry in Ulm with nearly twelve thousand employees) - they would have to find a partner, a foreign one, and an Italian one at that.

To expect the Germans (although, at the time, it would have been the same with the French, Unic apart) to accept that people from Italy could tell them anything about technology, design, diesel engines, organisation, factory planning methods and procedures was unthinkable. An inconceivable situation for which Magirus-Deutz was not quite prepared, because at the time, Italian industry did not exactly enjoy a sparkling image beyond its own borders.

It was difficult to persuade them to accept it, and much more difficult to explain the situation to others: to the workers at Magirus-Deutz, the people of Ulm, reporters, etc.

The whole thing was complicated by the fact that in any case, the starting point, that is the Gruppo Veicoli Industriali, was itself still in the formation stage with a whole series of pre-Iveco problems still unresolved.

It was still not possible to export a tried and tested Group strategy; instead, the situations within the group were still disparate and "dis-integrated".

FROM ONE LOT OF CUSTOMS TO ANOTHER

To discuss more specific problems, let us take a look at customs procedures - to show how the day to day administration of a company with a transnational structure can become something of a problem.

"Playing customs" for a company like Iveco did not mean (and still does not mean) merely ploughing through a certain amount of bureaucracy which - whilst awaiting a truly free Europe without frontiers - affected anyone who wanted to export or import anything. It is much more serious than that.

Because it was necessary to act as customs agents for everything: not just for imports or exports of complete vehicles, but also for the interchange of materials and parts intended for Iveco factories in different countries. A jumbled mechanism which took up valuable time.

It penalised the efficiency of the company management as a whole and created a serious burden in terms of the administrative apparatus. It locked up capital, raw materials, parts and vehicles ready for delivery which, to offset delays and any bureaucratic obstacles, had to be maintained at a higher level than physiologically necessary.

A situation which, although with some developments, still essentially exists today. Because, during those years, the Europe of the politicians had not succeeded the Europe of the market reality and no Community standard had yet been adopted.

AN ALL ITALIAN PROBLEM

To have a complete picture of the scenario into which Iveco was born, we should not forget how different the reality of the world of work was at that time in the three countries in which the holding company was operating with its national companies.

The problem was Italy which, as we have seen, was passing through the grey and unstable post war period.

For five long years, from 1975 to 1980, it was trapped between anarchy and violence both inside the factory gates and out, with serious consequences both for society and for industry.

As soon as Iveco had been set up, they became aware that they had to eliminate uneconomical practices, and that the company would have to be restructured and reorganised and certain surplus production capacity reduced.

But the labour market in Italy was controlled by many restrictions. All this created misunderstanding and anxiety with the French and German companies of Iveco. Because for example, in these countries the companies were able to adapt their workforce to the market trend, but since it was not possible to do something similar in Italy, there was the fear that the entire weight of the Iveco crisis would come to bear outside Italy.

Things were to go from bad to worse until, at the beginning of the Eighties, the Italian labour system was to find a more logical dimension with the setting up of social safety nets such as early retirement and the "integration fund" which was to give a new direction to industrial management. Within this new climate Iveco was able to close a factory: SPA Torino.

FOREIGNERS IN THE HOUSE?

Perhaps it is not obvious, but even the relationship between industry and the political powers becomes a problem where a transnational industry is concerned. It takes tact and diplomacy to have yourself accepted by the public as a compatriot and not as an immigrant.

The problem is two-fold. Every so often, a government contract or - worse still - a military contract is at issue.

And there is state aid: a situation where - as with any rationalisation project - it may be necessary to move the production location of a vehicle in order to be able to convince the authorities concerned that this is a local product.

Probably, in the case of Iveco, the member which had the easier life was Magirus: the German government has, by tradition, a somewhat more liberal attitude to industry, although when competing for an important military order (some tens of thousands of parts), Magirus-Deutz had to prove that a large slice of the added value of the goods was truly the fruit of German labour.

Things were even worse for Iveco's French company, whose "cri de coeur" was directed at the government because in France, apart from Renault, there was another national company: Unic.

This is a situation which still exists today, to the detriment of any claim to a "made in Europe" label.

Unfortunately, the local authorities still reason in terms of imports and exports without wanting to accept that an Iveco vehicle, for example, even if it is made in another country, is still the product of an industrial complex present in France as a major manufacturer of diesel engines.

A MERE TRIVIALITY: LANGUAGE

And finally, something which, at first sight, may appear trivial: the problem of language. Forget the better educated people. The Germans are like the Italians: they only speak their own language, or at least they do not speak another language sufficiently well to be able to use it every day, in the work place for example. In Italy, at the time when Iveco was born, you could find people with a good knowledge of French. But German, that was not of this planet!

To deal with this problem, it was decided that the official language of Iveco would be English. But that did not solve anything, because English was not familiar to many employees either.

So life went on, until the beginning of the Eighties when, with an unprecedented initiative in Europe, it was decided to organise English language courses for the several hundred directors and managers of Iveco's thirteen industrial establishments in France, Germany and Italy. They wanted to give the company management a "lingua franca" to be able to communicate inside the company and with the outside world.

The size of the initiative - christened the "VIP project" - was such that it was necessary to seek the assistance of language and communications experts.

A specialist institute was chosen, Riversdown Publications, which prepared the teaching texts for Iveco under copyright. In November 1980, individual discussions were held to form the "classes" and the lessons started immediately afterwards, these being held in the various factories. Certainly the possibility of making yourself understood either side of the national barriers was a problem which went way beyond mastering a common language, but this definitely was a step in the right direction.

Ample proof of this was provided six years later on the occasion of the negotiations concerning the Iveco-Ford joint venture when the English company, recognising that it was at an advantage by being able to conduct the negotiations in its mother tongue, expressed its appreciation for the fact that no Italian manager needed an interpreter.

IVECO:
FROM AN IDEA TO A SOLID
INDUSTRIAL REALITY IN FIFTEEN YEARS

So far we have retraced, step by step, the events and strategies which led to the founding of Iveco.

We have now arrived at the eventful day on 1st January, 1975, the one chosen as the "operational" date of birth of the holding company.

Iveco was on the road. A road built on hopes - and the unknown.

A road which, as we shall see, was to be conquered in a long and hard process of evolution and consolidation aimed at the company within rather than the world without.

But before we go on, let us pick up the thread of the story between the past and the future.

Iveco was born at a time when the European truck industry was still a "puzzle" of makes operating within national markets which all enjoyed direct or indirect protection in some way or another.

The starting point for the new company was the union of five companies in three countries which wanted to set up a large industrial complex to operate at European level.

The initial idea was based on the concept of Europe, even if Europe was still only half way between the conceptual and the political ideal: Iveco was born as a great "wager" which industry placed on Europe.

To respond to the merging requirements of a more modern and specialised European transport system, a drastic industrial renewal was necessary first of all.

Starting up a process of concentration between companies was the first step made by Iveco to ensure sufficient size to finance and feed this renewal process.

For this reason, the union of the five partners could not be regarded as a simple tactical alliance between independent makes.

Instead, Iveco was looking towards an industrial situation which was new and different even in qualitative terms and which was able to generate synergies and economies of scale appropriate to large volume production.

A production which alone could guarantee a balanced and constant absorption on a market of continental size.

Italy, France and Germany, the home countries of the companies merged in Iveco, suddenly opened up the large domestic markets needed for the take off of the new company whose homeland was now Europe.

Even while the political conditions within the EEC were quite unfavourable and actually impeded the development and integration of a transnational company, Iveco pursued this road with persistence, with a geographical and political vision way ahead of that of the politicians.

Iveco was being formed by means of a deep process of rationalistaon, by integrating factories, management and systems of the partner companies into a new supra-national corporate model.

1975 - 1979

The first task of the newly constituted holding company was to rationalise production by converting the factories and their respective specialisations in groups of components and finished product lines.

Rationalisation of production which was to complement rationalisation of the product, was initiated by the complex plan to standardise the ranges.

However, the process of integrating production and product is not conceivable unless it is accompanied by a similar integration of people and method.

The aim of a cultural homogeneity, which was to be created by integrating the corporate cultures of the different countries, was a priority and one of the most difficult to achieve.

Integration proceeded in successive steps with events which help us to define four major historical stages. In an initial period, from 1975 to 1979, the work of rationalistaion was done in a type of "federation: between the three national companies which maintained a "de facto" identity and independence, the only link being forged by a consultative committee (management advisory committee) at corporate level for coordinating the various activities. This committee was made up of the representatives of the national companies together with the managers of the central divisions.

Two vehicles from the "integrated" range, which came into production immediately after the formation of Iveco: the heavy "170/190" and, below, the light "S Range".

1980 - 1984

The move towards true corporate integration took place between 1979 and 1984, when a re-organisation of the key divisional management made it possible to harmonise strategic directions through the three national corporate bodies which constituted Iveco.

With the rationalisation of the product range and the gradual elimination of surplus capacity, the sales networks in Europe were also standardised, but the marketing of products and existing marks was left to each country.

At this stage, whereas the integration and renewal process proceeded successfully, the young company was still suffering from structural weaknesses which were reflected in the problems of transferring the image of the old marks to the Iveco mark and, in particular, the lack of image in the heavy road vehicle industry.

The company was faced with these problems against a serious market crisis which exacerbated the effects and demanded solutions which were neither temporary nor short term.

After five years in existence Iveco reinforced its presence in the "heavy" sector: the time had come for turbo engines, and at the top of the heavy range "TurboStar" was born (see photo) a vehicle destined to be a key player at a European level.

1985 - 1989

The end of the tunnel was reached in the third period, between 1985 and 1989, characterised by an intense product renewal process, the consolidation and extension of the sales network in Europe and the creation of subsidiaries in all the main markets.

The old national marks were removed from the product and replaced by the Iveco mark.

At organisational level, the various company departments were specifically re-organised in a series of strategic plans finalised when the company was back in the black and following the structural reinforcement of Iveco.

At the same time, the company was engaged in a massive investment plan with an ambitious project involving the complete renewal of all key product ranges with maximum rationalisation and a substantial generation leap in production technology with the extensive use of automation.

Having strengthened its structure, Iveco was also in-creasing its commercial and industrial presence in Europe and beyond.

The joint venture acquisition of the truck division of Ford of Britain resulted in the setting up of Iveco Ford Truck, a very important event which transformed the most important European market into Iveco's fourth domestic market.

There were then numerous commercial or industrial initiatives outside Europe in selected key countries - China, Turkey, India and in the then Yugoslavia - to consolidate and extend Iveco's presence outside the domestic market, as well as in Africa, Asia and Eastern Europe.

The second half of the eighties: on the front of trucks the Iveco name stood out alone. At the end of the decade, within the terms of the joint-venture with Ford, Iveco bought the British "Cargo" range (above).

THE NINETIES

We have now arrived at today, and the fourth major chapter which opens with a journey through the Nineties.

A chapter which sees the further expansion of Iveco in Europe, on the Spanish market, through the purchase of Enasa, and the finalising of an ambitious plan for the complete renewal of technologies and the product from Turbo-Daily to EuroCargo. In an unprecedented industrial effort within the sector, more than 5000 million Lire have been invested over a period of five years.

But in the meantime, Europe is proceeding at a pace towards economic integration, with the historic emergence of the Single Market in 1993. The transport market and its related industry is also undergoing far-reaching changes.

The loss of protection which vehicle transport previously enjoyed leads us to expect fierce competition which, on the one hand, will result in a reduction in the cost of transport and on the other, will force operators to reorganise and specialise according to the demands of their customers.

Unique as a truly European company, Iveco is an ideal situation to face this new challenge.

And it is doing just that; aiming to improve quality by initiating a global optimisation process, which integrates in an innovative way a whole series of corporate systems for the purpose of bringing the company ever closer to the customer. This will offer him an "added value" not just in terms of quality and completeness of the product, but also support for his own operating efficiency.

The nineties started with the marketing of the "Euro" ranges (above), a completely new generation of vehicles; and in the meantime, with the acquisition of Enasa, manufacturer of Pegaso vehicles, Spain became the fifth "domestic" market for Iveco.

*1975, Iveco became a reality. On the vehicles' front the "historic mark" was linked
with the characteristic 'I' chosen as the group's first "logo".*

1975-1979
A FEDERATION OF COMPANIES

Let us retrace the course of events and link them to that famous day, the 1st January, 1975. In its first five years of life, Iveco tended to work as a federation of companies rather than as a unitary organisation.

Each of the national companies controlled by the holding company - Fiat Veicoli Industriali SpA in Italy, Unic SA in France and Magirus-Deutz AG in Germany - retained each of its departments, from design to after-sales. And the management structure of the holding company, based on the national structures, did not exactly help towards achieving integration, either.

The first core management team, made up of the men from the Gruppo Veicoli Industriali, formerly OM, Fiat and Unic, together with representatives of Magirus-Deutz, found itself working in a situation where links were formed by coordinating committees. There were eight main departments - administration and finance, engineering, strategy and development, personnel, equipment, production, commercial sales, planning - and the management of each of these was entrusted to a management committee controlled by a director from the former Gruppo Veicoli Industriali. Subcommittees were also set up: local markets, exports, new industrial initiatives, and so on.

The coordination and supervision of these bodies was entrusted to a senior committee on which were represented the managers of the national companies plus those of the different departments.

It was laid down that several nationalities had to be represented on each committee and that if a committee decision was unanimous, it became an executive decision.

To sum up, the initial idea was that discussion by the committees would paint a full portrait of Iveco, would illustrate the structures and methods of the various national companies and how everyone operated. Once in the executive stage, the way would be open to integration and rationalisation.

This was the basic concept. In practice however, it did not always work as it should because of misunderstandings, a diversity of method and objectives and also because of conditions alien to pure management logic. This had the effect of limiting those ini-

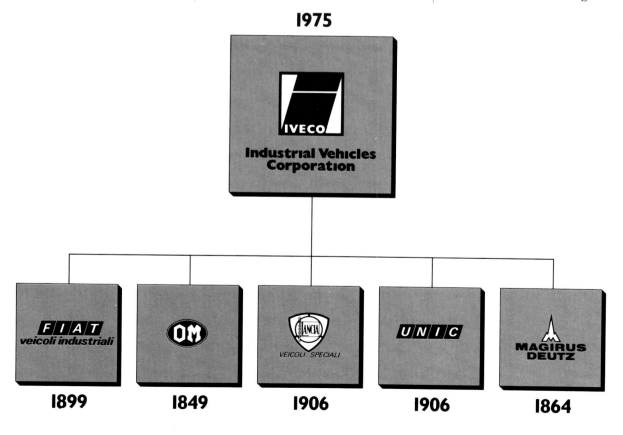

tiatives or strategies which could have actually modified the status quo of the holding company.

It came down to the capacity of the German parent company to put pressure on the Magirus-Deutz management which, according to the contract, was appointed by KHD, (except for a member proposed by Iveco). However, the holding company had the sole right of veto for the members it appointed.

And there were the constraints on the commercial and product strategies imposed when the holding company was set up (we will refer to this briefly later).

All this, for the five years KHD was to remain in the holding company, made the coordination work entrusted to the committees more difficult. Decisions and directives stopped - so to speak - at the surface, without reaching executive level, with the result that Magirus-Deutz continued to be managed in an almost autonomous fashion.

A BRILLIANT START AND THEN CAME THE CRISIS

In spite of the not insignificant internal problems, in the first three years, the financial performance of the holding company was satisfactory. Iveco seemed to have been born under a lucky star.

After the drop in demand which marked the early years of the Seventies, reaching a low in 1974 (more than 125,000 vehicles down compared with the previous year), the European market saw the trend start to reverse.

The effects of the first oil crisis had by now been absorbed and Europe was recovering from the general economic stagnation which had rendered it sluggish in the previous years.

The recovery in volume, uncertain between the end of 1974 and the beginning of 1975, was to continue with increasing vigour, reaching a peak of more than 400,000 vehicles in 1979. A number which, at the time, no one would have dared to predict. For Iveco, the prospect of an expanding internal market - Germany, France and Italy - was starting to open up with all the potential of its continental size.

Two historical pictures which record the supply of 10,000 Magirus-Deutz heavy trucks destined for use in the freezing temperatures of Siberian Russia.

The newly constituted holding company was also able to benefit from the positive effects brought by the innovative processes still active within the Gruppo Veicoli Industriali, with more attention dedicated to the market (remember the birth of the marketing division) and a shrewd commercial policy which had resulted in a substantial increase in profit. Other advantages were created by the process of rationalisation and standardisation which, as we have seen, involved the production divisions, the ranges of vehicles and the corresponding production allocations.

In those first years, the Magirus-Deutz management also performed well and had just been awarded a large order by the Soviet Union for the supply of more than 10,000 construction vehicles designed to operate in extremely low temperatures of 40 degrees below. Some of the largest companies in Europe had competed for the order and Magirus-Deutz had succeeded in getting it. This had happened before Iveco was set up (between 1972 and 1974), but deliveries started immediately afterwards and continued for two years. Throughout this period this order had a considerable positive effect on the results acheived by Magirus-Deutz.

So Iveco took off with a positive thrust. The first balance sheets were in the black with an upswing in the trading profit which leapt from approximately 3% to nearly 9% in the year from 1975 to 1976. This had an even more positive effect because it made it possible to pay a dividend to the shareholders, something which was important in order to achieve a good relationship with the minority partner, KHD.

The figures for the two years, 1976 and 1977, speak volumes: 105,000 vehicles and just less than 107,500 vehicles (trucks, buses and special vehicles for defence and fire fighting) with a billing of 7,285 and 7,342 million Dutch Guilders, respectively (an enormous figure if based on current values).

This result was translated into a net profit of 343 million Dutch Guilders in 1976, i.e. 4.7% of the billing. But the following year, in 1977, the figure was already more than halved: 109 million Guilders.

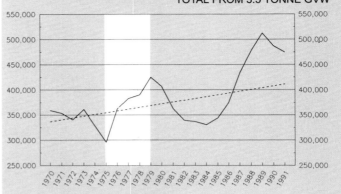

DEMAND FOR TRUCKS IN WESTERN EUROPE
TOTAL FROM 3.5 TONNE GVW

1975	....	2962
1976	....	3623
1977	....	3830
1978	....	3901
1979	....	4252

This was the warning sign of a crisis which was destined to last until the middle of the Eighties, apart from a brief respite in 1981. In the next three years, sales and billing continued to produce positive results: 108,890 vehicles and 7,284 million Dutch Guilders in 1978, 109,780 vehicles and 7,709 million Guilders in 1979 and then 109,600 vehicles and 8,600 million Guilders in 1980.

But the profit fell, and Iveco plunged into the red: the loss was almost 269 million Guilders in 1978 and reached a maximum (loss) of 425 million in 1979; 1980 showed a reasonable recovery, reducing the loss to 342 million Guilders.

What had happened? Why was the management of the holding company more and more affected by financial charges, by indebtedness? In fact, the escalation from the 928 million Guilders in 1976 is impressive: 2,565 million in 1977, 3,542 in 1978, more than 4,000 in 1979 and more than 4,420 in 1980 at the peak of the descending parabola.

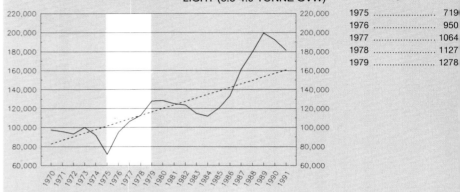

DEMAND FOR TRUCKS IN WESTERN EUROPE
LIGHT (3.5-4.9 TONNE GVW)

1975	....	719
1976	....	950
1977	....	1064
1978	....	1127
1979	....	1278

An ascending curve which kept pace with investments: (the bottom line): 418 million Guilders in 1976, 601 in 1977, 555 in 1978 and then the sharp fall, as evidenced by the 291 million in 1980.

Hence the crisis which the still young Iveco had to face was mainly one of indebtedness. What were the reasons? These were numerous, and not always directly the result of internal management choices. Management had to support the weight of investments, with relative depreciation, in order to buy some of the factories of the former Gruppo Veicoli Industriali - e.g. SPA Torino - for which the holding company had acquired the "right of use", but not the title.

It would take too long to explain in detail the reasons behind this situation.

We will only say that this was the result both of agreements made when defining the value of the shares of the two shareholders and of "technical" requirements on the part of Fiat which, when the Group Veicoli Industriali had already been set up, still had some common management and production structures with the various sectors.

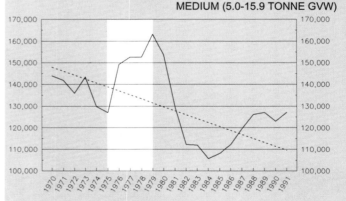

DEMAND FOR TRUCKS IN WESTERN EUROPE
MEDIUM (5.0-15.9 TONNE GVW)

1975	....	1271
1976	....	1493
1977	....	1527
1978	....	1527
1979	....	1632

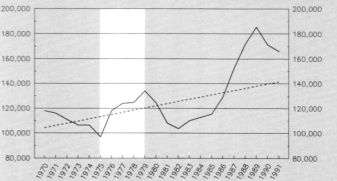

DEMAND FOR TRUCKS IN WESTERN EUROPE
HEAVY (FROM 16 TONNE GVW)

1975	....	971
1976	....	1180
1977	....	1239
1978	....	1246
1979	....	1341

DEMAND FOR TRUCKS IN WESTERN EUROPE
(BY COUNTRY FROM 3.5 TONNE GVW)

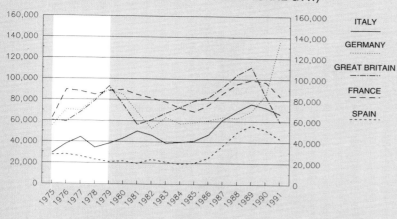

Legend: ITALY, GERMANY, GREAT BRITAIN, FRANCE, SPAIN

	ITALY	GERMANY	GREAT BRITAIN	FRANCE	SPAIN
1975	29372	55500	60614	63115	27671
1976	38142	70739	59257	89767	28062
1977	44330	69927	68635	88245	26271
1978	34511	80979	79338	88245	23199
1979	38525	89667	93175	88772	20879

1975 - IVECO (%) MARKET SHARE
FROM 3.5 TONNE GVW
EUROPEAN TOTAL = 15.5%

Once Iveco was born, it was a case of separating the various departmental responsibilities, following which the holding company was also able to take on these activities, too. This happened in the second half of the Seventies. And in fact, the investment quota reached its peak of 601 million Guilders in 1977.

However, this was only one of the causes which propelled Iveco's balance sheet into the red in those years.

An important role was also played by other factors such as the obvious difficulties of adopting a uniform approach to the very different operating and cultural positions.

All this was also affected by non-strategic choices, (which we have already mentioned), linked with the agreements made when the holding company was set up and which, in practice, did not achieve the results hoped for.

For example, the decision to equip Magirus-Deutz vehicles with Deutz air-cooled engines and the one to maintain separate sales networks for the Fiat, OM and Unic vehicles and for the Magirus-Deutz vehicles.

As we shall see, instead of emphasising the product and image - and therefore commercial - plus points of the Franco-Italian and the German elements of the holding company, these choices merely had the effect of creating inefficiency inside and confusion for potential customers outside. They had to wait until the middle of the Eighties to remedy this situation.

To complete the picture, we would mention the investments which were necessary to complete the process of integration of the production processes and the ranges, to include the factories and products of Magirus-Deutz. And those investments intended for the development of the initiative taken to seize industrial and market opportunities.

In spite of these internal problems, Iveco did not fail to look for new openings and opportunities right from the start.

An evocative picture of the Fiat 682, which has gone down in history with the nickname "African King" for its widespread use in markets outside Europe.

FROM AFRICA TO THE UNITED STATES, THEY INVESTED IN THE FUTURE

This stage includes the resources applied by Iveco to start up new industrial initiatives in Libya and Nigeria in 1976, in the United States in 1977, with the creation of ITONA as the bridgehead to the American market. The aim was to lay the foundations for a presence in "strategic" areas outside Europe. This was a commercial vision intelligently projected towards the reality of a future still some way off; one which was to be reaffirmed in time with the more recent joint ventures in China, India and Turkey.

But these proved expensive investments using finance in a strong currency which the exchange rate in the following years was to make even more burdensome, affecting both capital repayments and interest payments.

THE PRESENCE IN NORTH AFRICA IS REINFORCED

North Africa represented a traditional presence for the Italian part of Iveco dating from the time of Gruppo Veicoli Industriali. Suffice it to say that in the three year period, 1975-1977, 25,000 vehicles were sold in that area compared with the 4,500 delivered to the Middle East in the same period.

However, the possibility of trading in those countries was linked with types of participation and cooperation in the development of local production and assembly initiatives, a condition which practically all the local governments imposed on companies wanting to bring their products to those markets.

It is against this background that the joint ventures started by Iveco at the end of the Seventies in Libya and Nigeria, with the birth of Libyan Trucks and Bus Company and National Trucks Manufacturers Ltd., will be evaluated.

On the wave of the profits derived from oil sales, a desire to create a local industry emerged in those countries. International tenders were launched and Iveco was more or less compelled to compete:

otherwise, it would have left these markets open for its competitors.

In consideration of the envisaged volume, Libya had launched a tender with just one successful applicant and that was Iveco.

Nigeria, on the other hand, issued a tender involving three orders. All the major European manufacturers took part and finally, the contract was won by Iveco, Daimler Benz and British Leyland. At the last moment however, the orders were increased and a fourth contractor joined the consortium, the Austrian company, Steyr.

But the size of the Nigerian market was such that it would not allow four parties to "cohabit" and the consequences of this choice were serious for all of them. Particularly for Iveco which, not having the necessary financial resources at the time, was obliged to withdraw from the market.

This despite the fact that, at the outset, it was actually intended to make Nigeria a centre for export to other African markets.

IVECO LANDS IN THE USA AND ITONA IS BORN

Only two years after it was set up, Iveco also launched itself on the American market.

The idea of somehow ending up in the United States already existed in 1973, still within the Gruppo Veicoli Industriali.

There were numerous contacts with Mack and White which, for various reasons, did not bear specific fruit.

It was decided to use the spade work which had been done - both in connection with defining the range and studying the territory - to establish a presence in the USA, not within the scope of a cooperation arrangement with a local manufacturer, but in a purely commercial form with its own distribution network. And so they set up ITONA, Iveco Trucks of North America.

The idea resulting from the market research was to penetrate the US market in the medium or medium to low range, between 10 tonnes and 13 tonnes (classes 6 and 7, according to the American classification), creating a niche for diesel engines (which, at the time, were only used in the heavy

sector in America) and a European vehicle which was more sophisticated than the local product.

In order to take advantage of the good image which Deutz engines already enjoyed on the other side of the Atlantic, a Magirus-Deutz vehicle in the "Club" range was chosen and suitably Americanised: this was the M11 with an air-cooled engine.

Marketing started in 1978. Two years later the range was extended downwards to the 4.5 tonne category. This time the vehicle was chosen from the "Z" range, the Z 100 diesel, equipped with an air-cooled 100 HP, 5 cylinder F5L912 engine. In the years to come, new versions were gradually introduced with a higher GVW and water-cooled engines. 1982 - 1983 saw the birth of the 4.5 - 6.7 tonners, 110 HP and 125 HP 8060 aspi-rated engine and a 120 HP turbo engine. In 1984, a 7.9 tonner was launched with a 130/140 HP 8060 turbo engine. Between 1985 and 1986, vehicles were available in the entire range up to 10.9 tonnes.

Iveco had become the first foreign company to enter the United States and its vehicles achieved great success, thanks to the greatly superior quality compared with the American standard in that range.

So this "niche" began to gain substance. Operators were aware that vehicles of this type had to be able to solve transport problems hitherto dealt with by means which were inadequate and expensive (petrol engines) and not particularly comfortable for the people who had to work with them.

So, in the first years, Iveco's presence on the American market achieved a positive result both from the point of view of its image and its profitability. However, the situation was destined to change. This was due to two concomitant factors: on the one hand, there was the drop in the exchange rate of the dollar; on the other, the market was penetrated by Japanese manufacturers who, having deduced the potential of the new market - opened up, ironically, by the quality of the

Iveco product - entered the field with all their competitive might. As a result, the good initial profitability soon became a memory and the presence of Iveco in the USA settled at volumes of around 2,000 vehicles a year with very reduced margins. Until, at the beginning of the Nineties, it was decided to abandon the US market altogether.

COMMUNICATING TO CREATE A NEW SUPRA-NATIONAL IMAGE

Of the many problems which Iveco had to face in its initial period of life, one of the most acute was definitely that of creating an image for itself.

It was not easy to explain Iveco, but it was even more difficult to promote the new mark in an industrial sector where many competitors already had a very long tradition and a well established image.

It was undecided whether to move immediately to a new image to be created for Iveco, or to continue to lean on the marks of the companies merged in Iveco and if so, to what extent.

In this difficult process towards a secure identity, they also considered the possibility of mark specialisation: OM as a specialist manufacturer of light vehicles; Magirus-Deutz in the construction sector and Fiat for heavy road vehicles.

The specialisation theory is one which crops up frequently. However, the fact that a mark only has a raison d'être if it has its own precise commercial validity is also a market reality. Otherwise enormous investment is required to sustain it.

What should they do? The fame and the role of Fiat and OM on the Italian market were indisputable. So why renounce such an asset, the fruit of years of presence in the market, by destroying these marks at a stroke and replacing them with Iveco?

The same applied to Magirus-Deutz in Germany, and in other European countries; even outside Europe the German mark enjoyed a positive image, particularly in special sectors of the market.

On the other hand, Iveco was born as a multi-national company projected towards the European market with the aim of conquering an increased share of European truck sales.

As we have seen, Fiat was strong in Italy, but not sufficiently strong in Europe (and the same more or less applied to OM).

Magirus-Deutz might be what was needed to offset these shortcomings in terms of image. But the Italian side was interested in promoting the name Iveco. In the end they opted for a soft introduction of the Iveco mark onto the market.

Consequently, whereas in the communication campaigns (publicity, promotions and sponsorship) they specifically referred to the name Iveco, on the vehicles they restricted themselves to placing the Iveco logo - an "I" in a diamond - alongside the "historic marks", bottom right on the front.

A Fiat vehicle remained a Fiat vehicle, but was part of a corporation with an "I" as its logo.

It was intended that the name Iveco - which is an acronym for "Industrial Vehicle Corporation" - was to be perceived as a type of umbrella over the other national marks. But what was to be the "size" of this umbrella? Was it to be seen by the outside world as a large umbrella or a small umbrella? The solution adopted was that of the small umbrella, although in some cases it was decided to keep only the national mark in order not to "disturb" the image.

The realities of the market could not be ignored.

For example, look at the Fiat 682, a legendary vehicle which, in many parts of the world, and particularly in the African countries, was better known by the simple "682" symbol than as a Fiat product.

It was for the same reason that for the United States operation they decided on the Magirus-Deutz mark: Magirus-Deutz plus the "I" for Iveco.

Naturally, the time was to come when the company would act on the market with a single product; and then the different marks would simply become secondary manufacturers. But only then

and not before.

The first of the national companies which opted for abandoning its own make in favour of the Iveco mark was Unic, whose logo in any case had been Fiatised for some time (i.e. capital letters inscribed in a diamond).

This is explained by the fact that as a result of some product problems, Unic's image was somewhat "tarnished" in the latter years.

Magirus-Deutz on the other hand, remained a very independent company in terms of history, product, coordination of its image and also its mark which was immediately recognisable by the stylised shape of the bell tower of the famous Ulm cathedral. In the meantime, the Iveco mark was stylised to become more rounded and more pleasing to the eye and to improve its typography.

The support network in Europe

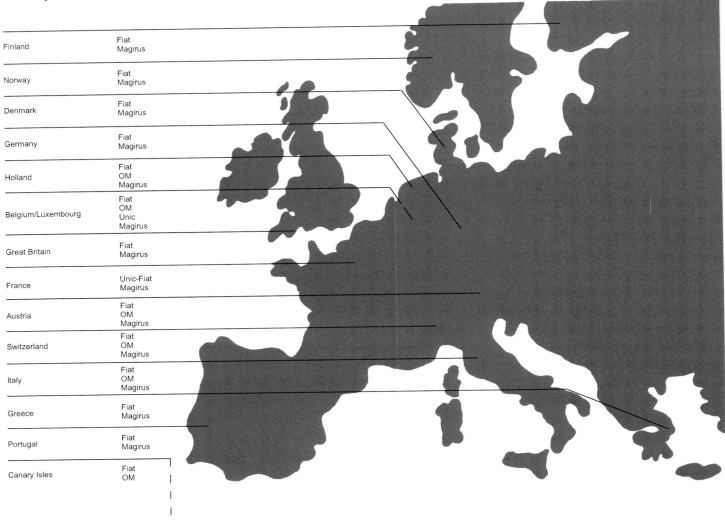

Finland	Fiat Magirus
Norway	Fiat Magirus
Denmark	Fiat Magirus
Germany	Fiat Magirus
Holland	Fiat OM Magirus
Belgium/Luxembourg	Fiat OM Unic Magirus
Great Britain	Fiat Magirus
France	Unic-Fiat Magirus
Austria	Fiat OM Magirus
Switzerland	Fiat OM Magirus
Italy	Fiat OM Magirus
Greece	Fiat Magirus
Portugal	Fiat Magirus
Canary Isles	Fiat OM

AN INTRICATE NETWORK

From image to network. The link is obvious, because in either case, a way had to be found - as easy as possible - to deal with the three-in-one reality of Iveco, particularly when its image was projected towards the outside world.

In the separate network versus single network debate, as we have already seen, the choice had already been made before Iveco went into operation.

Separate networks were chosen with the declared aim (but perhaps not the sole aim) of taking advantage of all the opportunities offered by one or other of the marks in the various markets: not to sell a standard product, but to utilise partial synergies in each country by selling in a network.

So Fiat V.I. opened its own establishment in Germany, Fiat LKW, with its head office in Monaco. In Italy, the uncontested domain of Fiat and even more of OM, Magirus-Deutz Italia was set up with its head office in Verona.

In England, where Magirus-Deutz UK had an assembly facility (because of customs barriers) it was necessary to have a product with a high local content in order to access the British market.

In the remaining European countries, very often two or more parallel networks existed. Examples of this are the Belgian market which had four separate sales organisations at the same time (one for Fiat, one for OM, one for Unic and one for Magirus-Deutz) and Austria where the situation was similar.

Obviously this was a situation to the detriment of all four networks but, also because of the highly protective legislation typical of this country, the problem to be solved was complex.

Only today can it be said that the process of network reorganisation has been well and truly concluded.

THE DESIGN AND PRODUCTION STRUCTURE

It can be said that in those years, the engineering and test centres coincided with the production locations.

In Italy, the former Fiat factories, Torino SPA and Cameri were in operation; the former OM factories at Brescia, Milan and Suzzara; the old Lancia factory in Bolzana. To these were added Foggia, belonging to the newly constituted Sofim, and the new bus factory in Valle Ufita towards the end of the decade.

Turin was concerned with the design and production of medium and heavy vehicles for road and off road use; series 8000 to 8280 engines and axles. Buses were concentrated at Cameri and then progressively transferred to Valle Ufita. The chassis were made in Turin.

Brescia was concerned with light vehicles in the "S" and "Z" ranges; CP3 and 8360 engines; gearboxes and hydraulic torque converter (for the Hydrotrans, a heavy construction vehicle); and axles. Suzzara made the "S" range vans (production only). Milan made the axles. Bolzana made the military vehicles. Foggia produced the series 8100 engines (production and testing).

Above: The SO.F.I.M. plant at Foggia equipped for production of the 8000 series engines. To the side, the "snapshot" of Iveco products, vehicles and components in the second half of the seventies.

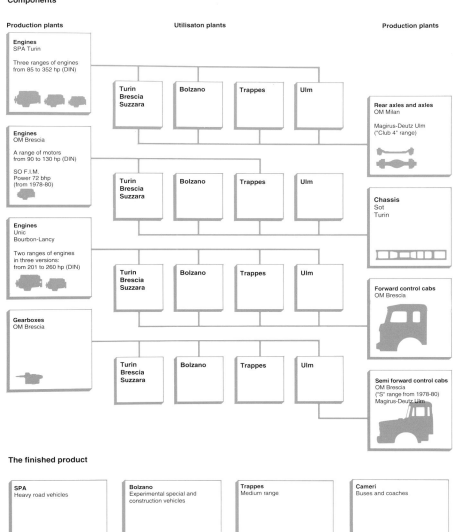

Italy:
Fiat Truck S.p.A. plants

France:
Unic-Fiat S.A. plants

Germany:
Magirus-Deutz A.G. plants

SPA Stura - Turin

Total surface area	1,150,000m²
Surface covered	330,000m²
Employees	9,500

Produces medium and heavy trucks, engines for trucks, buses and other applications.

OM Brescia

Total surface area	727,000m²
Surface covered	235,000m²
Employees	6,100

Produces light trucks, mechanical and hydraulic gearboxes, 3-4 and 6 cylinder engines.

Trappes

Total surface area	520,000m²
Surface covered	110,000m²
Employees	1,700

Produces medium and heavy trucks.

Ulm

Total surface area	835,600m²
Surface covered	271,800m²
Employees	9,950

Produces medium and heavy trucks and fire engines.

SPA Centre - Turin

Total surface area	105,000m²
Surface covered	80,000m²
Employees	2,300

Produces cylindrical and conical gears for truck differentials.

OM - Milan

Total surface area	191,000m²
Surface covered	141,000m²
Employees	3,350

Produces rear axles, engine axles and bearing axles.

Suresnes

Total surface area	63,200m²
Surface covered	58,000m²
Employees	2,500

Produces gearboxes and mechanical components.

Magonza

Total surface area	197,000m²
Surface covered	76,000m²
Employees	2,050

Produces buses, coaches and special vehicles.

Chassis - Turin

Total surface area	135,000m²
Surface covered	75,500m²
Employees	1,900

Produces chassis for trucks and buses.

Suzzara

Total surface area	230,000m²
Surface covered	64,000m²
Employees	1,300

Produces vans and twin cab vehicles.

Bourbon-Lancy

Total surface area	270,000m²
Surface covered	88,000m²
Employees	1,600

Produces engines and truck components.

Cameri

Total surface area	156,000m²
Surface covered	40,000m²
Employees	1,500

Produces buses and coaches.

Lancia:
Special Vehicle S.p.A. plant

Bolzano

Total surface area	223,000m²
Surface covered	110,000m²
Employees	2,700

Produces special vehicles, axle housings.

Fourchambault

Total surface area	80,000m²
Surface covered	47,000m²
Employees	500

Produces pressed components and parts for trucks.

In France, home of Unic, there was the new factory at Trappes and also the factories at Bourbon-Lancy and Fourchambault.

Trappes made medium and medium heavy vehicles. Bourbon-Lancy made the engines in the 8220 and 8210 series (production and tesing) and Fourchambault was responsible for engineering.

In Germany, Magirus-Deutz had the Ulm and Mainz factories. At Ulm they designed and produced vehicles including those in the "Club" range, axles (which were produced at Magirus-Deutz, at least to some extent), bridge laying military vehicles and fire fighting vehicles. They also designed buses which were then produced in Mainz.

IT IS ALREADY THE ERA OF THE COMPUTER AND TECHNOLOGICAL INNOVATION

It should be pointed out that right from the outset, Iveco has always paid due attention to the problems of technological innovation.

This attention was prompted by the transnationality of the holding company which allowed and promoted comparisons between different industrial worlds in a global vision of the realities of the time at European level.

So today, in the light of the revolution which accompanied the launch of the new generations of EuroCargo vehicles, it can be claimed that in matters of technology - this term being both the actual production equipment and the computer "instruments" used to control them - Iveco has always been able to invest the right amount at the right time, and is often ahead of its time.

COMPUTERISED CALCULATIONS IN THE INITIAL DESIGN STAGES

This has been the case with computer technology. It has been used at Iveco since the beginnings of its existence in the wake of a tradition which dates back to the end of the Sixties, when design was a main division of the group and shared human resources and equipment with the car division.

Then they used a network service via a telephone link with the United States (Cleveland in Ohio) offered by General Electric.

They were pioneering times with uncertain and difficult connections, few telex machines and a punched tape system for storing any data which was not typed in via the keyboard.

These facilities were used in particular for making calculations for the dimensioning of engineering parts. However, already at that time (in 1968), they succeeded in processing the calculation of a bus suspension for the 421 model which then went into production.

The first computers had already been installed at Fiat, but these were very expensive and were only used in connection with management activities.

The first programmable computers also existed, but their memory capacity was so limited (200 program steps in all) that there were practically no real possibilities of using them.

At the beginning of the Seventies there was a generational change with the installation at Fiat in Corso Marconi of a powerful main frame computer: a Univac 1106 which was advanced for those times - and which represented an enormous investment of several thousand million Lire to lease it - which was used by the technical and design offices.

This comprised the entire central computer structure in Systems Management in Corso Marconi which controlled the machine and the first programs. Fortran was the typical language used at that time. Between 1970 and 1974 this machine, since backed by a second with more or less the same facilities, was used to mechanise at least a thousand procedures: from dimensioning important parts to calculating gear ratios and the various kinematics, etc. Towards the middle of the Seventies, that is the time when Iveco was born, we saw the inauguration of the individual computer station based on Digital PDP 11/45 computers. At the Fiat group, the first technical offices to be equipped were those of the Gruppo Veicoli Industriali and then Iveco.

It is interesting to remember that this was the first generation of machines which was bought (up to then, computers had been leased, together with the necessary specialists for their management and maintenance).

It was on these machines that the first graphics attempts were made: i.e. the first CAD trials, even before CAD (computer aided design) was known as such.

To give an example, the design calculation of the connecting rod rotating inside the crankcase was made (an important step because the crankcase is then modelled on this).

This activity was conducted in parallel on the main frame computer and on the local PDP stations which supported practically all the calculation work which was done in the technical and calculation offices.

So this was the situation in 1975 when Iveco was born. In the same period, 1976 to be exact, computers were used for the first time in the testing area with Digital PDP 11/34 machines used to analyse experimental data. Three years later the first road simulator was commissioned for bench testing the cabs and bus bodies; the first step towards CAT (computer aided testing).

In the computer sector however, the most substantial change was to take place at the beginning of the Eighties when the company embarked on the road leading to modern computer systems, not just for engineering but for corporate management in all its varied aspects.

From the early days of its operations Iveco has been able to take advantage of modern design and testing facilities: from the research centres at Orbassano (Turin) and Ulm, to the test tracks in Turin, La Mandria, Nardò and Ulm (top).

PRODUCTION TECHNOLOGY: THEY TALK ABOUT CELLS AND CATAPHORESIS

With regard to the production technologies, one example of innovation of considerable interest is that of the Sofim factory in Foggia.

It went into production in 1978 designed to produce 700 engines a day but to be increased to 1000 on the basis of advanced design parameters.

First of all, the production cycle was organised into "cells", four interfaced assembly areas each dimensioned for a maximum capacity of 250 engines a day. The machining operations were performed with traditional transfer machines which were controlled electronically.

This was a basic form of control which could still only be programmed via the hardware (i.e. by physically modifying the electronic circuit boards), but nevertheless, it was a technological leap at the time and not just at the Iveco factories.

Developed by Comau of Modena, the system was a prototype and as such it did have some teething problems. It was also necessary to train the personnel. The Sofim factory at that time (naturally, today, many things are different) made a first important step towards modern style automation.

Still on the subject of technology, at about the same time in Ulm, a new cab division was being set up to be one of the most modern in Europe both in terms of machining logistics and technology.

The paint shop was already using cataphoretic dip coating for protecting sheet metal against corrosion, and the bodywork division was to have a robot welding line.

Advanced technology at all stages of production, to guarantee the high performance levels and reliability of the vehicles in all conditions.

RATIONALISATION OF THE RANGES CONTINUES

Whilst Iveco was still taking its first steps, between 1975 and 1978, it managed to implement the second stage of the plan to rationalise the range which had started in the time of the Gruppo Veicoli Industriali.

The standardised range was being succeeded by the Fiat, OM and Unic integrated range.

This was a new range which standardised the power trains in the various GVW bands: from now on, the only difference between the vehicles of the various "marks" was to be the individual identity.

This consisted of five details: apart from the model name, there was also the front badge and the mark, the licence plate and the stamping of the chassis.

The rationalisation process was carried out in three successive stages: first of all the heavy vehicles were launched, with design starting in 1971 and marketing in 1975; these were followed by the medium weight vehicles, with design in 1972 and marketing in 1976, and finally the "S" range, the new light vehicles from Iveco, with design in 1973 and marketing in 1978.

Regarding the medium light vehicles, the "Z" range was to be derived in 1977 with a series of adaptations to the "X" range.

In those years, a new range of civilian and military vehicles was also developed (identified as "P" and "PM" respectively). Specially designed for site and off-highway use and equipped with "gantry" axles (i.e. with the axle centre raised in relation to the wheel hub to increase the ground clearance) they were four-wheel drive vehicles in the 7 to 9.3 tonne category produced by Iveco.

1975 saw the launch of the 70P and 90P powered with the 122 HP version of the 8060 engine. In 1977, the 65P was derived from the 75P with an 85 HP, 8040 engine and 1979 saw the dubut of the 75P and 90P equipped with the new bigger 135 HP, 8060 version.

THE INTEGRATED RANGE OF HEAVY VEHICLES

The integrated range of heavy vehicles arrived on the scene more or less at the same time as Iveco made its debut. This was designed as a complete range with two and three axle vehicles, but in the initial marketing stage priority was given to 4x2 vehicles (in the tradition of the Italian market). The three axle configuration was produced by outside conversion companies).

This family of vehicles was christened the 170 and 190 according to the GWV.

It should be remembered that after more than 10 years of fruitless negotiations (started in 1962), the European code had still not been finalised. Therefore, the range was adapted to the 17.5 to 19 tonne category: the 17.5 tonne vehicles ran a mean course between the 16 tonner (for two axle vehicles) allowed by the British and German codes and the 19 tonner allowed by the French, Belgian and Spanish codes.

The GVW should have been 40 tonnes, extended to 44 tonnes for transporting containers (for developing combined transport).

However, in this way it was possible to derive lighter and heavier versions to satisfy the various national codes in force at that time.

The vehicle designations kept the code already used for the standardised range: the initial number indicates the weight in 100 kgs, the letters of the Fiat versions indicate the type of conversion: "NC" (normal cab) for the road vehicles, "NT" (normal tractor) for the road tractors, "PC" (heavy vehicle with cab) for the quarry/construction trucks and so on.

A further reference was added which concerned the power of the engine and which was indicated by a two digit number separated by a full stop: 170.26 for 260 HP, 170.33 for 330 HP and so on.

Aspirated engines were used: these were the 260 HP, 13.8 litre 6 cylinder 8210 engine and the latest 330 HP 17.2 litre 8 cylinder V engine, the 8280, produced at SPA. The chassis were new and were designed by Fiat.

Two new ranges born with Iveco.
LEFT: The off-road 4x4 vehicles
from the "P" series.
ABOVE: The heavy on-road
170/190.

The cab was the tilt version of the "H" cab with a raised roof (a solution which made it possible to conform to German legislation concerning the vertical distance between bunks, which had to be 55 cm).

But even while these vehicles were being launched, the new weight and dimensions law number 313, was passed in Italy. Effected in 1975 and in force from the following year, it mirrored more or less exactly the proposed European standard which we have mentioned; except for the weight, raised from 17.5 tonnes to 18 tonnes. The maximum weight allowed on the axle was increased from 11.5 tonnes to 12 tonnes and the GVW was fixed at 44 tonnes, but associated with a specific power of 8 BHP/tonne (from here emerged the famous 352 BHP minimum power: 44 tonnes multiplied by 8).

These variations imposed a modification of the 170 range just a few months after its launch on the market.

Apart from the approval modifications regarding the load on the axle and the total weight of the vehicle train, the most important modification required was for the engine whose power had to be increased from 330 HP to 352 HP. This was achieved by using a new injection pump and by changing the settings. As a result, the range was now as follows: 170.26, 170.35 instead of .33, plus the new 190.26 and 190.35. The 170.20 and the 190.20 were then added, equipped with a smaller engine, the 6 cylinder 8220 (the Unic X 200 produced at Bourbon-Lancy) which was a 205 HP 9.6 litre engine. This was because French legislation, which was different, also required smaller engines.

Finally, the 18 tonne weight fixed for Italy from the weight ad dimension law number 313 became law in Europe from 1990, except that it was changed to 7 HP/tonne.

However, these powers have already been well exceeded. In 1976, the 370 bus range was launched at the same time as the truck range. But we will discuss this separately.

The "Hydrotrans" on the left with hydraulic torque convertor transmission: a truck which is particularly suited to quarry and construction applications.
BELOW: The heavy "integrated" on-road truck in the "190" version.

THE INTEGRATED RANGE OF MEDIUM WEIGHT VEHICLES

The second step in the integration process concerned the medium weight vehicles. These vehicles were launched in 1976 with production already in progress at the new Trappes factory. As we have seen, from 1973, the standardised range already had a 110 and a 130 equipped with an HCS fixed cab. From 1975, the cab also became a tilt cab.

In 1976, the new 140 was launched equipped with a tilt cab and a choice of three engines: the 145 HP, 7.4 litre 6 cylinder CP3, the 168 HP, 8.1 litre 6 cylinder 8060 and the 205 HP, 9.6 litre 6 cylinder 8220. The 150 and 159 models were then derived from the 140.

All these vehicles were produced at the new Unic factory in Trappes. It was at this stage that Unic ceased production of all its old vehicles. The light vehicles were already OM; the first medium vehicles had been standardised in 1973; the heavy vehicles with the launch of the 170 range.

An integrated range was also to mean rationalisation of production. It was the "clean sweep" which Iveco had made ante Magirus-Deutz: all the light vehicles at Brescia, all the heavy vehicles at Torino SPA and all the medium weight vehicles at Trappes.

In fact, this had also happened to the components to some extent: shafts and axles at Milan, gearboxes at Torino SPA (first made at Brescia which gained the light vehicles but lost the gearboxes); the same with shafts and axles which were made at Brescia and were then transferred to Milan; all the chassis were made at Sot of Turin, whereas initially, all factories made their own.

Bourbon-Lancy produced the 6 cylinder in-line engines: first the 200 HP X200 of Unic origin and then the 260 HP 8210 of Fiat/OM origin which is another basic engine in the medium range still being produced at Bourbon today.

With this operation, Bourbon-Lancy changed the course of its history completely in 1975. We must remember that first they made the trucks (whose production was then concentrated at Bari), tractors (transferred to Modena) and some of the medium vehicles (concentrated at Trappes).

The 159, here below and on the left, the 150 and 140, below from the left: three trucks from the medium "integrated" range, in production at Trappes since 1976.

THE RANGES ARE INTEGRATED WITH MAGIRUS

As soon as it was set up, Iveco had a range which was already new and 80% integrated but one which was created during the life of GVI, before the arrival of Magirus-Deutz.

From 1st January 1975 or at least at the beginning of 1976, the problem of integrating ranges and production arose once more.

We should remember that Magirus-Deutz was, by tradition, a company specialising in the heavy construction vehicle sector, with the peculiarity of Deutz air-cooled engines. But it had just completed the development of the medium range (or rather medium to light range) within the "Club of 4" agreement.

These vehicles were destined to go into production in 1975, also equipped with an air-cooled engine, and were being added to the new medium vehicles development to a large extent by the GVI.

Since it was not conceivable to modify the agreements made by Magirus-Deutz in connection with the "Club", it was decided to make the vehicles in the "Club" range independent by integrating the range with vehicles in the Italian medium range where necessary.

Otherwise, it was a case of marrying two ranges and two completely different engines, one water-cooled and one air-cooled and, as far as production was concerned, of finding the right allocation to the Magirus-Deutz factories: trucks and fire fighting vehicles to Ulm and buses to Mainz.

The first thing they did, in 1976, was to give Magirus-Deutz the 50, 60 and 75 versions of the light vehicles (still the "X" range): these were models and conversions (vans, 6+1, 8+1, etc.) which did not exist in their "Club" range. This was the first time the Deutz air-cooled engine - the 87 HP, 4.1 litre 4 cylinder F4L913 - was used on vehicles originating from Iveco of Italy.

The following year, 1977, the "X" range was expanded upwards to include the 90 and 100 versions and at the same time it benefitted from the restyling of the cab and some engineer modi-fications (new gearboxes, shafts and axles).

The modified range changed its name to the "Z" range.

Two years later there were further modifications when the 1979 model was included in the range and a tilt cab was offered as an option.

Returning to the integration with Magirus-Deutz, the integration of the heavy site and road vehicles also started in 1976. Versions were made with Fiat engines and a Magirus-Deutz backward cab.

The 190 PAC 4x2 and 260 PAC 6x4 were launched (the latter initially for the French market only) with the 195 HP, 9.6 litre, 6 cylinder 8220 engine and 260 HP, 13.8 litre 6 cylinder 8210 engine. The Magirus-Deutz versions were equipped with a 256 HP, 11.3 litre 8 cylinder V engine, the F8L413F and a 320 HP, 14.7 litre 10 cylinder V engine, the F10L413F.

In 1977 the 4x4 and 6x6 versions of these vehicles were also made using the 260 HP 8210 engine.

At the same time, these air-cooled engines were used on the Fiat 170 road vehicle which became the Magirus-Deutz M16F (remember the German code limiting 4x2 vehicles to 16 tonnes).

In 1978 the integration process was to be completed by eliminating the range of Magirus-Deutz heavy road vehicles and the corresponding cab.

In the same period, the 6x2 and 6x4 versions of Italian origin were launched. These had completed the design stage but had never gone into production because, as we remember, in Italy it was normal for the third axle to be added by conversion companies.

The German market on the other hand, wanted the third axle as original equipment so the "220 6x2C" tractor, with a third central pneumatic axle, and the "240 6x2P" truck, with a third rear non-steering axle and individual wheels, were derived from the 170N. Both vehicles had pneumatic rear suspension and used the 352 HP, 17.2 litre V8 8280 engine; they were also produced in the Magirus-Deutz version under the M22F badge with 256-320 HP Deutz air-cooled engines.

Still in 1979, standardised vehicles with forward cabs went into production for use in the construction sector: these were the 190 P 4x2 and 260 P 6x4, with the 260 HP, 8210 engine and the 330 and 350 HP, 8280 engine and the corresponding Magirus-Deutz M19FK with a 256 HP, V8 engine and the M26FK with a 320 HP, V10 engine. Four wheel drive versions were converted from these vehicles: 190 P 4x4 with a 260 HP, 8210 engine and the 260 P 6x6 with the 352 HP, 8280 engine and the corresponding Magirus-Deutz M19-FAK with 256 HP, V8 engine and the M26FAK with a 320 HP, V10 engine.

The 330 series was also launched at the same time: the 330 P 6x4 with forward cab (devised from the 260 P) with a 260 HP, 8210 engine and 352 HP, 8280 engine, and the 330 PA 6x4 with backward cab with a 260 HP, 8210 engine. 1978 also saw the integration of the Magirus-Deutz power train in the bigger versions into the medium range: the 140 which also became M14F and the 159 which became the Magirus-Deutz M15.9F. At the same time the vehicles were equipped with new shafts and axles and the NC's tilt cab, a restyling of the HC's became standard for the European markets.

Specially conceived for quarries and construction, these are Magirus-Deutz vehicles with conventional cab and Deutz air-cooled engine. They were to be included in the "integrated" range with the name "PAC" and Fiat water cooled engines.

THE "S" RANGE:
A STAR IS BORN

The Seventies closed with an event of particular importance from the point of view of the Iveco product. This was the debut of the new "S" range in 1978 which was made up of light vehicles ranging from 3 to 5 tonnes. Since Magirus-Deutz made nothing in this range, there were no problems of integration.

We have already dealt with the events which accompanied the birth and the first steps of the "S" range and its engine, the Sofim. So now we are going to concentrate on the product. The "S" range was originally based on a weight of 3.5 tonnes with possible extension to 4 tonnes and a bottom limit of 2.8 tonnes. The engine was the 2.5 litre Sofim engine 8140, an 80 HP engine with direct injection and natural aspiration.

The basic specification of the vehicle was linked with a semi-forward cab structure which, apart from ease of access to the cab (very important for door to door vehicles) also meant a structure which would help the centre of gravity on the axle.

This allowed vehicles with different total weights without having to modify the front engineering. Consequently it was possible to develop a sophisticated front suspension with independent wheels to improve the steering and comfort of the vehicles.

With the "Daily" they wanted to make a small, strong industrial vehicle with the working capacity of an industrial vehicle, but also with the cab comfort of a car.

Hence the supporting structure with chassis, longitudinal front engine and rear wheel drive - typical of industrial vehicles - a front independent wheel suspension. This specification was one of the main plus points of the range, the key to a success which had not been expected at Iveco. The most optimistic assessment had been 20,000 to 25,000 vehicles in full production, whereas today, the figure has gone beyond 60,000 including CKD vehicles and is still growing.

An unimaginable success in terms of volume and also profitability, which was to become one of the financial strengths of Iveco in the years when it would be needed.

Destined for a truly brilliant future, in 1978 the "S" range light vehicles from 3 to 5 tonnes GVW were introduced, with a completely new 4 cylinder diesel engine, the 2.5 litre Sofim 8140.

1980 - 1984
FIVE YEARS TO BUILD ITSELF
A NEW IDENTITY

As we have seen, in the first few years, the process of integration between the national companies which had merged into Iveco was burdened by attitudes and uneconomic practices of all kinds; these were not only financial, but also operative both inside and outside the holding company.

In practice, in this initial period it was possible to work more specifically on rationalising the product and production.

As for the "true choices", the substantial innovations, all they could do was talk about them.

A stalemate situation arose which dissipated energy and resources inside the company instead of looking outside at the realities of the market place in order to seize the opportunities it offered.

Then, between 1979 and 1980, came the unexpected change.

The German minority partner, KHD, indicated its wish to leave the holding company and expressed this by exercising the right - laid down in the contract - to have its shares taken over by its majority partner, Fiat. This decision was to have important repercussions for Iveco which was to derive new impetus and opportunities to control its strategies from the new corporate position.

The basic problem was once again that of rationalisation.

In spite of the amount of work which had been done in the previous five years, a great deal still had to be done, starting with the choice of the internal management of the holding company.

It was a case of adopting a new position and being capable of making decisions and strategies through the three national companies with the necessary decisiveness to achieve the executive decisions directly.

The solution, as we shall see, was sought (and found) in a divisional type structure in which the management of similar departments at each of the national companies was transferred to a single, centralised body.

They also had to find new structures which would allow them to control and coordinate the Iveco organisation in all its complexity.

This was achieved by giving a decisive boost to the development of the network and of the computer systems. And they had to define the aims as a strategic priority. Basically, there were two. Firstly, optimised management of the market. This was to be achieved by using a new instrument called logistics, a science which controls the market/production flows. Secondly, by starting on the standardisation of the sales networks which, until that time, had been kept separate to maintain the identity of the Magirus-Deutz mark.

At the same time they again tried to satisfy the need to rationalise the range and production, primarily for the purpose of relieving the holding company of the financial burden created by including the double power train which resulted from the water-cooling and air-cooling of Deutz origin.

With regard to this last point, we should remeber that on the basis of the agreement signed when the holding company was set up, Iveco was to use the Deutz engines on the Magirus versions of its vehicles in the medium and heavy range. This, although it looked like a product "plus" on the one hand, in reality was found to be a penalising choice.

The Deutz air-cooled engines were known and appreciated both for industrial applications, either heavy duty or in extreme climates, and for fire fighting vehicles and construction vehicles (which was the specialisation of Magirus-Deutz). All these uses had one characteristic in common: that of not demanding the continuous operation of the engine at high speed and at maximum power output.

The situation was quite the opposite where road use was concerned particularly on vehicles where, with hour after hour at cruising speed and possible uphill climbs, the engine had to withstand completely different thermal stresses.

So Iveco was faced with dual problems, a technical one and a commercial one.

Because the road users were not willing to accept the idea of buying a vehicle equipped with an air-cooled engine they had to force sales of the Deutz engine. For Iveco, all this meant increased production costs through the need to duplicate the product and because the cost of an air-cooled engine is higher than that of a water-cooled engine. They had to resort to incentives and promotional campaigns within the network.

So when KHD - which, you will remember, had its core business in the air-cooled engine and had defended its use with all its might - withdrew from the holding company, the decision to eliminate the Deutz engine from the range was taken.

This could not be done in a short time because there was a basic undertaking according to which, for five years after KHD left the company, Iveco was to continue to install a considerable number of Deutz engines.

Of course they had to do so, but in the end it had a serious effect on the already considerable trading deficit of Iveco at the beginning of the Eighties.

IVECO CREATES A DIVISIONAL TYPE STRUCTURE

From 1979, Iveco decided to formulate a new internal structure for the holding company which would finally allow it to put in place an organic management over the three national companies. A study of the possible solutions was made in consultation with an American specialist company, McKinsey.

Two alternatives emerged.

To sum up very briefly, either to restructure Iveco in "divisions", mainly one for the core business, the truck sector, and one for components. Or to "divisionalise" the management of the holding company.

The second option was chosen with an added obligation to maintain the national companies in order to derive maximum advantage from the contributions of the national "cultures". From then on there was to be just one manager, rather than three, for each of the corporate divisions: engineering, production, purchase, networks, administration, etc. This was to create a central, global vision of the various corporate realities; an essential precondition for implementing a true process of rationalisation.

The aim (which was achieved) was to overcome the individualism of the three national companies and to create instead a horizontal system of control and decision making. As is easy to imagine, not inconsiderable difficulties and resistance had to be overcome to introduce this divisional structure. For many people, particularly within the national companies, were to lose their decision making powers.

But the choice had been made, and there was no going back.

The arm of this "revolution" extended to the entire company in all its aspects, both its internal relations and those with the outside world. Practically everything changed at management level. For example, one important consequence was to occur in 1982 when the legal structure of the holding company was adapted to the new trend.

The company changed to a "tree" structure where the three national companies were no longer directly connected with equal ranking to the parent company, Iveco B.V. From that time it was to be headed only by Fiat Veicoli Industriali S.p.A. which was to control Unic S.A. and Magirus-Deutz A.G.

This reorganisation was inspired not only by taxation requirements, but also by a management logic. Because, at that time, it was mainly Fiat V.I. which supplied Magirus and Unic with what they were selling on their respective markets in Germany and France, whereas the flow of supplies in the opposite direction was relatively modest.

Still in connection with the divisionalisation of the company, it was decided to coordinate the truck and engine-related sectors under a specific responsibility by setting up the divisions, particularly for market product lines.

A new coordinated engineering and production programme was started. And the idea to "deverticalise" the company and the component sector (joint venture with Rockwell) also took shape.

The purchase departments were centralised by a decision which was also highly controversial. Action was taken on the "image" strategies with the decision to use the name Iveco first and the marks second (Iveco Fiat, Iveco Unic, Iveco Magirus). Market management was also centralised.

THE COMPONENT SECTOR IS DEVERTICALISED

At the same time as the divisional reorganisation, between the end of the Seventies and the beginning of the Eighties, Iveco started to "deverticalise" its production by looking for joint ventures for components, particularly gearboxes and axles.

This idea was inspired by the American example except - as was to be realised much later - the context of the European market was very different. However, at the time, they thought that this was the right road to take.

There were discussions with Cummins, also with regard to engines, but (as was logical bearing in mind the tradition of Iveco and Fiat in the sector) nothing came of them and the engines remained the preserve of the company.

However, deverticalisation was achieved for axle production, at least for the medium and heavy single reduction axles.

The opportunity was offered by the need to use axles with single rather than double reduction on the new generation of heavy road vehicles, particularly the Turbo-Star. This was because longer ratios were required to reduce consumption and noise.

But Iveco's single reduction axles were very old at that time and not suitable for the new power levels which engines had reached with supercharging: 420 HP-450 HP. And so it was necessary to design a new generation of axles or to obtain them from an outside supplier.

They decided on the alternative of joint production and the partner found was the American company, Rockwell, which had excellent know-how in this field.

In 1982, a joint venture agreement was signed with Rockwell within the recently constituted Rockwell CVC-OMEVI SpA.

One important consequence of the event for Iveco was the solution to the problem of utilisation of the Cameri factory in Novara whose bus production had just been transferred to Valle Ufita.

The production of the new range of axles, initially destined for Milan, was assigned to Cameri.

The events of this joint venture are recent history. Whilst evolving in the market context, it was realised that the prospects of Iveco running a business as a components manufacturer in Europe could not be achieved.

Consequently, in the middle of the Eighties, a new agreement was made with Rockwell which took over Iveco's share and Iveco in turn gave an undertaking to buy axles for the next five years.

With the start of the 1980s Iveco adopted a new organisational structure on "functional" lines (see diagram), more suited to the aims of "integrated" management of the various national identities involved in the group.

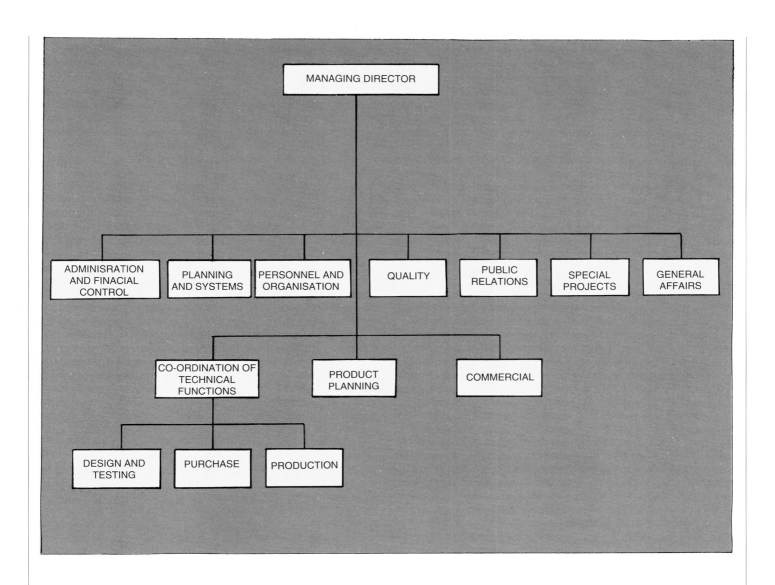

The organisation chart shows:

- MANAGING DIRECTOR
  - ADMINISRATION AND FINACIAL CONTROL
  - PLANNING AND SYSTEMS
  - PERSONNEL AND ORGANISATION
  - QUALITY
  - PUBLIC RELATIONS
  - SPECIAL PROJECTS
  - GENERAL AFFAIRS
  - CO-ORDINATION OF TECHNICAL FUNCTIONS
    - DESIGN AND TESTING
    - PURCHASE
    - PRODUCTION
  - PRODUCT PLANNING
  - COMMERCIAL

A SIGN OF RECOVERY, BUT THEN THE BALANCE SHEET GOES INTO THE RED AGAIN

Although the European market was showing signs of a recession, and in spite of the serious commitment assumed when choosing divisionalisation, the Eighties opened on a note of optimism for Iveco.

Production and billing remained in the ascendant, maintaining the positive trend which had been the mark of the previous period: 109,600 vehicles and 8,600 million Dutch Guilders in l980, 113,120 vehicles and 10,839 million Guilders (more than 2,000 up) in 1981.

The management result provided visible signs of improvement. 1980 still closed in the red, but with a consistent reduction in losses: 342 million Guilders compared with almost 425 in 1979. In 1981 the company went back into the black: 56 million Guilders, not much to shout about, but still 400 million better compared with the previous year.

To recover 6 profitability points with the European market taking a downturn - inflation running in double figures on the national market - is no mean feat. It was a satisfactory result to which several factors contributed:

Firstly the satisfactory performance of the Italian market and the good profitability of markets outside Europe, in particular Nigeria, Libya, Egypt, Algeria and Tunisia, which still showed no signs of crisis and which represented for Iveco a very important billing share mainly made up of heavy vehicles.

Then came the rationalisation of the ranges and commercial measures started in the previous years and also the start of a more radical reorganisation of production. The crisis made everyone understand that it was not sufficient to rationalise the structures, it was also necessary to eliminate production capacity which was not used.

The redundancy programme started in 1980 - approx. 3,000 people or 6% of the Iveco workforce in just one year - and continued in the years to follow.

1982 saw the first closure of a factory, the one in Mainz, which had employed 1,500 people.

In Italy, they could always go to the integration fund at the last

179

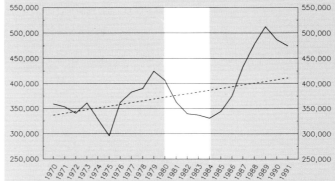

DEMAND FOR TRUCKS IN WESTERN EUROPE
TOTAL FROM 3.5 TONNE GVW

1980	....	407004
1981	....	363112
1982	....	339784
1983	....	336893
1984	....	330565

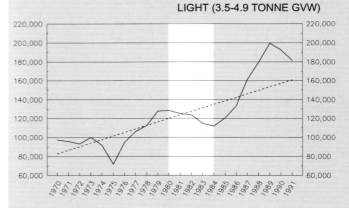

DEMAND FOR TRUCKS IN WESTERN EUROPE
LIGHT (3.5-4.9 TONNE GVW)

1980	....	128597
1981	....	125080
1982	....	123895
1983	....	114665
1984	....	111919

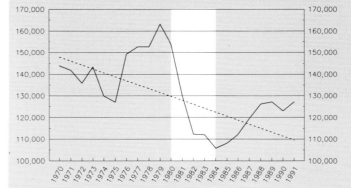

DEMAND FOR TRUCKS IN WESTERN EUROPE
MEDIUM (5.0-15.9 TONNE GVW)

1980	....	153867
1981	....	129744
1982	....	112277
1983	....	112100
1984	....	105746

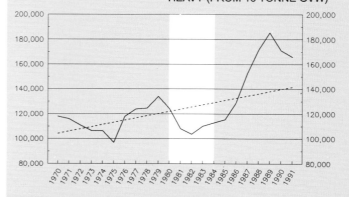

DEMAND FOR TRUCKS IN WESTERN EUROPE
HEAVY (FROM 16 TONNE GVW)

1980	....	124540
1981	....	108288
1982	....	103612
1983	....	110128
1984	....	112900

minute, but whilst the new factory at Valle Ufita became operative, there was the prospect of closing the factory at Cameri (which was then saved by the Rockwell agreement for the production of axles).

A rigid freeze on investments was also implemented. They dropped from the peak of 556 million Guilders in 1978 to 242 million in 1980 and 222 in 1981.

In spite of all this, the company's indebtedness was very high, more than 4,370 million Guilders in 1981 (compared with 928 in 1976, and just over 2,000 in 1977).

Since reorganisation is expensive, investments are also expensive, particularly if there is no self-financing opportunity, a chance to find the necessary resources from within the company.

This was the situation when the 1982 crisis descended on the market.

This was a crisis which not only hit the Western economies but also - for the first time - the developing countries, causing a drop in the markets outside Europe.

Iveco in particular suffered from the difficult recession which affected Nigeria, reduced the capacity of Libya and created problems in Egypt, Algeria and Tunisia.

The situation was further aggravated by the increased strength of the Japanese who, at that time, were starting to establish their light and medium vehicles in all the countries of North Africa and the Middle East.

So the crisis dealt a heavy blow to all the markets and, in particular, to Italy, constitutionally already weak through the chronic squandering of its resources.

For the industrial vehicle sector these were the years of the "price war", the discount battle with a reduction in margins to lure buyers.

It was also a very hard period for Iveco which suffered a drastic reversal in its turnover and billing trend and found itself in the red again within two years.

The decline was to last for the next three years: 102,000 vehicles (11,000 down, i.e. a drop of approx. 10% compared with 1981) and 9,538 million Guilders in 1982, still with a modest profit,

DEMAND FOR TRUCKS IN WESTERN EUROPE
(BY COUNTRY FROM 3.5 TONNE GVW)

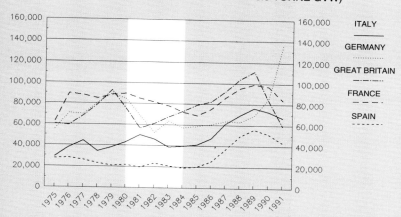

ITALY
GERMANY
GREAT BRITAIN
FRANCE
SPAIN

	ITALY	GERMANY	GREAT BRITAIN	FRANCE	SPAIN
1980	43363	84718	75361	89806	21710
1981	50279	68674	56516	85142	19748
1982	46562	52809	61363	85142	19748
1983	38829	63491	67572	81670	23528
1984	39821	57398	73310	72468	19158

DEMAND FOR TRUCKS
(TOTAL FROM 3.5 TONNE GVW)

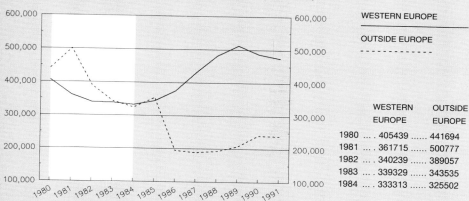

WESTERN EUROPE

OUTSIDE EUROPE

	WESTERN EUROPE	OUTSIDE EUROPE
1980	405439	441694
1981	361715	500777
1982	340239	389057
1983	339329	343535
1984	333313	325502

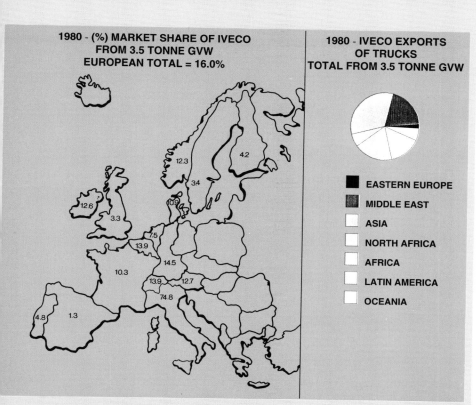

1980 - (%) MARKET SHARE OF IVECO FROM 3.5 TONNE GVW
EUROPEAN TOTAL = 16.0%

1980 - IVECO EXPORTS OF TRUCKS
TOTAL FROM 3.5 TONNE GVW

- EASTERN EUROPE
- MIDDLE EAST
- ASIA
- NORTH AFRICA
- AFRICA
- LATIN AMERICA
- OCEANIA

16 million; just under 96,000 vehicles and 8,266 million Guilders (1,300 less) in 1983, already with a loss of more than 230 million; and barely 90,320 vehicles in 1984, with a slightly increased billing, approx. 100 million, but with a loss running at nearly 395 million Guilders. Fortunately, the crisis had peaked and the recovery started the following year.

In those difficult times, Iveco defended itself as well as it could. It persevered with its policy to reduce costs: in 1984, the number of employees had dropped to 35,000, i.e. 30% less compared with the 50,000 in 1979. And it maintained its freeze on investments: from 600 million Guilders in 1978, they fell to nearly 190 million in 1984.

1983 saw a new peak - nearly 337 million Guilders (more than 4% of the billing), a result of the costs incurred to close the Trappes factory and for the investments in the new factory at Valle Ufita; and for those intended for Bourbon-Lancy, which was converted from producing tractor parts (transferred to Modena) to engine parts (originally made in Brescia). In the following years Bourbon-Lancy again was to benefit from considerable investment in automation.

In the meantime, to contain an indebtedness which in 1981 reached a peak of nearly 4,400 million Guilders, Fiat, the parent company, intervened with the issuing of a conditional loan between 1983 and 1986 ("conditional" because it was destined to be transformed into an increase in registered capital, which was to take place in 1987).

IVNET - IVECO'S COMPUTER NETWORK - IS DEVELOPED

When Iveco was set up a considerable degree of integration had already been achieved within the Gruppo Veicoli Industriali. This integration included methods and management tools.

The three areas of the group were more or less coordinated at the time, particularly with regard to the computer systems: Turin with the Fiat connections, OM in Brescia (which included Suzzara), Unic in France, which had come on stream later but was already at a sufficiently advanced level of standardisation.

Three computer worlds born of a common mother - the Turin production module was the same as that of Brescia, the same as the French one - but sufficiently autonomous: there were local programming units which personalised the procedures on the basis of the specific requirements.

Each factory had a certain number of computers connected to the production point for which they were responsible. The major part of this area concerned production control.

It must be remembered that at the time we had barely entered the era of computers with a certain processing capacity. We were at the stage of "mechanising" procedures in the production and administrative areas.

"Mechanising" meaning running existing manual procedures on a computer: the punched card was the first means of mechanisation.

The conceptual leap to "automation" was made when the computer was used to manage procedures which had not been done manually or which were done in a different way.

Typically, payments are still mechanised today because the procedure, imposed by the law, is more or less always the same: it is simply faster to work with a computer than manually. And the same applies to accounts.

However, if the programming of suppliers, or certain methods of processing orders are done by computer rather than manually this not only changed the speed, but substantially changes the amount and quality of the data which can be processed.

Returning to Iveco, the arrival of Magirus meant integrating a completely different production and organisational system into G.V.I.

The differences were substantial, for example the hardware systems were Honeywell at G.V.I. but IBM at Magirus (Brescia, which had used IBM systems originally, had been converted).

And since, at the time, the software was strictly correlated with the hardware, each of the parties used independent programs: for production, purchase, and everything generally connected with calculations.

The transfer of data from one area to another and from one point to another was done in a basic and traditional way. Consequently time and energy were initially lost in trying to transfer a Honeywell system to Ulm to process the software of Italian origin.

But this was always at a very marginal level. The core systems remained the original Magirus systems, which were based on IBM.

At the same time however, in around 1974 to 1975, the first experiments were carried out for transmitting data by telephone line. Data entry machines were used (where, instead of punching cards, data were recorded on magnetic tape) which transmitted the data from one to the other when connected by telephone. Until, in 1980, the first communications network emerged which was able to transcend the point to point connections concept, this simple transmission of data on line allowed a dialogue between automatic control systems.

And so the foundation of "Ivnet" (Iveco network) was laid, a network which emerged at the level of technological availability and as an immediate application for that technology. It linked both factories and countries.

At the time practically no one in Italy spoke of network in the strict sense of the word. Nor were they to do so for a considerable time to come. But, by its very nature, Iveco had been given a considerable impetus to integrate and to communicate, because the languages were different, the cultures were different and the distances were great.

To have an efficient means of communication was a strategic factor for the survival of the company.

In just a few years Ivnet expanded into a major network extending throughout Europe, integrating the public and private networks of the various countries passed through, allowing data to be transferred in any form and at any place in Iveco's territory.

For example, a terminal at a Belgian subsidiary which was working in real time with Turin had access to its own national network which was integrated into the French network, itself integrated with Iveco's Paris outpost. From here, the connection continued until it reached the end user. Apart from making it possible to communicate, Ivnet also assumed another very important task in the initial stage: that of allowing the different systems operating at Iveco to understand each other and to dialogue with each other in an intelligible language. At least in one direction. Ivnet was created as a superimposition of three different networks corresponding to the three processing standards initially operative at Iveco: IBM, Honeywell and Digital.

And Ivnet was structured so that it was possible to look inside the IBM network from any terminal, whether based on Honeywell or Digital technology.

Consequently, Ivnet became the instrument which allowed Iveco's computer process to make the first steps in the direction of effective integration. And it is on this that all future moves were based and developed.

In 1982 - 1983, the Ivnet network had already reached a significant size in relation to the systems of the time and all the Iveco processing centres - Paris, Turin, Brescia, Foggia and Ulm - had an infrastructure network, i.e. interconnecting hardware.

It was at this stage, in the full flow of divisionalisation, that it was decided to activate the Iveco information system - then called

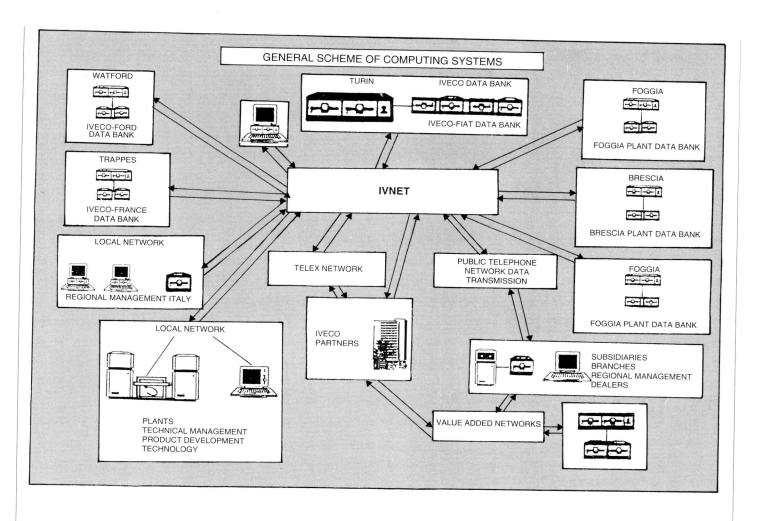

Information Resources (IR) - in order to improve efficiency in the computer sector too.

The aim was to make sure that if the company wanted to develop a certain processing program, certain software (let us say for marketing in France), this would be structured with aims and specifications which would make it suitable for use throughout the Iveco organisation.

This opportunity represented an integrated move towards achieving a single type of hardware throughout Iveco.

In the same period, following the development of the computer market, it was decided that the new standard would be IBM.

A gradual conversion was implemented. Then, from 1985, the conversion process was accelerated with the launch of the central database and the twin computer centre.

THE "LOGISTICS" FOUNDATIONS ARE LAID

Still at the beginning of the Eighties, whilst the computer network was being installed and the new hardware and software standards established, Iveco was laying the foundations of a new department destined to play a key role in the company's future.

1983 saw the birth of logistics, a "science" aimed at improving the control of the market production flow.

At the time, the link between the network (dealers and trade) and the production coordination centres was based on information provided by telephone, telex and the first faxes.

And the interface between the entire business world and the production world consisted of a structure which can only be defined as being of "cottage industry" standard.

So something else was needed to ensure the necessary efficiency and speed of response of an organisation of the complexity and size of Iveco.

A true generational leap had to be made and it was to be achieved in the second half of the decade with a substantial contribution being made by computer systems.

In the early eighties the development of IVNET started, the telecommunications network which towards the mid-eighties would enable Iveco to gain maximum advantage from the potential offered by the most advanced information technology.

LOGISTICS -
A NEW "SCIENCE"

But what is this new science, heralded as a true revolution in industrial management, and how does it operate? It is difficult to explain.

As already mentioned, the logistics department was set up for the purpose of optimising everything connected with the product and the market: the acquisition and analysis of data collected from the markets; the processing of forecasts; programming production and supplies from outside suppliers; the management of vehicles in stock; deliveries; spares management; etc.

The preliminary studies conducted in those years indicated two possible ways forward:

One was a system which combined production and management systems into a number of centres, each controlling a particular product range; to put it extremely briefly, a certain factory becomes a main contractor and has to deal with the markets as if they were its outlets for its product range.

Certainly a valid approach, but one which is only feasible when operating in an economic, social and legislative context which allows the "flexibility" in terms of production volumes, which is necessary to compensate for the inevitable fluctuations in the market.

It is known that the "cyclic" patterns of demand are never synchronised in all the markets and in all product sectors. It is quite normal for a surplus of orders in one sector to be offset by stagnation or recession in another. At a time when a given market or set of markets is not pulling in the right direction, it is necessary to be able to redimension the production centre concerned by reducing the production volume.

If this is not possible, it is necessary to reallocate production - i.e. to move it physically, tooling up another factory - a situation which is always very expensive for any industry not only in terms of finance and investment, but also because of the disruption from the point of view of organisation and production schedules.

But in the European context - and even more so in Italy - flexibility was thin on the ground.

And so it had to be realised that rightly or wrongly, it was not possible to impose a type of organisation based on an assumed stable production allocation over a long period.

This was true for the factories concerned with the final assembly and equipping the vehicles, whereas in the industrial vehicle sector, those concerned with machining did not have sufficient volume to allow multi-allocation. In the case of Iveco, the exception to the rule was the engine division which had separate factories for the Sofim, a "small" large volume engine, and the 6-8 cylinder engines with a bigger cylinder capacity.

So it was the assembly factories which mopped up more manpower and which demanded a greater organisational effort.

Let us remember that a single vehicle is made up of more than 4,000 parts and even if just one bolt is lost, the assembly work cannot be completed.

Going back to the problem of logistics, bearing in mind that multi-allocation is a real, historical requirement, and that there are no precedents for relying on stability, another way was chosen for the future of Iveco.

This was to have a single nerve centre for controlling the product/market coordination, equipped with the necessary tools for programming the vehicles independently of the allocation and the progress (forecast, order, machining, equipment, stocks, delivery, etc.) of production.

This was to be a commercial and production programming centre able to control multiple allocations at the same time, in other words, the allocation movements.

Chassis ready for the bodywork, in an evocative telephoto shot of the bus plant at Valle Ufita.

IVECO WORKS ON STRENGTHENING ITS IMAGE

The wind of innovation blowing through Iveco from the beginning of the Eighties also veered towards its image.

Whilst strengthening all the departments of the company, the need to restate its new identity to the outside world became more pressing.

This was done in various ways. They modified the ratio of strength between the Iveco mark and the historic marks both on the vehicles and generally at communication level.

They aimed to make the name of Iveco more familiar to the public - on its own, without complex references to parentage or kinship - by mounting a new sponsorship campaign.

As far as the identification of the vehicles was concerned, the first signs of change were seen after 1980 when the first stage (that of the diamond with "I" for Iveco) was followed by a second, when the historic mark was accompanied by the Iveco logo written in full.

At that time, neither the mutual positions nor the hierarchical relationship changed.

The change came two years later in 1982, when the roles were reversed: the Iveco logo was moved to the centre of the radiator and its size was increased.

At the same time, the historical Magirus Deutz mark was standardised, losing the bell tower and the Deutz part of the name.

In the years which immediately followed, the Unic mark was abandoned, so then there were countries and markets only using the Iveco mark.

In those years they also built up the campaign to promote the image and product of Iveco, this time in two directions: publicity campaigns and sponsorships.

Regarding advertising, the Iveco planets were gradually combined with the plus features of the product - i.e. the "turbo" adopted by Iveco for its engines from 1981 - or with a scene on whose background the planet turns and which captures the essence of the message to be communicated.

For example they used the English word "transport" when they wanted to highlight the idea that Iveco was working in the interests of transport; the words "research and technology" when they wanted to convey the idea of commitment in the field of research and technology. Sometimes there were other planets with historic marks of Iveco, this time to emphasise the transnationality and multi-cultural heritage of the holding company.

As a matter of interest, in 1983, Iveco's publicity campaign received the "best remembered" award of the American journal Business Week, as voted by its readers. The other road pursued by Iveco to communicate its image was that of sponsorship. Launched at the beginning of the Eighties, and then continued throughout the decade, it started with major sporting events and was gradually extended to expeditions, long distance races and scientific missions.

Couched in these terms, the subject became more complex, because it assumed the connotations of an image strategy aimed at persuading the people (in the broadest sense of the word) to perceive Iveco as a manufacturer producing for transport.

Bearing this aspect in mind, towards the end of the decade, they decided on a particular form of sponsorship which involved supplying the product directly to those involved and to the organising committees.

Typical examples are the support given to the Jacques Cousteau expeditions and to the 1990 World Cup event.

On the opposite page, through the "mark" displayed on the vehicle front, Iveco has developed its image from 1975 until the present day.

187

FROM WORLD SPORT TO MAJOR EXPEDITIONS

Let us quickly leaf through the diary of Iveco's presence on the scene of international sport and major expeditions.

It all started in 1978 when Magirus-Deutz sponsored the internationally famous football club Bayern Munich.

1980 was the year of the Moscow Olympics when Iveco sponsored an athletic team worthy of a US college with a long tradition - in fact three gold medals were awarded - with Maurizio Damilano, Petro Mennea and Sara Simeoni.

Still in 1980, the "Pigafetta Race" was completed after two years and eight months on the road and 184,000 km on the clock in Europe, Asia, Australia, Africa, South and North America, passing through 48 countries. The vehicle was the Iveco-Fiat 75 PC 4x4, the first truck ever to complete the round the world trip.

1981 was the first year of the big fight which saw Iveco sponsoring the boxing match between Leonard and Hearnes in Las Vegas: an event which was televised to some 400 million viewers in more than 50 countries. A month later, in October, there was a repeat performance with the double world championship in Chicago.

It was also the year of the expedition of the Castiglionni brothers, Angelo and Alfredo, in a 75 PC 4x4 and an off road car, following in the tracks of the 19th century explorers: more than 20,000 km from Timbuktu to Guinea, from Sudan to the Republic of Central Africa, emulating Caillé in 1827, Piaggia and Barth in 1849 and Nactigal in 1869.

Still in 1981, and in spite of heavy rain, 60,000 spectators watched the first 24 hour Le Mans for trucks. Iveco was the winner.

The early eighties: the still young Iveco name is brought to the public's attention through sponsorship of international sporting events and major scientific and humanitarian expeditions.

1982 was another boxing year, sponsoring Top Rank, a prestigious series of 64 matches; and it was the year of athletics, when the Iveco team was joined by Gabriella Dorio, the middle distance runner from Venice and holder of the Italian 800 m and 1500 m records. It was also the year of tennis, sponsoring the Davis cup.

And the year of the expedition. "Commander" Jacques Cousteau set off in the "Calipso" to explore the Amazon basin, a fresh water sea the size of an ocean. The expedition equipment included an Iveco "amphibian" produced at Lancia in Bolzano.

This brings us to 1983, another year filled with important events: sponsoring of the English football team, Watford; second place for the Iveco women's team in the athletic championships in Madrid and sponsoring of the first athletics world championship in Helsinki; sponsoring of the boxing match between Hagler and Duran, referred to as "the match of the century", and sponsoring of the world ski cup.

Iveco also tried its hand at Formula 1 with the Toleman Shield, but it was not to be a lucky season.

Two 75 PC 4x4 vehicles took part in the 83rd Paris to Dakar rally providing organisational support and transporting the press and television entourage. And in the truck competitions, Iveco also successfully competed in the second "24 hour Le Mans".

The next two years were dedicated to adventure. In 1984, again it was the turn of the Paris to Dakar race, with five Iveco trucks, three 190.26 NW and two 80.14 HW, used to assist the competitors, and also the Rally of the Pharaohs, which was assisted by three 40 PM 4x4 (for the judges and the press plus an ambulance) and one 90 PC 16 4x4 equipped as a mobile office.

1985 and again it was the Rally of the Pharaohs, this time with a complete range of vehicles from the 90 PC to the Daily 4x4 and

the TurboStar 190.42. The Venice to Pechino race was completed in three months and covered nearly 20,000 km. Three Panda 4x4s and a TurboDaily 40.10 WM were used, the latter powered by the new direct injection, turbo diesel version of the Sofim engine.

In 1986 Iveco took part in events organised in connection with European road safety year promoted by the EC. Iveco, Pirelli and Agip were the most important sponsors of the "truck driver of the year" competition, organised to emphasise the importance of correct driving habits to improve the truck driver's image with other road users.

In 1987 Iveco again sponsored the world light athletic competion in Rome but this time as a technical supporter, transporting the athletes in thirty 370 S buses, twenty four Orlandi "Pokers", two "Domino High Deckers" and two 315 "Pokers". In the meantime, the TurboStar starred in thirteen episodes of the TV serial "Two Axles for a Turbo" produced by the Italian Broadcasting Corporation.

In 1988 the Orlandi "Poker" was the vehicle used by Radio Pechino for its tour of Europe.

Finally, in 1990, Iveco again sponsored the football World Cup.

MARKET MANAGEMENT IS CENTRALISED

With the divisional reorganisation at Iveco, it was also possible to start on the reorganisation of the sales networks on the various markets.

The departure of KHD from the holding company had made it possible to remove certain basic obstacles and it was also possible to work more freely, as is emphasised by the necessary clean-up operations connected with the trade-mark strategy.

Everything had to fit into a complex framework and it soon became apparent that it would never be possible to improve the situation in one go.

So it was decided to operate in stages and 1982 saw the start of a plan for the rationalised management of the networks: apart from placing the networks of each of the markets under the control of a single centralised departmental director, the local managements were disbanded, entrusting each market to a single national manager.

This was the case with Germany for example where, at that time, a Fiat network and a Magirus network operated in parallel, each controlled completely independently by its own manager. As a first step towards rationalisation, the German "major market" was created and one manager was made responsible for both Fiat sales and Magirus sales within it.

And the same thing in France, where the Head of the Unic network was also made responsible for the management of Magirus France.

The next step was the actual process of standardisation itself and this was the responsibility of the Iveco subsidiaries.

It was not possible to adopt one criterion and a single timescale: on some markets the trademarks were standardised immediately, whereas on others, a more gradual approach was needed.

On the whole this process (which reached its peak in 1986-1987, ending in 1989 with the creation of the Finnish subsidiary) either resulted in achieving economies

of scale - in those countries where several Iveco makes were brought into competition with each other by different importers - or "planting the flag" for the first time as Iveco, as in the case of Switzerland and Spain. The strategy of replacing the importer by a direct presence was based on two factors.

On the one hand, with the market in crisis, the dealers were no longer able to sustain business. This happened in Holland, Portugal and later in Finland. And on the other, there was an awareness that this was the right way to achieve a closer and deeper relationship with the markets with a management aimed more at the customer than at the immediate benefits to the point of sale.

On the "domestic" market, this process more or less meant making the national company responsible for all the networks.

This happened in Italy where the Magirus network was added to the "historic" Fiat and OM networks; Magirus was to be closed, whilst the management of

the OM network was to be transferred to Turin, finally achieving the single Iveco network.

Likewise in Germany where the network of Fiat LKW was incorporated in that of Iveco Magirus.

And in France where the Unic network finally absorbed the Magirus organisation, a direct subsidiary of considerable size which was progressively re-dimensioned and finally removed. The newly constituted Iveco network became responsible for selling the Magirus product under the supervision of a manager with specific responsibility for Magirus.

Similar processes took place in England where Fiat Commercial Vehicles was integrated into Magirus UK, which then became Iveco UK Limited.

In Switzerland, with a separate network for OM products (via the Saurer network, within the tradition of cooperation between Saurer and OM in engine design), Fiat and Magirus were merged into Iveco Schweiz AG and

194

maintained separate marks for a certain time.

In Austria, where Magirus had two networks, one a direct sales network and the other an importer network, Fiat controlled a small network via an importer in the Southern part of the country and Steyr sold the OM vehicles. Iveco Austria GmbH was created in the process of integration.

In Spain, where the customs duties were prohibitive, vehicles were not imported and the national manufacturers were monopolists. Iveco Espana SA was set up and started to import Iveco Fiat products directly.

In Portugal, where there was one importer for Fiat buses, a Magirus importer and also an importer with a local assembly plant for OM vehicles, everything was integrated into Iveco Portugal Lda. In Belgium where there was an importer selling OM products, another for Fiat and a third for Magirus, SA Iveco Belgium NV was set up and the network was recreated to some extent.

In Holland, Magirus had a fire-fighting vehicle assembly facility (which was closed) and an importer. Although Fiat was not present, they set up Iveco Nederland BV and the entire network was set up more or less from scratch.

In Denmark, which was one of the countries which tended to import Fiat products and which had a limited Magirus presence, they set up Iveco Danmark AS.

In Ireland, where there was a Fiat importer, Iveco Ireland Limited was launched (later, bearing in mind the very small numbers, they were to resort to being an importer again). In Scandinavia, Iveco Norge AS, Iveco Sweden AB and finally Iveco Finland OY were launched.

This left Greece which was the home of Magirus Hellas which also assembled city buses. But because its performance was poor, it was closed, so from then on they relied on an importer. The same applied in Cyprus and Israel.

As far as outside Europe was concerned, the trend moved more in the direction of industrial agreements and joint ventures and therefore this development will be described separately.

RATIONALISATION ALSO REVOLUTIONISES DESIGN AND PRODUCTION

In the first half of the Eighties the design and production scenes saw major changes, a consequence of the new strategies initiated in connection with the "departmental" reorganisation of the company. This was followed by the creation of the divisions, rationalisation of the ranges and production and "deverticalisation" in the component sector, a cost-saving plan based on reducing surplus production capacity.

This resulted in the closure of three factories: SPA Torino (employing 3,500 people) in Italy, Mainz in Germany and Trappes in France. This was after transferring bus production to Valle Ufita and converting Cameri to the production of axles under the Omevi-CVC agreement. As a consequence of these events, design and production started to go their separate ways. Let us see what happened.

As far as vehicle and component design were concerned (testing was carried out more or less exclusively in Turin and Ulm), the medium range vehicles, including the former Trappes vehicles, and buses were concentrated at Turin. However, Turin lost the medium and heavy axles, which were transferred to Cameri, and the heavy on-and-off-highway vehicles which were concentrated at Ulm.

Ulm continued to make the "Club" vehicles, special vehicles, fire-fighting vehicles and buses.

Brescia kept the light "S" and "Z" vehicles, gearboxes, shafts and axles, but lost the torque converters. Milan had the light shafts and axles. Suzzara had no design facility.

Bolzano continued to concentrate on military and armoured vehicles. Engine design within the diesel engine division was at Arbon and Turin which were responsible for engineering and testing; small design facilities were still operative at Trappes and Brescia, whilst Foggia and Bourbon-Lancy tested the relative productions.

Aifo concentrated on special applications.

Let us look at the production allocation.

In Italy, Turin produced medium and heavy on-and-off-highway vehicles, the 8000 and 8280 engines, truck chassis and bus chassis. Cameri produced medium and heavy axles, Milan, light shafts and axles and Brescia, the "S" and "Z" light vehicles, 8360 engines, gearboxes, light shafts and axles. Suzzara made the van versions of the "S" range plus the Fiat 900 T commercial vehicle. Bolzano made the military and armoured vehicles, Valle Ufita the buses and Foggia made the 8100 engines.

In France, Bourbon-Lancy kept the 8220 and 8210 engines and Fourchamboult continued to produce buses.

Ulm remained operative in Germany, with the heavy on-and-off-road vehicles, the "Club" vehicles, special military vehicles and also fire-fighting vehicles and buses.

195

CAD ENTERS THE DESIGN STAGE

In the early Eighties, the ambitious "computerisation" plan heralded the arrival of CAD - Computer Aided Design - which was to become a key instrument for future design development.

The first experimental work in this field dates back to 1979 and the first "official" station was bought in 1980. More of these stations were already operative in 1981.

These were non-intelligent stations, i.e. VDUs controlled by a central processor made up of Vax 780 systems, each of which controlled four stations. In 1984 the first "intelligent" - i.e. independent - stations were installed and from then on, the growth was very rapid (today there are approx. 200 stations representing approximately 1 for every two and a half designers).

In 1980 Iveco also acquired a laser beam holograph developed by the Fiat Research Centre for the non-destructive testing of structures exposed to static or dynamic stresses.

In the years 1983 to 1985, the test benches for testing the engines were progressively automated both in terms of control and data acquisition.

Since the early eighties CAD (Computer Aided Design) has been on the Iveco scene, an invaluable systems tool for all aspects of design.

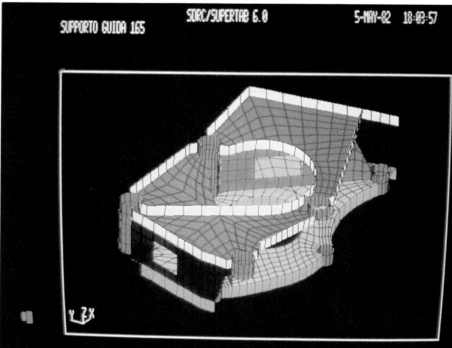

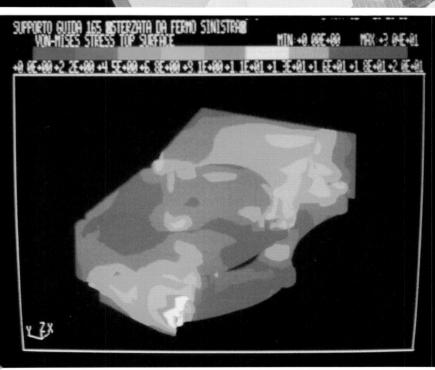

SUPPORTO GUIDA 165 ASTERZATA DA FERMO SINISTRA0
VON-MISES STRESS TOP SURFACE   MIN +0.00E+00   MAX +2.04E+01

+0.0E+00 +2.2E+00 +4.5E+00 +6.8E+00 +9.1E+00 +1.1E+01 +1.3E+01 +1.5E+01 +1.8E+01 +2.0E+01

LASER, PLASMA AND VIDEO CAMERA FOR QUALITY CONTROL IN PRODUCTION

In the same period, innovation was also concentrated on production technology. They talked about a "new way" of producing, about flexible manufacturing systems and Just-in-Time and new technologies for production control. Numerous pilot plants were commisioned at SPA Torino: a system for testing for superficial cracks in distributor shafts; a laser system for checking the roughness of the engine shaft pins; a video system for checking the drilling of the chassis members.

In 1983 - 1984, new production technologies were introduced.

Turin introduced plasma cutting in the stamping shop.

Turin also installed an acoustic signalling system for testing the strength of welding spots in the body shop, whilst Brescia introduced a robotised cell in the panel shop for assembling doors.

Brescia also introduced an automatic enamel spraying system using rotating cups and in Bourbon-Lancy, the running and diagnostic cycles in the engine test rooms were automated with the help of a central computerised system.

Brescia introduced robotised cells and automated the gear and shaft grinding lines in the machining shops. They also started to weld the clutch rings using an electronic beam. These years also signalled the first steps in the direction of computer aided manufacture, or CAM.

LIMO, a factory system for monitoring and supporting the production process by monitoring the assembly lines, started work in Turin, Brescia and Suzzara.

And the first flexible automation systems for machining parts of heavy engines were installed at Bourbon-Lancy.

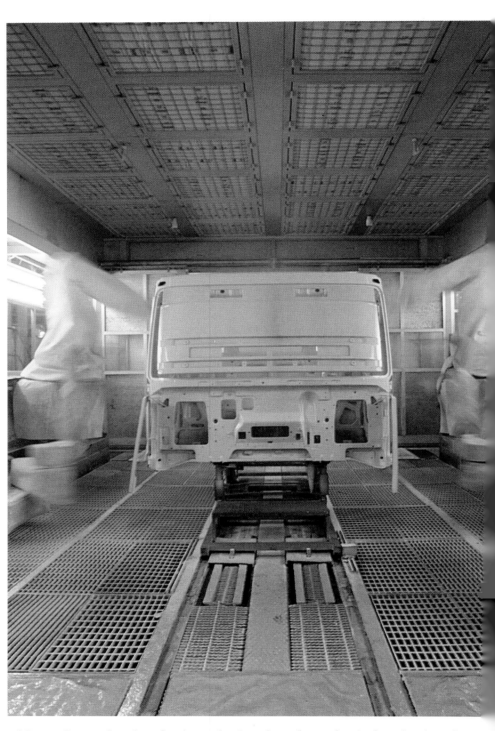

Advanced examples of production technology from the mechanical production of engines (top right) to electro-plating and the spray shop (bottom right and directly above, Brescia).

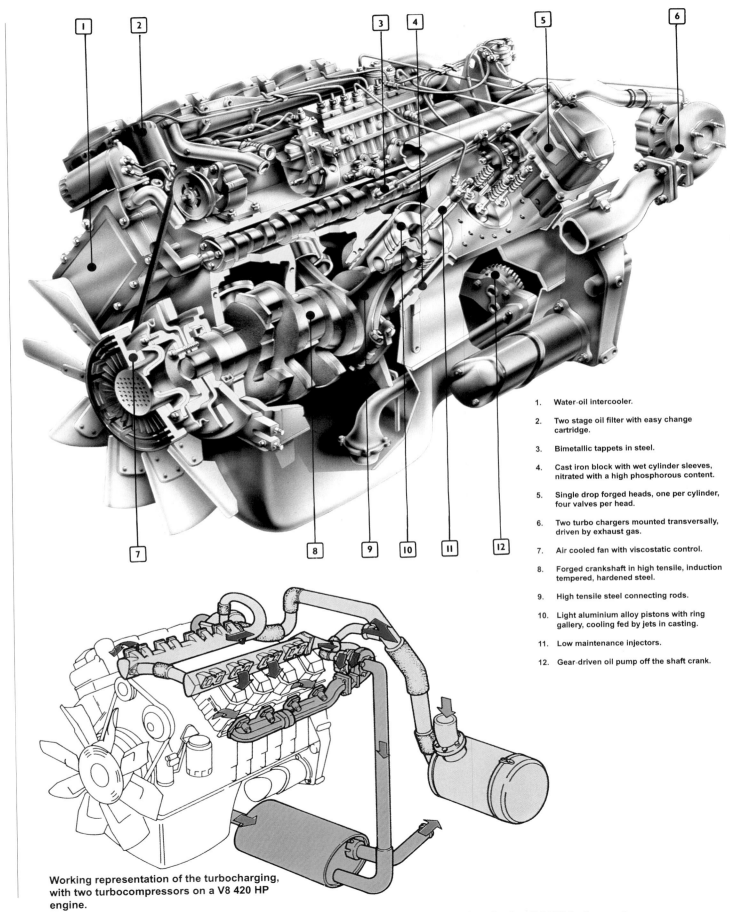

1. Water-oil intercooler.

2. Two stage oil filter with easy change cartridge.

3. Bimetallic tappets in steel.

4. Cast iron block with wet cylinder sleeves, nitrated with a high phosphorous content.

5. Single drop forged heads, one per cylinder, four valves per head.

6. Two turbo chargers mounted transversally, driven by exhaust gas.

7. Air cooled fan with viscostatic control.

8. Forged crankshaft in high tensile, induction tempered, hardened steel.

9. High tensile steel connecting rods.

10. Light aluminium alloy pistons with ring gallery, cooling fed by jets in casting.

11. Low maintenance injectors.

12. Gear-driven oil pump off the shaft crank.

Working representation of the turbocharging, with two turbocompressors on a V8 420 HP engine.

The 17.2 litre Iveco 8280 engine, with 8 cylinders in a "V" configuration, in the 420 HP turbo version.

FROM TURBO ENGINES TO THE DEBUT OF THE TURBOSTAR

The Eighties were highly innovative, especially from the point of view of the product.
Iveco purposefully embarked on the "turbo" supercharger, using it throughout its range from the heavy vehicles to the TurboDaily, in rapid succession.
This was also the time when, following the "nth" rationalisation process, the use of the Deutz engine was restricted - apart from its use in connection with the "Club" range - to site vehicles and special Magirus applications such as fire-fighting and military vehicles.
In the first few months of 1980, the Deutz engine was removed from the "Z" range and, at the same time, the air-cooled engine was eliminated from the "Club" vehicles destined for the American market.
The Deutz engine was then removed from the medium vehicle range, the Trappes range, whose production had been transferred to Turin in the meantime.
Finally, the Deutz engine was also removed from the heavy road vehicles, from the vehicles produced by SPA, and from the buses.
At the end of the process the Deutz engine was to remain with the "Club" range and with the forward cab and the "nose" versions of the heavy site vehicles.

RESTYLING OF THE HEAVY VEHICLES, A NEW GENERATION OF MEDIUM TO HEAVY VEHICLES

As far as the vehicles were concerned, in 1981, the cab of the heavy road vehicle range was restyled both inside and out with new versions and options added to the range, including rear pneumatic suspension on request.
In the same period the medium to heavy 180.24 and 180.26 - effectively the successors of the 684 and 160 of the Seventies - were launched.
These were powered by the 9.6 litre 6 cylinder 240 HP turbo version of the 8220 engine and the 260 HP, 13.8 litre naturally aspirated 8210.
In the construction sector, turbo engines were also introduced in this range from 1981, initially on the vehicles at the 19 tonne limit. The PA family was enlarged with the new 330.32, 6x4 and 6x6 with the Deutz 320 HP, 16 litre V10 aspirated engine.
From 1983, the 260.30 and 330.30 versions were introduced equipped with the 304 HP, 13.8 litre 6 cylinder 8210 turbo engine.

NEW INTERNAL FINISH AND TURBO ENGINE FOR THE DAILY

In 1981 there was also the first generation change for the light "S" range vehicles which, with the new cab interior, and having overcome the teething problems of the Sofim engine, were steering towards their brilliant future. In the years which followed, the range "grew" in tonnage and engine power, with the introduction in 1984 of the new 35.10, 45.10 and 49.10 models powered by a development of the Sofim 8140 engine: cylinder capacity increased from 2,440 cc to 2,499 cc and they featured direct injection rather than a precombustion chamber and turbo charging. They developed a power of 92 HP. The 4x4 military version was launched in the same year.
In 1984, the Daily also became "electric": it had a range of approx. 80 km, a speed of 55 km/h and the minibus version had 8 seats and a passenger capacity of 15. The transformation had been made from the forklift trucks.

RESTYLING AND NEW VERSIONS FOR THE 'ZETA' VEHICLES

1982 was the year when the "Z" range of light vehicles was given a new look. The cab was restyled both inside and out and this was accompanied by the introduction of the new 65.10 and 79.13 models with tilt cab.
The vans had a plastic roof which made it possible to increase the volume up to a maximum of 18.3m³.
In the early Eighties, versions of the "Z" range were also made for the USA: the Z100, 4.5 tonner with Deutz 100 HP F5L912 engine was followed in 1982 by 4.5 to 6.7 tonne versions with a 110 HP and 125 HP aspirated water-cooled engines and a 120 HP turbo engine. In 1984, a 7.9 tonne version with a 130/140 HP turbo engine was launched.

THE MEDIUM RANGE IS EXTENDED

1982 also saw a new rationalisation stage in the medium range which was connected with the closure of the Trappes factory.
The 110 was equipped with the 138 HP aspirated version of the 5.9 litre, 6 cylinder 8060 and became the 110.14; at the opposite end of the range, after the 159, they added the 165.24 with a 240 BHP turbo version of the 9.6 litre 6 cylinder 8220 engine, both in the truck and tractor versions.
A year later the 110 and 130 were replaced by the 115 and 135 (in practice, the same model but with different suspension and tyres), in both the cab and tractor versions.
The 5.9 litre, 6 cylinder 8060 engine was available both in the 138 HP aspirated version and in the 168 HP turbo version.
The 110.14 was also offered in the 4x4 version which was derived from the corresponding "Club" model and was equipped with the 8060 water-cooled engine.

A CHRISTENING WHICH WAS TO MAKE HISTORY: THE "TURBOSTAR" WAS BORN

In the summer of 1984 the TurboStar was launched with the 190.33 and 190.42 engines. This was a vehicle whose technical and "image" content tipped the scales in the heavy road transport sector. It was destined to become a best seller on the Italian market and score brilliant successes throughout Europe with 50,000 sold in seven years (by September 1991).

Even if it had been developed on the basis of the 190.38, the TurboStar was more or less a new vehicle, and not just in terms of its extremely spacious and comfortable cab.

It was necessary to develop nearly 2,000 specific components to make it . But, apart from its product content and its major image contribution, the TurboStar was a very important part of Iveco's history, because it was the first true embodiment of that consolidation of different cultures which had laid the foundations of Iveco.

The TurboStar was born as a product and grew as a commercial reality thanks to the knowhow and work contributed by several national entities: German engineering; Italian production technology and logistics and the particularly dynamic commercial thrust of the French market.

The highlights of the TurboStar were its cab and engine.

As far as the former was concerned, they had aimed at improved levels of ease and comfort, with an internal height of 1.70 m and a sophisticated suspension system for the cab itself. There were two engines: the 330 HP turbo after cooler version of the 13.8 litre, 6 cylinder 8210 and the 420 HP turbo version of the 17.2 litre V8, 8280.

WITH THE DEPARTMENTAL STRUCTURE CAME THE DIVISIONS

At the beginning of the Eighties, at the time when Iveco's management was being reorganised in departmental form, all the areas of activity of the holding company outside industrial vehicle manufacture were grouped to form a division solely responsible for their coordination.

This was a fortunate move which made it possible to optimise control of those activities which, together, represented less than 20% of the total billing of the holding company - forklift trucks, fire-fighting vehicles, defence vehicles, industrial and marine engines, and the buses - which, as small fish of a very special kind, had not been able to express their full product and market potential in the large Iveco pond.

An overview of the product sectors - engines or complete vehicles - covered by Iveco through the activities of the divisions.

ASTRA

Still on the subject of the divisions, a special role was also played by an industrial vehicle producer, Astra di Piacenza - to all intents and purposes a competitor of Iveco.

It produced off-road vehicles and specialised in concrete mixers (it had a 50% share of the Italian market), dumpers and defence vehicles, particularly special vehicles for the engineering corps. (This had been achieved in two stages, first with a holding of 40% and then, from April 1986, 100%). This was seen as a means of achieving greater market potential.

The birth and development of Astra is a curious story, a typical example of the post war Italian "economic miracle". It was founded by a Piacenza engineer, Mario Bertuzzi.

At the end of the war, the American army had abandoned in Sardinia all the vehicles it had used in Europe. Bertuzzi had the idea (and the means to put it into practice) of signing an agreement with the Italian government which would allow him to take possession of these vehicles and to use the mechanical components in exchange for supplying the Italian army with an Astra vehicle every so many units produced.

Still in 1955, the Piacenza company started to assemble dumper vehicles specially designed for tunnelling work, using "reconditioned" axles, gearboxes etc. of American origin. A technical aid agreement was also signed with General Motors.

In the Sixties, Astra tooled up for overhauling armoured trucks in a specialist unit, still in Piacenza.

It then started to produce off-road industrial vehicles. It produced its own chassis and bought in the engineering content: engines (from Fiat and Mercedes), gearboxes and axles (from the French company Soma). It also produced its own cabs by making optimum use of the versatile properties of a material like vitreous resin which allowed it to penetrate the market quickly with a new style cab and with limited investment.

These vehicles were over-

dimensioned for the use for which they were intended, and were therefore very reliable. They were also backed by efficient technical support.

To sum up, Astra had become a modern company with a good factory and a respected product, an established name on the market and an almost exclusive presence within the construction sector.

Also, thanks to the boom in the off-road vehicle market, the company managed to sell 1,300 vehicles a year between 1983 and 1984.

Then, out of the blue came the crisis. Mainly a liquidity crisis due to reasons outside the company's control.

At that point, the paths of Astra and Iveco crossed.

Once taken over, the crisis was overcome in a few years, with an increase in jobs, an increase in sales (1,500 vehicles per year) and a return to a respectable profit.

Quarry and construction vehicles from the "Astra" range and, on the opposite page, a powerful motorised crane truck, the 173 kw Iveco-Aifo (engine 8361) 17.3 kw SRI 10 which has been in service with the Italian Air Force since 1990.

THE IVECO AIFO DIVISION

The task of this division is to market, for the most varied applications, the engines produced at Iveco's three engine plants, intervening, when necessary, with even significant changes to the product.

This is explained by the fact that Iveco's strategy in the diesel engine sector was not to produce for internal requirements alone.

Looking at today's figures, Iveco produces and sells approximately 300,000 engines each year (146,000, about half the total, made by the Sofim plant in Foggia; approximately 30,000, i.e. 10%, made at Bourbon-Lancy and 114,000, approximately 40%, at Torino SPA).

Of these, approximately 135,000 are installed in Iveco vehicles (130,000 for commercial vehicles and trucks, 2,000 for buses and 2,500 for forklift trucks); approximately 130,000 are intended for Fiat companies (68,000 for Fiat Auto, 59,000 for Fiat Geotech tractors, 5,000 for earth moving machinery); and approximately 50,000 are sold outside, some 30,000 or so through Iveco Aifo. Consequently, Iveco also sells engines on the market both directly and through Aifo.

Aifo is a company which specialises in industrial engines and para-vehicle applications - site/-quarry vehicles, concrete mixers, tractors, small hoists, pump sets - and which today converts and sells around 30,000 engines a year with a good profit, in spite of strong competition (companies like Perkins, Cummins, etc.) which keep the margins under tight control.

Aifo is also proof of how strong a brand image can be.

Because, thanks to the world records achieved in the nautical sector in the Eighties, everyone thought of Aifo as a manufacturer of marine engines (true, the Venezia steamers have Aifo engines), even if these are but a very small part of its activities.

SIX "FAMILIES" OF ENGINES" FROM 50 TO OVER 1,000 HP

The current range of Iveco engines divides up into six "families", differentiated by cylinder capacity, number of cylinders and taring character-istics and "specialized" according to the applications.

There is the 2.5 litre 8140 series engine, with four cylinders in line, direct injection and precombustion chamber, offered in a 75 HP normally aspirated version, 103 HP turbo version and 115 HP turbo-aftercooler version.

This engine, which is produced at the Foggia plant, is not only fitted to the "S" range vehicles but also has many other applications where its merits of lightness, limited dimensions and lively performance are appreciated. This is therefore an engine which has been used widely, including in the car sector.

It is also produced in special versions, for generating sets and marine and industrial applications.

Then there are three Series 8000 engines which are in line and of 3, 4 and 6 cylinders respectively: the 3.9 litre 8040, with four cylinders, in the 102 HP LTC (light-turbocharged) version, the 116 HP TC (turbocharged) version and the 136 HP TCA (turbocharged-aftercooler) version and the 5.9 litre 8060, with six cylinders, in the 143 HP LTC version, the 177 HP TC version and the 207/227 HP TCA version. These, which are pro-duced in Turin, are fitted to the light and medium-weight ranges of the EuroCargo, from the 60 E 10 to the 150 E 23.

They are also used for city and long distance buses, special vehicles, agricultural tractors, generating sets, marine and industrial applications and earth-moving machines.

There is the 7.7 and 8.1 litre 8360 series, with six cylinders in line, in the power range from 50 to over 300 HP.

This series, produced at Bourbon-

Lancy, is fitted to the EuroCargo medium to heavy weight range, from the 175 E 24 to the 179 E 27. This engine is also used for city and long distance buses, agricultural tractors, marine applications, industrial applications and earth-moving machines, in a power range from 180 to over 400 HP. There is the 9.5 litre 8460 series, with six cylinders in line, in the versions TCA and TCA (sic) from 220 to 500 HP.

This series, produced at Bourbon-Lancy, is fitted to the medium-heavy weight vehicle versions of the EuroCargo range, the 176/-179 E 30 and the 176 E 34, and the Eurotech heavy vehicles, throughout the range of versions. It is also used for city and long distance buses, generating sets, marine and industrial applications, earth-moving machines, crane trucks and agricultural applications.

There is the 13.8 litre 8210, with six cylinders in line, in the normally aspirated, turbocharged and intercooler versions from 260 to over 500 HP.

This series, produced at Bourbon-Lancy, is fitted to the heavy ranges. It is also used for long distance buses, special vehicles, industrial and marine applications, generating sets, earth-moving vehicles and railway applications.

There is the V series, with 8 and 12 cylinders which are 17.2 litre engines and 25.7 litre engines respectively. The 8-cylinder engine is used for Iveco's most powerful trucks, giving 517 HP. The power range covered by this family of engines starts at 350 HP and goes up to over 1,000 HP. This series, produced in Turin, is fitted to the heavy vehicles.

This engine is also used for long distance buses, special vehicles, generating sets, industrial and marine applications, earth-moving machines and railway applications.

The diesel engines produced by Iveco are used in widely differing sectors: in addition to trucks (top left the 8360 with 6 cylinders in line) also in industrial, agricultural, and earth-moving applications and in cars, including top of the range saloons such as the Thema (here on the right).

THE "VEHICLES FOR DEFENCE" DIVISION

The insertion of the Divisions into the group has meant a major leap in quality for Iveco's activity, including, in the field of vehicles for Defence, a sector which as, hist-orically, always experienced an active presence of the makes which have subsequently come together in Iveco, with Fiat and Magirus being prominent.
In these ten years, Iveco's D.V.D. has boosted production of special vehicles.
Now, there are not only "logistical" vehicles, versions "derived" from civilian vehicles, but also "tactical" vehicles. In addition, there are armoured and armed vehicles such as the Centauro 8x8 armoured vehicle (now in production), the Ariete tank and the VCC 80, an infantry and combat vehicle, covered by the Iveco Fiat - Oto Melara Consortium programme.
A major development is involved in this as it entails a valuable enhancement of technical know-how.
Think of the fundamental aspect of quality alone: in the military field, "zero defects" quality is a foregone conclusion.

THE "BUS" DIVISION

For the bus sector, too, the insertion of the Divisions into the group has meant a stimulus for a vigorous push to invest in product research and development, new technologies and production processes and more incisive sales action.
It has offered the opportunity of realising the basic role played by collective road transport vehicles in modern society, characterised by ever-increasing requirements for mobility and for effective solutions to the environmental problems which beset this society.
Buses offer lots of opportunities for meeting these requirements, it not being forgotten that they are and will remain supplementary vehicles compared with other passenger vehicles.
Today, the Bus Division represents not only the original activity of Iveco but also that of Orlandi/Sicca, Pegaso and Altra, companies which, at various times and with various roles, came in to form part of the Group.
Special city and long distance buses are produced at the Valle Ufita plant and minibuses and chassis derived from the "S" and "EuroCargo" ranges are produced at the Brescia and Suzzara plants.
Orlandi production covers the "quality end" of the range of Gran Turismo long distance buses. Orlandi is the oldest bus bodywork company in business, after Daimler-Benz. The com-pany, founded in what is now a far-off 1859 by Angelo Orlandi, has had its headquarters in Modena since 1881 and has been part of the Fiat Group since 1970.
As for Vittorio Veneto's Sicca, this has represented for Iveco the acquisition of consolidated experience in making chassis for both city and long distance buses.
From the merger of the two companies in the second half of 1991, Orlandi-Sicca S.p.A. appeared and the companies' respective activities came together in this.

Through the divisions Iveco's activities range from the bus sector to military vehicles: from the top, the "Centauro" 8x8 armoured car and the 90.17 WM 4x4.

The acquisition of Pegaso, which took place in January 1991, was the opportunity for Iveco to strengthen further its position as a full-range manufacturer. Long distance bus and city bus chassis and also complete city buses are produced at the Barcelona plants. The Altra company of Genoa, only formed very recently (1991), carries out activity aimed at the development of and prototype work on electrically driven buses.

As a result of this subdivided, constantly expanding structure and in spite of the difficulties of an industry which is particularly exposed to external conditioning (linked with the socio-economical situation of the various different markets) and which has, in recent years, been hit by an economic recession in many countries, Iveco has been able to consolidate its position among the world's full-range manufacturers.

This has been a positive trend, confirmed by the sales details of the last two years, a period in which Iveco sales at world level progressed from 11,200 units in 1991 to 12,100 in 1992.

In Europe, the background of crisis which hit important countries such as Italy, Great Britain and Spain - where Iveco is in the position of leader or, in any case, has a considerable presence - brought about a fall in sales for the Group from 3,100 to 2,200 units and, consequently, a fall in the market share, which went down from 14.0% in 1991 to 11.0% in 1992.

Nevertheless, Iveco was able to consolidate its position on the world market, due to an activity policy of penetrating the non-European markets which made it possible to increase the 8,100 units sold in 1991 to the 9,900 units sold in 1992.

THE DEVELOPMENT OF THE BUS RANGE

Structurally, the bus market is divided into three sectors: city vehicles, intended for use in urban and suburban areas, long distance vehicles, intended for non-urban use in regular or tourist services and multipurpose vehicles, derived from chassis or vans from light and medium-weight commercial vehicle ranges. Iveco is one of the few world level manufacturers which offer products in all three sectors.

CITY BUSES

Iveco has a presence with the TurboCity 480 and 490 range. These vehicles are the most advanced expression of a school of designers and technicians which put down its roots back in the 70s; from the 421 and 418, to the 470 ranges, to the EffeUno ("F1") vehicles of the 80s.

It was the 470 range, comprising the city (470), surburban (570) and the short radius inter-city (670) versions, which was conceived with the combined back-up of the design experience of Magirus (chassis), Unic (engine) and Fiat Commercial Vehicles (bodywork). This range complied with Italy's new regulations for regular public transport services.

In 1981, these vehicles were replaced with a generation which was completely new, both in the chassis and in the bodywork; the family of the 471 - 571 - 671, also known as "EffeUno" or, in other words, Federtrasporti 1, as they had been developed on the basis of the indications in a set of terms signed by Federtrasporti and ANFIA (National Association of Italian Motor Industries).

Today, we have the TurboCity generation of city and suburban buses, consiting of models 480 and 490 - with a floor height of 700mm (3 passenger steps) and 550mm (2 passenger steps) respectively - offered in 10.6/12/18 metre long versions, giving 90 to

180 passenger capacity.

From 1993, for the whole range, new generation diesel engines have been used which not only easily conform to the emission limits imposed by EEC regulations 91/542 (EURO 1) but also satisfy the regulations required for the "Ecological Bus" brought in by the Italian Ministry of Transport Order of 26.10.1991 (particle emissions of less than 0.20 g/kWh).

In addition, being aware of the growing demands for environmental protection in urban areas, Iveco offers the possibility of fitting the particle filtration system to the TurboCity and Effe-Uno ranges already in service.

TOURIST BUSES

Iveco is present in the tourist sector with a varied range of bus models and bodies, from 7.5 to 12 metres long and with seating capacity from 28 to 57. These are the result of the exceptional wealth of experience acquired during the years on the international scene by Fiat V.I. (Fiat Commercial Vehicles), Magirus, Orlandi and Pegaso.

This experience dates back to the early 1970s when, within the Commercial Vehicles group, together with the projects for light, medium-weight and heavy trucks and the Daily, the project for the 370 bus was started.

Presented along with the 170 heavy road vehicle, the 370, like this vehicle, was in line with the new weights and dimensions regulations brought in by Act 313. With reference to buses, this Act increased maximum length from 11 to 12 metres.

As was only natural, the birth of Iveco set the pattern for the development of subsequent ranges. In the field of the long distance buses, the 370 was also produced by Magirus in the version (named the M2000) with a KHD air-cooled engine.

In the 7.5 metre sector, production of the 314 was stopped, this having been a vehicle of Fiat origin, and it was replaced with Magiru's model 160 R81,

although fitted with a KHD engine, and the 315, fitted with a Fiat engine (still available now, in a radically updated version).

When KHD left the holding company, production of the models with air-cooled engines, M2000, and 160 R81, stopped. The 370 was updated and re-named the 370 S. The rest is a modern-day story.

The growing specialization required by users for regular and tourist services entails ever-increasing diversification of the product in terms of performance, space and equipment.

In this sector, the bottom of the range supplied by Iveco comes in the form of model 315 which, at 7.5 metres long, is on sale as a shorter special bus marketed in Europe. This vehicle, offered in regular and tourist service versions with Orlandi Poker bodywork, is particularly suitable for routes which call for maximum manoeuvrability.

The 370 S range, available in versons 9.7, 10.6 and 12 metres long and with bodies by Iveco (produced at Valle Ufita), Poker and Domino Sicca/Orlandi, is structured to meet the most varied requirements of regular and tourist service.

These models also feature new generation engines. The emissions from these are appreciably lower than the limits imposed by EEC - Euro 1 regulations and come within the Italian Ministry of Transport "Ecological Bus" category.

Iveco-Pegaso too, with the Podium models which are 12 metres long, have engines ranging from 260 to 370 HP and three types of body (normal, high and extra-high) is responding with variety to the diversification called for by the various different uses in the sector.

The pride of current Iveco bus production comes in the form of the new EuroClass range, a family of buses designed specifically for the European tourist market.

The EuroClass - a vehicle of totally new conception - designed, calculated for and produced by means of innovative process technology, represents the best which can be supplied today in terms of comfort, safety, performance, reliability and environment protection.

It is supplied in two versions; normal and high, in two lengths (12 and 10.6 metres) and three engine power choices: 290, 345 and 380 HP. The EuroClass is instantly recognizable due to the innovative styling of the front which is as modern and pleasing as it is functional; the excellent aerodynamic properties actually favour both quietness of travel and lower fuel consumption.

The innovative content of the EuroClass includes the structure of the body, made with synthetic resin outer panels bonded to a strong steel supporting frame. With this technology, it has been possible to obtain excellent heat/sound insulation, favouring comfort inside the vehicle, ease of maintenance and good anti-corrosion characteristics.

In the event of damage to the protective coating, the structure of the body with open sections made of "corten" self-passivating steel prevents the processes of uncontrolled corrosion from being triggered off.

Maximum quality and precision of the structure are ensured by a computerized process which controls special machines for plasma cutting of sheet metal, profiling lines, assembly carried out by means of robotized spot welding.

Inside, the EuroClass offers comfortable, functional fittings, with seats of a design which is new in terms of shape and the choice of materials. Hand luggage can easily be placed in spacious hat racks with built-in handrails and more bulky luggage can be stored in a roomy compartment which passes under the floor.

To give maximum comfort, special attention has been paid to sound-proofing, the chassis suspension characteristics and the air conditioning unit.

With regard to the mechanical content, two 9.5 litre turbo-intercooler straight 6 cylinder engines are available, in two power alternatives: 290 and 345 HP. Designed in accordance with the cycle of use of a long distance bus, like all current generation Iveco engines, their emissions are appreciably lower than the limits imposed by the EEC - EURO 1 regulations and come under the Italian Ministry of Transport's "Ecological Bus" category.

The suspension is of a new design; front wheel independent suspension, favouring both comfort and road-holding, and conventional suspension for the rear wheels but with the four air springs moved outwards a great deal, favouring stability in motion. An electronically controlled ride levelling device is provided as standard. The chassis safety equipment also includes ASR acceleration anti-slip and ABS anti-lock braking.

For manufacturing the Euro-Class, the Valle Ufita plant has benefited from major innovations in production processes and technology.

The body frame is welded by automated robots and treated against corrosion by means of cataphoresis in a tank. The mechanical, electrical and pneu-matic units are mounted in ad-vance on trolleys - a front one and a rear one - and are then assemb-led with the completed body.

DERIVED BUSES

In the sector of bused derived from others, Iveco has a presence in the form of the TurboDaily and EuroCargo chassis.

As the abbreviated names indicate, the TurboDaily A 40.10, A 45.10 and A 45.12 are based on the 4 and 4.45 tonne total road weight chassis. These vehicles, fitted with turbo and turbo-aftercooler engines with direct injection, giving power of up 115 HP, are nimble, comfortable and suitable for the most varied service; schools, sport, hospitals and tourist/hotel service, whether in the city (at historical centres, for example) or for special long distance transport requirements. The A 40.10 and A 45.10 school

buses come in four versions, from 31 to 41 seats for elementary schools and from 20 to 28 seats for secondary schools. They are all fitted with an electrically operated rotating-sliding service door.

The A 45.10 and A 45.12 regular service buses are capable of carrying 19 seated passengers. The 16-seater A 40.10 turbo and 19-seater A 45.10/12 turbo and turbo-aftercooler models, with rotating-sliding door, are marketed for private use.

Also available are 16 and 19-seater Executive versions, characterised by particularly comfortable, well thought out fittings (velvet covered reclining single seats, co-ordinated hat racks, air conditioning), and fittings "by Orlandi", in the "Top" version with 12 seats (Shuttle) and 16 seats for regular and tourist service.

The range is completed by the 49.10, 49.12 and 59.12 body makers' chassis, with a total road weight from 4.7 to 6 tonnes, left or right-hand drive, wheelbase and dimensions for fitted bodies up to 7.5 metres long. These vehicles are particularly suitable for fitting out as city minibuses and school buses.

Finally, for special uses, there is the four wheel drive 40.10W model which is capable of reaching a top speed of 70 km/h and carrying up to 20 passengers.

In the higher total road weight band, from 6 to 16.5 tonnes, Iveco has a presence in the form of the shielded chassis which are derived from the EuroCargo range.

These are the heirs to a tradition associated with names which have become legendary; historically, in fact, this type of bus has always followed the development of the original range.

The well-known, widespread Fiat 625 and 329 models, together with the OM, Leoncino, Lupetto and Tigrotto models, were bus chassis derived from the EuroCargo truck counterparts, with production in the 1970s which ran to something like 5,000 units a year; a truly high number. The following generations wer the 60-70-80 AI, de-

rived from the "X" range vehicles, and the A60 - A70 - A90, derived from the "Z" range vehicles.

Going up in total road weight, at the origins of the story of the Iveco bus, there are the 110 and 130 AI medium-weights, derived from the corresponding trucks, plus the medium-heavy 331. With the formation of Iveco and the rationalization resulting from the inclusion of Magirus, from 1976, there was the addition of the family of the 120, 140 and 160 A/AP, with front mounted and rear mounted engine, respectively.

In 1981, with the closure of the Mainz plant, production of the 120 - 140 stopped. However, this was not the case with the largest, the AP160, linked to the "Libya" project and destined to go down in history as the biggest-selling Iveco chassis. When it comes to the 110-130 AI, with the transfer of production from Trappes to SPA and the start of production of the new 115-135-175, it would be from these models that the shielded A 135.14 and .17 and the 175.24 would be derived.

The story continues now with the bus versions derived from the EuroCargo ranges. These are high performance, comfortable vehicles, fitted with turbo and turbo-aftercooler "ecological" engines delivering 115 to 240 HP, with seating capacities ranging from 22 to 52 and capability of accepting bodywork from 6.2 to 11.5 metres in length. They are available in versions for Europe and outside Europe and offer left or right-hand drive manual or automatic gear change and mechanical or full-pneumatic suspension.

ADVANCED RESEARCH FOR THE BUS OF THE FUTURE

The purpose of this research is to improve the quality of service offered by the bus to make ever-increasing improvements in the environmental compatibility of this type of vehicle. Some time ago, Iveco took on board the urgent requirement for environmental protection and, having made this cause its own, has

allocated effort and resources to research into and experimentation with increasingly ecological buses intended for specific niches in use. In this context and as an alternative to vehicles with diesel engines, from which polluting emissions are progres-sively and rapidly falling, due to the continuous design and technological action taken to comply with the ever more stringent regulations for environ-mental protection, Iveco has developed, in parallel, two types of innovative drive: on the one hand, the electric and hybrid system and, on the other hand, the system with methane suppply

The ElectricDaily is a 6 metre long vehicle fitted with a 22 kW DC motor, supplied exclusively by batteries. In the version for city transport service, it has capacity for carrying 20 passengers, reaches a speed of 55 km/h and has a range of up to 60 km, depending on the service procedures and when using lead batteries. Quietness, manageability and the absence of gas emissions make this the ideal vehicle for the care of areas with special environmental and architectural constraints.

One solution for overcoming the present constraints imposed by batteries is represented by the hybrid vehicle, in which the drive, provided by one or more electric motors, is separated from generation which is obtained from a small heat engine operating at a constant speed and therefore with negligible levels of gas emissions and noise.

The heat engine drives an alternator which generates the power necessary for operation of the electric motor. Between the two functions there is a power lung of batteries which supplies additional power when power peaks are demanded from the electric motor, such as when moving off and climbing and, vice versa, stores excess power produced during deceleration, downhill driving and stops. Iveco's solution is the AltroBus, supplied in two versions. One version is derived from the ElectricDaily, from which it takes all its components, and this vehicle is 6 metres long, is capable of carrying 25 passengers, has a generator and a Fiat Fire 1000 engine, catalysed with Lambda probe. The other version is derived from the TurboCity 490; it is 12 metres long, is capable of carrying 100 passengers, is fitted with a 128 kW AC electric motor and a 2.5 litre Sofim diesel generator which supplies 30 kW.

The AltroBus is the ideal vehicle for city traffic as it embodies the ecological advantages of electric drive and the advantages of the heat engine's flexibility and long range.

With regard to the system with methane (CNG) supply, Iveco offers a version of the TurboCity powered by the 165 kW 8469 engine, specially produced for this type of supply with a three-way catalytic exhaust and a Lambda probe.

The system employs electronic management which ensures optimum proportions of the air/methane mixture with the result that gas emissions are minimized in the exhaust. In October 1992, field trials were started in Ravenna - carried out jointly by Iveco, the Ministry of Transport, SNAM and ATM Ravenna - with five 12-metre TurboCity "480" buses. It is planned for such vehicles to be available on the market by 1994.

THE FIREFIGHTING
VEHICLES DIVISION

Magirus has been established as a vehicle manufacturer in Germany for over 125 years, and today - as Iveco Magirus, an integral part of the Iveco Group - continues that long tradition as home of the Firefighting Vehicles Division.

With an annual production of around 600 vehicles and an annual turnover exceeding Dm-100 million, the firefighting business makes a substantial contribution to Iveco Group, both in terms of economics and image.

Today, about one third of all the Fire Service vehicles in the Federal Republic and over half of all the fire escape vehicles in service around the world are supplied by Iveco Magirus.

This dominant position has been achieved by the advanced design of the vehicles themselves, and the continual development of materials and control systems.

The Division controls and co-ordinates the operations of two companies; Iveco Magirus AG, which was formed in Germany in 1989 and Iveco Mezzi Special S.p.A., which was established in Brescia in 1992, following the acquisition of Societa Baribi. Production is concentrated at three plants located at Ulm and Weiswall in Germany and at Brescia in Italy, with 65% of the output going to Germany, 25% to the rest of Europe and the remainder to countries in Asia, Africa and South America.

The Iveco Mezzi Special plant in Brescia covers an area of 40,800 square metres, more than half of which is given over to production. The workforce of 150 operates a flexible and integrated production system which maintains high quality standards while meeting varying production schedules.

Iveco Magirus firefighting vehicles are designed to meet the needs of many different users. Specific vehicles are built for civil use in residential areas; airport vehicles satisfy ICAD and NFPA standards and typically have high capacity foam cannons controlled by automatic systems; rapid intervention vehicles

equipped with specialised systems fight fires in refineries, chemical plants and power stations and dedicated vehicles with all-wheel-drive are used to reach difficult sites and forest fires. Perhaps the most specialised vehicles of all are those developed for rescue operations in underground railways. These unique vehicles drive on the railway track, permitting the maximum mobility within the restricted space of the tunnel.
Apart from the front line fire escape trucks, some of which have escape ladders which can reach as high as 53 metres, Iveco

Magirus makes a variety of auxiliary equipment such as water tankers, self-contained portable water pumps, and hose winding trailers.

In its range of vehicles and firefighting equipment Iveco offers sophisticated powered ladders able to extend to as much as 53 metres and specialized vehicles for rescue in restricted spaces, eg underground railway tunnels.

1985-1989
TOWARDS TOTAL INTEGRATION

On its 10th anniversary in 1985, Iveco found itself at the starting point of the most fertile and flourishing period of its history, especially from the financial point of view.

At last they were able to harvest the fruits of the continuous rationalisation projects put into practice in the previous years and, at the same time, loosen the grip of indebtedness. The balance sheet was back in the black.

The reorganisation stage had been completed and they were able to start the process of placing the company on a more substantial footing by implementing all the changes which were to embody the original concepts on which the holding company was based: multi-nationality, integration, rationalisation at all levels.

The sales network was gradually assuming its final shape; they were refining the management and financial tools; the image of the company, now consolidated, was to make it possible to use one trade mark, the Iveco mark.

Following major investment in computer equipment, technology and organisation, logistics and computer science were to facilitate the design and implementation of an absolutely innovative system for the integrated management of the company in all its aspects, both commercial and industrial. From an in-depth analysis of the market to the order/production flow, to the production cycle in all its stages including the procurement of raw materials and components, everything was now coordinated.

Working on a Just-in-Time basis resulted in a drastic reduction in stocks and inevitably, the money tied up in them. At the same time, plans were taking shape for developing the new generation of integrated and rationalised ranges, together with the technology and layout of the lines on which the vehicles were to be produced.

In this respect, two basic strategies adopted during this period should be highlighted.

First of all, the impetus given to increasing the degree of integration of the company, ridding itself of the dever-ticalisation in the component production sector which had led to the joint venture with Rockwell.

Why was this choice made? Because they had become aware of the importance of using their advanced know how - technological and technical - in the components sector too.

There were at least three reasons why this transfer of know how to the component market was necessary: to be able to withstand the pressure of the market concerning the characteristics and performance of the vehicles; to be able to adapt the vehicles - within the necessary limits and times - when standards changed, particularly with regard to environmental pollution (emissions, noise, etc.). And - no less important - to be able to guarantee adequate control of the spares market from the point of view of quality.

Secondly, product development was set up to coordinate not simply the developments of product, but also quality; naturally they wanted a central quality division as a reference point for all the local engineering and production divisions.

All this was within Iveco. However, in those very years, there was also a vigorous continuation of the push towards the outside world, towards globalization of the business.

Major stages on this road were the joint venture with Ford, in which Iveco was able to establish solid bases for itself in one of the largest European markets, and the industrial and participation agreements with China and India, a basis for a direct presence, from within Iveco, in vital geographical areas and in markets with enormous potential.

Finally - and we are now up to 1990 - there would be the acquisition of Pegaso, an operation which would make Spain Iveco's fifth "home" market.

THE JOINT VENTURE WITH FORD

"Iveco Ford Truck Ltd" was formed in July 1986, with Iveco and Ford of Britain, each holding a 48% share and the remaining 4% being held by the Merchant bank, Credit Suisse First Boston. The new company was responsible for the production and sale of the Ford Cargo range and the marketing of Iveco vehicles in the UK. This was a very significant agreement, which in one move gave Iveco leadership of an important fourth European market. The agreement provides for the distribution, sales and after sales back-up in the UK of the joint vehicle ranges via a unified dealer network formed from existing Ford and Iveco franchise holders.

In addition to the Iveco Ford Truck range, Iveco Ford dealers are also franchised to sell the long wheelbase versions of the Ford Transit.

The new company also supplies "Cargo" trucks to the Continental Ford sales companies, which they continue to sell in turn, through an existing dealer network.

Ford's former Langley truck plant in Berkshire has become one of the biggest resources of the company and importantly, the joint venture happened at a time when Ford had established its modern and very successful Cargo range.

Since January, Iveco's presence on the UK market has been further strengthened by the purchase, under an agreement with Pegaso, of Seddon Atkinson Vehicles Ltd, a British company which had been owned by the Spanish group Enasa since 1983. Based in Oldham, Lancashire, with a workforce of about 260, Seddon Atkinson boasts a long tradition of over 86 years in the commercial vehicle business. Today, the plant builds trucks in the 17 to 44 tonne GVW range.

With its integration into the Iveco Group, Seddon Atkinson has benefitted from the Group's expertise and, for example, the company's "T5" 17 tonne model now uses a cab from the new Euro range. Future Seddon Atkinson models will also embody the Iveco theme.

LANGLEY, HOME TO THE HURRICANE AND THE CARGO

The Langley plant is located 25 kilometres to the west of central London, close to Heathrow airport, and 50 kilometres from Ford's Dagenham estate. The plant's history dates back to 1936 when Hawker Siddley, now part of British Aerospace, bought a property known as Parluant Park Farm on which it built an aeroplane factory.

Two years later, with the threat of war very real, the new works started production of the Hawker Hurricane Fighter plane. By the end of the war, some 3,700 Hurricanes were built and such was their success that they shot down more enemy aircraft than all the other air and land defences combined, including the more formidable and manoeuvr-able Spitfire.

In 1949, about 300,000 m^2 of the main Langley site was bought by Ford and used as an engine reconditioning centre, a production area for parts and warehousing. Ten years later, Ford bought the remaining area and, for an investment of £3.5 million, restructured the whole site ready to take over commercial vehicle production, which had previously been located at Dagenham.

By 1960, Langley was building the 400E light van and by March of the following year it was building the Trader as well. This was a semi forward control truck with a two/three tonne payload.

This was a busy time for Ford and several new models soon followed. In 1964, the Trader was replaced by the all-new "D" Series and in 1965 the 400E was replaced by the Transit. The Transit was to became a best seller and within its first year of manufacture became the market leader, with production exceeding 32,500 units.

In 1967, Ford extended the "D" Series range and bought extra land about 1.5 kilometres to the

north of the main site. Two years later in 1969, the move from Dagenham was complete and all of Ford's British commercial vehicle production was concentrated at Langley.

The early 1970s saw the start of a massive new rationalisation and modernisation plan involving Southampton and Langley, culminating in the launch of the Cargo in 1981.

In 1972, to make room at Langley, Transit production was moved to Southampton. In 1973 the "A" Series was launched, going into production at the satellite Langley B plant. The "A" Series was a medium weight vehicle which filled the gap between the Transit and the "D"

Series. In 1974 a new building equipped for the inspection and final approval of all trucks was completed and commissioned. A unique "D" Series derivative for Germany called the "N" Series, which had been built in Amsterdam, was transferred to Langley in 1976.

In 1977, work got underway to transform Langley into a major industrial complex at a cost of £150 million in readiness for the cargo.

Ford purchased extra industrial premises, adjacent to the main site, from Firestone and turned it into a warehouse serving the plant. This freed valuable space within the plant, which in turn was used to assemble "D" and "N"

Series cabs which had previously been built at Ford's Southampton plant. This transfer was accomplished in 1978. During 1979, the cab build area was completed, including the installation of four robot welders and a very accurate three axis measuring machine for checking the dimensions of anything from individual panels to complete cabs. Elsewhere in the plant, a new paint shop was installed which included cathodic electrocoating by total immersion of the complete cab.

Cargo production started in November 1980 and the new range soon proved attractive to operators because of its modern appearance and wide choice of models and options. Among the many possibilities were four and six cylinder in-line and Vee-8 engines of up to 280 horsepower.

In a few months, Cargo became Britain's top selling truck and altogether some 100,000 units were built in its 12 year production run.

The first light and medium "Cargo 1" models in the range 6 to 15 tonnes GVW were introduced in January 1981, and these were followed in September by the medium weight multi axle vehicles and later still by the heavier Cargo 2 models. These models had gross weights of up to 32 tonnes, the maximum weight permitted by UK legislation at that time.

Following the establishment of the joint venture in 1986, the Cargo range benefitted from innovations such as the introduction of the Rockwell drive axles and the fitting of all round disc brakes on the 6 to 8 tonne models.

LANGLEY TODAY

When the New Cargo was introduced to the Langley plant (1991), which builds vehicles for Britain and Northern Europe, the opportunity was taken to introduce the latest technological and management standards common to all Iveco production sites.

Together with Brescia, Ulm and Madrid Valladolid, Langley is now an integral part of Iveco's European wide production facility sharing the same equipment and layout and linked by on-line data communications.

The Iveco Manufacturing Information Systems (IMIS) data link, centred in Turin, coordinates and controls all of the commercial operations of the Group. An investment of £25 million, including £5 million for cab assembly alone, has made Langley one of the most modern industrial plants in Europe.

Advanced Statistical Process Control (SPC) systems and fully automated robots are used to ensure that none of the "quality" achieved by CAD/CAM techniques at the design stage are lost in production.

Many operations are automated and have automatic gauging linked to SPC monitors to track and maintain quality.

Brescia has a very modern press shop and supplies Langley, Ulm and Madrid-Valladolid with chassis and cab panels. Brescia also produces and supplies cab panels made from plastics Sheet Moulding Compound (SMC).

Cab assembly at Langley uses the most advanced robotised welding installation in the UK, equipped with the latest generation of Comau robot. The Italian Comau company is a world leader in industrial automation. The pneumatically operated welding robots have six degrees of freedom and interchangeable heads, which are changed automatically to suit the operation.

Cab build starts with the pressed steel panels being loaded into a large three dimensional jig and locked in place by pneumatic clamps. The jig, complete with its cab panels, then moves off to the welding station. Here, two type 6100 robots start by tack welding the cab floor in place.

At another station, two type 7100 robots, which have an extra seventh degree of freedom, load in more panels such as the rear and front panels, door opening surrounds and so on and tack weld them in place.

Finally, two more type 6100 robots make over 500 precision structural spot welds, checking all the time that important parameters such as supply voltage, electrode temperature and tip pre-load are correct. At the end of the assembly phase, completed cabs are scanned by a laser system to check that the required tolerances have been met.

Right from the start of the "Euro" range programme, the utmost attention has been paid to combatting corrosion with a view to maximising service life, and for this reason much time has been spent perfecting the paint process. Langley has a first class paint process. Even before they are assembled, individual panels go through a three stage cleaning/protection process which eliminates any traces of grease or dirt, protecting even the most critical areas, such as corners and sharp edges from oxidation, and forms an excellent key for the paint.

Once assembled, the completed cabs undergo a four-stage wash cycle using demineralised water, before receiving a cathodic electrocoat primer which builds to a thickness of 42 microns. This very advanced process is carried out with the cab totally immersed in the paint solution, guaranteeing that every surface and cavity is coated. Excess paint is washed off and the cabs move on through the system, past an infra red pre-heating station and then on through a drying oven where they spend 10 minutes at a temperature of 190°C.

As they leave the oven, the cabs are quickly cooled by jets of air and the panel joints treated and protected with a special sealant. Thermo-fusible sound-proofing panels are fitted to the floor before the cabs enter a second oven for a further ten minutes, this time at 165°C.

This careful pre-treatment phase is followed by the final painting which is completely robotised. Pairs of ABB Tralfa TR 5000 robots with seven degrees of freedom, apply a base coat, 40 microns thick, followed by two finishing coats.

The whole system is electronically controlled to ensure the maximum uniformity of application; the quantity of paint, its viscosity and the spraying time are all constantly monitored and the parameters varied to suit the covering power of the different colours used. Cabs can be painted in any chosen colour sequence and, when necessary, the change from one colour to another can be made in less than 70 seconds. The cabs then pass through a heated tunnel where the paint is baked at 140°C. Finally, structural box sections are injected using a hot wax spray as an extra anti-corrosion precaution.

Under the Iveco-Ford agreement, signed in 1986, the new generation "Cargo" first appeared at the Langley plant in England.

At this stage the cab roof, which is made from lightweight, corrosion proof SMC material, is selected and fitted to the cab structure. The roof panels are conveniently assembled alongside the main track, complete with trim, and hoisted into position on the cab. To make the fixing easier, the operators work at a comfortable height using a mobile platform. The edges are first cleaned with distilled water, then joined with a special high strength adhesive which forms an elastic, yet impermeable joint, ensuring a perfect seal over a long service life.

In the plant, cab and chassis build are separate activities and the two completed assemblies only come together on the final track. With the structure now completed, cabs are transferred to another area for final build and trimming.

Moving along a floor level track, the cabs are gradually built up. Rear and side windows are fitted, the door windows and regulators, windscreen, wipers and washers, internal trim panels, cab wiring loom and finally the dashboard. Like the roof panels, the dashboard is built alongside the line and tested for electrical integrity. Once assembled into the cab it is tested again using an automated system that quickly checks for the proper operation of 100 different functions. During the final inspection at the end of the production line, the complete electrical system of the whole vehicle will be tested and checked yet again.

The cab assembly continues with the fixing of the door trim panels, floor covering, driver's seat, bunks, passenger seat and so on. When the inside is complete, the cab is lifted into the air so that the remaining components mounted low down on the cab can be fitted more easily.

Finally completed, the cabs move away on an overhead conveyor ready to join up with the correct chassis which has been built up elsewhere in the plant. The job of tracking cab and chassis build

and co-ordinating them to produce the complete vehicle is handled by a dedicated computer. Chassis frames arrive at Langley ready built and where possible use is made of pre-assembled sub-units. The chassis is loaded onto the line upside-down making it easier to install the suspension, axles, steering and prop shaft. The electrical harness and the braking system is also installed at this stage.

With this major work completed, the chassis is turned the right way up ready to accept the engine and transmission which are prepared on a separate loop line close by. As a chassis passed, the correct engine and transmission is selected and transferred by overhead crane and lowered into place. As the line progresses, the last chassis items such as the radiator are assembled and it is ready to receive its cab.

As the chassis line continues to move forward, the selected cab, suspended from an overhead track, positions above the chassis and with their speeds synchronised, the cab is lowered onto the chassis and secured in place.

So, after a four kilometre journey the vehicle reaches the end of the production line. The engine is started, and the truck moves for the first time under its own power and on its own wheels to a test area for the final sign off.

Each vehicle is "run" on a dual lane rolling road dynamometer, which is the most advanced of its type in the UK. The inspector enters the vehicle data into a computer terminal and from then on the test procedure is computer controlled. A series of prompts displayed on a monitor in front of the driver takes him through a number of tests including measuring the power and torque of the engine, the gearbox efficiency, the accuracy of the tachometer, and the efficiency of the braking system; even a hill start can be simulated.

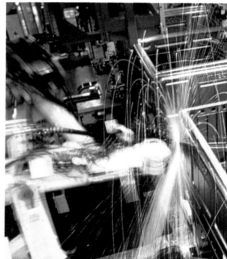

For the production of the New Cargo the Iveco Ford plant at Langley in England has been completed re-equiped with the most up-to-date technology and extensive automation.

THE DAILY DISEMBARKS IN BEIJING

An important date in the history of Iveco is the 17th August, 1991, the day when the first assembly line for the TurboDaily went into operation at the factories of the Nanijng Motor Corporation in China. This was the first fruit of the licence and technical aid contract signed in 1986 between Iveco and the Nanijng Motor Corporation to produce light vehcles in the "S" range, the 3 to 5 tonners, under licence in China. The agreement is based on a production forecast of some 30 versions, including the 4x4, with an annual volume of 60,000 vehicles. After an initial CAD assembly stage (but already with a high local content, up to 40%), the vehicles and the corresponding components, including the 2.5 litre diesel engine, will be produced almost entirely in China.

The project includes the gradual reorganisation of 19 factories in the Nanchino area, with a contribution of 260 million dollars from the Chinese government. Apart from technology, Iveco signed a contract to supply all the technical aid and the necessary knowhow, including training courses for more than 400 Chinese technicians.

The agreement with Nanijng assumes particular importance, even beyond purely industrial aspects.

First of all, it is the recognition of the qualities of a vehicle and a range, because the TurboDaily was chosen in competition with well proven Western products.

And secondly, because it allows Iveco to achieve an advantageous position on the oriental chessboard, both directly as far as China is concerned (a closed market of major potential) and throughout South East Asia, a traditional land of conquest for Japanese industry.

The latest TurboDaily has already landed in China. On the 17 August 1991 the first assembly line was opened at the Nanijng Motor Corporation plant.

IVECO INCREASES ITS PRESENCE ON THE INTERNATIONAL MARKETS

At the beginning of the 1990s, with the none too easy period which characterized the five years from 1984 to 1989 having been overcome, Iveco set about boosting its presence on the large international markets.

It set its mind on consolidating the sales in countries which were traditionally important to Iveco, such as Africa and South America, on strengthening the relations with industrial associates and on establishing a distribution presence in the countries of Eastern Europe and the Far East and on recovering shares of Middle East markets, jeopardized by warfare. For this purpose, in Turkey, for example, a joint venture was finalized with the Koc group, at Otoyol which has a capacity of 8 - 10,000 units a year in the light and heavy weight sectors and is leader in the 3.5 to 8 tonne sector (it is also the leader in the market for 20/25 seater buses). Something similar was done with Z.K. and T.I.V. in the former Yugoslavia, both with production capacity of 7 - 8,000 units a year and the market leaders (approximately 70/75% market share).

In India, in association with the Hinduja group, Iveco bought the relative majority share of Ashok Leyland, India's second-ranked manufacturer, with potential for producing 25 - 30,000 units a year, with a strong vocation for the passenger transport sector and good prospects for exports to the closest areas.

In Australia in 1992, Iveco took over leading local manufacturer, Ital, which was already assembling and marketing the Turbotech and Turbostar to supplement their (sic) range. This was a strategic move in order to have a presence on a continent which is a test laboratory for harsh use of vehicles and where there is the fullest competition and, in the medium term, it may become a strategic and tactical base for the markets

Iveco in the world

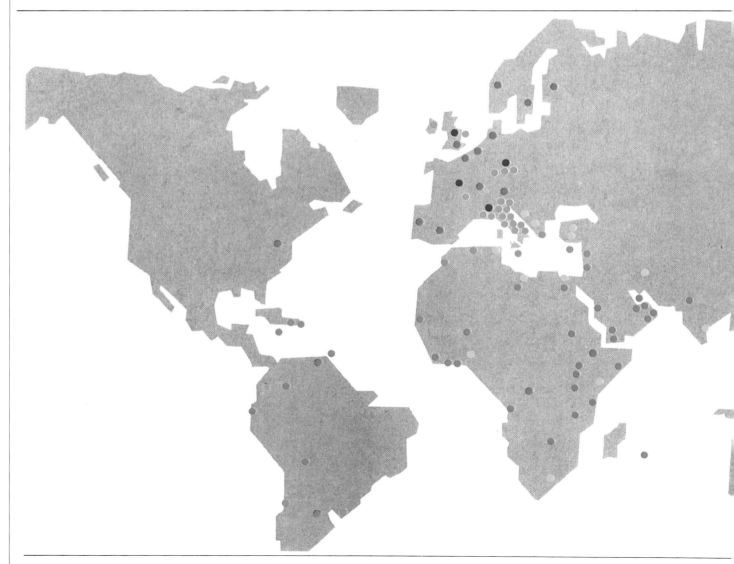

● National companies   ● Production centres   ● Affiliated companies

of South East Asia.

In Russia, a co-operation scheme was finalized with Uralaz; first for assembly and subsequently for production of heavy Arctic vehicles (continuing a tradition under which 15,000 Magirus vehicles have been used in harsh conditions over a period exceeding 15 years).

At the same time, there was a renewal and strengthening of the traditional industrial co-operation in Libya, Tunisia, E g y p t a n d I r a n w i t h Khodrowsazan in the light bus sector. As far as the "heavy vehicles" are concerened, new agreements with Zamyad (again in Iran) and Halla (in South Korea) opened up new areas for Iveco products.

Licensees   ● Importers

In the markets which were free to imports of commercial vehicles, forceful penetration action was taken, with significant results being obtained in Saudi Arabia, the Emirates and Chile. All this action, with the presence in China, India and Australia greatly improved Iveco's image in the Far East, making it possible to have an organized presence, of substantial - and growing - proportions. In the former Communist countries such as Hungary, the Czech - Slovak Federation and Poland, an increasingly European type of sales network has been developed, marketing the full Iveco range.

In this way, there has been a return to volume growth, from 13,000 to 21,000 units, with the most recent acquisitions of Pegaso, in European activities, and Ital, in international activities, being turned to account.

THE MARKET: EUROPE STARTS TO LIFT BUT THE MARKET OUTSIDE EUROPE COLLAPSES

As far as the market is concerned, when the recession of the early Eighties had passed, a period of expansion resurged towards the middle of the decade in Europe, culminating in a new historical record in 1989.

However, the rot outside Europe could not be stopped and this was followed by a ruinous collapse. This was to change the market scenario completely.

The figures speak for themselves. Let us look at the figures concerning Iveco. In 1987, the first year of recovery, a total of 117,790 vehicles was produced, 4,000 up compared with the 113,120 vehicles in 1981 (the last good year before the crisis). But the 28,200 vehicles sold outside Europe in 1984 became just a memory: in 1985, the figure had dropped to 18,600, then 12,400 in 1988, less than half, and down even further in 1989, to 11,300.

Therefore, in the Eighties, it was the boom in demand in Europe which had to sustain the market, having to top up the drop in exports (reduced by almost two thirds in five years) with a totally different product mix.

It was a great disappointment in the third world which, let us remember, for the sector at the time meant almost all the heavy and medium to heavy trucks, in effect, any high value product.

In spite of this depressing situation, the second half of the Eighties represented a period of exceptional boom for the Iveco management. They were to harvest the fruits of all the work done.

As we have seen, in the previous years, they had adopted an austerity policy to contain management costs and excessive production capacity - remember the integration fund, early retirement, the freeze on investments.

But they had also worked very hard - obviously with excellent results - on the efficient management of the working capital, loans and stocks.

On the loans side, improved control was introduced and the company entrusted the financing of the network to finance companies to reduce the level of indebtedness.

And on the stock side, they drastically reduced the capital tied up: in 1989, the appreciated value of the stocks was almost half compared with 1980.

In ten years, Iveco had organised a system of rotating the stocks more quickly - both the production materials and the stocks of finished products. Having previously reached stock levels of 26 - 27 thousand vehicles, in 1989, following the incorporation of the English activities of Iveco Ford and with 136 thousand vehicles sold compared with 100 thousand in 1982, stocks fell to around 19 thousand vehicles. This was mainly due to the organising capacity of the Logistics department.

And in the future - if the market manages to re-establish a minimum equilibrium within a reasonable time after the serious slump at the beginning of the Nineties - these measures will allow Iveco to self-finance its ambitious five year investment plan for 1988 to 1992 launched in association with its structural projects.

5,000 million Lire is a very large sum of money!

Let us look at the number of vehicles sold in the five year

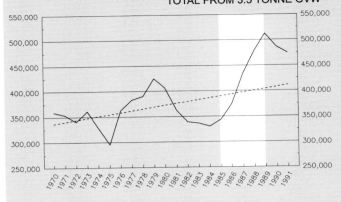

DEMAND FOR TRUCKS IN WESTERN EUROPE
TOTAL FROM 3.5 TONNE GVW

Year	Value
1985	344388
1986	375144
1987	433304
1988	477967
1989	512432

period 1985-1989. In 1985 there was an increase - 99,000 units, nearly 9,000 up on the previous year. In 1986, a slight drop, 94,580 vehicles, followed by a constant increase in the following years: 117,800 vehicles in 1987 (the newly acquired production of Iveco Ford with the Cargo range represented approximately 15,-000 vehicles), 129,330 in 1988 and 136,000 in 1989.

The billing kept pace with these figures: 8,900 million Guilders in 1985, approximately 600 more compared with the previous year; more or less the same figure in 1986 and then a marked increase: 10,390 million in 1987, 11,320 in 1988 and 12,420 in 1989.

After the heavy loss suffered in 1984 - nearly 395 million Guilders - the company was back in profit in 1985 with 120 million Guilders net. Then came the upswing: a little less than 284 million Guilders in 1986, 435 in 1987, 516 in 1988, more than 590 in 1989, a new historical record (4.8% of the billing).

The fact that the situation had not merely recovered but was positively blooming is also evident from the rapid reduction in accrued liabilities: from 2,300 million Guilders in 1984 to 1,500 in 1985 and 1,378 in 1988; for the first time in the history of Iveco, 1987 marked the transition to a credit situation with 186 million Guilders, rising the following year to the historic record of nearly 870 million.

In the next few years there will be a progressive redimensioning of the company, justified by the almost dizzy growth in investment which reached 8% of the billing in 1989.

Let us take a look. From a situation still more or less frozen in 1985, with investments of 198 million Guilders compared with 193 the previous year (2.2% of the billing), the situation changed to 261 million in 1986. And then came the explosion: 553 million in 1987, 663 in 1988 and 1,000 million in 1989.

There were investments in the product, with a continuous stream of new engine and equipment versions. And there were investments in engineering, technology and factory plant for the new

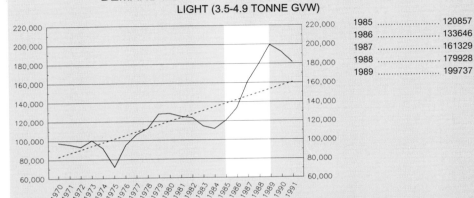

DEMAND FOR TRUCKS IN WESTERN EUROPE
LIGHT (3.5-4.9 TONNE GVW)

Year	Value
1985	120857
1986	133646
1987	161329
1988	179928
1989	199737

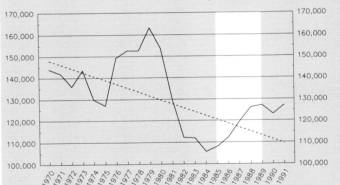

DEMAND FOR TRUCKS IN WESTERN EUROPE
MEDIUM (5.0-15.9 TONNE GVW)

Year	Value
1985	108162
1986	112344
1987	119557
1988	126226
1989	127247

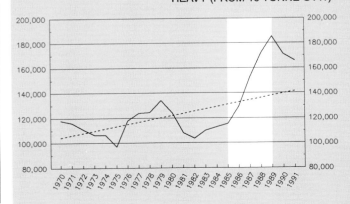

DEMAND FOR TRUCKS IN WESTERN EUROPE
HEAVY (FROM 16 TONNE GVW)

Year	Value
1985	115369
1986	129154
1987	152418
1988	171813
1989	185448

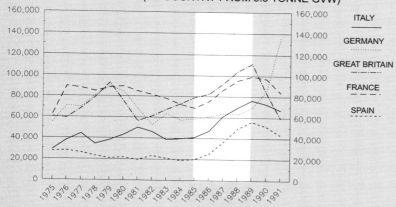

DEMAND FOR TRUCKS IN WESTERN EUROPE
(BY COUNTRY FROM 3.5 TONNE GVW)

ITALY
GERMANY
GREAT BRITAIN
FRANCE
SPAIN

	ITALY	GERMANY	GREAT BRITAIN	FRANCE	SPAIN
1985	41283	58931	79298	69120	20197
1986	47350	60831	82558	75498	25101
1987	61405	63685	92494	86600	36479
1988	69528	63352	104442	95463	49562
1989	76669	69485	111587	99544	56028

DEMAND FOR TRUCKS
(TOTAL FROM 3.5 TONNE GVW)

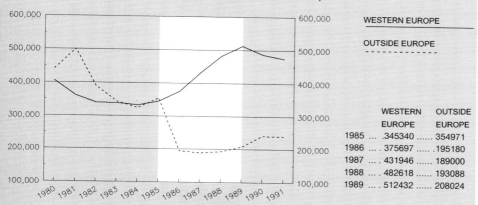

WESTERN EUROPE

OUTSIDE EUROPE

	WESTERN EUROPE	OUTSIDE EUROPE
1985	345340	354971
1986	375697	195180
1987	431946	189000
1988	482618	193088
1989	512432	208024

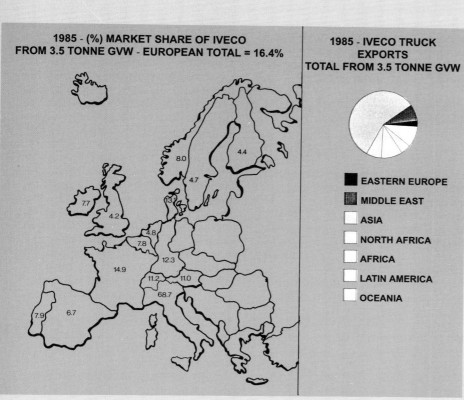

1985 - (%) MARKET SHARE OF IVECO
FROM 3.5 TONNE GVW - EUROPEAN TOTAL = 16.4%

1985 - IVECO TRUCK EXPORTS
TOTAL FROM 3.5 TONNE GVW

- ■ EASTERN EUROPE
- ▨ MIDDLE EAST
- □ ASIA
- □ NORTH AFRICA
- □ AFRICA
- □ LATIN AMERICA
- □ OCEANIA

generation of vehicles to be launched in the early Nineties. The efforts of the company had reached their peak.

THE PROCESS OF CONSOLIDATION OF THE IVECO IMAGE IS COMPLETED

The wave of innovation which revolutionalised Iveco in the second half of the Eighties was also projected outside the company.
The time was right to offer the markets a specific image of a company with a well-defined and consolidated personality.
In 1984 the TurboStar was launched still with the label of the national marks. But one year later, the Iveco logo braved it alone on the front of the vehicles in some markets.
The specific nature of some product lines is in the balance here, for example the fire-fighting vehicles and less so the defence vehicles. And history, which is being repeated, is also in the balance.
In 1986 there was the joint venture with Ford, and the acquisition of Pegaso in 1990.
And now both the English market and its Spanish counterpart find themselves on the horns of that dilemma once more: Iveco or Iveco-Ford, Iveco or Iveco-Pegaso? Deciding if and when to abandon a historic mark on any market is no easy matter and there is no clear cut answer.

A NEW IDENTITY FOR THE NETWORK TOO

In the process of consolidating Iveco's identity in the outside world, the removal of the national trade marks from the front of the vehicles was a fundamental step for the purposes of communication, not less in a historical context. That was not the only thing. Something similar had happened about the same time in the sales network which, on its road towards integration and rationalisation, had gradually emphasised the united Iveco front rather than identificaton with one or other of the historic marks.

The company was now on the threshold of the '90s and was fully aware that this was not going to be enough.

A quantum leap was needed in this area, too.

The industrial vehicle side was now a mature business with a market which was more or less a pure replacement market.

In fifteen years, the sales strategies and the profit margins had radically changed.

And the needs and application of the user had changed a great deal too, with competitors offering him a much wider choice.

Today, compared with fifteen years ago, if dealers are to do their work properly, they are going to need much more space and a considerable investment in premises, fixtures and fittings.

The client had to be presented with the right image, one which expressed efficiency and competence, adequate service capacity, a feeling of solid, but not ostentatious prosperity.

To sum up, it is the dealership with its premises and its aesthetics which gives the customer his first impressions of this contact with Iveco itself. This goes beyond any label.

It was these considerations which gave rise to the identity project in the Nineties, aimed at unifying the identification systems for anything to do with Iveco.

This identity programme was to touch on communications, the product and the physical embodiment of the sales network. As far as the network was concerned, the aim was not just to standardise the image of all the Iveco points of sale throughout Europe. Instead, it offered the network an advisory service to help it make the right choice when setting up a new showroom rather than helping to reorganise an existing one. Very many factors are involved. For example, when choosing an area and designing the infrastructure, it is important to make sure that any investment is safeguarded in the future. Property has to be chosen carefully from the point of view of local appreciation and the possibility of using the infrastructure for activities other than the sale of industrial vehicles.

Even the position of the site and of the internal infrastructure in relation to the adjacent road system is important, because this will help - or hinder - the overall view of the complex for those who come to look, or those simply passing by.

The premises are designed as an integral whole, integrating the internal and external environments: the face of a commercial activity is its visiting card, but that first impression also has to be confirmed inside.

With its identity project, Iveco planned to offer its dealers useful support with problems of this kind: from layout studies to building plans, Iveco developed standard, but not rigid guide lines, using the range of prefabricated industrial buildings on offer.

A NEW WAY OF HANDLING SALES

Naturally a company's image is important, but it is not everything. And the same is true of the dealer who, first and foremost, is an entrepreneur who, if he is to survive in the market place, has to be in a state of financial equilibrium which will allow him to operate with adequate margins and reasonable risk cover.

The costs are numerous and onerous: he has to run an efficient office and garage; he has to invest in the purchase of vehicles and spares; and then there are the costs of financing customers bearing in mind that a cash sale is a rarity. This is where the liquidity problem starts.

Usually, a dealer is able to finance the running of the company and also the spares store. However, he often finds it difficult to be self-sufficient when it comes to buying stock vehicles and financing sales to customers. Therefore, to ensure the good health of the sales network, the parent company has to provide positive financial support. In the second half of the Eighties in connection with new strategies to improve efficiency and reduce the burdens imposed by locked up capital, Iveco took on the problem of financing the network sales both to dealers and to end customers.

It did this on two fronts: directly, using mechanisms to facilitate payments for buying the vehicles; and indirectly by offering the dealer favourable financial conditions, for example when

vehicles are ordered over a long period.

Why was all this necessary? Because efficient planning on the part of the network is an essential pre-condition for optimising the sophisticated logistic system which Iveco had set up and which allowed the factories to operate with minimum stocks. And if this objective was to be achieved, the active support of the dealers was indispensable and had to be adequately rewarded.

Secondly, this direct support was complemented by easier finance which Iveco offered through finance companies on terms which differed from market to market (also depending on the specific regulations in force).

This could enable the dealer to buy his stock vehicles and also to find the type of finance his customers want.

Iveco had a dual role in all this. Generally speaking it had to find the best finance at the most favourable rates. On the other hand, in some cases, it arranged finance assuming the role of guarantor vis-à-vis the investor and also assuming some of the risk.

THE ORGANISATIONAL PLANS TAKE OFF

As far as the product is concerned, it was during those years that Iveco also implemented its plan to market a completely new and extremely wide range of vehicles using the progressive "just in time" system for production.

The implementaton of this ambitious programme raised the problem of having to develop a completely new method of producing.

It was necessary to invent organisational and technological methods and instruments capable of ensuring maximum flexibility and speed of response in all stages of the commercial and production process. But at the same time, methods which were capable of providing the necessary economies of scale despite extreme diversification of the product and volumes typical of the industrial vehicle.

It soon became clear that this could only be achieved with a high investment in technological automation, and not just at the factories. Iveco was to be run in a completely different way compared with the past. A new generaton of products would also produce a company which was radically different from its former self.

Under the large "umbrella" of the logistics division, a series of innovative plans and organisational projects was set in motion. There were twenty or so lines of action ranging from the rationalisation of production to interfactory material flow and, for the first time since Iveco had been in existence, these involved the connective tissue of the company, in other words its management systems. Not that they were not already interfaced, although this was barely apparent; or should we say there was only a small token of interfacing radiating from a central nucleus which, as we will remember, had started to revolve around logistics.

The result was that at the end of 1985, the logistics concept was not only confirmed but extended, through interfacing, to a whole series of other company processes following major investment in computer systems. In fact, the

company advanced from the era of organisation which saw it as a set of structural blocks to one where it was regarded as a body interfaced by processes and procedures.

LOGISTICS ARM IN ARM WITH COMPUTER TECHNOLOGY

The philosophy of logistics is based on the concept that if the sales forecasts are correct, enabling the factories to supply the right product at the right time, it is possible to obtain a consistent reduction in stocks, that is the number of vehicles produced and awaiting a buyer.

This is very important as far as profitability is concerned. Reducing the stocks means compressing the order-production-delivery-billing times, which also reduces the amount of capital tied up. This then becomes a form of self financing: the company achieves its liquidity from within itself.

But how can stocks be reduced? The problem is certainly a complex one and requires an overall corporate effort involving the markets, the dealer network, production, factories and suppliers. It is necessary to have a system which can gather and process this mass of information, transforming it into forecasts and production scheduling. The basic requirement of this is the ability of the various areas to dialogue, to understand each other and be provided with uniform data.

This is where the massive power of advanced computer technology comes in. Projects concerning data processing took off at Iveco in the second half of the Eighties.

The first years of the Eighties saw the standardisation of the hardware and the beginnings of the computer dialogue via Ivnet, whilst between 1985 and 1990, the company made the qualitative leap generated by interfacing the engineering centres and centralising the databases following the inauguration of the data processing centre in Turin.

This was a major innovation in data processing terms: centralisation of the systems (and of the databases); until then, they had thought along the lines of a single data processing system, but one that operated in three different regional areas.

So, for the first time in the history of Iveco, they managed to overcome the idiosyncrasies of the national companeis once and for all.

There was one fundamental concept: that of having a single datasource for all of the departments concentrated at a single station which could be updated by the user in real time wherever he happens to be. The idea of the database as a company asset became rooted in company thinking.

This in turn triggered the impressive growth of the Turin computer centre using the most up to date development methods. The main brain of the company was centred in Turin backed by a series of processing centres at Ulm, Brescia, Watford and Trappes. Ivnet was still making this possible.

Between the end of 1983 and the beginning of 1984, the new processing methods were developed, as were the software and the organisational factors.

The first to be implemented were the processes for specifying product which had two databases: the EBOM (Engineering Bill of Material) and the product sub-routine system which concerned planning and product marketing. Then there was the system which became the Order Processing system. And finally, IMIS, the Iveco Manufacturing Information System for controlling the factories and production. It is important to emphasise that in this context, the transnationality of the company offered opportunities, and they were shrewd enough to seize these. For example, EBOM, with its close links with engineering, was mainly developed on a Magirus base with Unic components and a modest contribution by Fiat. Why? Because the bill of material system developed at Magirus had proved to be the one most suited for defining the industrial vehicle in all its components. On the other hand, the part of the system associated with marketing methods was developed on the basis of the Unic culture, because the

French are, by tradition, the acknowledged leaders in marketing methods.

Finally IMIS, which concerned the factories and production, availed itself of the Fiat culture to develop a system which was highly innovative compared with anything which had gone before.

A significant example of the innovative spirit in which the problem was approached is given by the distinction introduced between the purchase department, which remained the preserve of the purchase contract department and the new materials and components procurement system which followed the purchase contract but which became the responsibility of the assembly works.

It is interesting to note that this logic was used to balance the supply relations both with outside suppliers and with the Iveco factories which produced components.

THE SYSTEM FOR GATHERING ORDER DETAILS IS REORGANISED: ORDER PROCESSING IS BORN

Having made the basic strategic decisions and established the centralised databases, they started to translate the plans into working instruments. To do this they started from the leading end of the chain, from the commercial sector and the markets. A truck is an extremely complex product. The aim was to achieve a maximum level of uniformity when dealing with orders for all markets. What is the main task of a dealer? To find out what customers want and need so that he can promote his sales in the best possible way through marketing and product support campaigns.

And, of course, it involves ordering the products from the production centres.

This required forecasting and reservations sytems, ordering systems, systems for physically moving the finished product; target management; product dialogue; billing; financial systems, and so on.

Obviously it would not be acceptable for each market to

operate with its own system without finding a common language.

If there was no uniform method for acquiring the data relating to the pattern of the various markets, the central departments responsible for scheduling the order-production flow would not be able to make reliable forecasts. They could not objectively decide whether, and to what extent, to expand one production area compared with another, or whether to favour one market at the expense of another.

Apart from these considerations, they were also aware that one day the development of data processing would allow each and every dealer to be able to access not only one market, but also to find out the situation regarding an order, to ask for changes, and so on.

So they decided to make a major leap at operational level so that all the markets would have a uniform system for providing information on product, forecasts and orders. The result was Order Processing, the new system for dealing with orders at Iveco. Conceived in 1982, Order Processing took its first small steps along its operational road between 1984 and 1985. The three main markets, Italy, France and Germany were included in 1987, and from 1989, the other European countries where Iveco did not have a production base were also covered. Today, Iveco's computer is one of the first which, in terms of structural organisation, is ready to operate as if Europe were already a single market.

On the opposite page a telephoto shot of the Data Processing Centre in Turin, the "nerve centre" of the computerised telecommunications network to which the management of the sophisticated Iveco logistics system has been entrusted since the early nineties.

FOUR CENTRALISED DESIGN LINES

At this stage, the department-alisation process within Iveco was complete and the management responsibilities were centralised with four design and testing lines: trucks, engines, drive lines and components, coordinated by a chief engineer.

As far as the trucks, drive lines and components are concerned, these remained at Turin, Brescia and Ulm.

Turin made the medium vehicles, including the future range which was being developed at the time, and the gearboxes (testing only). It also gained component innovation, i.e. the part relating to the pneumatic, hydraulic, electric and electronic systems, etc.

Brescia had the light "S" and "Z" ranges and the gearboxes. Ulm was responsible for the heavy vehicles, including those to be included in future ranges; it also had the "Club" vehicles and the fire-fighting vehicles. As far as the engines were concerned, these were concentrated at Turin and Arbon, with a small nucleus still at Trappes (which did not include testing). Bourbon-Lancy and Foggia were still responsible for testing.

Then there were the divisions. Bolzano had the defence division and the military vehicles (but not testing, which was done at Turin). The fire-fighting vehicles remained at Ulm. The bus division was centred at Turin and Ulm, linked by computer. Orlandi, in Modena, which specialized in tourist coaches was also included in the division.

Production was distributed as follows; In Italy, Turin had the TurboStar and the medium range vehicles, the 8000 and 8280 engines and bus chassis. Brescia had the light "S" an "Z" vehicles and the light gearboxes. Suzzara made the van versions of the "S" vehicles. Milan made the axles, Valle Ufita and Modena made the buses. And Foggia made the 8100 engines.

Bourbon-Lancy in France made the 8210, 8460 and 8360 engines. Ulm in Germany made the heavy road vehicles in the T-range and all the off-road vehicles, both forward cab and nose versions,

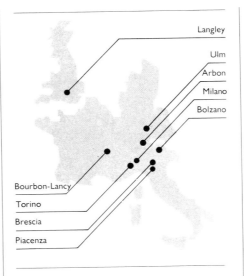

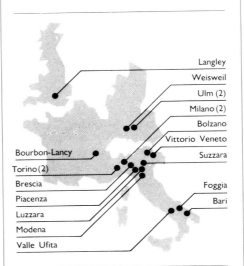

and also the axles.

Towards the end of the decade, the scene started to change. Langley was added, with the engineering and production facilities for the Cargo 1 and Cargo 2 range. Milan acquired a small axle production line.

A new name appeared on the engine scene, that of Iveco, rechristened Iveco Motoren Forschung (Iveco M.F.), whilst the testing department in Brescia all but disappeared.

There were also changes in the divisions. Ulm no longer made buses, whilst the division gained Sicca di Vittorio Veneto, which designed and produced chassis. Bolzano acquired the testing of the defence vehicles formerly at Turin and, at the same time, the division acquired Astra of Piacenza with its production and design facilities.

ENGINEERING AND TESTING SUCCUMB TO THE COMPUTER

On the subject of computers, you have seen how right from the outset, Iveco made every use of the resources available including for the design and testing of new products.

It is a tradition which was continued throughout the Eighties, particularly in the second half of the decade, with an explosion in the use of CAD and the next logical step, CAT (Computer Aided Testing). This was used for simulating fatigue tests, both in the laboratory and on the road, with obvious benefits in terms of costs and quality. Being able to simulate the testing of not just one mechanical component but also complex assemblies, eg. a suspension system, means being able to test a large number of solutions in a relatively short time, resulting in greater optimisation of the final solution.

It was CAT which, in 1988, led to the installation of a power train bench in Turin which made it possible to test the complete drive line: the engine, gearbox, shaft and brakes. In those years systems were also introduced for measuring engine emissions, particularly fumes, which were previously only used for engines intended for the USA.

The location of the main Iveco research and development centres (above) and production plants in the latter half of the eighties. On the right hand page, trucks in track and road trials.

AUTOMATION OF PRODUCTION TECHNOLOGIES IS EXTENDED

During those years there was also considerable activity in the field of production technology.

A particularly important event in July of 1987 was the inauguration of a new plant at the Iveco Unic factory at Bourbon-Lancy which represented a change of technology for producing the Iveco engines.

It was the epilogue to a process which started in 1983 as a forerunner to the launch of the new 8460 engine.

It was decided to abandon the traditional production systems and develop a flexible manufacturing system using NC machines. At that time there was practically nothing of this kind, apart from equipment at Sofim.

This was an idea which would be progressively refined: first there was just one machine, then a group of machines. And then, to increase the overall efficiency, they arrived at a system for supplying the production plant automatically using pallets.

From here to the concept of flexible cells controlled and connected by computer was but one short step, integrated in the logic of the new machining operations. And so FMS was born (Flexible Manufacturing System), a system allowing the flexible automation of mechanical machining operations. The flexibility achieved at Bourbon-Lancy is flexibility in its truest sense.

Each set of machines is independent but, at the same time, each is also universal in relation to the other. In this way it is possible to program (in different quantities and order) the machining of different parts: exhaust and intake manifolds, distributor caps, crankcases, cast iron or aluminium covers, for example. The system was designed for a production of between 20 and 30 thousand engines a year. If Bourbon-Lancy was the important event of those years, the innovations gradually introduced at the various Iveco factories were also a milestone.

For example, a COMAU flexible transfer line was installed in the press shop at Brescia (the first of its kind in Italy). A press line was automated with robots operating between presses and a laser cutting system was installed in Turin. In the panel shop, the cab and chassis spot welding method was automated at Brescia and Suzzara and a system for transporting cabs on skids was introduced at Brescia.

In the paint shop, a system of rotating cups with a high build cataphoretic cycle and the application of stone-throw resistant enamels was installed at Brescia and Suzzara.

As far as the mechanical machining operations were concerned, there were many innovations which involved the engines: new robots for deburring the cylinder head, centralised control of the assembly process and a pilot plant for the dynamic measurement of engine noise at Foggia. A pilot plant for the laser hardening of the valve seats, optical fibre control of the induction hardening process, the automatic checking of pilot equipment for laser hardening of the valve seats, optic fibre controls for the induction tempering process, automatic control of the surface of the cylinder liners, crankshaft dimensions and the micro-structural precision of the crankshaft journals, at Turin, for the 8000 series.

For the gearboxes, laser welding equipment capable of making gears and gearshafts, in Brescia. For the axles, robot welding arms and test robots, in Milan.

CNC machines for flexible production and sophisticated control methods (bottom right, system to check the manufacture of profiles) for consistently high quality.

THE WHOLE RANGE STRUCTURE IS COMPLETED

While Iveco was committed with all its resources, both human and financial, to this process of "transformation" in every area, including the development of the new product generation. Iveco did not neglect, obviously, to push ahead the development of the ranges of vehicles already in production.

As we have seen, the process of integrating the products and rationalising production facilities had been completed. It was now a question of allowing the various ranges to "mature", in a physiological process of technical development and widening of the choice with a view to ever more pressing "specialisation". Let us look at the salient facts.

Starting from the "S" range, a 35.10 combi and van versions 35-45-49.10 were introduced in 1987 with a new long wheelbase (3950mm) for a payload of 15.4 m³. In autumn of the same year the civil version of the 40.10W 4x4 came into production, with a 100HP Sofim 8140 direct injection turbo engine in rigid, van, combi and crew cab options. In 1988 the combi 40.10 and crew cab 40.10W were included in the range.

In 1989 the range received major style and technical updating, with external and internal restyling of the cab and a palletised side door for vans: the addition of a powerful 103 HP version of the Turbo Sofim engine and a new naturally aspirated 75 HP version; the addition of a new gearbox (Iveco 2824).

The "Z" range benefitted from a new external and internal cab facelift, coupled with numerous mechanical changes; larger cc and HP 8000 series engines (3.9 litre and 88 HP 8040: 5.9 litre and 138/177 HP 8060 respectively in turbo version), new Rockwell single reduction axles, front disc brakes (model 79.14).

In 1987 there was another external cab facelift and at the same time new versions were introduced, the 60.11-65.12-79.12 with 8040, 4 cylinder 3.9 litre engine in 100 HP LTC and 115 HP TC. Parabolic suspension was introduced on the whole range.

THE PRODUCT IN BRIEF

On road

Tractors
GCW from 44 to 17.5 tonne
From 420 to 128 horsepower
34 models 6x2P, 6x2C, 4x2

Rigids
GVW from 26 to 3.5 tonne
From 420 to 72 horsepower
174 models 6x4, 6x2P, 4x4, 4x2

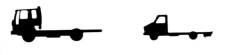

Vans
GVW from 8 to 3.5 tonne
Load volumes from 18.3 to 7m³
From 138 to 72 horsepower
12 models 4x4, 4x2

Off road

Tractors
GCW from 82 to 38 tonne
From 352 to 256 horsepower
11 models 6x6, 6x4, 4x2

Rigids
GVW from 33 to 12.5 tonne
From 352 to 130 horsepower
44 models 8x4x4, 6x6, 6x4, 4x4, 4x2

The "light" vehicles from Iveco range at the end of the eighties: From the top: The latest TurboDaily, in the 4x2 and 4x4 version and the "Z" range lorry.

In the medium sector, yet again in 1985 there was another step forward, with the introduction of the new 145 model, with the 8060 in the NA version with 138 HP and TC with 177 HP, which in practice replaced the previous 130, 140 and 150 models.

Simultaneously the components of the 115 and 135 models were rationalised with the more powerful 8060 engine in naturally aspirated 138 HP and turbo 177 HP versions.

In 1986 the 175 was born, offered with 177 and 240 HP engines (the latter is the 9.5 litre 8460, with six cylinders in line in turbo version): new ZF and Fuller gearboxes were adopted along with Rockwell axles.

1987 saw the marketing of the 175.24 RSU version with automatic transmission, specially designed for refuse collection. The rear pneumatic suspension was introduced in 1989.

This was the configuration of the Iveco medium range vehicles before the EuroCargo. We have now arrived at the heavy road vehicles.

In 1985 the chassis of all the vehicles was standardised to that of the new TurboStar. The "T" range versions had different cabs and also less powerful engines. New models were added to the range such as the 220.30 PT 6x2, with a central steering third axle and the 140.26 powered with the new 260 HP turbo 8460 engine.

Between 1987 and 1989 the range - both the "T" and the TurboStar - benefitted from constant development with the addition of specialist versions: the 6x2P with a rear steering third axle plus individual wheel and pneumatic suspension; the .36 versions with the 360 HP, 13.8 litre 6 cylinder in-line turbo after-cooler variant of the 8210 engine; the (large volume) .30 and .32 versions, still with the 8210 engine but without after-cooler, developing 304 HP and 317 HP respectively; and the municipal version, the 190.24, which had a 241 HP, 9.5 litre turbo engine in the 8460 series.

In 1989, the TurboStar 190.48 went onto the market with an V8, 8280 engine in the 476 HP turbo after-cooler version and the new

.32 models powered with the 318 HP turbo after-cooler version of the 8460 engine (6 cyliner, 9.5 litres).

In 1990 the development of the range culminated in the launching of the Turbotech, the last generation before the Eurotech, which had a slightly restyled cab and a 377 HP engine.

In 1985 they also rationalised the range of site vehicles, both those with forward cab and the nose versions. Another important event was in 1987 when the forward cab was standardised with those of the "E" range road vehicles, with important benefits in terms of comfort.

Finally in 1989, the air-cooled engines were improved to take into account the regulations concerning noise and environmental protection.

Still from the late eighties, (to the right) are the Iveco trucks 145.17 and 175.24 from the 'top' ranges, above the TurboTech with a 337 horsepower engine.

TRUCK OF THE YEAR 1992

EuroCargo

IVECO

AG 44005

1990... IVECO :
EUROPE IN A COMPANY

We are now in the Nineties. An important time, and not just for Iveco.

During the twenty years covered by our story, events have evolved constantly and the situation today is seen as a radical change - for the better certainly - but not always, and not in every way. Many equilibria - political, social and market - have been upset and the search for new positions has found no quick and easy solution.

The repurcussions on the scene which interest us are vast and incisive. The cyclic nature of the markets has produced the "nth" recession stage to coincide with the start of what is the last decade of this century; a recession which, in the middle of 1991, reached dramatic proportions in some markets: a drop (compared with 1990) of around 50% in Britain and 20% in France.

The situation is less serious in Italy, not exceeding 7% - 8%, but in Germany the market is going into reverse through the effects of reunification and there the drop exceeds 15%.

In a situation which is already difficult, industry is further burdened by the uncertainties and problems associated with a dual transition stage: the arrival of the single market in 1993 which is likely to change the rules of the game, and the environmental legislation which is becoming tougher, imposing stricter limits on vehicle emissions, noise, "clean" technologies and the recycling of materials.

As far as vehicle manufacture is concerned, all these measures mean planning problems and enormous investments to renew not just the product, but also the production technology.

This is why, almost twenty years after the beginning of our story, the agreements and concentrations between industries are not yet complete. The examples of Daf-Leyland, Volvo-Renault and of course Iveco-Enasa are worthy of note.

Why? Because they have tried to achieve economies of scale, to spread the enormous investment needed to remain competitive in the market.

What is happening represents the latest affirmation of how right the vision of the future was which inspired Iveco to conceive and implement the idea of a large company with a transnational soul.

We have traced the events from the first unsteady steps until the vigorous maturity reached at the threshold of the Nineties.

Iveco is faced with an open challenge at the start of the last decade of the century.

If companies think that the present situation is in a constant state of evolution, then the future must surely hold a panorama which is just as different with regard to the market and the relationship between manufacturer and customer.

We have to expect considerable changes due to the opening up of the European market and the spread of coastal trading.

Such deregulation will have the effect of generating strong competition, favouring the more efficient transport companies and, inevitably, a reduction in charges. And even if we choose not to expect a marked reduction in the demand for vehicles (there will, after all, be more goods to transport), industry must not forget that it will be faced with a much more demanding user, one more conscious of his choices, and one more demanding in terms of product and performance.

Vehicle manufacturers will have to present themselves to the customer as "purveyors of added value" rather than just suppliers of goods, and try to satisfy the needs of the "customer's customer" too, in order to allow transport of companies to improve their income structure.

The Iveco of today has established all the structures and ground rules needed to sustain a leading role in this new context: the size of the company and its share of the market, the efficiency of its management, production organi-sation and its sales network.

And also in terms of the technological, technical and performance characteristics of the product and the size of the range offered.

As we have seen, a determining factor in achieving these goals was the five year investment (1988/-1992) of 5,000 million Lire to be made in plant and technology.

This plan is aimed at the development of an entirely new, highly innovative generation of products and a full range at world level.

This plan has been implemented with the widespread introduction of the most up to date factory automation systems aimed at achieving the quality and flexibility which are essential if a company is to compete in the market of the Nineties.

A NEW CHALLENGE: GLOBAL OPTIMISATION

But in a market situation which is becoming more competitive and sophisticated, product quality alone will not be sufficient to guarantee the future.

Performance, diversification, price, and quality will be the things to watch. It will be necessary to offer that bit more.

And Iveco is translating the intellectual concept of global optimisation into practice.

What does this mean? It means that the process of optimisation will also be extended outside the company to the customer, to offer him a product within the global product-service concept which will allow him to secure his competitiveness within his working environment.

The aim is no longer merely to produce vehicles which provide the user with a competitive plus.

It is also that of supplying the customer with a service which is better in global terms. And that means everything.

For example, the cycle between the time when the order is placed and when the goods are delivered needs to be as short as possible to minimise the capital in circulation and to give the customer a tailor-made product within the shortest possible time. This is obtained by involving suppliers and by making them operate in close liaison with the end factories and according to a strict timetable.

But the financial aspects also need to be improved.

The customer has to be provided with the financial service he needs and it must be ensured that each invoice arrives at its destination as quickly as possible.

Systems also need to be overhauled in the administrative field so that staff can concentrate more on work with a greater added value and less on work with a low intellectual content.

In this sence, this can be defined as total quality or global optimisation.

The targets are two fold: on the one hand we need to achieve new levels of efficiency, indispensable for generating the necessary internal resources to build the future and, on the other, a coherent use has to be made of the resources generated for renewal of the product and of the production processes.

The concept is also valid for globalisation of the business which means having a presence on all major markets in the future.

We are talking about consolidation in Europe and a precise strategy for the markets outside Europe with industrial agreements or joint ventures; for example, if a company wants to enter closed markets, the only way is to become a local manufacturer.

BRINGING THE PRODUCT TO THE MARKET

The desire to bring the product, that is the industrial vehicle, as close to the customer as possible, is expressed in tangible form in a new rationalisation measure involving the company management which was completed at the beginning of the Nineties.

This rationalisation measure involved both design and production, and market management, by defining specific sets of responsibilities.

On the one hand there is the industrial vehicle "product", i.e. the engineering content of the final product and the commercial aspects, and on the other, we have the mechanical components, from the engine to the power train and the chassis.

In practical terms the new style of management is seen as a deverticalisation operation performed by Iveco on itself, with the main components regarded as specific engineering and business products which are then sold to the vehicle assembly companies.

The management of the markets is viewed from a different perspective.

The territorial responsibilities of the different areas are reorganised to overcome the sub-division between the domestic markets of Iveco and the rest of Europe.

The Italian and French market management teams remain separate. England is responsible for the Scandinavian markets (excluding Sweden) and Germany for the markets of Central Europe, (Benelux, Sweden and Austria).

The importance of this operation is clear: Europe today is a large single market and Iveco intends to avail itself of its opportunities in the most efficient manner.

A NEW WAY OF LOOKING AT INDUSTRIAL ORGANISATION

The needs of the end customer must be satisfied by implementing a suitable product, marketing and sales policy. The product must be brought nearer to the market and the time taken for the commercial network and the factories to respond to the changing needs of the user must be reduced. At the same time, stocks - a huge financial burden - must be contained using a style of management which is optimised in all its aspects and a logic which embraces the ideal of Just in Time.

Ambitious objectives which, if they are to be achieved, require suitable structures and resources which can respond sensitively to the needs of the market and perceive the symptoms of each new trend at the earliest possible stage.

And they require a system of management of the order-to-production cycle which is able to respond quickly and flexibly to the demands of the sales network.

For Iveco, this means globalisation with Marketing and Logistics as the driving forces, backed by the power of the computer. We have seen how the foundations for this innovation were laid in the Eighties, first with the development of the databases and the Order Processing System.

And now, with advanced computer technology established in all the technical and commercial departments of the company, the grand project to integrate production and the market which started to take shape at the beginning of the Nineties.

A PRIORITY AIM: TO KNOW THE MARKET INSIDE OUT

In the commercial sector, the problem has been taken on by Maisy (Marketing Information System), a sophisticated integrated system used to formulate objective sales forecasts.

As we have said, we use the term forecasts to quantify in terms of volume, the difference between the orders and the sales forecasts formulated by a certain commercial area.

But remember, the difference between the two terms is important.

An order is a request to produce a vehicle which has been effectively sold to a customer.

Therefore, an order is represented by a physical entity, a vehicle (even if not yet physically in production) and therefore an order can only be considered as such if the agreements have been defined between the seller and the customer with regard to the delivery of the vehicle, the contents of the vehicle itself and the financial arrangements for its payment.

A forecast on the other hand represents a quantification of the expectations concerning the sales in a given territory over a certain period of time. Therefore, it is only a hypothesis.

The task of Maisy is to allow its users to formulate hypotheses (in other words forecasts) which are as objective as possible. To do this, Maisy operates on the basis of a detailed monitoring of the markets both nationally and in individual areas.

The registrations are recorded and analysed according to the type of vehicle and territory, as are national and local traffic levels, the type of vehicles and the characteristics of the vehicles. On this basis it is possible to schedule customer contact at the right time and in the right way. But also, once negotiations are in progress, they must be concluded in the most advantageous way for both parties.

The right knowledge of the needs of the potential user enables the seller to give the best possible advice on the choice of product.

Using the Sapac sub-routine (sales activity planning and control), Maisy also makes it possible to monitor the progress of dealer/customer contacts in the various areas.

The sales forecasts are then formulated with all this information area by area. These, together with the order, are forwarded to the Central Logistics System at Iveco (Order Processing) which uses the rolling process to transform these data into a production schedule for a given period.

THE LOGISTICS WEAPONS ARE PRIMED

So, having started the dialogue with the markets, the next step is to integrate and process the data acquired to produce the production schedules.

These have to reflect the market situation as closely as possible. And they have to be managed with mechanisms which guarantee a parity check between the order started in the factories and the forecast grid for the product. The problem is a very complex one. Each market operates with a few dozen basic models in each range, each of which have different wheelbases, equipment and facilities, some standard, some optional.

Consequently, in theory, the possible combinations tend towards the infinite. But this variety of combinations is measured against a finite quantity of sales.

Therefore it is necessary to lay down the ground rules, the operating methods and the limits which make it possible to define a reasonable probability framework on which the factory production can be scheduled.

However, this type of scheduling cannot be rigid, at least not for a long period: it is necessary to establish stages in the time arc spanned by the schedule in which the forecast can be checked and the schedule adjusted as required.

This happens for a minimum period, after which it is no longer possible to modify the production schedule.

All these functions are subject to the rolling process, a method with which the forecasts (sales forecasts

and orders together) are made to roll in a strictly controlled process of checking and adjusting the production/sales balance sheet.

Each rolling cycle covers a period ranging from 20 months maximum to 12 months minimum, including the month during which the markets make their forecasts. The minimum period of time for transferring orders from the market to the factory is 3 months.

This mechanism is used to define a standard stock - how much is to be produced each month for each market and for each product line.

To be able to operate the rolling mechanism, it is necessary to interact with a well defined production system and product grid.

This is where the computerised product system comes into its own. This system is responsible for managing the product, with the principal task of checking that the production requests are congruent with the product grid. In simple conceptual terms, the product system defines the content and characteristics of the product in detail. This process takes place within two classification sub-routines, the VCB (Vehicle Country Block) and the VM (Vehicle - Market).

Let us explain. A range of vehicles is built up on a certain number of basic models available with a certain number of different features (weight, engine, wheelbase, type of cab, suspension, etc.). Each vehicle can also be personalised according to the demands of the given market and, obviously, of the end user. Whereas the VCB gathers together the design specifications of the basic versions and of the variants of each range (range "S", EuroCargo, etc.), the VM system defines and applies constraints in terms of specific engineering and equipment for a given market. These constraints either concern legislation or commercial opportunities defined for the market concerned.

All these specifications define the mix of characteristics which transform a given vehicle in the production grid into a vehicle which is either compatible with a given market or not.

The entire system is structured so

that an order for a certain vehicle intended for a certain market is rejected automatically if one or more of the characteristics requested for the vehicle do not conform to the product grid defined by the VCB or the constraints established by the vehicle-market system.

This system should provide computer support for sellers in the near future as a product database on CD-ROM (a digital disk similar to the compact disk which we all know). It can be read and processed using a portable computer and a software package which, by means if simple logic codes, allows the product grid to be exploded into its infinite possibilities in order to obtain the precise vehicle configuration the customer wants. Yet another step.

It is also worth considering calculating the price of the vehicle configuration directly and printing the contract form which, once signed by the customer, will automatically have the satus of an order ready to be input into the rolling system and then into production.

FROM IMIS TO CIM, COMPUTER AIDED SYSTEMS FOR THE WORKS TOO

To sum up; with Order Processing, we have gathered the order and sales forecasts from the markets and have input them into the logistics system.

The orders are checked against the product grid for parity by the product system. The rolling program then processes the sales forecasts for a given period of months and transforms it into a schedule for the factories and for the procurement of materials and components.

At this point, the production instrument comes into its own: IMIS, the Iveco Manufacturing Information System.

This is a complex computer system involving a set of procedures, data and automation developed with the aim of allowing the integrated control of all the activities relating to the product.

Its task is to harmonize design, production and material flows according to the requirements of

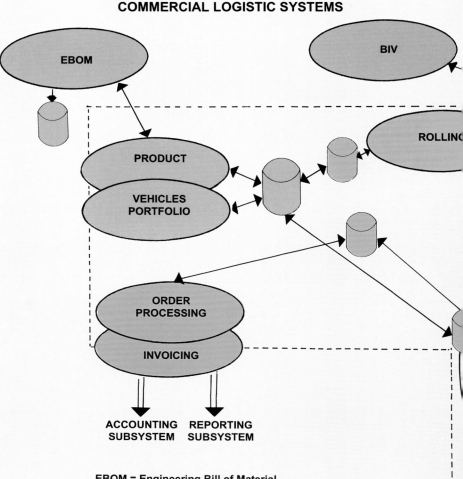

COMMERCIAL LOGISTIC SYSTEMS

EBOM = Engineering Bill of Material
BIV = Warranty Systems

The diagram shows the logistic organisation adopted by Iveco for the coordination of all activities relating to the product: from gaining an order to the organisation of production, to the management of the delivery to the final customer.

Here above, the areas relating to commercial activity, in which the characteristics of the product-market are defined, with interface to the distinct planning base (EBOM). The system, starting from the short and medium-term forecasts (Rolling), manages the portfolio of customers' orders and the availability of vehicles until the final customer is invoiced, with interface to the accounting systems. The vehicle is then loaded into the systems which follow it during the guarantee period (BIV).

On the right, the areas relating to production, from programming, including the supply of materials and stock management, to the control of the flow on the production and assembly lines (LIMO). The whole system provides for the necessary interface between the accounting and purchase systems.

PRODUCTION LOGISTIC SYSTEMS

Master production
schedule

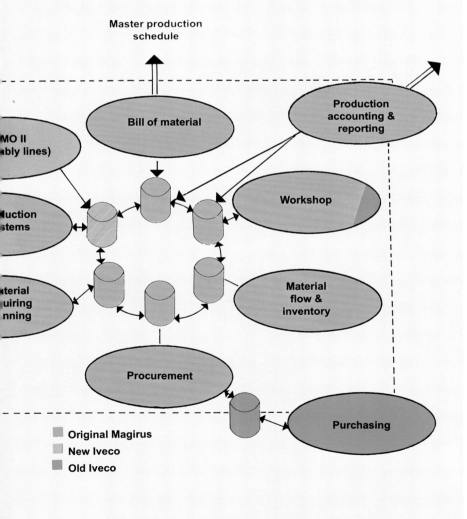

Bill of material

Production
accounting &
reporting

MO II
bly lines)

Workshop

duction
stems

terial
uiring
nning

Material
flow &
inventory

Procurement

Purchasing

◼ Original Magirus
◼ New Iveco
◼ Old Iveco

that order (purchase, supply and transport), reduce the timescale and allow small product batches to be put into production in sequence.

The capacity of the system to acquire valid peripheral data allows a fast and coherent control of the production process, from the purchase stage to the factory and on to supplier scheduling stage with monthly, weekly and real time cycles.

Consequently, this is not simply a concentration of control processes, but a system based on compatibility between maximum coordination and maximum decentralisation.

The IMIS requires other computer-based control and management sub-routines.

One of the main sub-routines is IPIS - the Iveco Purchasing Information System - which has the task of integrated purchase management using standardised procedures and an efficient interface between the purchase, administration, logistics and production departments.

This is an "on-line" system which is able to respond to practically any request in real time, thereby making it possible to refine the analysis and control methods and to have an extremely detailed view of events.

IMIS completed its running-in cycle at the Brescia, Turin and Ulm factories with the launch of the new "Euro" ranges.

The order from the customer boots the complete system. When an order is received, IMIS, assisted by the lateral support systems, defines the bill of quantity for the vehicle required, makes sure that the parts needed are supplied to the machining shops, controls the stocks and workshops, programs the assembly sequence for the vehicles according to the orders and monitors the process right up to the time when the goods are despatched.

The information network which interconnects all the Iveco factories using a single language and a single data file allows a constant interaction between market, front end factories, end factories and suppliers.

The needs of the market are transformed into orders which IMIS sends to the end factories

Automated technologies and a high level of standardisation in component engineering: Iveco chose this strategy to guarantee the quality and competitiveness of its new ranges for the '90s.

(which the finished vehicle will ultimately leave) and also to the front end factories which produce the components. The front end factories notify their suppliers of their requirements and the operations then start.

IMIS allows the work to be scheduled weekly both for the factories and for the suppliers. In this way, the flexibility of the end factories is increased, the production times are reduced and the response to the customer's request is faster.

Each day, the main computer in Turin - the clearing point for orders from the entire Iveco sales network - transmits the production schedule to the processor at each end factory both for the finished vehicles due to roll off the line and for the sub-assemblies intended for other factories. Based on the production schedule received, the processor calculates the requirements for the cells which assemble the sub-assemblies, checks the facilities and sends the production instructions (for the body panel cells) and the transport instructions (for the automated stores and the transport system) to all the terminals in real time.

Therefore, the reorganisation has been total and has involved the factory in all its aspects: layout, production line technology, management logic and computer systems to support and integrate this logic.

The dual aim of flexibility and quality has been sought in maximum integration between all the activities inside the factory and also at the interface between these and the external production points (the suppliers) and commercial points (the Iveco logistics system).

That which has been achieved - and is still going on to some extent - is the total computerisation of the industrial organisation, from the commercial sector to design and production, using the processing instruments which have developed so rapidly during the Eighties and up to now: the Ivnet data network, the computerised logistics of Order Processing, computerisation of the engineering processes using CAD and all subsequent developments,

from CAT (Computer Aided Testing) to CAE (Computer Aided Engineering) and finally CAM (Computer Aided Manufacturing).

The combination of all these systems has created CIM (Computer Integrated Manufacturing), the computer controlled instrument which, when interfaced with IMIS, aims directly at the heart of the Just-In-Time process, making the order - purchase - production flow completely transparent and coordinated.

AUTOMATION AND MODULARITY FOR AN ADVANCED FULL RANGE

The present Iveco range is the fruit of a very ambitious project involving the total renewal of the product and the production technologies which started in the second half of the Eighties.

The aim was the development of a completely new range, characterised by an extreme diversification of basic models and a very high degree of standardisation at component level.

This standardisation is seen from two aspects.

As far as the company is concerned, it is an instrument for improving the quality of the product and achieving interesting synergies at the same time. As far as the user is concerned, it is an innovation in terms of product content and diversity which is being built up to a worldwide range with the introduction of versions not available at the moment: different engine powers, pneumatic suspensions, vehicles with three axles and four wheel drives in the medium and medium to heavy ranges, electronics, diagnostics, etc.

The development of the range has constantly referred back to the needs of the user, based on strict standards with regard to minimising running costs by reducing fuel consumption, refining the aerodynamics of the vehicles, improving reliability, enhancing product quality, reducing maintenance and repair costs.

To achieve this, they have not only worked on the product; the project has also involved the factories with technological innovation and

logistic organisation of the processes aimed at a close coordination between the commercial part of the business and production. The result is an extremely diverse range, modern in its engineering and right at the forefront of production technology. There are three main families: the light "S" range, in the 3 to 6 tonner band; the medium and medium to heavy range, from 6 tonnes to 16 tonnes; and the heavy vehicle range, from 16 tonnes up to the limits allowed by current European legislation.

SPAIN ALSO BECOMES A "DOMESTIC" MARKET

Let us talk again about "globalisation" and markets. This time in terms of joint ventures.

1990 was an important year from this point of view too. Under an agreement signed on 12 September between Iveco and INI (the holding company owned by the Spanish state) Iveco acquired 60% control of Enasa, the producer of Pegaso commercial vehicles. The agreement provides for an industrial development plan for the Company and the integration, with immediate effect of Pegaso and Iveco.

It is an important new step in Iveco's European development strategy, and similar, though in a different industrial size, to the English joint venture. It was an excellent opportunity for Iveco to increase its penetration of the Iberian market, and gain an efficient sales network and a good local product.

"PEGASO" A MARQUE WITH A LONG HISTORY

The history of the Pegaso marque began in 1946, but to understand its intricacies it is necessary to go back to 1936, to a Spain badly scarred by the consequences of the Civil War of 1936-1939 and stunned by the devastation of the second world war.

It was in these circumstances, on 25 September 1941, under the direct control of the Spanish Ministry of Industry, INI, that the Instituto Nacional de Industria was created, with the objective of putting the economy of the country back on its feet, supporting with largely public capital the rebirth of a competitive national industry.

As far as the transport and automobile sectors were concerned, there was at the time only one industrial entity of any size in Spain; the prestigious mark Hispano-Suiza. The company is remembered today all over the world because of its superb cars, and because for most of its history it also produced commercial vehicles and buses.

Spain's domestic crisis also affected Hispano-Suiza as the government concentrated almost exclusively on armourments and ammunition for war and withdrew any financial support.

So, in spite of having ambitious plans in the pipeline to develop new vehicles and engines and from the early 1940s, having resumed production of its prestigious V12 aero engines, the Company found itself in serious financial difficulties. This was the situation then, when in 1946, INI began its first industrial reconstruction programme.

Responsibility for the automobile department was entrusted to the brilliant engineer Wifredo P. Ricart, who for political reasons had left his job as manager of Alfa Romeo's technical department.

In the private car sector it was decided to aim for co-operation with a foreign company and later this plan was to lead to the creation of SEAT, Sociedad Espanola de Automoviles de Turismo, and the production of cars under licence from Fiat.

Commercial vehicles and buses were considered to be of strategic importance and it was decided to establish a nationalised industry. To help in the process, the Centre De Estudios Tecnicos de Automocion (CETA) was set up in Madrid in January 1946 and entrusted to Ricart. CETA was to study and test vehicles and internal combustion engines and everything relating to their production.

On 23 October that same year, with an initial capital of 240 million Pesetas, Enasa, Empresa Nacional de Autocamiones S.A. was launched, with its management and design centre in Madrid and technical offices, test laboratories and production plant in Barcelona.

The works in Barcelona were none other than the old Hispano-Suisa at la Sagrera works, which were acquired by INI, together with the designs and licences of the company in the industrial vehicle and bus sector, in October 1946.

The agreements between Enasa and Hispano-Suiza di not iclude the marque and so in 1947 Enasa was looking for an identity for its models. On 30 January the name Hispano was registered and six months later the final name was chosen, Pegaso, the horse from Greek mythology, a symbol of lightness and power. Just why Pegaso was chosen is a long story. Hispano-Suiza was also renowned for its aero engines. Its V8 engines, designed in Barcelona and manufactured under licence by Itala and Scat of Turin, were fitted to the aircraft of the legendary "Squadriglia" of the French aviation ace Francesco Baracca, and he had used a "little horse" for his insignia.

But the coincidences did not stop there. Ricart, the Technical Director of Enasa, had worked for the aero engine division of Alfa Romeo, and it so happened that at the time, Alfa also overhauled Bristol "Pegasus" engines. And so the Enasa vehicles designed by Ricart were baptised "Pegaso" and the mythical "little horse",

Artillery Captain Emilio de La Cuadra Albiol, who founded the motor vehicle manufacturing company in 1898, which some years later in 1904 gave birth to Hispano-Suiza.
ABOVE: The 4-door La Cuadra 4.5 HP of 1900.

strangely without wings, became the Pagaso 'trademark'.

HISPANO-SUIZA
A LEGENDARY NAME

The Hispano-Suiza's roots go back to the end of the last century, when in 1898 the artillery captain Emilio de La Cuadra, together with the Swiss engineer Carlos Vellino, owner of an electrical accumulator factory, founded the Compania General Espanola de Coches Automoviles E. de La Cuadra, Sociedad en Comandita in Barcelona.

The objective of the new company was to produce electrically-driven vehicles. They were, more correctly, hybrids, since it was planned to drive them by two electric motors supplied by a dynamo operated by a petrol engine and accumulator batteries. The driving power was to be supplied directly by the dynamo or the accumulators. Under special conditions, for example starting on steep slopes to obtain more power, it was planned to use both the direct supply and that of the accumulators simultaneously.

But De La Cuadra had over-estimated his financial resources of the enterprise and he was forced to relinquish the company to a group of creditors. J. Castro Soc. en Comandita, Fabrica Hispano-Suiza de Automoviles, was launched.

This was the first time that the name Hispano-Suiza had appeared in the company title. It indicated the Spanish nationality of the firm and the presence in the com-pany itself of the brilliant eng-ineer Marc Birkigt, who was hired by Vellino in August 1899.

The first Castro car, a 10 HP, was ready in July 1903 and on 22 November of that same year a 14 HP was presented with a 2.4 litre engine.

But, in spite of the interest aroused by these cars, once again the company found itself in financial difficulties and in

March 1904, having sold only five vehicles, it was no longer able to meet its payments. It was clear that to guarantee itself a future, greater financial stability was needed.

The partners decided to set up a new limited liability company with a capital of 500,000 Pesetas, consisting of 1000 shares of 500 Pesetas each. On 14 June 1904, the Hispano-Suiza Fabrica de Automoviles S.A. was set up on this basis. The underwriters included the most important figures in the world of industry and finance in Barcelona.

It was the start of an adventure destined to turn the name Hispano-Suiza into a legend and, not only for cars. For it is a fact that as well as for its superb cars, Hispano-Suiza also won acclaim for the production of sophisticated aviation engines in six countries: Spain, France, Great Britain, Italy, United States and Japan. This engine was also the king-pin of a generation of 4 and 6 cylinder engines which gave the Hispano-Suiza a place of absolute supremacy in automobile industry.

By virtue of this presence in the aeronautical industry, at the end of 1919 there appeared on the radiator of Hispano-Suiza vehicles, not only the cars, but often also the lorries and buses, the "Swan", the mascot of the Guyneme fighter air squadron. The first cars of the newly formed Company were introduced in 1906 at the Paris Motor Show.

In 1907 Hispano-Suiza introduced its first 6 cylinder engine, an 11.1 litre, 60/70 HP consisting of three blocks of two cylinders derived from the 40 HP. This was an enormous engine, with a power output of 76 HP; only 8 units were produced. In 1908, a new engine and a new chassis for motorcars were produced; 12/15 HP with a four cylinder block, which by virtue of the low consumption and low price were considered to be forerunners of the utility vehicles.

In view of the success of this model, the management of His-

pano-Suiza decided to create a passenger transport vehicle which could increase the development of communications and employment in areas where the absence of railways made it necessary to modernise the transport system.

The first Hispano-Suiza bus was launched. The technical approach was the same modern and highly successful approach as for the motorcars.

Again in 1908 a new 25/30 HP bus was launched, developed on the mechanical basis of the 24 HP car. Apart from the technical aspects, it is an interesting fact that Hispano-Suiza created a system very similar to the present leasing system to support the launch of the new transport services management companies.

If the initiative was successful, the customer duly became the owner of the vehicle, otherwise Hispano-Suiza simply took back the vehicle in the condition as it

stood. For this reason, many Spanish bus service companies included the name Hispano in their company name, alongside that of the geographic region in which they were operating.

In parallel with the birth of the buses, the Hispano-Suiza chassis began to be used for lorries and, both in Spain and in France, many 12/15 HP chassis were adapted for vans, while in France they were used primarily within the Company's works. They were also marketed from 1908. In 1910 two new lorry models, 12/15 and 25/30 HP, were ready for sale.

The success of the motorcars and the new buses was such that the

The Hispano-Suiza 24 HP engine (1905-1907) on the test bench. An outstanding technical characteristic, in view of the period, is the double ignition.

Company could not meet the demand. In July 1911 the head office was transferred to larger premises, though still in Barcelona. Meanwhile, the operations of Hispano-Suiza had crossed the frontiers of Spain, and motor car chassis were dispatched to Belgium, Egypt, the Philippines, Greece, England and even to the Soviet Union and South America. The lorries were also sold on the export markets, mainly in Spanish-speaking countries.

In the following years the design of lorries and buses followed the growing demands of the market and the engine capacities increased. Between 1929 and 1931 all the models were renewed.

New engines were developed with separate cylinder heads and from 1935 Hispano-Suiza began the design of its diesel engine. But meanwhile, because of the social situation within Spain, the financial situation of Hispano-Suiza became more and more difficult. Events were precipitated from the early Thirties with the fall from power of Primo de Rivera at the end of 1929, followed in 1931 by the abdication of King Alphonso XIII and the proclamation for the Second Republic.

The sales of Hispano-Suiza fell virtually to zero and the company succeeded in supporting itself only thanks to income from royalties and the sale of parts and machine tools.

This brings us to the Forties. In spite of the difficulties at the La Sagrera works, the development of a new chassis for a seven tonne lorry proceeded. The prototype was produced in 1944 with the name 66G. The engine was a 6 cylinder 5.1 litre, 110 HP. The vehicle provided a pay load of 7,000 kg. A bus version was also produced, called the 66GA.

Based on the chassis the first trolley buses were also produced, many of which remained in service in many Spanish cities until the end of the Fifties.

In those years Hispano-Suiza developed a version equipped with a diesel engine, named the

66D. The engine was a 6 cylinder 8.5 litre, 128 HP, a development of the T69 of 1930. The vehicle had a pay load of 7,000 kg with a gross weight of 13,000 kg.

The whole series of 66G vehicles were equipped with a spacious

A view of the celebrated Hispano-Suiza omnibuses and lorries. From the top, the 12/15 and 25/30 HP buses of 1908; the 25/30 HP lorry, also of 1908, produced for a Portuguese company; two 40/50 HP buses of 1929.

cab built entirely of steel and with a flat front design, the one which a few years later was to be the first cab of the Pegaso vehicles.

In 1944 and 1945 Hispano-Suiza took part in the exhibitions in Valencia and Barcelona, exhibiting the 66G in the 7 tonne lorry and 55-seater bus versions and its military products, from the famous 20 mm gun to the V-12 aero engine.

THE FIRST PEGASO VEHICLE WAS LAUNCHED IN 1947

Ceta's first design on behalf of Enasa was, an advanced three-axle lorry which was developed in Madrid in 1947. This was the Z-201, and since production had been planned in the future new Madrid-Barajas factory, it was also nicknamed Barajas. With a 6 cylinder 120 HP petrol engine, it was designed for a pay load of 10-12,000 kg. The engine had an aluminium engine block and an integral gearbox, both located between the differentials of the rear axles. The front axle was equipped with independent suspension and the braking system was powered by air. All these solutions were too expensive for mass production. In fact, the design only resulted in one prototype, which was probably never fitted with an engine.

While these studies proceeded, in 1947 the last lorry developed by Hispano-Suiza, the 660 and now called Pegaso I, went into production again in Barcelona.

At the end of this same year the first Pegaso 2 lorry, called the Z-203, came off the line at the Barcelona works. Its engine was a 6 cylinder 5.65 litre petrol engine of 110 HP, it was a heavy vehicle (8,000 kg pay load) with its modern flat fronted cab. This same cab was introduced by Hispano-Suiza in 1944 on the prototype of its 66 lorry, but it never reached production.

In 1949 the first Pegaso Diesel engine was launched, a 6 cylinder 9.3 litre 125 HP developed on the

TOP: The Pegaso 1, the first lorry produced by Enasa, at the Barcelona Exhibition in 1947.
CENTRE: Entrance to the Hispano-Suiza La Sagrera Works in Barcelona. Beside it, the first trademark adopted by Ensa for its Pegaso vehicles.

basis of the similar Hispano-Suiza 66 engine. Because of its fuel consumption, 26-28 litres of diesel per 100 km, compared with almost 50 litres for the petrol engines of the time, it immediately aroused great interest among operators and rapidly replaced the petrol version. The economy and good performance, 72km/h maximum speed of the new engine were possible thanks to the direct injection, developed by Bosch, whose pumps were imported initially from Germany and later produced under licence in Spain. The Pegaso II Z-202 Diesel provided a pay load of 8,000 kg.

By 1954, when the cab of the Pegaso II was re-styled using double side windows and rear-opening doors, the Diesel was already confirmed as a reliable and economic engine, and four years later in 1958, over 2,100 units had already been produced.

In 1949 an innovative 70-seat bus body was fitted to the Pegaso II lorry chassis. Named the Z-410, it could either have a 110 HP petrol engine or the new 125/140 HP Diesel engine. Subsequently five, 40-seater coach prototypes were produced; the Z-402, as it was called had double square headlights.

We come to 1950, the year which marked an important debut: bearing the name Z-403, the Pegaso Monoshell (Monocoque) coach was born. Its innovative design marked a significant development of this type of vehicle, both in terms of safety and comfort. The basic version was equipped with a radio, bar and a small show window for newspapers and tourist brochures.

A unique feature of the Monoshell was, however, the body structure: a revolutionary solution for the time, which by abolishing the traditional chassis made the vehicle lighter and freed more useable space. Also, all the mechanical parts were mounted below the floor, isolated from the passenger compartment. To ensure greater comfort, a front suspension with independent

suspension was used.

The Monoshell was fitted with the new Pegaso III D diesel engine of 125 HP mounted centrally under the floor. With a kerb weight of 7,800 kg and a top gross weight of 11,800 kg, it reached a maximum speed of 80-85 km/h.

From 1952 a second version of the Monoshell was produced which caused a stir with its panoramic rear windows. In March 1952 the vehicle won the first prize, the Golden Rose and an honourary diploma, in the 5th competition for buses in San Remo, Italy.

From 1950 to 1957, 1,186

From the top, the guns pulled by Pegaso II lorries in the Victory Procession on 1 April 1949 and the Pegaso Z-406 petrol-engine bus.

Monoshell coaches were built, showing how much this vehicle was appreciated in the as yet little developed sector of the market. In 1952, based on the structure of the Monoshell, Pegaso also fitted out an articulated vehicle which was probably the biggest coach of its time.

During the same years, based on the Pegaso II chassis, prototype electric lorries and the first Pegasus trolley buses were developed. While the former never reached production, the latter were destined for considerable commercial success. Purchased by many Spanish cities, they were still in regular service up to the end of the Sixties.

Also in 1952, Enasa introduced its first cars, the fruit of a programme which had begun back in 1949. The model Z-101 was a 6-seater limousine which was to be fitted with a 12 cylinder 4 litre engine. The car was designed in all its details but never went into production, in spite of the insistence of General Franco.

There was to be a different fate for two sports cars models, the Z-102, Ricart's favourite and the Z-103. Both used 8 cylinder 90 V engines of 2.5 litres and 160 HP.

They were short-stroke engines - with a bore greater than the stroke - made entirely of light alloy, with hemispherical combustion chambers, oil-jet cooled aluminium pistons, an innovative system for the time but still used today in high-performance engines and double overhead camshafts. It had a 5-speed gearbox, De Dion suspension, and inboard drum brakes.

Spider versions of these cars were also produced with Touring Superlight bodywork and, from 1953, a "Pan-american" Touring Saloon and a record-breaking "Bisiluro".

The Bisiluro was powered by a 360 HP 6000 rpm engine. This was a 3.2 litre engine using two supercharges driven from transmission.

In 1953 the styling was modified,

replacing the horizontal grille with the cross motif destined to identify the Marque for the next thirty years.

And in fact the "Pegasines", (as they were familiarly called by the Pegaso men because of their reduced dimensions compared with the lorries and buses) in 1953 were better known abroad than in Spain itself. This was due to numerous successes both in shows and in sports competitions, even obtaining a few speed records. This was in spite of the fact that only 86 examples of the Z-102 and the Z-103 were produced.

It should, however, be said that the six short years of production of these sports vehicles, represented for Pegasus a unique opportunity to acquire a precious wealth of technical experience, and at the same time constituted a stimulating challenge for all the design and development staff. In December 1953, in reply to a journalist who asked why Pegaso did not produce family cars, Ricart answered that the firm's objective was to solve the problem of heavy transport, and that the fact that Pegaso had produced two such exceptional sports cars intended for the export markets was only the spin-off of such an advanced school of thought.

Towards the end of 1954 the new works at Madrid-Barajas finally went into production. Its construction, planned since 1946, had been delayed by the difficulties imposed by the post-war period in obtaining construction materials and getting them to the site.

All that time the steel for the production of the engines and chassis was imported from abroad, not without some difficulty. The works began to produce the Z-207 lorry and chassis for buses and coaches.

In the Pegaso story, an important part was also played by military vehicles: here is the M-3 truck of 1954, towing a piece of ordnance.

The Z-207 Barajas was the first vehicle to be developed and produced completely by Pegaso. Neither its new V6 110 HP engine nor its cab design were reminiscent of the years of the Hispano-Suiza. The structure, lighter than that of its bigger brothers from Barcelona, gave a pay load of 5 tonnes for a maximum gross weight of around 11,000 kg.

The bodywork was made from corrugated steel sheet, which became a characteristic of Pegaso vehicles, such that even today people call this type of steel sheet a "Pegaso sheet"

The vehicle was fitted with a new 120°, 7.5 litre V6 engine which produced 110 HP. This was a very advanced engine, for the time, with a light alloy cylinder block, two interchangeable cylinder heads, cylinder liners of special steel and direct fuel injection. A real refinement was the use of a counter-rotating balancing shaft, positioned below the engine shaft to reduce vibrations. Another distinctive characteristic of this vehicle was its independent front suspension, which gave an excellent ride.

From 1957 a version of the "Z-207" Barajas was produced with a greater carrying capacity a 120 HP engine. Thanks to a series of im-provements and the adoption of a rigid front axle, the payload increased to 6,250 kg for a maximum gross weight of 10,320 kg.

The Z-702 articulated lorry with semi-trailer and a pay load of up to 10 tonnes, was also included in the range. These vehicles remained in production until 1962, reaching a total production run of 4,412 units.

Meanwhile in 1955, based on the Z-207 Barajas chassis, the prototype of the first rear-engined, Pegaso bus, the Z-407, was built. The engine and transmission were enclosed in an isolated compartment in the rear of the vehicle.

Again in early 1955, in Madrid, the design of the new Z-207 Barajas was being completed, the design centre in Barcelona was

"authorised" to develop an updated version of the Pegaso II diesel with a greater capacity.

In actual fact, the objective of the operation was to develop a completely new lorry and it was conducted virtually in secret under the name Z-206.

This was to be a vehicle adapted to carry a pay load of 8,000 kg with the possibility of further increases. The cab, also developed in secret, was a completely new design based on Z-207, but with a modified rear wall to give more internal space.

The 6 cylinder, 9.3 litre Z-202 diesel producing 140 HP was selected, but subsequently the vehicle had to be fitted with a new 165 HP engine. A pay load of

8,300 kg was planned with a maximum gross weight of 14,800 kg.

Once finished the prototype was presented to Ricart, who realising the bold initiative of his engineers but also the quality of the work carried out, solved the embarrassing situation by saying

TOP: View from the air of the Enasa works at Barajas, Madrid, which entered production at the end of 1954. CENTRE: The Pegaso Z-206 8 tonne lorry during a road test; note the direction indicators, characteristic of the period.

"very well done, you interpreted my wishes perfectly". In fact, this project was to consolidate the role of the Barcelona team as a new technical centre of the company.

Together with the Z-206, chassis were developed for buses and coaches and used by the most important body builders in Spain. At the end of 1955 Pegaso introduced at the Paris Motor Show a prototype 6x2 vehicle with twin front steering axles. This was one of the first lorries in Europe to use this configuration, with the engine positioned in the centre of the chassis in the horizontal position.

It was equipped with a 165 HP new diesel engine with four valves per cylinder (Pegaso IV). Developed from the model Z-206, the cylinder capacity was increased to 10.17 litres.

The vehicle used a tandem front suspension system with interconnected axles, thus giving a constant weight distribution. The maximum pay load was 12,000 kg for a maximum gross weight of 20 tonnes.

We thus reach the Sixties. The first development phase of Pegaso can be considered completed. The company knew how to demonstrate its ability to develop vehicles and engines with avant garde characteristics. The start of the new decade signalled a substantial change in the strategy of the company.

Although the Ricart age was characterised by advanced but expensive projects, from now on the Company was to commit itself to more competitive production from the point of view of industrial costs with the aim of achieving bigger sales volumes.

The technical responsibility of the company was transferred to Barcelona where from now on, all the vehicles were to be developed. 1960 was a year full of events. Above all from the point of view of the corporate condition of Enasa, with the purchase of an interest by the English company Leyland Motors Ltd.

In 1957, Enasa had signed a preliminary agreement with Leyland for future co-operation in

areas to be defined. Initially the co-operation comprised the importation and distribution on the Spanish market of a number of Leyland models by Pegaso.

Then a few hybrid models were launched, which used Spanish technology and a number of parts produced in England, such as the 5022 bus, equipped with the Leyland engine. This was a

In the early 1960's the technical management of Ensa moved to Barcelona and plans for a new generation of vehicles began, bearing new company name; from the top, the 1060L lorry of 1962 and the fleet of 5020A buses delivered to the City of Barcelona in 1961.

model designed by Pegaso with an English double reduction rear axle, which were then sold on a number of foreign markets.

With the entry of Leyland into co-partnership, the Spanish proposed an upgrade of the smaller vehicle in the range, the Z-207 Barajas. A model which, though technically very advanced, had no future because it cost at least twice as much as the competing light vehicles on the market.

Enasa also aimed to produce under licence the Leyland Comet engine, less advanced compared with the Pegaso engine but technically sound and more economic to produce.

The Pegaso Comet "1090" was launched, equipped with a 6 cylinder 6.55 litre engine of 125 HP. With a pay load of 8,000 kg and a maximum gross weight of 16,000 kg, the vehicle was equipped with a totally new panoramic cab, that featured a single piece windscreen.

The styling did however retain the two characteristic elements of the mark: the bodywork in corrugated steel sheet and the two identifying Pegaso front panels, the stripes and the broad cross on the badge, which was made even more prominent.

Based on the Comet 1090, a truck with a pay load of 10,000 kg, the 2030 tractor, able to tow 16,000 kg and an off-road vehicle with integral transfer box, called the 3040, designed to work on difficult sites and for off-road transport, were produced.

The 3040 could cope with 100% slopes with a load of 3,000 kg. Based on the Comet, various models of buses were also developed, like the 5060 and its successors the 5061 and 5062, which were adapted for inter-urban transport. They had a high maximum speed, over 100 km/h.

With the idea of offering an even smaller vehicle, in 1965 Enasa developed the 1100 range, with a gross weight of 10,750 kg and a pay load of 7,000 kg. The engine, a 4 cylinder version of the Comet, was 4.4 litre, 90 HP. These vehicles remained in production, with their typical cab, until 1977.

In the coach sector, based on the model Z-408/1, an urban version was developed called the 5010, which was equipped with a Wilson semi-automatic gearbox. The engine was mounted at the front in the vertical position.

In the same year a very different model 5020 was introduced which had a maximum length of 10,990 mm and maximum permitted weight of 16,500 kg. The engine was mounted horizontally below the chassis, which improved the floor level.

In fact the 5020 was the leader of a whole new generation of passenger vehicles. Based on this model the Pegaso bus and coach chassis began to be different completely from those for lorries. It had now become clear that the requirements of the two transport sectors were completely different. As far as the engines were concerned, there was a significant development towards horizontal engines, the structure of which was increasingly different from those with vertical cylinders. Returning to 1960, another vehicle intended to mark an important development of the Spanish bus was the Pegaso Monotral-Viberti. The aim was to offer even greater comfort to the passengers and to achieve even

lower kerb weight for the vehicles.

Thanks to the good relations between Pegaso and Officine Viverti Spa of Turin, the Spanish coach-builder Giorsa signed an agreement with the Italian firm to build vehicles with monocoque bodywork of the Monotral type under licence.

Ten metres long, the Pegaso Monotral-Viberti bus was produced with a monocoque body structure, made of very strong welded steel tube. An important contribution to the lightness came from the Pegaso mechanics, for example, thanks to the balanced weight distribution of the two axles, it was possible to use a rear axle with single and twin wheels. The gross total

The 1066/2 4-axle lorry in the tanker version.

weight was kept below 10,000 kg. It was, in practice, a modernised new edition of the Pegaso-Monocasco (Monoshell) design of 1950.

The engine, located under the floor at the front, was the Pegaso-Barajas 120 HP used in conjunction with an automatic gearbox. The vehicle was also equipped with Pegaso-Vire power steering, exhaust brake and a centralised lubrication system.

In 1967, the 6035 A was introduced, a vehicle 16.5 metres long, designed with a central platform. This design was very important for meeting the increasing demand for larger vehicles for urban use.

An important technical feature was the adoption of pneumatic mechanical suspension, which gave the advantage the constant height of the entrance and exit platforms. Like the normal version, it was equipped with the Pegaso 185 HP engine fitted in the horizontal position.

Based on the same structure, a series of touring coaches was developed, like the 6045 with the Pegaso 170 HP engine giving a top speed of 112 km/h

At the end of 1969, based on the Pegaso Comet 1090, a very special truck was built, the 6011 Monotral, fitted with a self-supporting structure similar to that of the buses. The bodywork was of light alloy and the front panel of the cab of fibreglass-reinforced polyester, which gave the cab a completely different look to the rest of the vehicle.

The vehicle was in great demand and remained in production for a number of years, because its lightness (6,300 kg kerb weight) permitted a high carrying capacity, 6,800 kg for a maximum gross weight of 13,100 kg. It had single rear wheels, a choice which permitted a lower toll to be paid on the motorways.

But as we return to the commercial vehicle, going a step backwards, to 1964, the year which saw the introduction of a new generation of Pegaso heavy vehicles. For the first time in Spain a lorry was to be equipped

with a 200 HP engine.

Launched under the slogan "bigger than the biggest, more powerful than the most powerful" the 1061 4x2, the 1063 6x2 were launched, with maximum gross weights of 20,000-35,000 kg, and the 2011 4x2 tractor, the real father of modern tractors, with a total weight of 38 tonnes in accordance with the new Spanish legislation of 1967.

The engine of all these vehicles, called the 9105, was a 6 cylinder /24 valve, 10.5 litre 200 HP, derived from the 9100 of 165 HP, with an increase in piston diameter.

The naturally aspirated version was soon followed by a turbocharged version, the first turbo Pegaso engine, with a capacity of 260 HP. For this version a cast-iron, as well as an aluminium, cylinder block was used, a solution which was subsequently extended to the 200 and 170 HP versions.

This engine was used on a new vehicle fitted with double front and rear axle, the 1066 8x2, which offered a payload of 25,900 kg with a maximum weight of 34,000 kg. A special feature of the vehicle was the fourth steering axle, with a pneumatic locking system to facilitate reversing. Using the 200 HP engine two new tractors were also developed, both with three axles: the 2041/1 6x4x2 and the 2045 6x2x4, double steering.

In June 1966 Enasa acquired 52.7% of the shares of Sociedad Anonima de Vehicluos Automoviles (SAVA), which marked the entrance of Pegaso into the sector of vans and light vehicles up to a maximum weight of 10 tonnes.

SAVA produced medium-sized vehicles and agricultural tractors under licence to the British Motor Company and heavy trucks under licence to the French company Berliet (some of which, like the Berliet-SAVA GPS, with an engine of 200 HP and a pay load of 16,200 kg, were in direct competition with the Pegaso products).

The production of the SAVA models continued regularly, while Pegaso centred its interest on the range of light and medium-sized vehicles, starting

The extended family of the Enasa Group at the Barcelona Exhibition in 1970: Pegaso, Sava, Monotral and Allis-Chalmers.

with the J4, a van with a payload of 850 kg and a gross weight of 2050 kg, having the same design of the original Austin vehicle and equipped with the diesel engine of the long-standing English company.

Two years later, in 1968, Enasa was to increase its shareholding in SAVA to 82%, and in that same year the J4 was finally fitted with a more modern engine, a 4 cylinder, 1489 cc unit developing 46 HP, giving a maximum speed of 98 km/h - which gave it a brilliant commercial future, up to the end of the Eighties.

Derived from the Austin range, SAVA also produced another van with a payload of 1,500 kg, fitted with an English 2.2 litre 56 HP engine. On this basis, the Pegaso Cosmos was developed, similar in design but fitted with two new engines: a 2.5 litre 71 HP and a 3.8 litre 77 HP.

The 2.5 litre Cosmos reached a speed of 86 km/h and could carry a payload of 1,700 kg with a gross weight of 4,000 kg. The 3.8 litre Cosmos had a speed of 80 km/h, a pay load of 3,375 kg and a gross weight of 6,000 kg.

In the range of medium-sized vehicles, in the first phase the agreement with SAVA covered the marketing of the Pegaso 215, 315, 415 and 515 models, derived from the SAVA-BMC S-66 and S-76, with maximum gross weights of 4,500 and 6,400 kg respectively, and the SAVA-BMC A-404 and A-504 models, which had an advanced driver's cab and engines of 125 HP and maximum weight of 10,200 kg.

At the time, SAVA also had a series of buses and coaches in production, some for urban and inter-unban services with capacities ranging from the 14-plus-one to the 28-plus-one seater. In accordance with the agreements, all these vehicles were equipped with the Pegaso 90 HP engine.

At the end of 1965 the 1065 was introduced, a vehicle designed in line with the new maximum gross weights authorised by Spanish law, for vehicles with two axles: it did in fact permit

the maximum utilisation of the authorised weight for each axle and offered a greater useful length in relation to the wheelbase.

Because of the modern cab, the long version of the Comet, was known as the "Super Comet", with a new version of the 9100 engine, now with only two valves per cylinder and again with an aluminium cylinder block, which developed 170 HP at 2000 rpm and had a big engine torque.

It was coupled with a six speed gearbox with sixth overdrive and a double reaction axle.

The 1065 was launched with a gross weight of 18 tonnes, but soon was developed into the 1065A of 19 tonnes and the 1065B of 20 tonnes. A light tractor with semi-trailer was also introduced into the range, the 2020 equipped with a 170 HP engine and with a maximum gross weight of 29 tonnes. Versions were also produced with lengthened and re-inforced chassis and special versions with gross weights up to 26 tonnes, intended above all for the markets of the Middle East and South America. In 1966 the engine was fitted with a cast-iron block.

The success of these vehicles was

demonstrated by the fact that they were still in production in 1977, fitted with a 170 HP engine or, on request, a 200 HP engine.

In 1972 Pegaso brought on to the market a new rationalised range of vehicles, designed in line with the European legislation for the maximum permitted axle weight.

With a view to production of 15,000 to 25,000 units/year, and with the possibility of large numbers for export, it was vital to reduce manufacturing costs and to adapt the total weight, the weight/power ratio, the engine emission characteristics, safety, to the standards of various countries.

The new 1080 range, in its different versions - two axle 1080 and three axle 1083, four axle 1086 and 2080 tractor - were presented at the Barcelona Motor Show in 1972. Their special features included the new cab and a new 12 litre engine.

The new cab, developed with a

The 1065 lorry of 1966, a new generation of vehicles with panoramic cab and one piece windscreen. The vehicle styling retains the two characteristic themes of Pegaso: corrugated sheet panelling and cruciform radiator grille.

very advanced design, was styled by the Italian Aldo Sessano, who developed the traditional features identifying the Pegaso vehicles, like the parallel stripes, which were wider and less deep, and the cross motif on the front of the vehicle, now more stylised and made independent of the double square headlights. Also the "logo" of the marque changed, using a more readily readable "baston" character.

The cab was constructed completely of steel and suspended on silent rubber blocks. An access flap made working on the engine very easy.

To reach the 9-10 HOP/tonne permitted by the various European standards it was necessary to develop new engines. So the 10 litre 170-200-260 HP engines were followed by a new 6 cylinder 12 litre naturally aspirated version of 230-250 HP and turbo-compressed version of 352 HP, respectively called the 9154-9151-9156. All had a cylinder head with four valves per cylinder and the maximum rated speed increased to 2,200 rpm.

The Pegaso 1080 was equipped with the naturally aspirated 250 HP engine, the capacity of which was soon increased to 310 HP, equipping it with a Pegaso-Bosch injection pump. The vehicle had a payload of 13,630 kg to 29,665 kg with a maximum total weight of 20,000 to 38,000 kg.

In June 1974 Enasa began the design of a new tilt cab. Similar in design to the cab used for the rationalised heavy range, which improved accessibility to the engine bay, thanks to the 70° angle. Production started towards the end of 1975 for the new 1180 model, and it was subsequently used for the whole Pegaso range.

In 1976, in the bus sector, the new 6055 was presented, equipped with automatic gearbox and transmission with hydraulic retarder. Based on the small Sava-Pegaso, the 5020 model was developed with a 90 HP engine, which was also available in the school bus version.

By the end of the decade Pegaso

buses were equipped with more an more powerful engines, from over 275 HP of the prototype "5036" to the 310 HP of the turbo engine for the new 6100 range.

As a result of the first big energy crisis, in the second half of the seventies, Pegaso had to cope with a serious fall in the Spanish market and growing competition, a situation which led to negative balance sheet results for a number of years.

In 1980, Enasa signed a co-partnership agreement with the American company International Harvester, which acquired 35% of the Enasa shares, and placed some of its staff on the management team.

The aim of the agreement was to develop and produce a heavy range of vehicles based on the experience of Pegaso in the heavy vehicles sector. An ambitious plan was also studied for the construction of a works able to produce 100,000 diesel engines per year, which were to be built in Spain, at Torrejon de Ardoz.

The site was even purchased (376,000 m²), but because of the serious economic problems which were also afflicting the American industry the project never matured. It had to be abandoned, with heavy losses by Enasa too, who also lost precious time in the development of new Pegaso products because of this project.

In 1981, Enasa signed an agree-

ment with the German company ZF to produce in Barcelona, its famous gearboxes for industrial vehicles. The agreement related to synchronised gearboxes with 6:9 ratios, providing that the Spanish production would both equip Pegaso vehicles, and be exported with exchanges of parts between the two companies.

Pegaso customers were thus able to choose between ZF synchronised gearboxes produced by Enasa and the classic Fuller range.

In 1982, studies began for the development of new T1 range, with the aim of improving the reliability, the rationalisation and simplicity of parts, to cope with the increasing competitiveness of the market. The performance and reliability of the 12 litre engine was improved.

At the same time, production of a new bus started, model 5036-S, equipped with rear turbo engine of 270 HP and integral air suspension.

A new chassis for buses and

Prototypes of the Pegaso-International Harvester heavy vehicle, developed under a partnership agreement with the American company, not yet in production.

coaches was also introduced, intended for developing countries: equipped with a front engine, there were versions of 10-11 and 12 metres and capacities form 170 to 224 HP.

In 1983, at the Barcelona Motor Show, the rationalised T1 range, heavy vehicles from 14 to 40 tonnes gross weight, was introduced. The engines were 6.5, 10.5 and 12 litre, naturally aspirated or turbo, with outputs from 135 to 310 HP. The ZF gearboxes produced by Enasa in Spain were incorporated, using the S-130 16 ratio gearbox units for the first time in Spain. Disc brakes were used along with moisture-proof electrical system. Compared with the previous generation, over 2,000 modifications were made.

For these models new nomenclature was introduced, composed of four figures and a letter: the first figure stood for the number of drive axles, the second the total axles, the third and fourth the engine capacity in BHP, the letter indicated the type of vehicle: R for road truck, T for road tractor, K for quarry/site vehicle.

Going back to some extent to the origins, the cross motif on the front was abandoned, and replaced by a more sober grille with horizontal slats, felt to be more consistent with modern styling. Also the Pegaso "little horse" was re-stylised, becoming more muscular to give a better expressive force.

In February 1984, Pegaso introduced the prototype 6420 bus, a model developed in co-operation with the German industrial company MAN. A vehicle which introduced a new technological concept into the design and production of urban buses, because of the design of a mono-crane structure with rear engine which gave a floor level of around 17cm lower than the previous vehicle. The transmission comprised an automatic gearbox with hydraulic retarder, it had air suspension and independent front suspension. The equipment included air conditioning as standard.

Following the welcome received by this vehicle, co-operation with MAN in the field of buses developed and in 1989 a new modified version was presented, called the 6424, fitted with a Pegaso turbo engine of 240 HP.

We now come to 1985. At the Barcelona Motor Show Pegaso presented its new top vehicle, the Tecno, equipped with an even more spacious and comfortable cab than the "T1", and a turbo version powered by the 340 HP, 12 litre engine. The transmission was a ZF 16-speed and the suspension used a new design of parabolic springs. To ensure the necessary reliability in the face of the higher performance the engine was radically revised, using an air-to-air intercooler, oil cooling of the pistons, modified intake and exhaust valves and a special injection pump.

Considerable interest was also shown at the exhibition in the prototype of the 8.7 metre "5317"

TOP: The 6424 bus of 1989, developed in collaboration with the German MAN company and equipped with Pegaso 240 HP turbo-engine.
CENTRE: A line-up of Troner vehicles, weighing up to 44 tonnes GVW with cab designed by Giugiaro.

bus. Equipped with integral air suspension, a vehicle designed to meet the requirements of a quality service in medium-sized transport. The 6.55 litre engine was mounted vertically in front of the vehicle.

With this bus and the modern 6420 developed with MAN, Pegaso had competitive products available to meet the great competition provided by the foreign manufacturers following the entry of Spain into the European Common Market.

In the bus sector the 6100 and the more popular 5036-S, a model with integral air suspension and electric retarder which from 1985 was equipped with a 310 HP engine, continued to be very successful.

In 1984, Enasa together with DAF created the company CAB-TEC, with shared capital of 50%, aimed at the development of a completely new cab. To produce it a new works was also planned, located in Madrid-Barajas and production started in 1986.

Designed by Giugiaro, with a very modern concept the new cab was intended for the new top of the range Pegaso vehicle the Troner, and later the DAF 95 range.

The Troner, a heavy vehicle at the limit of 44 tonnes fitted with the new 12 litre, 24 valve 360 HP engine, was the star of the Barcelona Motor Show of 1987. Bearing the name 1236.38, the vehicle had a maximum gross weight of 38 tonnes, the maximum speed was self-limited to 120 km/h.

Special attention was paid to driver comfort and safety. All the versions offered as standard, air conditioning, computer and check control. For this model Pegaso developed a new hypoid design of rear axle.

Two events characterised 1983. For the token figure of £1 Enasa acquired from International Harvester the English company Seddon Atkinson, with registered office in Oldham, Lancashire: a marque rich in tradition, with almost ninety years of operation in the heavy commercial vehicle

sector, from 17 to 44 tonnes total weight. From this operation in 1988 was born the new Strato model, equipped with Cummins, Gardner or Perkins engines and the Troner cab re-stylised at the front.

In co-operation with MAN and Volkswagen, Pegaso presented the range of light Ekus vehicles in the version personalised for the Spanish market. The new vehicles replaced the old J4 and the light 215-315-415-515 trucks of SAVA origin. In 1988 a new bus chassis was introduced, the 5231 which replaced the old 5036 S, having the advantages of a significant reduction in weight and a greater engine output (310 HP).

At the Barcelona Motor Show in 1989, Pegaso presented as a surprise the Solo, an innovative experimental prototype of tractor and semi-trailer. Not simply an exhibition exercise, but a laboratory-vehicle for experimentation in the use of new concepts and

materials, including composites derived from the aviation industry, with the aim of reducing the number of components and the total weight of the vehicle. Solo 1, presented in 1989, was followed a year later by the new design, Solo 2.

Again at the Barcelona Motor Show in '89, in the range from 20 to 26 tonnes, Pegaso intro-duced the medium-weight "Mider", with a 257 HP version of the well known 10.5 litre Pegaso engine.

We now come to the present day. On 13 September 1990 INI and Fiat signed an agreement which brought Pegaso into the Iveco

Above the EuroCargo in the Pegaso version. On the facing page, two highly significant "baptisms": from the top, in the Iveco-Pegaso works in Valladolid and Madrid-Barajas, the first Daily and the first EuroTech (cutting the symbolic ribbon is King Juan Carlos of Spain in the presence of Gianni Agnelli and Cesare Romiti) marked with the characteristic "colt" at the exit of the respective assembly lines.

Group.

For Iveco this was an important contribution, which was worth a 30% share of the Spanish market in the segment above 16 tonnes; six production plants in Madrid, Barcelona, Barcelona-Valladolid, Mataro, Oldham (England) and Cumana (Venezuela); a vehicle fleet of over 80,000 vehicles in Spain and 15,000 in the rest of the world; a wealth of one hundred years technology and a unique know-how on the market of the industrial vehicle in Spain.

After the union of the two groups the new Iveco-Pegaso actively committed itself to the integration of its range with the other vehicles in the Group.

In the segment from 6 to 10 tonnes, the Ekus was replaced by the Daily range, partly produced directly in Spain, partly imported from Italy. In the segment from 10 to 15 tonnes, the Tecno was replaced by the light EuroCargo and the 330 and 340 HP versions of the Mider.

In the segment of heavy vehicles, the top of the range vehicle, the Troner, is equipped with a turbo-inter-cooled version of the 400 HP 12 litre Pegaso engine, which rightly puts it in the class of super-powerful lorries.

In the sector of site vehicles, the presence of Pegaso is being extended with the Trakker range, trucks, isolated vehicle and tractor, with two, three and four axles.

Finally, in the field of buses, Iveco-Pegaso offers two chassis: the 5226, with a 10.5 litre 257 HP engine and a 12 litre 320 HP engine, and the 5237 with 370 HP engine.

From the middle of 1992 the Barajas works began a total renovation of the equipment in the assembly lines of the heavy Eurotech range.

*Well established and with a good reputation on all the major markets, not just European,
the light vehicles in the "S" range are one of the traditional forces behind the Iveco image and product.*

A HIGHLY SUCCESSFUL FAMILY: THE LIGHT "S" RANGE

The Iveco range of industrial vehicles starts with the "S" range - the Daily and the Turbo-Daily.

These are light commercial vehicles ranging from a 3 tonner to a 6 tonner, designed to perform like an industrial vehicle but with a level of comfort and handling more typical of a car. They are of limited size (maximum width 2 m) for use in urban areas.

These vehicles are specifically designed to solve urban and interurban distribution and light transport problems.

The success of the "Daily formula" is witnessed by the number of vehicles sold - more than 450,000 - and also its European market share of around 25%. This success is due to the wide diversification of the types offered backed by high quality and performance: from the chassis to the dual cab/front suspension concept and the power train.

The Daily and TurboDaily vehicles are available in a range made up of more than 50 versions developed from 6 basic models: 30-35-40-45-49-59 (the number usually indicates the approximate weight) with three versions of the Sofim 2.5 litre, 4 cylinder direct injection diesel engine: 75 HP aspirated, 103 HP turbo and 115 HP turbo-intecooler, rear wheel drive (4 x 2) or four wheel drive (4 x 4) which can be engaged (for the 40 model), and there are five wheelbase versions (2800-3200-3310-3600-3950mm).

There is a wide range of variants. It includes original vans, including the type with raised roof or the large volume version with the longer wheelbase and with four heights (1500-1880-1930-2100 mm). There are three wheelbases for vehicle weights from 3170 kg to 6000 kg and a payload of 15.4 cubic metres for the tall van (height 1930 mm, wheelbase 3950 mm) and 17 cubic metres for the large volume version (height 2100 mm, wheelbase 3950). These vehicles have a sliding side door with a clearance of 1060 mm.

There are also the versions with cab, with standard or double/triple cab, 6 + 1 and 8 + 1 seats, two wheelbase versions (2800 mm or 3310 mm) and a choice of heights (1500 mm or 1880 mm) to satisfy a wide range of uses, including moving people as well as equipment and materials (forestry work, work on power lines, telephones, building sites). The bus and minibus versions have 16-19 seats, the school bus between 20 and 41 seats.

Finally, special chassis are available - including a long wheelbase version (3950 mm) for leisure type conversion.

The strength of the vehicles is the chassis with longitudinal members. This is a typical "truck style" solution, guaranteeing both strength and reliability even under severe conditions, and one which also has the advantage of versatility and "customisation", allowing imaginative conversions for any type of use. The cab chosen in this case is the semi-forward type which is both practical and comfortable.

The result is improved accessibility (there is no longer the bulk of the wheel housing) and habitability (the engine is outside the compartment), also with the advantage - very important for a vehicle used for deliveries in town - that it is possible to pass from one side of the compartment to the other without any problem.

This type of cab also makes the vehicle more comfortable when driving, because it is quieter (insulated steel bulkhead separates the engine compartment from the passenger compartment) and it absorbs the irregularities of the road surface because the driving seat is behind the axle, not over it.

In this respect, an important contribution is made by the vehicle's independent wheel suspension at the front and the entire cab is suspended elastically on the chassis by means of rubber shock absorbers. The equipment, which is similar to that of a car, includes an instrument panel which blends elegantly with the door panels, ergonomically designed seats complete with head restraints, seat covers coordinated with the door and roof coverings.

The ventilation/air conditioning system with air recirculation, four speed fan and nozzles (also used for demisting the side windows) also helps to enhance the comfort of the vehicle. The driver has access to fully electronic modular controls and instruments. The numerous options available also include the Iveco check system, which provides information on the levels of engine coolant, engine oil, brake fluid, front and rear brake lining wear.

The power train used on the Daily and TurboDaily is the Sofim 2.5 litre direct injection diesel engine.

This engine, which is both compact and light, is modern both in terms of technical design and the production technology used. One of the main benefits of an engine in this class is the direct injection - the diesel is injected directly into the combustion chamber rather than into a pre-chamber made in the head - a solution which improves the thermodynamics with a reduction in fuel consumption of 15%.

The cold start also has advantages; the pre-heating typical of diesel engines with pre-chamber is not required for temperatures above 15°. As far as the other technical characteristics are concerned, the drive line has a fully synchronised five speed box designed and produced by Iveco - also the fruit of advanced production technology.

The availability of versions with four wheel drive which can be engaged offers additional versatility for use in particularly difficult environmental conditions, including on loose soil and off-highway.

Under these conditions, the special chassis construction with longitudinal members enhances the key features of mobility (optimum adhesion and traction on bumpy or difficult terrain) and reliability (fewer stresses transmitted to the superstructure and to the equipment).

The suspension systems are mixed: independent wheel suspension at the front, with an original architecture which uses torsion bars and rigid axle at the back, with fully flexible, semi-eliptical leaf springs or parabolic springs. All the versions have series 75 tyres, with the advantage that the loading platform is not so high off the ground.

The steering is rack and pinion (variable ratio on the 45.10 and 49.10) with hydraulically assisted steering, standard or as an option, depending on the version. The brake system - a hydraulic system with independent dual circuit (EC standard) and vacuum servo brake supplied by a vacuum pump - with disc brakes at the front. The rear brakes are drum type brakes with large surface linings and automatic adjustment. The rear axle is equipped with a load-sensitive braking corrector and the linings are of the ecological type - no asbestos.

Strength, good price/performance ratio, a wide and diverse range of versions - these are the "secrets" of the third generation of the TurboDaily light vehicles.

Iveco turns the page for the '90s: the debut of the Euro ranges heralds a completely new generation of vehicles at the leading edge of producti technology and engineering with an exceptional choice of versions.

THE EURO RANGES:
A CHOICE OF MORE THAN 400
MEDIUM TO HEAVY VEHICLES

Iveco's other large family of vehicles is the Euro range which covers the weight range from 6 tonnes up to the legal limits. This is a completely new range developed in the second half of the Eighties on the basis of highly innovative criteria: integration/modularity aimed at an extreme diversification of the product grid; design technology using computer aided design and calculation; production technology developed in parallel with the vehicles for the purpose of achieving advanced automation wherever possible.

Development also involved many technical characteristics of the product: from the design of the cab to the disc brakes for the light and medium to light ranges.

This was the result of an ambitious project aimed at establishing a "full range" presence on world markets and the new generation of Iveco vehicles was launched with a product grid embracing more than 400 versions (weight, engine settings, cabs and equipment).

A figure which speaks for itself and whose "feasibility logic" is due to the enormous memory and processing capacity of the computer system which Iveco had installed.

We have discussed this at length. For Iveco, "innovation" meant finding a completely new approach to the organisation and control of the production process and all its aspects: from the market to the factory, between factory and supplier, inside the factory, between computer centre and individual cell or machine tool.

So logistics combined forces with the computerised control of all stages of the production process for the purpose of achieving improvements wherever possible (to reduce timescales and stocks, to remain competitive and to lock up as little capital as possible) but also to achieve real time control of a product grid of this complexity).

FOR VEHICLES FROM 6 TONNES TO THE LEGAL LIMIT

These ranges represent a classic division. First of all we have the light vehicles ranging from 6 tonnes to 7.5/8.0 tonnes, depending on the legislation concerned (translated into practical terms, these are vehicles with payloads ranging from 2,500 to 5,000 kg); this range then has a medium-light extension with weights up to 10 tonnes.

Then we have the medium vehicles, from 12 tonnes to 17.5 tonnes, perhaps the most diverse range from the point of view of use, with numerous applications in the transport sector.

This category is followed by the medium to heavy vehicles, at around 17-5 tonnes for a twin axle vehicle and 35 tonnes to 40 tonnes for vehicle combinations.

And finally, we have the heavy vehicles, from single 18-19 tonners up to the limit of 40-44 tonnes for vehicle combinations and heavy duty vehicles.

These are mainly triple axle vehicles (from 26 tonnes to 38 tonnes for single vehicles), characterised by a high level of standardisation with the road vehicles, but designed for particularly taxing applications.

The vehicles intended for markets outside Europe and product lines intended to cover the demands of the other sectors in which Iveco has a presence - from buses to military logistics vehicles and firefighting vehicles - are derived from these ranges.

MODULAR DIVERSIFICATION IN SEARCH OF COMPETITIVENESS AND QUALITY

As we have seen, Iveco has used two instruments to deal with a product range of this size and diversity: computerised control of all the functions and processes and modularity in product design both in the form of a grid and in the form of vehicle components.

Let us look at the logic which guided the designers and analyse the key elements of this incredible "puzzle": the cabs, chassis and engines.

A SPECIALIST LINE OF CABS FOR THE JOB

The cabs first of all. For its new range Iveco developed a family of modular cabs all of the tilt type, made in cooperation with Italdesign. These are characterised by an intelligent industrial design mix both with regard to the structural design and the choice of materials, with specific advantages for the user.

An important aspect is the modular design with which, using a type of hi-tech meccano, the desired versions can be put together with a considerably reduced number of components.

This resulted in an extreme form of rationalisation, going down from the 9 cabs of the previous generation of vehicles (including the "Club" or "Cargo" vehicles) to just three basic cabs for the present range: "EuroCargo", "EuroTech" and "EuroStar".

Each of these vehicles has a short and long version, a top sleeper, the medium or low roof (for the EuroTech and the EuroStar) and the high roof (for the EuroStar).

The EuroCargo is used to equip the 16 tonne to 17.5 tonne vehicles, i.e. the light and medium ranges plus the first vehicle in the medium to heavy range. The short version is 2090 mm wide and 1520 mm long and the long version with bunks is 2100 mm long. The medium vehicles have a special skirt (mud flap and bumper combined). It is higher, with two steps and bigger wheel arches. The EuroTech cab is used both on medium to heavy and heavy vehicles. It is wider and longer than the light version, 2280 mm and 1670-2100 mm.

The EuroStar cab is reserved for heavy vehicles for TIR and transport services; it is the same length as the EuroTech cab, but it is wider, i.e. 2460 mm, to provide a bigger compartment.

To facilitate body manufacture the rear part of the cab is completely free of projecting parts. Even the 'snorkel' has been made as small as possible, providing a solution which is both aesthetically pleasing and practical.

MODULAR CONSTRUCTION

Structurally, the cab can be regarded as a set of three parts one on top of the other: the bottom part (delimited by the bumper and wheel housings), which contains the mechanics, the working area in the middle and the rest area at the top.

The bottom bumper section and the rest section at the top are made completely from synthetic materials. The working area consists of a robust pressed steel construction lined with steel panels (the surface exposed to aggressive agents is galvanised) or an SMC material.

As far as the components made from synthetic materials are concerned, bumpers, mud flaps, front panel and spoilers are made from SMC and are produced at Iveco.

Basically, the modular concept is based on the standardisation of the doors and corresponding structural rings which are identical for all the cabs, a solution which has made it possible not only to robotise the panel work, but also the door assembly process.

ACCURATE AERODYNAMIC STYLING

Apart from stylistics, the design of the cab is also concerned with aerodynamics.

By working on the details, they succeeded in achieving a very interesting Cx value (0.45), which has not only benefitted fuel consumption, but also safety and comfort: improved visibility in bad weather (because the side windows do not mist up) and quieter running at speed.

Particularly important from this point of view are the front/side connections and the spoiler connection, which alone gained more than 9 points, sealing of the edges of the front grille and spoiler (2 points), the cab sides (nearly 12 points) and the uprights (5 points).

COMFORT IS ALSO A SPECIALITY

When this new generation of cabs was designed, particular attention was paid to comfort and safety.

The problem was confronted at general level and also according to the job which the vehicle had to perform. The design of the cab as a whole is very important from this point of view.

They wanted to improve the ergonomics of getting out of the vehicle, both by giving the doors a very big opening angle (90°, with an intermediate closed position), positioning the door handles at the bottom, reducing the height of the first step from the ground and increasing the number of steps depending on the type of cab (the height of the wheel housing from the ground varies from 815-946 mm for the EuroCargo to 1098 mm - 1450 mm for the EuroTechand 1331 mm for the EuroStar).

The inside of the cab received similar attention.

This is a spacious compartment both in terms of internal width and the space available above the driver and the passengers which allows excellent visibility enhanced by the large wrap-round windscreen. The windscreen wipers are in a protected position and the special shape of the side windows is also designed to improve visibility.

A great deal of work was done on the ergonomics of the driving seat. The angle of the steering wheel can be adjusted on all the vehicles. On the medium to heavy and heavy vehicles, the steering wheel has two adjustments: angle and height. The seats adjust along the three axes, fold down and contain a lumbar support.

Still in search of maximum comfort and practicality, the layout of the compartment varies depending on the job the vehicle has to perform. For the EuroCargo and EuroTech cabs, the priority is to be able to cross the cab and a traditional style of dashboard has been developed which leaves the floor completely clear.

For the EuroStar cabs however, they have aimed more specifically at achieving a control seat, choosing a wrap-round configuration for the dashboard with the central part directed towards the driver and equipped with instruments both for control and comfort.

The designers based their work on homogenous criteria resulting in the highly rational instrument panel which combines instruments and controls in separate functional modules according to requirements.

A sophisticated array of equipment is provided throughout the range (for example, the check control and electrical headlamp adjustment are standard) and can be personalised with a very wide range of options, from the trip computer to the electric windows, air conditioning (standard on the EuroStar), and additional heater, etc.

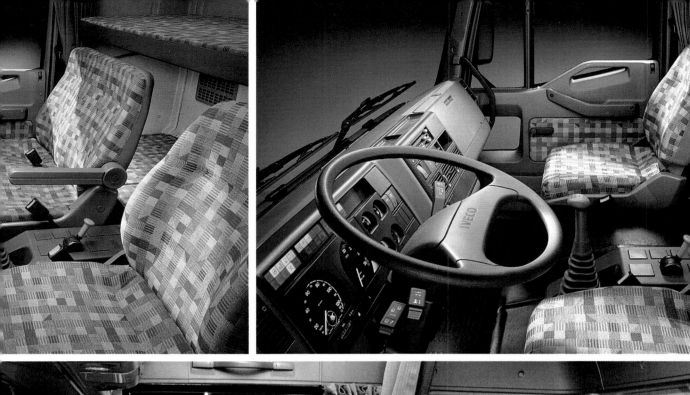

THE SAFETY OF A "PROTECTED" ENVIRONMENT

Comfort and safety are not only practical and ergonomic, they also help to insulate the compartment from the vibrations, noise - and temperature - of the outside environment.

To guarantee safety, it is important to find the right compromise between comfort and safe driving and the solution is derived by balancing a series of components, starting with the wheels and extending to the driving seat, with a double filtering effect of the vehicle and cab suspension systems.

As far as the chassis is concerned, an important and innovative contribution is made by the pneumatic suspension (full suspension on some vehicles), whereas different solutions have been adopted for the cab, depending on the model. Rubber shock absorbers are used for the light vehicles up to the 75 model; springs at the front and McPherson struts (spring and shock absorber) at the back with cross bracing for the remainder of the range. The option of pneumatic suspension is also available for the heavy vehicles.

Safety also means a quiet working environment. The present Iveco range has reduced the sound levels by between 5 and 10 decibels compared with previous levels.

This is a considerable advance if you remeber that a reduction of 3 dB is equivalent to halving the sound effect.

The company has also worked on the engines to reduce the noise at source, and also on the outside of the cab (secondary bulkhead between cab and engine, side panels). It has also worked on the cab structure and equipment: cab suspension, door and window seals, floor and wall insulation, improved air conditioning and aerodynamics.

For all the vehicles the range and capacity of the heater have been practically doubled compared with the previous series.

The system now includes a recirculatin function, independent controls for the upper and lower

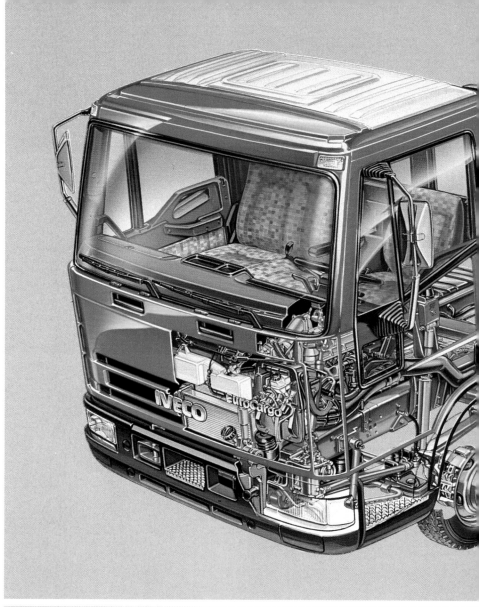

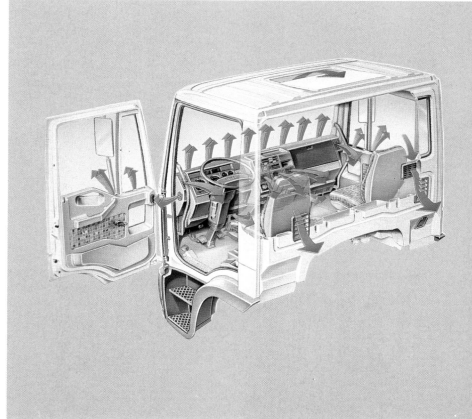

282

sections of the compartment and for the driver/passenger sides.

The air is distributed by a large number of nozzles at the bottom of the windscreen, in and underneath the dashboard and also on the doors so that the side windows can be quickly demisted. Depending on the versions and the equipment, the roof flap is controlled electrically on vehicles with a top sleeper. The EuroStar cab is equipped with automatic air conditioning as standard and this is also available for all the other versions on request.

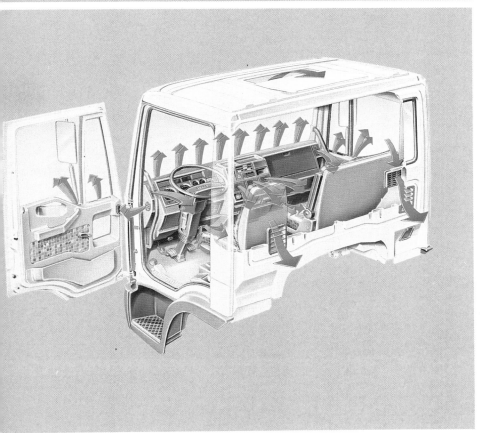

The "Euro" cabs have optimum comfortable and ergonomic design to provide a safe and "protected" working environment.
Particular attention has been paid to sound-proofing and air-conditioning, which uses a highly efficient, sophisticated installation.

MODULAR CHASSIS

The chassis are modular. The configuration used is the classic one: longitudinal and cross members assembled by riveting. Design effort has been focussed on improving the ground clearance and the weight, using high strength steels (type FEE 420/FEE490) which has made it possible to reduce the size of the sections. The top of the chassis is completely flat to facilitate conversion work.

The concept of modularity was developed according to the technical requirements connected with the weight of the vehicle and also the installation dimensions of the mechanical systems.

This has resulted in a range of chassis divided into three main families: light, medium and heavy. Straight section chassis have been developed for light and medium vehicles ranging from 6 tonnes to 17.5 tonnes. The distance between centres of the longitudinal member allows 4 and 6 cylinder in line engines to be installed, from the 8040 to the 8360.

Single bottleneck chassis have been developed for medium to heavy vehicles, limited to 20 tonnes for the separate vehicle. This means that the front part of the chassis is widened to accommodate larger engines and radiators. Therefore the 8360 and 8460 engines can be used. At the back, the chassis maintains a standard distance between centres to allow maximum conversion flexibility. A chassis with a double bottleneck has been developed for the range of heavy vehicles from 18 tonnes to 26 tonnes.

The front section is also widened to accommodate the top-of-the-range engines, including the V8 820 and the radiators; however, the distance between centres has been reduced at the back to accommodate single ratio axles whose box is large and at the same time accommodate large suspension units like the tandem cantilever. All this whilst still remaining within the maximum track limits allowed (normally 2.5 metres).

The result of this rationalisation measure is 160 complete chassis versions in five families compared with the 221 chassis in 13 families of the previous range.

Sufficiently robust to carry large loads, and with flexibility to deal with any concerns a the guarantee of reliability and the long service life of the vehicles. For maximum dri comfort and for the most fragile goods, the "Euro" ranges offer pneumatic suspension o rear or both axles.

PNEUMATIC SUSPENSION FOR COMFORT AND DELICATE CONSIGNMENTS

Extending the concept of modularity to suspensions has made it possible to offer pneumatic suspension as an alternative for all the ranges, starting with the light vehicles.

This type of suspension offers optimum comfort both for the passenger and for more fragile merchandise. It also offers specific advantages when transferring loads, because the vehicle loading bed can be lowered to the ground to facilitate the handling of "swap bodies".

Two alternatives are available: rear pneumatic suspension with front parabolic leaf springs or complete pneumatic suspension, front and back.

It is interesting to note that as the range develops, full pneumatic suspension systems will be available for practically all vehicle configurations, i.e. not just the 4x2, but also the 6x2 and 6x4, both vehicles with cab and tractors. There are also two types of mechanical suspension: highly flexible parabolic leaf springs or semi-eliptical springs for heavy duty use.

A notable development has also taken place in the triple axle sector and in two directions: on the one hand, instead of the traditional self-steering third axle, the 6x2 can also have a hydraulically controlled steering axle at the back (synchronised with the front axle).

On the other hand, the range includes 6x2 and 6x4 vehicles featuring rear cantilever suspension with single or twin wheels for extreme demands made by exceptional applications. This programme also includes friendly suspensions (i.e. with non-aggressive natural response frequencies reacting to the road surface) in line with the new European standards for 26 tonne 6x2 vehicles and 19 tonne 4x2 vehicles. By developing a suitable suspension configuration, it has been possible to achieve this result without using a pneumatic suspension.

ADVANCED TECHNOLOGY FOR AXLES

As far as the drive axles are concerned, a single ratio solution has been chosen for the entire road vehicle range.

For light vehicles up to the 100 model, two new Iveco axles have been developed: the 4517 (three weights: 4000/4600/5200 kg) and the 4521 (5800 kg).

There is also a wide range of ratios to satisfy all uses, also depending on the type of vehicle equipment. A pneumatically controlled differential lock is available on request. This is standard on the tipper versions.

All the light vehicles have twin wheels at the back, using low profile tubeless tiles (not for the tippers), 16" from the 60 to the 75 and 17.5" from the 80 to 100.

The use of low profile tyres has made it possible to reduce the height of the loading bed above the ground.

The medium and heavy road vehicles have Rockwell axles (a development of the series already in use) and Iveco axles designed in Madrid with the addition of a tandem axle for the 6x4 vehicles.

There is then a third type of drive axle, a development of the axles with reduction at the hub, designed by Iveco and intended for site/quarry vehicles. As far as the other axles are concerned, the principal features are the wider track, which helps to stabilise the vehicle, and the steering angle which has been increased to 52 degrees (compared with 43°-46° of the previous generation), which reduces the turning circle and therefore makes the vehicles more manouverable. Wheel bearings which do not have to be adjusted and which are lubricated with oil (rather than grease) have also been introduced. The oil level is controlled via the hub.

Completely new designs have been developed for all the ranges: for light vehicles with a capacity of 2670 kg/2900 kg and 3200/3500 kg, the medium vehicles with a capacity 4800 kg and 5300 kg and the heavy vehicles ranging from 7.5 tonne and 8 and 9 tonne (depending on the legislation in force).

Among the key features of the Iveco "Euro" trucks integral disc braking (i.e. front and for the medium to light range.

DISC BRAKES ON ALL FOUR WHEELS FOR THE LIGHT VEHICLES

The brakes are another important development for these ranges.

The light vehicles now have disc brakes front and back. The system is a hydro-pneumatic type (complete with energy saving air compressors) with floating calipers and individual self-ventilating discs. The engine brake is supplied as standard for 6 cylinder engines.

A pneumatic system with disc brakes at the front and drum brakes at the back - the Simplex type - has been chosen for the medium to heavy range, whilst the heavy site vehicles have drum brakes at the front too.

287

FIVE FAMILIES OF ENGINES FOR POWERS RANGING FROM 70 HP TO 500 HP

The creation of the present generation of vehicles has also meant rationalisation and improvements of the engines.
Iveco still has its 6 classic families: apart from the 2.5 litre Sofim 8140 used on the "S" vehicles, there are two engines in the 8000 series, the 3.9 litre, 4 cylinder 8040 and 5.9 litre, 6 cylinder 8060; the 7.7 litre, 6 cylinder 8360, 9.5 litre, 8460 and 13.8 litre 8210; the 17.2 litre V8 8280. However, the performance has been changed, with an average increase in power of 10%, and the power development has also changed.
The light vehicles use the 102 HP light supercharged version, the 116 HP standard turbocharged version and the 136 HP turbo-intercooler and also the four versions of the 8060: 136 HP, 177 HP, 207 HP and 227 HP.
The medium vehicles are equipped with the 240 HP and 266 HP turbo-intercooler ver-sion of the 8360.
The medium to heavy and heavy vehicles have three engines: the 300, 345 and 375 HP versions of the 8460; the 306, 420 and 470 HP versions of the 8210 and the 514 HP 8280.

EVOLUTION WITHOUT REVOLUTION

An interesting example of evolution is the 8360 which, of all the engines in the current Iveco range, has undergone the most significant changes.
The increase in performance brought about by supercharging with intercooler has coincided with a slight reduction in cylinder capacity, from 8 litres to 7.7 litres, obtained by reducing the bore.
With the same distance between cylinder centres, the circulation of water around the cylinders has been increased, improving cooling. This has made it possible to guarantee reliability even with the increased stresses generated by supercharging.
In more general terms, the work of updating the engines concerned increasing the performance and improving efficiency, reducing both fuel consumption and emissions.

The increase in power, obtained by adjustments to the injection system (greater pressure) and the use of the intercooler, has allowed the company to achieve higher commercial speeds or a reduction in tare.
In some cases, whilst maintaining the same performance, it has been possible to install an engine with a smaller cylinder capacity, thus saving around 200 kg in the case of heavy engines (e.g. between the 9.5 litre engine and 14 litre engine).
In terms of fuel consumption (an important factor if running costs are to be reduced), the improvement in quality has been not as much in absolute terms as in the efficient use of the vehicle.
This is because the graphs have changed; the torque curves have been improved (traditionally high with Iveco engines) in the move towards low engine speeds.
Naturally, all these measures have had positive repercussions on emissions and noise to reflect the new environmental legislation.
All the engines have been officially approved in accordance with the future EEC directive on emissions (91/542), in force from 10/93.
The improvements obtained derive from work done both on the structure of the engine and on the fuel supply.
The following have been adopted: pistons with high-turbulence combustion chambers, piston rings positioned very high up, to reduce clearance volume and fibre inserts to increase resistance to high pressures.
In addition, the fit between pistons and cylinder liners has been improved, with benefits in terms of emissions and noise, and automated control systems have been introduced for engine timing.
An important contribution came from adopting injection systems with higher pressures and - for the 375 HP engine which is top of the 8460 range - from electronic control, favouring better control of the torque curve.

Iveco produces for its trucks six groups of modern engines, offered in a wide range of sizes. Here from the top the 2.5 litre 4 cylinder 8140, used in the "S" range and the 6 cylinder 8060 and 8360. On the opposite page, the powerful 8280 V8 and, below, details of the 6 cylinder 8210 and 8460.

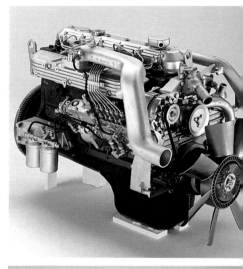

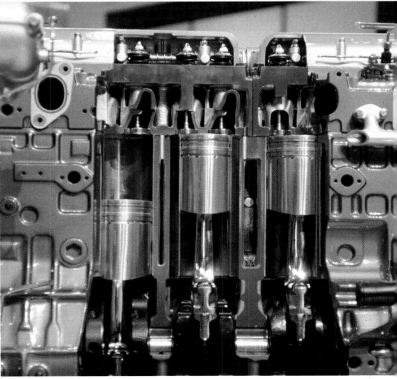

A GENERATION OF HI-TECH GEARBOXES

The drive line of the present Iveco range is also inspired by the concept of modularity.

The light and medium to heavy vehicles are equipped with a new generation of gearboxes with 5, 6 and 9 speeds, some designed and produced by Iveco and some the fruit of a joint design project with Eaton and produced by Iveco.

One very interesting characteristic for the user (mainly large fleets with several versions of vehicles) is the high level of modular components used (forks, synchroniser rings, bearings, etc.) within each family.

Equipped with fully synchronised forward gears and helicoidal gears designed to reduce noise, they are also distinguished by the light alloy clutch housing and very light gearbox, making them ideal for use with Iveco engines.

However, the range of heavy vehicles continues to offer a choice between Eaton Twin Splitter gearboxes and ZF Ecomid, both with 9 and 16 speeds or the Ecosplit 16 speed box. The application depends on the engine torque and the job for which the vehicle is intended.

Innovation has also been possible in this range: the weight has been reduced (aluminium boxes for the ZF systems) and there is a semi-automatic version using electronic control systems.

Iveco offers a wide range of gearboxes for its trucks, adapted to the GVW class and the intended use.
DIRECTLY ABOVE: The newest with 5-6-9 gears designed and produced by Iveco for the EuroCargo.
LEFT: The groups with 13-16 gears developed in collaboration with Eaton and ZF for medium and heavy trucks.

RELIABILITY AND LOW MAINTENANCE COSTS

When it designed the new range, Iveco paid considerable attention to the problem of reliability and ease of maintenance - ordinary and extraordinary - so that the vehicle is off the road for as short a time as possible.

These design measures include the check control in the cab, which means that the main functions of the vehicle can be checked directly from the driving seat.

The normal checks (engine oil, engine coolant, screen washer liquid, hydro-pneumatic brake circuit) can be made directly and easily by lifting the large grid on the front of the cab which is balanced by two shock absorbers and has an opening angle of 120°.

There is complete access to the engine and all the mechanical components at the front of the vehicle because the cab tilts 60° and has a convenient hydraulic control (also available with electric pump on request) and a double safety system (on the instrument panel and in the pumping area).

The Iveco engine tester plugs into a socket in the cab to diagnose the efficiency of the engine (torque performance), calculated on the basis of data transmitted by three sensors, two on the flywheel and one on the distributor.

Particular attention was also paid to the electrics. The main control unit with the fuses is inside the cab, directly accessible through a flap in the dashboard.

So that the cab can be detached quickly from the rest of the vehicle, a multi-pin macroplug is used which is made in two parts, with one half permanently connected to the front wall of the cab and the other half to the chassis wiring.

All the cables, which are sheathed, are coded for easy identification. An interconnecting control unit is also placed at the back of the chassis which is useful if any modifications are needed as a result of vehicle conversion. The various parts of the equipment are connected by captive studs. The batteries used are the maintenance-free type with different capacities depending on the engine and the type of vehicle.

Maintenance has generally been simplified. The oil changes are now made at 30,000 km for 4 cylinder engines and 40,000 km for 6 cylinder engines (equipped with a dual filter on the lubricating circuit).

Otherwise, the only lubrication points to be checked are the wheel bearings, the transmission shafts and the steering linkages. The leaf spring attachments do not require maintenance.

The brakes do not require periodic adjustment and a light on the dashboard indicates wear of the front pads. These can be relaced much more quickly than drum brakes.

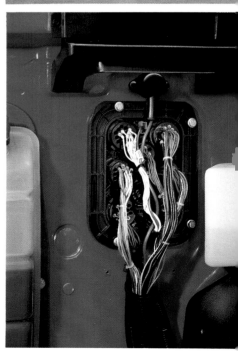

Rapid intervention to reduce "stopping times": everything is under the direct control from the driving seat or simply by lifting the front grille; for more difficult operations the cab tilts and the electrical installation can be isolated by the removal of just one multi-pin plug.

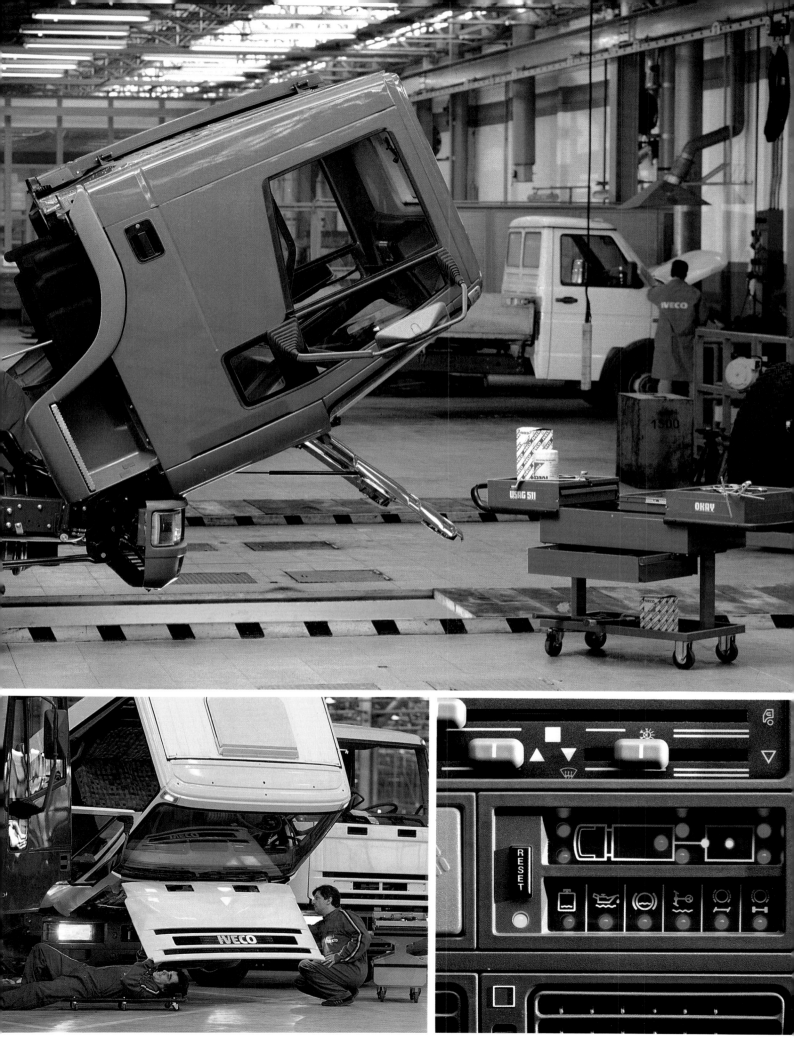

THE EUROCARGO
MEDIUM - LIGHT VEHICLES

This covers the 6 tonne to 10 tonne band which, in Europe, represents approximately 65,000 to 70,000 vehicles per annum, with 30% to 35% in Germany, 25% to 30% in Great Britain, 10% in France and Spain, 7% in Italy and just over 15% in the other markets.

Iveco occupies second position with approximately 25% of the total European market with national shares of 75% in Italy, 35% in Great Britain, 20% in France, 16% in Germany, 15% in Spain and approximately 12% in other markets.

In the latter years of the Eighties this market expanded consistently. It is a competitive market in which all the major manu-facturers compete and which is now beginning to feel the presence of the Japanese who hold approximately 10% of the market.

These vehicles perform a wide variety of jobs including local and long distance delivery and various service activities.

They are used to maintain public utilities (water mains, electricity, gas, telephones, etc.) and services provided by local authorities (street cleaning, refuse collection, etc.). They are also used as mobile shops, by building contractors, for passenger transport, i.e. minibuses and school buses.

On the British and French markets, an important share of the business is in the hire sector.

Iveco is represented in this sector with its light EuroCargo range which replaces the previous "Z" range and also complements the lower end of the "Club" and "Cargo" ranges.

The range is centered on five weight categories: 60-65-70-80-100, divided into more than forty basic models differing according to weight, engine and version (single version with cab/trailer, tipper, tractor). The basic cab is the light, short version. A short cab with top sleeper and a long cab are also available, depending on the version.

With regard to the engines, three options are available for all models: the 60E and 65E use the 102 HP LTC (light turbocharged) version, the 116 HP TC (turbocharged) version and the 136 HP TCA (turbocharged after-cooler) version of the 8040 (4 cylinders, 3.9 litres).

These are combined with two gearboxes, both designed and produced by Iveco: the 2838 5 speed and the 2845.6 6 speed).

The 75E has the 116 HP TC and 136 HP TCA version of the 8040 or the 143 HP TC version of the 8060. There are three gearboxes, all Iveco: the 2838, the 2845.5, 5 speed and the 2845.6, 6 speed.

The 80E and the 100E have the 143 HP LTC, 177 HP TC and 207 HP TCA versions of the 8060. Here there are four gearboxes, also designed and produced by Iveco: the 2845, 5 speed and 6 speed plus the 2855 and 2865, both 6 speed boxes.

The alternative offered by the 75E and 80E, (also approved at 7.5 tonnes) is important from the point of view of the range: two complementary vehicles, one of which is particularly economical (lighter, 4 cylinder engine), and an 8 tonner with 6 cylinder engine and a particularly brilliant performance.

As far as the equipment is concerned, there are versions with cab, tilt cab, truck with original Iveco light alloy box body and tractor, all with mechanical and pneumatic suspension (including full suspension for the trucks).

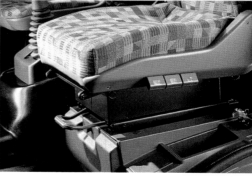

In the medium to light band from 6 to 10 tonnes GVW, Iveco offers the EuroCargo, in a range of five basic models from 60E to 100E, subdivided into over forty variants.

THE EUROCARGO MEDIUM WEIGHT VEHICLES

This extends from the 10 tonner and 12 tonner to the 16 tonner representing approximately 35,000 to 40,000 vehicles per annum on the European market, with 20% to 25% sold in Germany, 20% in France, 15% to 20% in Italy, 10% to 12% in Great Britain and Spain and approximately 22% in the other markets.

Iveco is the leader in this vehicle range with 22% to 25% of the total European market, 70% in Italy, 30% in Great Britain, 18% to 20% in France, 10% to 12% in Spain, 5% in Germany and approximately 10% in the other markets. This market is characterised by a variable volume, sharp competition and a modest presence of the Japanese who have a share of just over 4%.

These vehicles are also used for a wide variety of jobs, involving all areas of haulage and services. They are also used for maintenance work on public utilities. The range includes tippers, tankers, vehicles suitable for local authority work, road sweepers, transport of live animals etc.

The basic van version is converted to the type of vehicle required: insulated or refrigerated van, large delivery van, etc.

Compared with the light vehicle market, these vehicles tend to run up a much higher mileage, with an average of 50,000 to 54,000 km/per year and even up to 150,000 km/per year.

Buyers range from the small businessman to the large fleet owner and hire companies, which are becoming more and more important in markets such as France and Great Britain. Local authorities and construction companies are also customers.

The result of the diversification of use is the demand for a specialist product with selected power trains, axle load, etc.

It is also significant that the different markets are interested in different conversions.

Legislation also varies: in France, contract transport is limited to 13 tonnes and to 11.5 tonnes in Italy (with a useful load of less than or equal to 7 tonnes on the box body). So a 13 tonne model has to be converted specifically for France, whereas the equivalent for Italy is the 120, a vehicle with different characteristics both in terms of weight and load.

Iveco has introduced a new range on the medium vehicle market, the EuroCargo (the name does not change in relation to the light range) which replaces the previous vehicles in the "M" range, plus the "Club" range and similar versions in the Cargo range.

The range is centered on three weight categories: 120-130-150 for the truck versions, which become 260-280-320 for the tractors, made up of more than 30 basic models which differ according to weight, power train and engine. The basic cab is the light model which is available as a short cab, short cab with top sleeper and long cab.

As far as the engines are concerned, the 120E and 130E use the 143 HP LTC, 177 HP TC and 227 HP TCA versions of the 8060 (5.9 litre 6 cylinder in-line); the 150E is also equipped with these engines, plus the 266 HP TCA version of the 8360 (7.7 litre 6 cylinder in-line). The 260E and 280E tractors have the 227 HP TCA version of the 8060, whilst the 320E is equipped with the 266 HP TCA version of the 8360.

There are 6 gearboxes, all designed and produced by Iveco: the 5 speed 2845.5, for the 120E only; the 6 speed 2845.6, 2855.6 and 2865.6; the 9 speed 2870.9 and 2895.9, which are used on the tractors.

As far as the conversions are concerned, this range also includes versions with cab, tilt cab, truck and trailer (with original Iveco light alloy box body) and tractor, all with mechanical and pneumatic suspension (also full pneumatic suspension for the truck).

Compared with the previous range, considerable improvements have been achieved in terms of load carrying capacity. The 150E reaches the 32.5 tonne limit (compared with the 28 tonnes of the previous 145), when combined with trailer versions from the 120E (whereas the previous 115 did not have this facility).

The body length has also been increased, ranging from 4,400 mm to nearly 8,600 mm. This has been achieved both by improving the dimensions of the cab and the wheelbases - five for the previous generation and now seven - with a better distribution and wider range.

THE EUROTECH MEDIUM - HEAVY VEHICLES

This covers the range from 16 tonnes to 20 tonnes, equivalent to 35,000 to 45,000 vehicles per year in Europe, i.e. nearly 34% of the total European market for vehicles equal to or greater than 16 tonnes. Of these, 35% are 4x2 trucks, 30% 4x2 tractors, 25% 6x2 trucks, 10% 6x2 tractors.

The distribution of the various markets is 35% to 40% in Germany, 20% to 25% in Great Britain (65% of all 4x2 articulated vehicles and 71% of all 6x2 articulated vehicles), 5% to 10% in France (43% of all 4x2 trucks), 5% in Italy (30% of all 6x2 trucks) and in Spain, 30% in the other markets and more than 10% for Northern Europe alone.

Iveco (Iveco, Ford and Pegaso) are in second place in this sector, with approximately 15% of the total European market.

In recent years, this sector has seen a modest upward trend. Only manufacturers who are also involved in the heavy vehicle sector compete in this market.

As far as the use of these vehicles is concerned, again they are used by local authorities, for transporting vehicles, long distance transport, including TIR. Single vehicles, articulated vehicles and tankers are available (up to the 40 tonne limit). In this sector, Iveco is replacing the previous medium to heavy 175.24 and partially covers the lower band of the heavy range.

It is a wider range in terms of load capacity and engine versions with more comfortable and habitable cabs. This range represents a specific step forward both in terms of performance, modularity and standardisation.

There are also the 170E 18s and 170E 23s, which are in the low band of the medium-heavy sector, closely related to the medium weight vehicles and sharing the work missions of the latter but obviously in heaver roles.

These three vehicles are the ony ones in the range which have the same cab as the "EuroCargo" vehicles. All the other medium-heavy vehicles have the "Euro-Tech" cab; the same one as is used for the heavy vehicles.

For vehicles intended for heavy use over long distances, practicality in every detail and an ergonomic working environment, with a full range of features and maximum comfort.

To continue analysing the range, as the first medium-heavy vehicle in the true sense, there is the MT 180E 24 which is immediatley recognizable as a replacement for the previous 175.4. It is the typical vehicle for twin councils, in general; as a vehicle for refuse collection, rather than road cleaning, cesspit emptying, liquied carrying, etc.

Then there is the MT 180E 27, designed for transport over medium distances, especially as an independent vehicle, (truck with body, van, kipper, etc., consistent with the EEC reg-ulations relating to the 18 tonne total road weight limit), but also as a light trailer vehicle, for transporting cars, for example.

There are the MT 180E 30s and MT 180E 34s, intended for medium and long distance transport, which we could define a "medium TIR trucks", either as trailer vehicles or articulated trucks, for a total road weight of 40 tonnes.

The applications are of the most varying types: van, ATP for perishables, car transporting, large volume loads, containers and swap bodies.

There are the MT 190E 27s and MT 190E 30s, vehicles for medium distance transport, which, as "independent" vehicles, conform to the regulations fo countries such as France, Portugal, Spain and Belgium in relation to the 19 - 20 tonne total road weight class. Trucks with bodies, vans, kipper, etc., are typical versions.

In addition, there are the MT 400E 30 T and MT 400 E 34 T tractor units, for transport over medium and long distances, including international transport (particularly in the 5 and 6 axle lowbed configuration, ie. with body and low bed). Finally, there are the 6x4 three-axle vehicles; trucks 245E 23 and 245E 27 (derived from the 170 two-axle vehicle), all these being special vehicles for quarries.

With reference to engines, in accordance with the respective designations, the vehicles are fitted with the 8060 (5.9 litres, 6 cylinders in line) in the 177 HP TC version and 227 HP TCA version, the 8360 (7.7 litres, 6

cylinders in line) in the 240 and 266 HP TCA version and the 8460 (9.5 litres, 6 cylinders in line) in the 300 and 340 HP TCA version. There are four gearboxes: the 9 + 1 speed Iveco 2895.9, the 16 + 1 speed ZF-Ecosplit 16S-151 and the 12 + 3 speed Fuller TS 11612 Twin Splitter (with single "H" gear selection gate).

With regard to fitting out, it is of interest to hear about the

possible body lengths, which have been optimised in accordance with the transporting of pallets, 20 foot containers and swap bodies, covering up to a maximum of 9,200 millimetres, which is the maximum permissible length.

Maximum versatility combined with cost-effectiveness, safety and comfort: these are the requirements in the group of medium to heavy trucks, destined to operate in the toughest conditions over medium and long distances.

THE EUROSTAR HEAVY VEHICLES

We have now arrived at the range which is the queen of the road. This is the heavy vehicle range with weights from 18 tonnes up to the legal limits.

This part of the market is analysed according to the engine power classes: 280-309 HP, 310-349, 350-389, 390-449 and over 450 HP. The development is very interesting.

The numbers clearly indicate how, since 1986, the European world of heavy on-road vehicles has rapidly polarised around the 350 to 390 HP engine category.

This has been at the expense of the lower engine range, which is being gradually relegated to the specialist vehicle niche, whilst long distance transport and the major international routes are demanding ever higher engine powers.

This trend is easily explained by the need to have adequate torque reserve both for the various mountainous regions of the trans-European routes and from the point of view of limiting the use of the gearbox with extreme load configurations.

Let us look at the trends in Europe since 1986. The 280 HP to 310 HP range is showing a downward trend after reaching a peak of approximately 20,000 vehicles. On the other hand, the 310 HP to 349 HP range is growing from the 17,000 vehicles registered six years ago.

There are at least two reasons for this: the changing demands of the band immediately below, which now wants more power, and secondly because this power range is exceeding regional transport limits and is becoming increasingly more inter-European, operating between countries where there are no constraints in terms of engine power for each tonne transported.

The next power category, the 350 HP to 389 HP, has experienced a true upswing, not least through the effect of the maximum weight allowed of 44 tonnes with the constraint of 8 HP per tonne. Consequently, the 13,000 vehicles sold in 1986 have more than tripled today.

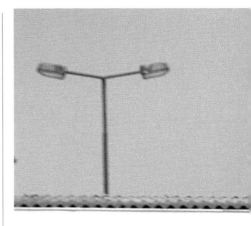

The 390 HP to 450 HP category is also on the increase (7,000 in 1986), as is the range above 450 HP, with a few thousand vehicles being regis-tered today. The analysis of the heavy market also provides interesting information regarding the type of configuration.

The trend of the last few years clearly shows how, above 320 HP to 360 HP, the articulated configuration - tractor with semi-trailer - has progressively esta-blished itself: in the case of the 4x2 vehicles for example, today the articulated vehicles represent 60% compared with the 40% of the truck and trailer.

This explains why Iveco decided to make a range of heavy vehicles (remember, strictly integrated with a very large medium to heavy family) which would be able to cover most of the niches which characterise the market today and will certainly do so in the future. It is no longer the time of multi-purpose vehicles.

Which criteria were used? First of all, they looked at the job of the vehicle: domestic transport, regional transport, interregional transport, long distance inter-national transport.

Having established the job, they then looked at the running costs in general terms, in other words fuel economy with high commer-cial speeds (allowed by suitable axle ratios).

They then worked on the land/tare aspect, offering vehicles at the then European limit of 18 tonnes with an extremely low tare and also vehicles which, whilst conforming to the 18 tonne European configuration, could also be used in countries with different legislation, like the 19 tonnes in France or 20 tonnes in Spain by adapting the chassis, suspension and, in some cases, the front and rear axles, at the same time maintaining the standard drive line and cab configuration.

As far as the cab is concerned, this has also become an im-portant specialist area. As we have said, the type of transport is significant: domestic, regional or international.

This division has resulted in the manufacture of two types of cab

based on completely different philosophies both in terms of dimension and comfort. Obviously, this does not mean that the cab used for inter-regional transport is any less comfortable than the long distance cab.

Quite simply, the cab specification has been improved (reduced width and height) depending on the specific requirements of the user and the job to be done.

Finally, they tried to divide up the transport sector according to the job or end use. To give but one example, let us look at the transport of fuel. An extremely light vehicle is needed for a tanker conversion. This requires a narrow cab, improved chassis and engine weight, using supercharging to achieve the performance required with a smaller cylinder capacity. They also tried to design equipment which would further reduce the weight of the vehicle: light alloy wheels, aluminium air and fuel tanks, etc.

The result of all this work is a range of more than 240 basic models which differ according to the type of cab - EuroTech or EuroStar - and come in various configurations: engine, number of axles and type of traction, equipment, and, of course wheelbase.

We have the 180E-190E 4x2 truck and 400E-440E tractor (6x2 C) with central third axle.

We also have the 240E and 440E (6x2 P), truck and tractor with rear third axle, the 260E and 440E 6x4 truck and tractor and the 340E (8x4) and 360E (8x2) trucks.

The range uses three engines with five power classes: the 345 HP and 375 HP TCA version of the 8460 (9.5 litre, 6 cylinder in-line), the 420 HP and 470 HP TCA version of the 8210 (13.8 litre, 6 cylinder in-line), the 520 HP TCA version of the 8280 (17.2 litre, 8 cylinder V engine).

There are six gearboxes: Eaton Twin Splitters 11612 - 13612 - 15612, with 12 + 3 speeds (with single "H" gear selection gate), the ZF-Ecomid 16 S 109, with 16 + 2 speeds and ZF-Ecosplit 16 S 151 / 221, with 16 + 1 speeds and twin "H".

In the heavy band above 16 tonnes GVW Iveco offers the EuroTech, in a range of over two hundred and forty basic models from the 180E - 190E 4x2 to the 260E - 440E 6x4.

EUROCARGO AND EUROTECH VOTED "INTERNATIONAL TRUCK OF THE YEAR" 1992 AND 1993

In 1992 and 1993, Iveco's Euro-Cargo and EuroTech achieved a unique double by becoming the first two vehicles in the history of the "International Truck of the Year" to win the award in consecutive years.

Iveco won the awards against the best European competition and the jury of International Truck Journalists commended Euro Cargo and EuroTech on the grounds of:-
- an unprecedented range of vehicles built from a set of modular components
- the ability to meet both national and international standards and technical require-ments in the given time-frame
- The choice of six power outputs from engines, all of which meet current EC emissions regulations, which together with a choice of transmissions are able to suit a wide range of applications
- a significant reduction in kerbweight for vehicles in specific power categories
- a quicker and cheaper vehicle rescue service and reduced service costs
- the high standards of active and passive safety built into vehicle at the design and development stage
- an excellent driving position which suits the widest range of vehicle duties.

The Truck of the Year Award was established in 1975 and the following year became a truly prestigious competition with an international jury representing 13 European countries. The rules state that each Member State has a maximum of 12 votes, of which no more than seven may be given to any one vehicle.

Judges are asked to cast their votes on the basis of the "contribution to the efficiency of goods transport by road" made by the candidate vehicles. Today, this contribution is expected to take into account not only the actual cost of the vehicle but operating factors such as safety standards, fuel economy, environmental impact, driver comfort and payload.

EUROSTAR, IVECO'S INTERNATIONAL FLAGSHIP

The flagship of the Iveco fleet is the new Eurostar which builds on the success of its predecessor, the Turobostar.

Iveco holds a share of around 15% of the European "heavy" market as a whole, but this increases substantially to 25 and 30% for tractors and trucks respectively in the 440 to 485 HP segment. In Italy, the 190.48 TurboStar achieves 47 and 60% respectively of these market segments.

The new EuroStar capitalises on the heredity and image of the TurboStar and will appeal to operators running in excess of four to five hundred kilometres on inter-regional or international haulage. This category of operator requiring engine powers of between 380 and over 500 HP, accounts for 40% of sales.

Typically, these hauliers demand high power outputs allied with ample torque at low engine speeds in order to achieve a relaxed driving style and improved fuel consumption. To meet the various needs of the market, the new EuroStar used three engine types offering four horsepower ratings of 340, 380, 420 and a new top-of-the-range 520.

The complete EuroStar range includes tractors, which are now the most popular type, and trucks, which continue to suit important niche operations.

EuroStar cab construction shares many features with the EuroTech, being a combination of a strong steel structure and lightweight corrosion-proof panels. The hinged front inspection panel, bumper, step wells and wings are made from sheet moulding compound (SMC), while the major roof panels are of glass reinforced plastic (GRP).

EuroStar's cab is a full width design and measuring 2460mm overall, is 10 mm wider than that of the TurboStar. The cab length remains the same as EuroTech at 1670 and 2100 mm, but new wider front, rear, floor and roof panels are used.

Four different roof options are available; the short cab takes a top sleeper and the long cab takes either a low, medium or high roof. As a result, the designers have achieved the best use of space yet in this class of vehicle. The medium roof version gives a headroom of 2.0 metres (compared with 1.70 metres for the TurboStar), while the high roof version has a remarkable 2.70 metres.

Access to the cab is particularly easy. The door handles are mounted low down within easy reach and three well arranged steps provided. The lowest is just 300 mm above the ground and all three are of a safe non-slip design.

The well accepted and logical layout of the TurboStar dashboard has been further enhanced for the EuroStar. The dashboard curves towards the driver with the controls grouped conveniently, immediately to the right of the instrument panel. Traditional analogue type dials are retained, but they are operated by the latest electronic controls.

To achieve maximum comfort for a wide range of drivers, both the driver's seat and the steering wheel are adjustable. The steering wheel is adjustable for height and rake while the driver's seat adjusts vertically and horizontally. The seat back is also adjustable for rake and the headrest can be raised and lowered to suit the individual.

Optional equipment includes an athermic blue tinted windscreen, the latest generation of automatic air conditioning (which does not use ozone depleting freon gas), central door locking and remotely adjustable mirrors with electrical defrosting.

The EuroStar has a large console between the front seats which has a recess to store personal belongings at the front and a closed compartment at the rear. The lid of the console is designed in such a way that when lifted up acts as a step, making it easier to climb on to the bunks in the sleeping area.

A moulding mounted above the windscreen houses the remote mirror controls and dual speakers and has provision for a radio and a CB unit. The high roof version also has a series of useful

lockers either open or protected by doors.

To suit a wide variety of operational requirements, the Euro-Star is available with four different power outputs ranging from 345 to 514 HP, delivered by three engine families, all of which meet the latest EC Euro 1 emissions legislation.

The type 8460 9.5 litre, turbocharged and aftercooled six cylinder in-line engine develops 345 HP in conventional form and 377 HP when fitted with electronically controlled fuel injection.

For operators requiring more power, there is the type 8210 six cylinder in-line 13.8 litre engine, which in turbocharged and aftercooled form produces 420 HP. For those operators wanting the ultimate output power for use in arduous conditions there is the type 8280 17.2 litre V8, which in turbocharged and aftercooled form develops 514 HP, matched by a massive torque of 224 kgm between 1100 and 1700 rev/min.

This level of performance has been achieved by the application of a whole series of technical modifications. For example, the injection equipment uses special injectors and pumps; the combustion chambers have been reprofiled to develop greater turbulence and a new design of oil cooler has been introduced. As a direct result of the new cooler and the lower oil temperatures achieved it has been possible to increase the oil change intervals from 30,000 km for the TurboStar to 50,000 km for the EuroStar and EuroTech model ranges.

This engine is also equipped with Iveco engine tester diagnostic system, which is common to all Euro ranges and is based on data supplied by three sensors. Two of these are located on the flywheel and one on the distribution box. Signals from these sensors can be used to dynamically compute the torque, both in individual cylinders and in total. By connecting the special tester to the socket in the cab, it is possible to assess the state of health of the engine, identifying any anomalies such as uneven compression between the various cylinders.

At the top of the Iveco range is the prestigious EuroStar with on the road weights up to the highest GVW class. Powered by 345 and 514 HP turbo-intercooler engines, one of its outstanding features is the luxurious and extremely spacious cab, with exceptional comfort and equipment levels.

EUROTRAKKER FOR CONSTRUCTION SITES AND OFF ROAD WORK

Off road and construction work demands a particularly robust vehicle design. In this sector of transport, applications range from the classic cement mixer and tipper, which can be based on three or four axle rigid chassis or tractor trailer combinations to specialist vehicles such as concrete pumpers, salt spreaders, and snowploughs. The group also includes vehicles for moving heavy plant, such as earth movers and agricultural machinery, and for hauling heavy loads such as marble.

This is a diverse but, nonetheless, important part of the market, which throughout Europe accounts for some 25,000 units annually (based on vehicles of over 250 HP for 1991) and 15% of the total market over 16 tonnes (166,000 units). Having earned a good reputation in this sector over the years, Iveco holds a share of nearly 22% of the total European market and 60% of the Italian market.

Iveco has two significant new models in this market sector, "EuroTrakker" and "Eurostar". These two ranges represent the very latest results of the commitment and investment made in the early 1990s.

EuroTrakker comprises an extremely extensive range of individual models covering the weight categories 19 to 40 tonnes. Sharing much of the same technology and modular design embodied in the current "Euro" models, these "heavy" vehicles are identified by the letter H. Heavy tractors and heavy all-wheel-drive vehicles are designated HT and HW respectively. EuroTrakker models include 4x2, 4x4, 6x4, 6x6 and 8x4 configurations.

Individual models are also designated according to their gross weight. Two axle vehicles with a maximum design weight of 19 tonnes are designated by the model type 190, three axle 26, 33 and 38 tonne vehicles by 260, 330 and 380; and four axle 32 and 40 tonne vehicles by 340 and 410.

The 340 and 410 models have each been designed to meet specific requirements. The 340 is optimised to meet the EC requirements for operation at 32 tonnes and is, thus, particularly well suited to markets such as Germany and Spain, where the four axle rigid is popular.

For Italy, where it is possible to operate these vehicles at up to 40 tonnes, a derivative of the 340 - 410 - has been introduced. To cope with the higher gross weight the frame thickness has been increased from 7 to 10 mm, while the braking performance and rear bogie capacity have been upgraded.

Articulated vehicles and truck-trailer combinations range from 40 tonne 4x2 tractors to 88 tonne combinations derived from the 380 model. Heavy combinations are designated 440, 560 and 720, referring to the maximum gross weight. For example, the 560E37HT is a 56 tonne tractor with a 370 horsepower engine.

For the most part, the cab of the EuroTrakker is the same as the heavy on-road models but there are some notable differences to suit it to the severe conditions for which the vehicles are intended. The front bumper is a new stronger, shallower design, which improves the angle of attack. It is made in five pieces, making it easier to repair and to cater for special front-end mounted equipment.

Some of the cab interior trim has been changed to suit the Euro-Trakker's construction role. The cab flooring and engine cover are made of rubber and the cab side and rear panels are finished in a tough vinyl which is easy to clean. Otherwise, the trim level is the same as other vehicles in Iveco's "Euro" range. In all other respects, the EuroTrakker is equivalent to the on-road Euro models with excellent driver comfort provided by both cab and seat suspension, and sound insulation. The driving position and the level of equipment are to the level expected of on-road vehicles and, thus, outstanding by normal site vehicle standards.

In the 19-40 tonne GVW quarry-construction site sector, Iveco is present with the EuroTrackker range. Recognisable by the different layout of the cab front and equipped with engines from 300 to 420 HP, they offer interior features identical to those of road vehicles.

EuroTrakker shares the same engines and gearboxes with the heavy on-road EuroTech range while the chassis, front and rear axles and the braking system have been specifically developed for site work.

Four engines are available, 300 and 345 HP turbocharged and aftercooled versions of the six cylinder, 9.5 litre, type 8460 - together with 370 and 420 HP turbocharged versions of the six cylinder, 13.8 litre, type 8210. The 370 HP version of the 8210 has been specially introduced for this construction role. Each of these power ratings has been certified to the Euro 1 emission standard.

Behind these engines comes a choice of ZF or Eaton transmissions. Depending on engine type, either ZF Ecomid or ZF Ecosplit designs are used. The Ecomid types used are the 9S109 nine-speed or the 16S109 16-speed, which uses the double "H" shift pattern. Two versions of the Eaton Twin Splitter are also offered, the 11612 and 13612 - both of which have 12 speeds selected using a simple "H" shift pattern. The all-wheel-drive HW models use a new Iveco transfer box which has been designed to transmit particularly high torques. Additionally, there is a wide range of power take-offs to suit applications such as concrete mixers, tippers and snowploughs. For concrete mixers in particular, Iveco has developed a sandwich PTO which fits neatly between the engine and gearbox offering an economic alternative to the normal solution. This new innovation is made at Iveco's Bolzano plant.

The chassis are of traditional ladder frame construction and made from a high tensile steel (FE 490) and fliched for extra strength. The rear axles are a new Iveco design and feature double reduction to give increased ground clearance and a more uniform torque distribution. The suspensions are also new designs; parabolic springs have been developed for the front suspension but more conventional semi-elliptical springs are optionally available. The rear suspension is a two-spring design which, depending on the model, may have parabolic or semi-elliptical leaves. Either type can have anti-roll bars fitted.

The braking system uses drums on all axles in conjunction with Simplex type units. A choice of either twin or wide single rear wheels and tyres is available to suit individual operator requirements.

With structural and mechanical characteristics designed according to particularly severe operating conditions, the vehicles of the EuroTrakker quarry-construction site range are available in a flexible range of versions adapted to the widest varitey of operating requirements.

VEHICLES AND SERVICES IN LINE WITH THE USER'S REQUIREMENTS

In the previous pages, we outlined the strategy and technical content of the current Iveco range. In the chapters which now follow, we will give a view of the industrial organis-ation and production technologies which the holding company has obtained in order to control such a complex programme.

However, first of all, it is important for us to spend some time on the concept which is the basis of Iveco's corporate philosophy of the '90s: providing a complete service to the customer.

The effect of the revolution has, in a few years, radically changed the Group's very essence: with the completed simultaneous development of the product range, the design and production of new technologies; and with the birth and development of "logistics", i.e. co-ordinated com-puter management of all the company's activities, both in-house and in dealings with the outside world.

At the heart of it all is the clear vision of a future dedicated to increasingly developed competitiveness, with the pointer on the scale being quality, taken in the widest sense of the term.

There is quality of the product, from which the following are required: profitability, compliance with the environmental requirements, high exchange value and reliability and all over a period of time. However, to an ever increasing extent, there is also quality in the relationship with the customer: from the choice of vehicle and of the financial support for purchasing, to ordinary and special after-sales service. As we have seen, Iveco has moved in this direction with a new determination. The commitment has been huge, in both technological and financial resources, and has reached its peak at a very critical stage in all the continental markets. However, all this has constituted a massive investment. Iveco is now ready to take advantage of market opportunities as it is in the best competitive shape from every point of view: in production technologies, functional and technical characteristics of the vehicles, and in its policy of back-up to the network and the customer, in respect of all sales and after-sales service requirements.

The latter are aspects which are worth examining further in order to understand how the relationship is evolving between the manufacturer and operator.

OBJECTIVE: CUSTOMER SATISFACTION

In the Iveco of today, everything is directed towards the operator, the end customer. He is the result of a combined effort by the company and its sales and service network and is in fact called upon to play an active part.

With this in mind, the Concessionaires, the Iveco points of sale and service, are developing and are building up equipment so that their role can be upgraded from "dealers" to "truck centres", the intention being for this description to summarise a new completeness of the relationship with the customer, from sales of new and used vehicles to financial consultancy concerning support for purchasing, to workshop service and supplying parts.

Iveco asks its network for a steadfast professional commitment, the object being the end customer, his satisfaction, which may mean his faithfulness to the make and so to the individual point of sale and service. All this constitutes the ultimate objective of an overall, integrated operation which starts from the customer, goes right back to the designers and back to the customer again.

The concept is clear. In the transport industry, operating costs are having an ever-increas-ing impact on accounts. It is therefore important to supply users with instruments which are suitable for reducing these costs. This can be done at both stages of the relationship with the custo-mer: at the time of sale of the vehicle, whether this is new or used, and in after-sales service, with everything which relates to assistance/service.

NEW COMPUTER INSTRUMENTS AVAILABLE TO THE NETWORK

For the "truck centres", Iveco has developed innovative computer instruments which are appearing for the first time in the world of trucks in which place Iveco at the forefront, strengthening its competitiveness; instruments designed to change the relationship with the concessionaires and sellers, converting this to an active partnership with a precise central objective: user satisfaction.

WITH MICOM/SAPAC: MORE EFFICIENCY IN CONTACTS WITH CUSTOMERS

Iveco has developed the Micom/Sapac system to help the sales network organise relations with customers in the most systematic way, and therefore the most productive way. This is not simple computer support but a true sales methodology.

On the basis of a computerised data-bank, the system can prepare optimised scheduling of contacts with customers, at

321

monthly and/or weekly intervals, taking into account negotiations in progress and expiry dates already scheduled.

This also means the possibility of co-ordinating visits in a single given area, with a reduction in unproductive travelling time, preventing overlapping and internal competition; the individual customer is entrusted to one salesman only.

The data-bank can be used for targeted promotional initiatives (from telemarketing to mailing) and - via analysis of companies and of the efficiency of the actions carried out - for identi-fying the possibilities of improve-ment of the sales results.

TECHNICAL DETAILS AND LISTS ACCESSIBLE ON SCREEN WITH ICAST

In a market which is increasingly complex, both seller and custo-mer find they have to evaluate more and more information.

With modern information tech-nology, data and pictures can be stored on a single small disk and can very easily be controlled and processed with the aid of a computer.

On this basis, Iveco has deve-loped Icast - Iveco Computer Assisted Sales Tool - a computer-ised instrument which replaces conventional sales manuals, showing all the equipment poss-ibilities for the vehicles and calculating the relevant lists.

With Icast, it is possible to "match up" each customer with the vehicle wanted, by having a direct dialogue and responding in real time to the requirements he expresses. It is a computerised programme which, in real time, puts together the offer of the "custom-made" vehicle.

It is possible to equip any vehicle on the screen, deciding on dimensions, loading capacities, power units and optional extras and it is possible to prepare a detailed direct order to be sent to the production plant.

For the customer, all this means a purchase proposal which is fast, detailed and up-to-date, based on what he himself finds acceptable and on his own requirements.

Using Icast is simple and intuitive; it is not necessary to have a knowledge of computers but it is necessary to have a knowledge of trucks! The config-uration of the vehicle can be obtained by means of four different methods.

Choosing, in succession, the various different characteristic components of the vehicle: the system always offers only those which are congruous with the previous choices until the structural and technical archi-tecture of the vehicle has been completely decided.

Determining the performance required, both in mechanical terms and in dimensional terms: the system automatically offers the vehicles in the Iveco range which meet the requirements.

Simply keying the commercial abbreviation which identifies a given vehicle: in this procedure, the salesman and the customer have an accurate idea of the vehicle needed and the system "recalls" all the information connected with it.

Finally, keying the alphanumeric order code (P.I.C.): in this case, too, the system supplies all the information relating to the corresponding vehicle.

Whatever the route taken, in addition to the information req-uired on a given vehicle, the following are obtained at the end of the search: the standards of supply, the optional items, list price and identification code for correctly giving an order.

Operating in the Icast environ-ment at any time, it is possible to gain access to the data-bank of the technical characteristics, which will supply all the avai-lable information relating to the specific component - engine, gear-box, wheelbase, cab, etc., involved in the configuration process.

When the model is complete, the complete array of information relating to every single vehicle included in the Iveco range is available: weights, dimensions, sketches, technical drawings of parts, photographs and illu-strative diagrams.

Each piece of information and each drawing can, naturally, be reproduced on paper, via an ordinary printer which can be connected to a PC.

AN INVESTMENT FOR THE FUTURE: MANAGEMENT OF USED VEHICLES

The management of used vehicles forms a primary element in the sales network's activity. With statistics to hand, the used truck market is even larger than the market for new trucks; in Europe in 1991, the figure of 500,000 units was topped, compared with 475,000 new vehicles and the same ratio was recorded in 1992.

There are companies which change their vehicles even after just one year; this is the case with hirers, users who, at the time of buying, want ti know at what figures their vehicle will be valued after one or two years' use.

There are countries where heavy trucks cover over 150 thousand kilometres a year and thesee are replaced with new vehicles after three or four years. In other countries, however, with different economic realities and with lower annual use of vehicles, times between renewing fleets of trucks are longer. In any event, trucks are capital goods and, during their life, before being scrapped, they are re-sold at least once. In addition, there is a large parts market which should not be under-valued.

SPECIALISED CONSULTANCY FOR PURCHASE FINANCING

Commercial vehicles are capital goods and, as such, are subject to financing in most cases.

In various different forms, de-pending on the characteristics of each market and the custo-mer's specific requirements, 85% of purchases are financed.

Through external and high-quality finance companies, Iveco has a network of financial specialists at its disposal in the principal markets and is there-fore in a position to offer terms

ICAST is a computerised programme which, by having a direct dialogue with the customer, makes it possible to put together in real time the offer of the vehicle which meets his requirements.

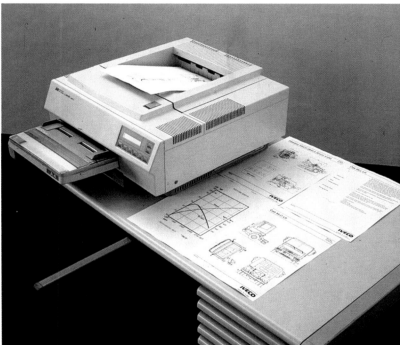

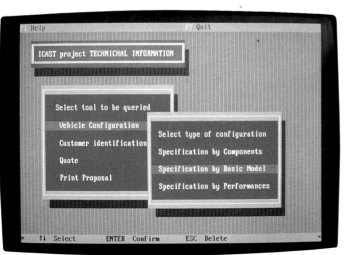

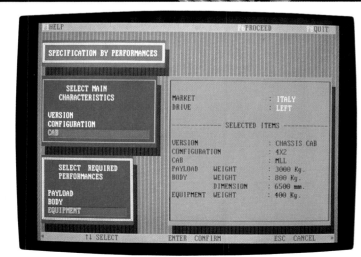

and formulae which allow for market conditions and which are suited to the particular situation in each country.

For the sales network, all this forms important added value in the overall supply for customers; in many cases the opportunity to close a deal faster and more effectively.

To optimise this aspect of customer service, it is important that the sales forces have sufficient basic knowledge of financing techniques and procedures. For this purpose, Iveco runs special training courses; one more instrument for raising the salesmen's profes-sional ability.

Customers who take advantage of the financing consultancy can benefit from terms and conditions which are personalised according to their specific requirements.

In the most complex cases, defining the operation can take place with consultancy direct from the specialists of the finance com-pany which the department calls in.

CUSTOMER SATISFACTION BEGINS AT THE DESIGN STAGE

In the product - service "quality" chain, after-sales service takes a role of primary importance. It is fundamental that this should offer efficient services, managed by qualified personnel. The instruments used are numerous and they are all important.

With regard to the product, the following become crucial: scheduled maintenance, diagnostic instruments which can be used for checking the operational condition of vehicles and the standardisation of replacement parts.

When it comes to the organisation of the service network, the following are important: training of the personnel, particularly in specialist fields, the organisation of parts and workshop management and of the services offered to users, with prominence being given to 24-hour assistance.

Profiting by the experience amassed with the vehicles in use, a great deal can be done up-stream, back at the vehicle design stage, in terms of optimis-ing the serviceability of the product,

which must be designed according to criteria such that maintenance work is - to the greatest possible extent - fast and, at the same time, reliable.

In these terms, too, after-market service takes on a very important active role, having a niche as a route between the end user, the customer, and the designers, to point out the operational critical items found in use and to put forward possible solutions.

This has the double advantage of intervening "upstream" from the problem and in a systematic way, as a result of an organised method of work management and not as a response to a single incidental event.

All this is summarised in the concept of serviceability, given the goal by Iveco of improving the running and servicing capability of the vehicle. What does "serviceability" mean in reality? It means a great deal and many things together. One example of this is improving the ergonomics of particular controls or components of the vehicle to give the advantage of shorter mainten-ance times. A better guarantee of quality of maintenance work, and also the reduction of the number of special tools needed are further benefits.

In order for the sytem to work, it is necessary for the designer to be informed of the problems pointed out by users and also for him to be able to see the case histories available when he is preparing to decide on the solution to use. For this purpose, a data-bank relating to the "Serviceability Standards" has been formed. This is the result of the experience of the Iveco After-Sales Technical Support technicians, who are constantly in touch with service and maintenance problems.

The Standards system is organised for large mechanical subassemblies - engines, chassis, etc. - and can be consulted in real time by all the Iveco design centres via the Iveco electronic mail network, "Ivnet".

Similar rationalisation work has been done to restrict the number of special tools for the new ranges, limiting the number to about ten for EuroTech, for example which means less invest-ment for the

service network.

WITH "MODUS", PREVENTION IS BETTER THAN CURE

Another important aspect in design aimed at simplification of servicing is offered by the reduction in times for scheduled servicing, diagnostics integrated systems and computer instru-ments of use for selecting parts. Iveco has done a great deal of work in this direction.

The reduction in machine stoppage times is a key item for reducing carriers' operating costs. Therefore, even ordinary main-tenance must take up as little time as possible. This can be achieved on the one hand by increasing the specified intervals between maintenance operations and, on the other, by speeding up as much as possible the oper-ations to be carried out.

Iveco is now heading the field from this point of view as well. In the case of the EuroCargo, for example, the servicing intervals have been set at 30,000 to 40,000 km and, in the case of the EuroTech, at 40,000 to 50,000 km. An important contribution to rationalisation of maintenance work has also been made due to Modus - Maintenance Outboard Diagnostic Unified System - an inter-active diagnostic system relating to the engine, braking system and on-board equipment controlled by electronic units.

Modus, which is available for all the Euro ranges, is an instru-ment which improves the quality of servicing in all its aspects: speed, precision and profitability. It can cut maintenance costs by around 20%, halving diagnostics times and providing a uniform quality standard for the whole network's maintenance operation.

How does Modus work? With one sensor on the engine timing system and two on the flywheel, connected to the Iveco Engine

MODUS is a diagnostic inter-active system relating to the engine, braking system and on-board equipment controlled by electronic units.

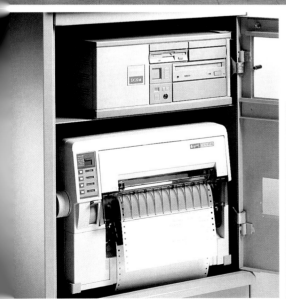

Tester at the Modus station (where the reference parameters are stored in the memory), it is possible to obtain a "driven" diagnosis on the screen. A considerable effort has been made to simplify communication between technician and computer, with programmes which are easy to use and which are available in several languages.

Modus, which was conceived at the vehicle design stage itself, investigates the nature of a problem, following the shortest logical course. By this means, the operations to be carried out are simplified and reduced in number. It guarantees the certainty and accuracy of the measurements recorded.

Hand-in-hand with the technical advantages, there are many economic advantages. The first of these is the appreciable saving of time; the joint effect of certainty and speed of diagnosis and the speeding up of operations.

Also very important is the simplification of the work of collecting data, which allows the expert technician to delegate this to others, giving a more efficient and productive distribution of the workshop's professional resources.

Equally important is the fact that, due to the speed of investigation, with Modus it is possible, for example, to carry out those preventive checks (which are uneconomical with the slower conventional methods) by means of which wear or faults can be found even before the symptoms appear.

COMPUTERISED PARTS SEARCH

Again with a view to cutting down maintenance times, Iveco - before any of the other European manufacturers - has developed the Compact Catalogue, a general parts catalogue on Compat Disc.

This is an instrument with which it is possible to automatically search for parts, cutting the time needed by up to 60%, eliminating possibilities of error and indicating the time requested for the repair.

Compact Catalogue is based on CD-ROM - Compact Disc Read Only Memory - computer technology with which it is possible to store on memory all the parts of Iveco's vehicles on a single small digital disc read by a laser beam. Compact Catalogue has been developed so that it can be used without any particular special skills.

With the menu search system, it is possible directly to select the part requested, or to carry out a search, using the code number or even starting with incomplete information, going by a graphic route. Search time is very short and mistakes are unlikely.

All parts are displayed in exploded view. The illustrations can be enlarged, so the drawing is displayed with greater clarity and the search for the component is simplified.

With the system, it is possible to print all the items displayed on screen; both text and graphics, so that the copy can be used to speed up, facilitate and optimise the operator's work.

The electronic catalogue of parts is up-dated every two months, by the simple action of sending the network a new disc, with considerably lower costs compared with conventional systems; paper catalogues or microfiches.

CHRONO SERVICE FOR THE DAILY

Iveco provides the Chrono Service for users of the Daily range. This service is a preferential channel giving fast service without booking in, at all-inclusive prices.

The following can be changed: engine oil and filters, alternator drive belt, cooling system hoses, silencer, shock-absorbers and brake pads and discs.

All this is with the guarantee of quality of "original" servicing: genuine parts, professional fitting, guarantee of the work and, (an aspect which is in line with modern times), compliance with ecological standards.

Of course, all this is also advantageous for the network because the minor maintenance operations become opportunities to meet the user, inspiring in him trust for when more extensive repairs are carried out and because, in each case, all this represents a presumed opportunity for widening scope for co-operation.

The Chrono Service point is marked with special signs both indoors and outside and is located close to the workshop entrance, so as to be clearly in view and to allow rapid access. Special notices prominently display the services provided and the relevant "all-inclusive" prices: Iveco Genuine Parts and labour.

SAFE EVERYWHERE WITH NON-STOP ASSISTANCE

As a rule, ordinary maintenance can be scheduled at the usual servicing point. However, when a vehicle is being used, unforeseen events are always possible and even the most common of failures - a broken belt or a blocked injector - can bring a vehicle to a stop in awkward situations.

Vehicles are becoming increasingly complicated and, to have the due guarantees of quality, each piece of work done to them must be carried out by specialists who have a thorough knowledge of every mechanical and technical detail, from the engine to the on-board electronic equipment.

Servicing at this level can be guaranteed only by Iveco concessionaires and specialised workshops, where trained technicians work and where there is suitable equipment and parts cover.

For this, the Iveco After Sales Marketing department has prepared the "Non-stop assistance" programme. This programme is managed by Green Flag, a company which , from Strasbourg, for the account of Iveco, replies to calls on a special telephone number and co-ordinates assistance to truck drivers throughout Europe.

Iveco's assistance service is capable of dealing with situations of this type, too, by making use of approximately 350 selected assistance points spread throughout Europe and available to customers 24 hours a day, every day of the year. Day and night, working day or non-working day, the network is connected to the Strasbourg call-reception and communication centre, which can be reached by telephone by using a "freephone number" with which you can telephone from every part of Europe, a reply being received in your own language.

The centre identifies the Iveco workshop which is closest to the vehicle for which assistance is to be provided. Normally, the assistance vehicle arrives within an hour of the call.

However, the service does not restrict itself to this. The operator is available to the person in contact with him also for sending messages to whomever he wishes: the depot, the place of delivery, his family. Until he has set off again, the user whose truck has broken down and the truck itself will remain under the full protection of the Strasbourg assistance centre.

Enrolment for the service is free of charge and no annual membership charge is requested. Even the telephone call to the opera-tional centre on the freephone number is free of charge.

Each piece of work done is covered by substantial credit which is sufficient for the greater majority of cases. The carrier does not have to have large sums of money with him; an important additional security feature and convenience.

If the repair comes under the guarantee terms, there is nothing to pay. Otherwise, a normal invoice is sent to the carrier's base, in his currency.

NO SHOCKS WITH "M&R CONTRACTS"

For those users who wish to obtain cover for every possible unforeseen event, Iveco offers the "M&R Contract" (Maintenance & Repair Contract) methods of assistance. These are personalised agreements with the individual customer, under which Iveco undertakes to guarantee, for a period of time, the correct and complete maintenance and repair of the vehicle through its national and international Network of Concessionaires and Workshops.

It is possible to choose from two different types of contract: Full, with cover of all the vehicle's components, or Drive-Line, relating to the engine, transmission, gearbox and axle gears.

The length of cover is also

variable, from two to seven years, as the customer wishes.

Payments are in instalments, monthly or two-monthly, of a fixed amount, unchanged for the whole duration of the contract, or variable in relation to the age of the vehicle.

With the M&R Contract, maintenance and repair costs no longer represent an unforeseeable variable but a balance sheet entry known right down to the last pound. Also, the administrative work involved is simplified: 6/12

invoices in the year, with complete clarity of the accounts.

The contract can be made with any Iveco Concessionaire, who will attend to personalising the agreement by incorporating a set of data (vehicle model, equipment, use, expected annual distance covered, duration of the contract, etc...) which will be processed by the computer.

Chrono Service is a preferential lane which makes a fast, no-booking, all inclusive price service available to Daily users

IVECO ENGINEERING IN THE '90s AND THE ENVIRONMENT

We have seen that, with regard to engineering, Iveco has implemented a policy of constant updating in relation to innovations, as they are made available.

Therefore, against this background, the arrival of the new ranges does not coincide with any particular leaps forward in technology. Rather than that, what changes is the objective of research, which is increasingly aimed at the subject of the immediate future: ecology.

This does not alter the fact that the "divisional" reorganization of the truck line, decided on at the beginning of the Nineties, brought about a complete shake-up, including the Design and Testing sector.

To give a quick recap of the picture, for final assembly of vehicles we have: Ulm, Madrid and Manchester for the heavy vehicles, both on and off-road, Brescia, Suzzara and Valladolid for the "S" range light vehicles, Brescia for the light (6 - 10 tonne) and medium-light (11 - 15 tonne) ranges of the EuroCargo and Turin and Langley for the medium-heavy range of the EuroCargo (around 16 tonnes). Support structures for designing new ranges are in operation at Iveco-Ford, Langley and Iveco-Pegaso, Barcelona.

With regard to production of sub-assemblies, (chassis, cabs, engines, gearboxes, drive axles and other axles, under Turin's supervision), this is caried out at many centres. The pressing of chassis and cabs, including the synthetic material components (SMC) of the latter, is concen-trated in the very modern Brescia industrial centre.

The engines are produced at Turin, Foggia and Bourbon-Lancy, with development and testing centres at Bourbon-Lancy, Foggia and Arbon, in Switzerland.

When it comes to gearboxes, production is at Turin, with designing at Brescia and testing at Brescia and Turin. Drive and other axles come from Turin, plus support at Barcelona.

On the subject of the Divisions, the design and production of buses involves the industrial centres of Turin, Vittorio Veneto, Modena, Valle Ufita and Barcelona. The design and production of mine/quarry and military special vehicles involves the Astra main office at Piacenza and the Bolzano plant and that of fire-fighting vehicles involves the centres at Weismeil, in Germany, and Brescia.

THE ENVIRONMENT: THE ROAD TO THE FUTURE

The environment is not a choice, it is an obligation. And it has to be approached on two fronts.

The first is engineering, aimed at achieving certain technical standards. For example, on ana-lysing US legislation, it is evident that there are major problems which also require the active participation of the oil companies who need to produce better fuels (free from sulphur and aromatic compounds). The second front requires a political world which must set clear and uniform objectives for everyone at Community level.

Industry has to liaise with legislative bodies on environmental protection for the purpose of agreeing targets which are ambitious, but realistic. But since the development of a new model takes anything between 5 and 7 years, Iveco is not in a position to await events and has initiated a plan to renew its entire range of engines.

This plan will require investments of 1,500 million Lire. And even today, more than a third of Iveco's investment in engine design is concerned with research aimed at controlling emissions.

The aim is to make vehicles which satisfy environmental legislation without the loss of performance. Like the opening of the single market, the environment can be seen as a barrier, but it can also be viewed positively as an opportunity.

Any change can also be an opportunity!

To design engines fit for the future means improving the combustion cycle and thinking about electronics for controlling the fuel supply. It means working on supercharging systems and on the use of new materials and ceramic coatings on engine components (cylinder liners, pistons and cylinder heads) to reduce the heat loss through the cooling system.

Environmental aims in connection with engines also mean continuing the development of the fume precipitation systems, the so-called "particulate traps", which Iveco has already used on the first series for some years.

To achieve the targets set in this field will mean designing the most ecological engine in absolute terms. The diesel engine per se is clean (except for the particulate which will be removed) and has the best thermal efficiency, consuming less fuel and reducing the emissions of carbon dioxide, thought to be responsible for the greenhouse effect. It can be expected that a leading role will be played by the development of the bus, both the traditional bus, fitted with a trap (and this type has enough room) or, in the more distant future, a non-conventional bus, for example a hybrid type.

Iveco is already trying out one solution in the area of Genoa together with the University and Ansaldo.

And we must not forget the

electric vehicle, another area in which Iveco has gained considerable experience. The first prototypes of the electric Daily date back to 1982. An initial trial programme was set up in Turin in 1986 and is being continued today in Trento with some electric minibuses in operation in the historic centre of the city.

IVECO ENGINEERING FOR ENGINE DEVELOPMENT

For its research and development work in the engine sector, Iveco is using three main centres: the Fiat Research Centre in Orbassano (Turin), which works for the entire Fiat group, and two Design and Testing centres dedicated exclusively to engines at Turin and at Arbon in Switzerland.

These are backed by peripheral units at the various factories and the staff of Iveco Aifo di Pregnana Milanese which specialises in the design and manufacture of special conversions.

The facilities are considerable: 130 test benches, 4 climatic cells operating at -50°C for cold start and emission tests, 3 acoustically insulated cells for recording noise levels under load and an anechoic chamber for recording noise levels in the remote and near fields.

There are also rolling roads for analysing vehicle emissions, rolling/braking circuits for simulating the limit conditions of the engine (running downhill, braking torque, efficiency), CAD and CAE systems for finite element analysis, laboratories specialising in fluid mechanics and electronic injection plus gas cromatography systems for analysing the particulate.

With a long track record in the diesel engine sector for auto traction and also for industrial purposes, Iveco has set up research and development facilities at the forefront of their field.

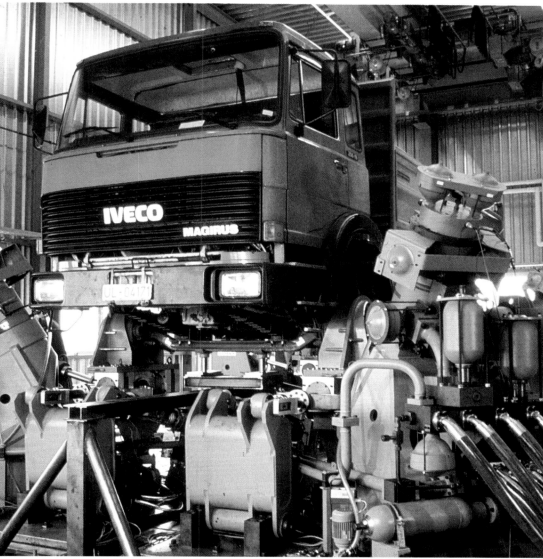

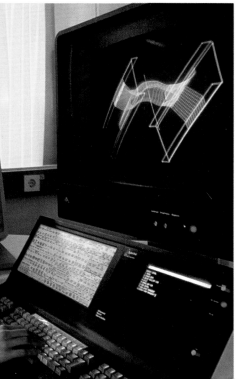

Quality and cost-effectiveness must be incorporated at the design stage. To achieve this Iveco has focussed on computerised calculations and established sophisticated test facilities: from the wind tunnel to computerised road simulators and modern test tracks.

PRODUCTION TECHNOLOGY: A COMPUTER REVOLUTION

To start production of the new product ranges, Iveco had to mastermind a technological and logistic revolution at its factories. The first renewal measures were initiated in 1989 and completed in 1992, when the first medium to heavy and heavy vehicle ranges went into productin at Turin and Ulm.

In view of the wide range of products with small numbers for each version and also the need to respond promptly to market demand, the first objective was flexibility as a means of improving the production lead time, that is the time taken by the factories to put in and the work entrusted to them.

Another priority was quality, not just with reference to the product, but also the machines used in the factory for the purpose of guaranteeing a constant quality of production over a long period.

A third objective - which complements the first two - was to install automation wherever economically feasible, with the relative advantages both for quality and for reducing costs.

Obviously, the latter is also a priority aim as a means for maintaining competitiveness in a market which is already very difficult.

All these measures involved enormous investment to reorganise the factories and automate the processes in the press shop, the body shop and in the machining shops. And also in technology, spear-headed by the strategic choice to produce SMC parts in-house, because these will be an important part of the cab structure in the future.

We have already discussed some of the computer aspects of this work. We will now describe the technological innovations which have been introduced.

We will divide these into two parts corresponding to the two main areas where Iveco has rationalised control of the industrial vehicle: a vehicle which involves presswork, body work, machining parts made from synthetic material (SMC), painting, assembly and inspection, and mechanical components, the engines, gearboxes and axles.

As far as the production allocation is concerned, we merely need to remember that the rationalisation plan is being completed at this stage.

The third generation of the Daily is still being made in Brescia and Suzzara (vans, buses, multi-purpose vehicles, pick-ups, etc.). The light and medium to light versions of the EuroCargo are being made in Brescia and Langley (right hand drive versions and for northern Europe).

The medium to heavy Cargo is produced at Ulm and Langley and the heavy Eurotech vehicles at Ulm and Madrid.

As far as the other product lines are concerned, the major innovation concerns the bus, with the transfer of chassis production from Torino SPA to Sicca di Vittorio Venneto. The activities at Valle Ufita and Orlandi in Modena remain unchanged.

The military vehicles are still being made at Bolzano and the fire-fighting vehicles at Ulm.

A TECHNOLOGICAL REVOLUTION IN AUTOMATION TERMS

With regard to assembly of the vehicles, the technological innovation has mainly involved Brescia, the production centre at which are concentrated the sheet metal presswork, chassis production and also the manufacture of SMC parts for all Iveco factories. Automation has also been introduced in the body shop, whilst the preparation cycle uses off-line pre-assembly processes (instrument panel and doors).

PRESSES: FIVE THOUSAND TONNES COMPLETELY AUTOMATED

We have seen that flexibility and quality of production are among the basic objectives which guided the product and technology designers in the development of the new Iveco vehicles and the corresponding production facilities. Since an automated assembly process needs to be supplied with parts which are geometrically perfect if it is to be able to operate correctly, the press shop had to be provided with equipment able to supply the best quality possible.

Therefore, investments have also been made in automation for the press shop. The jewel of the shop is a Weingarten 4,800 tonne transfer press, the most powerful transfer press in Europe.

"Transfer" means that the various operations (drawing, blanking, trimming, drilling, etc.) are not performed on different machines, but on-line, at successive stations: the pack is loaded on an automatic feed system at one end and the stamping leaves the line at the other.

This machine, which cost around thirty thousand million Lire, plus another sixty thousand for the dies, is able to produce as much as four traditional lines loaded manually and accounts for approximately two thirds of the entire production of cab panels.

Equipped with three hammers for six work sessions, and designed to work at the rate of eight to fourteen blows a minute, it is controlled by nine on-board computers which allow self-diagnostics and automatic die change (for 47 different parts) in just 15 minutes.

In view of the numbers which are typical of the industrial vehicle, it was possible to consider using a machine with these features because of the speed with which the dies can be changed. As is easy to imagine, the installation of a giant like this required major engineering effort: suffice it to say that the tolerance allowed for the supporting plates is only 4/10ths of a millimetre!

The machine foundation, designed by Ford Engineering, required

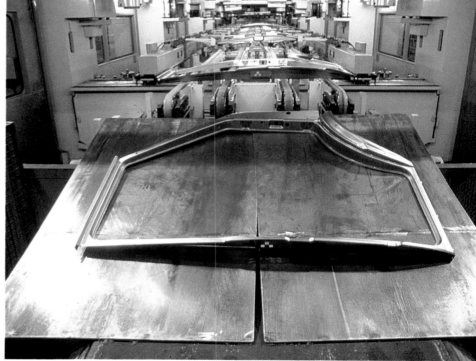

The start of the production of the new "Euro" ranges has coincided with a major leap forward in production technology.
Here the powerful 4,800 tonne transfer press, the most powerful in Europe, installed Brescia for automated cab stamping.

an excavation approximately 10 m deep and a reinforced concrete slab 3.5m thick. The ground underneath was strengthened with a diagonal concrete frame injected to a depth of 17 metres.

FLEXIBILITY AND QUALITY WITH ROBOTS

Everything is automated in the body shop too. There are 11 lines, 5 with automatic feed, on which 52 robots operate, 19 of which have a double welding/handling function.

A total of 3000 spots are welded automatically.

Support lines are used to prepare the main sub-assemblies: the sides, rear and front walls and floors. The cab is assembled in a completely automated and robotised cell where the tongs are changed automatically and the cab transferred along the various stations. Five robots work here, two of which have a seventh axis (for complete movement), capable of welding 14 different basic types. The plant is able to assemble 130 cabs per day.

Of the most important technical innovations introduced at the plant, we would mention the welding control system which allows approximately 95% of the welding spots to be checked automatically.

A basic characteristic of the body fixtures at Brescia and Ulm is their versatility, which not only means the capability to produce several different types in the required sequence, but also to recover 70% to 75% of the investment in tooling when a new production series starts up.

The change is usually made simply by reprogramming the robots and suitably modifying the masks for positioning the various parts to be assembled. After the fabrication work, the completed cabs and sub-assemblies undergo statistical dimensional checks (a certain number of cabs and parts per shift) on a Fenice type NC machine similar to the one used by Lancia and its Chivasso factory.

Using laser sensors, which operate without contact with the part, and mechanical transducers, the machine checks whether the geometric dimensions of the complete cab, or of the individual sub-assemblies (floor, side walls, front and back sections), correspond to the design specifications. Approximately 3,000 spots are checked in 45 minutes. The values recorded are displayed on screen or printed out.

Automation is also introduced into electro-plating with the use of "Robogate" installations which allow maximum flexibility and a consistently high level of production quality.

SMC:
ADVANCED COMPOUND
TECHNOLOGY

The double choice of making important parts of the new cabs from synthetic materials and producing these parts in-house meant that Iveco had to make a considerable effort in this particular technological sector to acquire the know-how.

A new system completely dedicated to SMC products, from the raw material to automatic stamping of the components, was set up at Brescia.

Another major problem, which was solved brilliantly, concerned the ecological aspect. It is necessary to control waste and residue, starting with the exhaust fumes. By using recirculation and recovery devices it is possible to achieve emission levels way below those demanded by current legislation.

Producing the plastic parts in-house was an important step for Iveco for two reasons.

First of all, because in this way it achieves a greater flexibility and speed of response in the event of modifications or the introduction of a new series.

And secondly, because it achieves optimum control of the quality. All the panels are checked 100% to guarantee the quality of the surface finish. An integrated factory has been set up to produce the parts in SMC.

For the tooling, Iveco went to one of the leading American companies in the sector to acquire the necessary know-how, searched the market for the most suitable production facilities and trained the necessary personnel to implement the project.

SMC - sheet moulding compound, is a strong but light thermosetting synthetic material whose structure is characterised by the presence of glass fibres arranged in a continuous but random fashion. The entire production process is governed by a single computerised station which controls the entire system for metering and mixing the compound automatically.

The compound is made on the basis of three different formulae: for embossed parts, aesthetic parts and structural parts (which have properties similar to those of steel). A continuous sheet 3-4 mm thick is obtained which is then stamped.

The stamping operation, which guarantees uniformity of the part's mechanical characteristics, takes place under vacuum with a pressure of 120 kg per cm^2 in dies heated by steam up to 150-160°C. Through the effect of the heat and the pressure, the compound fluidises and diffuses rapidly inside the die where it hardens through polymerisation. The subsequent finishing operations are carried out with mechanical machining processes performed automatically by computer-controlled, five-axis robots.

The plant is designed to produce up to 70 different parts, working with two to five metres of compound a minute, i.e. 31 tonnes of compound a day or 7,000 tonnes a year (figures which are twice those of the Italian SMC market).

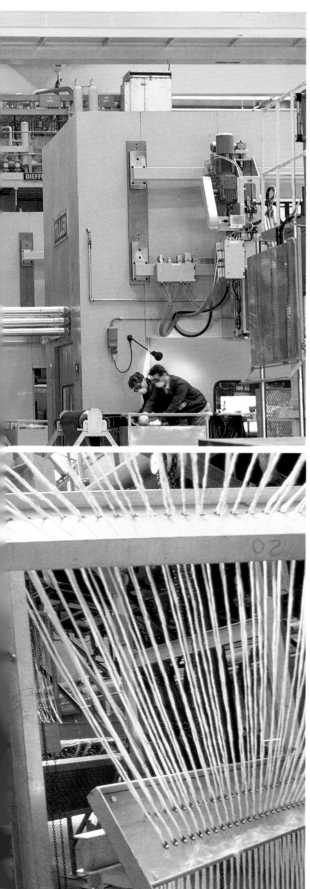

To produce the new "Euro" range cabs Iveco has also acquired the necessary equipment for stamping and finishing parts in the synthetic material SMC.

AUTOMATIC AESTHETICS (AND PROTECTION)

Another process which has been considerably modified for the new Iveco range concerns the painting process and the protection process before painting.

As far as the cab is concerned, all the various preparation stages before cataphoresis are dip rather than spray processes. The cataphoresis is a high build process: 40-50 microns rather than 15-20. The same treatment (high build cataphoretic dip process) is also used for the chassis. The actual painting process as such is completely automated. Three stations are provided for the cab with 12 robots, 8 of which have 7 axes and a double function (opening the doors and painting). The work sequence includes opening the doors, painting inside the cab, closing the doors and painting the outside of the cab.

This is done at three successive stations, which guarantees maximum uniformity of deposition of the paint film and also the quality of the final aesthetic result.

To avoid any impurities, the floor of the paint shop is ceramic and the air is continually purified by a system of filtering extractors.

The plant is designed to allow different colours to be used in a highly flexible manner, from pastels to metallics.

The fact that this process is completely automated is important for environmental reasons, both inside, for those who work in the factory, and outside, because when robots are used, the process consumes a constant quantity of paint, thereby reducing the quantity of solvents required.

In the production cycle an area of fundamental importance to achieve quality and t service life of the trucks is that of the paint finish, starting from protection of the raw against corrosion. For this reason Iveco has concentrated maximum attention on th technology, adopting the most advanced techniques available today.

IN SEARCH OF FLEXIBILITY FOR THE PREPARATION STAGE TOO

With regard to the preparation lines, both for the cabs and the complete vehicles, the numbers of industrial vehicles do not allow automation of this stage of the process. It is however, possible to achieve rationalisation with positive advantages.

Innovations here have mainly been aimed at achieving flexibility by two means. First, by designing lines with variable pitch, allowing optimum saturation of the individual machining processes and then positioning pre-assembly work at the side of the line, creating lungs with independent rhythms dedicated to more complex sub-assemblies, namely the roof of the cab, the doors and the instrument panel.

The mechanical components are also assembled according to sub-assemblies: the complete power train, axles, and also the air tanks, cable harnesses and pipework.

In this way, on the one hand they have tried to reduce the number of people employed on the assembly lines, improving the working environment, and at the same time they wanted to make sure that various assemblies are checked before they are fitted to the vehicle.

Returning to the preparation of the cab, a particular feature is the fact that the roof, made from synthetic material (but not SMC and therefore produced outside) is fitted by bonding after painting.

This is done for two reasons: because the top opening in the cab structure is used by the paint robots to do their work and secondly, because the roof is supplied already complete with its internal coating (which therefore should not pass through the paint shop without protection).

There are three types of roof: the low, medium high and high roof. Whereas the low roof is bonded immediately after painting, the other two are bonded to the finished vehicle because of their size.

As far as the doors are concerned, these are removed at the start of the line, complete with winders, glass and panels, and refitted at the end of the line. Finally, the dashboard is assembled at the side of the line together with the electrics, which then undergo a first functional test. The instrument panel is then installed in the cab and the electrics are checked again at the end of the line.

When the preparation work is complete, the cab is picked up by an overhead system and the process of mounting it onto the chassis for which it is intended starts up automatically.

We would like to mention another innovation introduced with these vehicles for the benefit of quality: the complete separation of the electrics installed in the cab and those on the chassis.

This solution is provided by bulkhead type male/female connectors, with one end attached to the front wall of the cab and the other connected to the chassis wiring.

In modern industrial cycles, one of the most difficult sectors to automate even now is assembly work, in which the large number of operations to be carried out and the diversification of the equipment to be fitted still call for work to be done by an. In this area, too, Iveco has made a great effort to rationalise.

ADVANCED MODULAR TECHNOLOGY FOR THE CHASSIS

With regard to the chassis, first a few words about the press shop, again an area where large amounts have been invested in automation and quality control. Three presses operate in this shop, two semi-automatic 3,000 tonne presses and one fully automatic 5,000 tonne press.
This is the only hydraulic press in the world capable of performing the entire stamping cycle automatically, including the loading of the blank and unloading of the machined longitudinal members. In just a few minutes, it stamps, blanks and draws sheets up to 9 mm thick and up to 11.50 metres long. It is able to operate at up to 3 blows a minute (2600 blows a day): it takes little more than a minute to complete a chassis. The machine is able to cope with approximately 200 types of longitudinal members which are different in terms of thickness, height of the core and holes.
The cross members are produced on automated lines with robots operating between the presses to transfer the parts. All the stampings are checked with gauges to guarantee that the parts arriving at the assembly stage are perfectly geometrical.
The assembly of the chassis - of the longitudinal cross members - is automated using robots. The only operation which is done manually is tack welding the rivets.
The chassis shop also has a painting area: the chassis are immersed in enormous tanks to receive cataphoretic anti-rust treatment before the robots enamel them.

The modular approach is the key element to guarantee the necessary flexibility in production to respond quickly to requests from the market. For this reason Iveco focussed on standardisation in the design of the new "Euro" ranges, starting with the chassis typology.

IN DIALOGUE WITH THE COMPUTER FOR FINAL APPROVAL

At the end of the line, each vehicle undergoes an operating test. All the stages of the test are coordinated and monitored by a central computer which transmits all the test instructions, via the monitor, to the inspector who has an infrared remote control for the dialogue.

In the first stage, the vehicle is identified with regard to type, wheelbase and structural characteristics.

The test bench adjusts automatically according to the distance between centres of the rollers and the test cycle required. After making the necessary connections for the test (rev counter, tachograph, exhaust pipe connection, etc.), the vehicle is taken into a soundproof booth and placed on the rolling road.

The second stage then starts in which all the necessary functional tests are carried out: heating of the engine, gearbox/speed test, speed governor, engine brake, decelerator, clutch, brakes, warning lamps, running and fume opacity. When it leaves the booth, the vehicle moves to the part of the test bed which checks the wheel track.

The last stage is the brake test (circuit pressure, braking force) with the vehicle positioned first with the front axle and then with the rear axle on a pair of motorised rollers.

The electrical and pneumatic tests of the trailer circuits are also carried out (stop lights, lamps, pressure, etc.).

Finally, with the aid of a special test program, the ABS/ASR system components are tested: any defects are displayed on the monitor and a sheet with the results is printed at the end of the test cycle.

From the drawing board to the production line, to the time when the truck is passed as ready for delivery: computers are an integral part of the whole production cycle, in which they play a decisive role in reaching "quality" objectives.

ADVANCED TECHNOLOGY FOR THE COMPONENTS

Development of the new Euro ranges resulted in a generation leap, not just in the production technologies used for vehicle assembly - press work, body work, assembly - but it also had a profound effect on the machining operations, from the engines, particularly at Bourbon-Lancy and Foggia, to the gearboxes at Turin.

FLEXIBLE AUTOMATION IS EXTENDED TO ENGINE PRODUCTION

As far as the engines are concerned, the design of the new Euro ranges strengthened the existing families.
Therefore, there was no major revolution from a technological point of view. The fixtures vary, from rigid systems of the transfer type used for high volume engines (for example the Sofim at Foggia rather than the 8000 engine at SPA) to traditional type fixtures, stand alone machines, for the Bourbon-Lancy engines and the 8280. An exception was the 8360 engine. Having decided to transfer production from Brescia to Bourbon-Lancy, it was decided to experiment with flexible automation using FMS technology to produce relatively small numbers of numerous versions. Some of the operations for machining the base and cylinder head were changed and were done on the same machine line.
The control architecture is typical of FMS system developed at three levels.
At level 1 you have the individual NC machines; level 2 is dedicated to control of the production cell (control of the individual machines with transfer of the necessary data to level 1; control of the transfer system to the modules from the loading/unloading or buffer station; integrated tool control of the cell).
At level 3, a central computer controls the various FMS cells by programming production on the basis of the orders received and planning machine utilisation by checking the capability and availability of the fixtures, materials, tools, with centralised preparation in the tool room.
One of the aims to be achieved by using an FMS system was to improve the quality of the product by making it easier to detect, and therefore remedy, the tendency of a process to move outside the pre-established tolerance limits. At the end of the machining cycle, after unloading the part which has passed through all stages, two control robots automatically measure each dimension of the component and

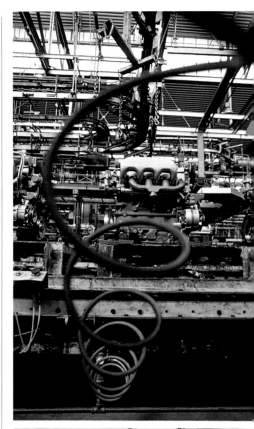

Engine production has been at the forefront in the whole move towards flexible automisation and it remains one of the most advanced sectors at the heart of the technology adopted by Iveco.

353

record in a corresponding table, the values and tolerance deviation. The aim of improving product quality was also centered on the assembly process. A high quality line was used for the more delicate assembly operations (assembly of the connecting rod) where each engine is loaded by an operator who carries out all the scheduled assembly stages. In addition, the engine test room at Bourbon-Lancy was replaced completely and became one of the most highly automated test rooms in Europe.

It has 16 cells (14 production cells and 2 endurance test cells) completely equipped to carry out the operations automatically (power, consumption, emission) with recording of the data and statistical processing.

The engine and the assembly are transferred to the finishing stage by AGVs which direct the engine to the dedicated cell which is free; the main computer monitors the entire system.

Automation of the cycle has also bought about an improvement in working conditions in that the operators only work outside the cells.

The entire production is tested, first on cold benches to check the seals and joints, and then on hot benches.

On average, the tests last between 40-45 minutes and 2 to 2$\frac{1}{2}$ hours.

High efficiency, low consumption, reliability and a long service life.
We certainly ask a lot of a truck engine, and in this case as well the quality of the end
is entrusted to a great extent to systems technology, which allows the management
sophisticated test cycles, both by "batch sampling" and on the entire production.

AUTOMATION OF THE GEARBOXES

In the case of the gearboxes - and axles in future - the advent of the Euro ranges coincided with a radical generational leap in production technology. The machining and assembly operations of all the Iveco gearbox lines (light and medium sectors) were concentrated at Turin at a completely new factory set up on a flexible automation basis similar to the one developed at Bourbon-Lancy for engines. It is fully computerised for the complete production cycle. A system of computers controls the programs transmitted from the Iveco centre, various machining cells and individual machine tools. The system is designed for producing more than 100,000 gearboxes a year on 12 different production lines and represents a very important technological advance compared with anything in the past.

This is truly a first application of CIM (Computer Integrated Manufacturing) which is the complete computerised integration of the company, from the control centre to the individual machine tools, whilst also interfacing with the design services.

The cycle starts in an area where the blanks are received and prepared.

The parts are moved fully automatically by means of loading units, each consisting of six pallets on which the parts to be machined (shafts, rings, hubs, sleeves, etc.) are placed in homogenous groups.

The loading unit is picked up by an AGV (Automatic Guided Vehicle) and taken to the machining lines.

All the operations, with the exception of those carried out on the output shafts, are carried out according to process, not product (e.g. the grinding of shafts, rings, hubs, etc.).

Once the machining operations are finished, an AGV takes the parts to the corresponding inspection unit, connected directly to the machine tool. When all the parts on a pallet have been machined, the gantry picks up the pallet and places it on top of the previous one. This continues until all the machining work has been done. The pallets are then taken to a washing station and from there are transferred to the heat treatment bay.

This process is controlled by a computer which automatically maintains the chemical and physical parameters of the process within the predefined limits. Apart from an improvement in quality through the constancy of the treatment parameters, automation also ensures greater operating safety and better working conditions for the operators who no longer have to operate on the equipment.

After the heat treatment the finishing processes take place, followed by inspection. The final destination is the automatic warehouse for the finished product, also served by AGVs which unpack the loading units in a reception area and allocate the individual pallets to the shelves. These have a total capacity of approximately 7,500 pallets which are transported by means of two trucks operating in a single lane.

Machining of the gearboxes and the assembly operations is done in another factory. This is divided into two separate cells: one for light gearboxes and one for medium to heavy gearboxes. Machining is done in cells consisting of a series of automatic or manual stations where the various components and sub-assemblies are assembled in the gearbox.

There is a certain number of buffer stores which allow the necessary flexibility for the machining cycle. Both the cells and the buffer stations are served by a robotised AGV system.

The main components of the gearbox are placed on pallets at the inlet station for each cell.

A certain operation is carried out at each station. Each station can contain up to 5 pallets, one being machined, two waiting to be taken to the next station and two waiting for machining (in practice, another lung in addition to the buffer stations).

At the end of the assembly operations, the complete gearboxes are placed on roller beds to be transported to the test benches.

100% of the production is tested and this is done fully automatically. The test cycle is set automatically on the basis of the data recorded by the magnetic card which accompanies each gearbox.

The test starts by introducing the lubricant into the gearbox at a temperature of approximately 40°C. The gear shift and noise tests are then carried out according to cycles operating at predefined speeds. The values are displayed on consoles and compared with predetermined reference data. If everything is correct, the gear box is approved with the issuing of a certification document.

Two views of the brand new centre for gearbox production located at the Turin plants. Completely automated and computerised, it is a real "cause for pride" for Iveco.

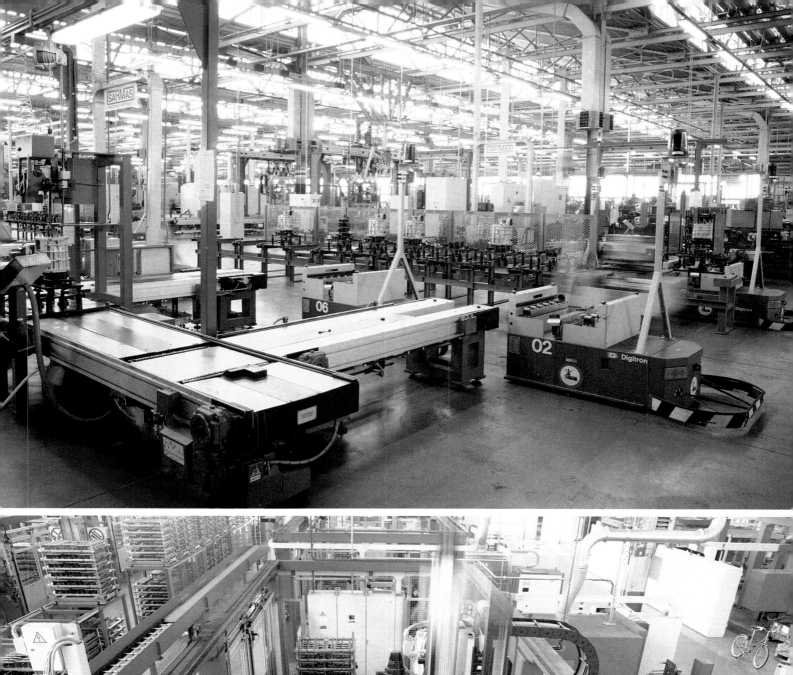

INNOVATION
AND A COMPETITIVE SPIRIT FOR
MEETING THE CHALLENGE OF THE '90s

With the quick glimpse which the previous pages have provided of the products and technology of the Iveco of the Nineties, we have come to the end of our story.

By this, we mean that we have to come to the end of our narration but certainly not to the end of Iveco's "story" which, instead, is running along fast; so fast that it cannot be 'pursued" with the pages of a book. The reality of "today" is in fact something which has already "passed" when its story can be told.

This is an inescapable rule, as a modern company which wants to be competitive and remain so in a market which is increasingly competitive and tough is forced to live "in the future" all the time. If you "go out" on to the market with a an innovative product or "strategy", you can be sure that, in the offices of the "decision-makers", other products and strategies are already being studied. This also holds good for the facts and vehicles "narrated" on these pages, even though our story ends at a very special time for Iveco.

This special time is a turning-point which involves practically all the management aspects of the company and, at the same time, the products in their en-tirety. Iveco's "bet" on its future and that of the market, (not just the European market), has been a committed and courageous one, and the significance of what has been sought and achieved is now there for everyone to see.

With the progress of an international scene in develop-ment which is deeper and faster than ever before, future events will tell whether - and to what extent - the theories which were used as starting points and the forecasts which were drawn from them can be objectively confir-med. Whatever the scene set in the nex few years, Iveco can be credited with the merit of having been able to "dare" and act, taking advantage of a partic-ularly favourable time in its development to start and carry through, at high speed, a sub-stantial "regeneration' in the field of strategy and advanced technology.

So there has been a true "generation leap" which, in all probabil-ity, will prove decisive for its future stoy.

As a company's primary reason for existing is that of "serving" the market, the first objective is always that it should have a product capable of beating the comp-etition.

Due to this, Iveco has directed all its innovative action towards manufacturing the products of the 1990s. It has not failed and today, at the beginning of the decade, Iveco can offer all sectors of the commercial vehicle and bus market ranges of vehicles which are extremely varied and at the highest level of competitiveness.

As we have seen, the commit-ment to the products has been accompanies and sustained by a radical renewal of production technology and of the structure of the company as a whole; the Iveco of today is an organization which is profoundly different from the Iveco of only five years ago.

It is larger but also much more "integrated" in its supranational character. It is more open to the market and, due to the resources of advanced computerisation, it is quicker to grasp, "in real time", re-quirements and take opportunities.

It has an instruments and stra-tegies package which is aimed at keeping pace with an increas-ingly wide, competitve market context. Having been founded in Europe with a far-sighted, supra-national vision of the concept of enterprise, Iveco is today ready to meet the challenge of an even larger scale; that world scale which is the only one which can enable it to take the new oppor-tunities of the emerging markets, wherever they may be.

The Editor and the authors would like to thank everyone who has contributed to this book and also those who, on reading it, will provide further useful information for improving and updating the history of the company reconstructed here, by pointing out any omissions or inaccuracies.